Franchising

Franchising

Martin Mendelsohn

Robin Bynoe

Solicitors
Partners, Eversheds

LAW & TAX

Martin Mendelsohn and Robin Bynoe have asserted their rights under the
Copyright, Designs and Patents Act 1988 to be identified as the authors of
this work

ISBN 085121 7478

Published by
FT Law & Tax
21–27 Lamb's Conduit Street
London WC1N 3NJ

A Division of Pearson Professional Limited

Associated offices
Australia, Belgium, Canada, Hong Kong, India, Japan, Luxembourg,
Singapore, Spain, USA

No responsibility for loss occasioned to any person acting or refraining from
action as a result of material in this publication can be accepted by the
authors or the publishers.

A CIP catalogue record for this book is available from the British Library.

Printed and bound in Great Britain by Biddles Ltd, Guildford and King's Lynn

Contents

Foreword

I am delighted to have been asked to write the Foreword to this book. Martin Mendelsohn is a renowned expert in the field of franchising. He is well known not only in the United Kingdom, but also internationally.

Franchising has become an increasingly popular and important service to the business world. The benefits of franchising in mature economies are well documented. But we should also recognise the crucial role which franchising can also play in developing countries.

The practical guidance which this book offers will, I am sure, greatly assist those who are unfamiliar with franchising to develop an understanding of the subject. And it will also significantly contribute to the information currently available.

Franchising provides a refreshing approach to the subject through its blend of the law with practical business experience. The resulting study should appeal to business people and lawyers alike. I commend it warmly.

LORD ALEXANDER OF WEEDON QC

Preface

This is a book about franchising and the law; however, there is no such thing in England, or indeed anywhere else, as franchise law.

In the United States of America, both at federal and state levels, there is legislation and regulation of aspects of franchising. If there were a version of this work in the United States it would look very different from this, with substantial sections on registration, disclosure requirements and so on. Only in three or four other countries would one find any franchise-specific legislation. In the European Union there is the Block Exemption Regulation for categories of franchise agreements; despite its name this is actually a deregulation measure, since it provides exemption from Article 85(1) of the Treaty of Rome.

There is an ambiguity about the areas with which a franchise lawyer should be concerned; even about what franchising is. The word 'franchising' is commonly used to cover a wide range of business relationships which are not at all what the franchising community regard as franchising: television 'franchises', a British Rail 'franchise', the Star Wars 'franchise'. We disregard these too. Franchising at its core, and for the purposes of this book, is a method of marketing goods and services; it crosses the dividing lines between the normal industrial categories and in its most popular and relevant form is called business format franchising. There are many variations on the concept which we have tried to identify in the work.

Partly because of the ambiguity and the hybrid nature of franchising, many different areas of law are involved. These are covered in the chapters of this work. Some, such as tax, are relatively discrete; others less so. It will be immediately apparent that we have not tried in these chapters to give definitive accounts of the areas of law covered. It would be impossible anyway to do so, or even to attempt even-handed summaries, given the diversity of subject matter and the practical limits inherent in any one volume work. Indeed our brief from our publishers was to concentrate on the business concept and how the law intrudes. What we have attempted is determinedly biased towards the interests of the franchising community. For a more comprehensive account of the various areas of law covered readers should consult the definitive text books.

Our aim has also been to err on the side of practicality rather than jurisprudential nicety. Where we have been pedantic (as for example in the discussion of medieval manorial privileges in Chapter 2) we have tried to be wilfully so.

We have been very considerably assisted by our colleagues at Eversheds. We particularly thank Tom Daltry for the tax chapters, Linda Lawrence for the chapter on real estate and Ros Kellaway for work on the two chapters on competition law. We also had invaluable contributions from Tim Maloney, Charles Lambrick, Isabel Davies, Paul Heatherington, Helga Breen, Tim Morley, Neil Matthews, Caroline Temperton, Catherine Bond, Susan Ormrod and Karen Poole. We are grateful to the Rt Hon Lord Alexander of Weedon for his felicitous foreword. Finally thanks to Jeffrey Boloten for having the patience to stay with us until and even after the manuscript was eventually delivered.

The law is stated as at 31 December 1994 (except for tax when it is 1 May 1995), but some events since then have been referred to.

Martin Mendelsohn
Robin Bynoe
April 1995

Table of Cases

Table of Statutes

Table of Statutory Instruments

Table of EC Materials

Chapter 1

What Franchising Is

Chapter 1

What Franchising Is

1.1 Introduction

Franchising is a method of marketing goods and services. If there are any reasons which can with confidence be identified as the explanation for its remarkable success they would be:

(a) the need for successful business operations to grow; and
(b) the ability to achieve that growth by linking up with others who possess the capital and manpower to do so.

The blending of these two interests has produced a powerful combination which has made a considerable impact in the marketplace. A study of what are essentially simple concepts reveals that these concepts are the tip of the iceberg. This becomes evident as one appreciates the elements with which one becomes involved in order to achieve the reality of the successful establishment and longevity of a franchise. These elements may be separated into the basic structure and the techniques which are employed to manage the network.

In this chapter we shall be examining the underlying nature of franchising. The techniques will be described in later chapters. In Chapter 4 we will bring together many of the points raised in this chapter to demonstrate the legal issues which arise in franchise transactions and at what stages they arise.

1.2 Basic structure

It is probably sensible, when considering the basic structure, to review how a franchisor would become established. All franchise systems must be based on a business which is successful in practice. The prospective franchisor could be in business as a manufacturer, a wholesaler or a retailer, he may not be involved at all in the manufacture or distribution of goods; or the business may consist of the provision of services (though it is possible that goods of some sort will be involved in the provision of some services). Whether or not the prospective franchisor is involved in dealing in goods or services, or both, the same basic structure will be found.

The franchisor's business will be identified by a 'brand name'. This may be the same as the trade mark which is applied to the goods which the prospective franchisor manufactures or causes to be manufactured or to the services provided, and which may or may not be registered, or it may be a trade name which is not strictly a trade mark.

The business will be developed by trial and error as is the way with new businesses. This is not to say that only new businesses can be franchised. An existing business which is long established may still be franchised—it would just be further developed than a new business. What the new business owner will be doing is making mistakes in establishing and running the business; he will be correcting his errors and fine-tuning his business system until he achieves the success for which he is aiming. Out of that process will emerge the business system which will have been developed along the route to success. The reason why so many new businesses fail is that they run out of capital before they have solved their problems. The fact that a franchisor has gained this experience and risked his capital to prove that his system is successful means that franchisees can open a business with the risk inherent in the trial and error of developing a business system for a new business virtually eliminated. That does not mean that there are no risks. The system is only one of the risk areas which has been dealt with. There are always risks involved in running a business and the franchisee will have to face those risks in the continuing conduct of his business; in addition he will also be bearing the risk of the franchisor not proving as good as he needs to be.

The prospective franchisor of an established business has developed:

(a) the branding for the business; and
(b) a business system: a method of conducting the business and know-how for which the franchisor will claim confidentiality and exclusivity.

If franchisees are to be recruited, the prospective franchisor must be able to achieve more:

(1) He must be able to persuade would-be franchisees that they should invest their money in establishing a similar business.
(2) He must also persuade these would-be franchisees that they should invest their labour in running the business.

Having managed so to persuade a prospective franchisee, the prospective franchisor has to transform an ambitious but novice would-be franchisee into a businessman capable of running a business according to the franchisor's system. The franchisor will need to train the franchisee and to help him establish the business to the point where he is ready to commence trading.

Since the relationship involves the use by the franchisee of the franchisor's branding and system, it will be necessary for the franchisor to retain a continuing interest in the franchisee's business to ensure that:

(a) the standards associated with the franchisor's branding are maintained and the system is correctly operated;

(b) so far as possible the franchisee is successful, so that the goodwill associated with the franchisor's branding and system is not harmed; and

(c) the franchised business system is kept up to date and the business is competitive with similar businesses in the marketplace.

The franchisee must expect to pay for the privilege of joining the franchisor's system and enjoying the benefits which flow from membership, as well as for services which the franchisor will continue to provide during the relationship. Payment may be made by one of the methods described in Chapter 7.

There have been a number of definitions of franchising. Definitions rarely explain the underlying concept; rather they are introduced to assist in the achievement of a particular objective. We shall look at definitions which have been coined by commerce and industry, as well as those which have been used in legislation.

1.3   Features of business format franchises

It will be seen that approaches differ widely, but that the issues which emerge from the explanation given above are taken into account. There are five basic features which appear in all definitions (with one or two notable exceptions) whatever else they may deal with. These five basic features are:

(a) branding in one form or another;

(b) a system;

(c) the grant of the right to use the branding and system;

(d) the payment of some form of direct or indirect consideration by the franchisee to the franchisor;

(e) the investment in, and ownership of, the franchised business by the franchisee.

There have been many attempts to categorise franchising, so many that they confuse. The suggested categories include:

(a) first generation franchises;

(b) business format franchises;

(c) job franchises;

(d) mobile franchises;

(e) investment franchises;

(f) service franchises;

(g) industrial franchises;
(h) trade marks/trade name franchises;
(i) product franchises.

Many of these are business format franchises but have had labels attached to them to describe either the nature of the business ('mobile franchise') or the nature of the franchisee ('job franchise', 'investment franchise').

To add to the confusion, many business people use the term 'franchise' generally to mean pure licensing transactions. The government legislates to establish authorities which grant franchises, such as the Radio Authority and the Railway Licensing Authority. Car dealerships are called franchises, as are many other traditional agency and distribution arrangements. In Chapter 5 these other arrangements will be discussed, but this work is principally concerned with what are described as business format franchises; that is to say those franchises which involve the five basic elements described above. Those basic elements do not, however, cover the whole range of features of the business format franchise which have been identified as including the following:

1 A franchise relationship is founded upon a contract which should contain all the terms agreed upon.
2 The franchisor must first develop a successful business format (the system) which is identified with a brand name which may be a trade mark and/or trade name.
3 The franchisor must initiate and train the franchisee in all aspects of the system prior to the opening of the business so that the franchisee is equipped to run the business effectively and successfully and assist in the opening.
4 After the business is opened the franchisor must maintain a continuing business relationship with the franchisee in the course of which it provides the franchisee with support in all aspects of the operation of the business.
5 The franchisee is permitted under the control of the franchisor to operate under the branding (trade mark, trade name) the business system developed and owned by the franchisor and to benefit from the goodwill associated therewith.
6 The franchisee must make a substantial capital investment from his own resources.
7 The franchisee must own his own business.
8 The franchisee will pay the franchisor in one way or another for the rights which he acquires and for the continuing services with which he will be provided.

(M Mendelsohn, *The Guide to Franchising*, 5th edn (Cassell, 1992).)

1.4   Commercial definitions

The definition of franchising which has been adopted by the British Franchise Association (BFA) is the first to be examined:

> A contractual licence granted by one person (the franchisor) to another (the franchisee) which:
>
> (a) permits or requires the franchisee to carry on during the period of the franchise a particular business under or using a specified name belonging to or associated with the franchisor;
>
> (b) entitles the franchisor to exercise continuing control during the period of the franchise over the manner in which the franchisee carries on the business which is the subject of the franchise;
>
> (c) obliges the franchisor to provide the franchisee with assistance in carrying on the business which is the subject of the franchise (in relation to the organisation of the franchisee's business, the training of staff, merchandising, management or otherwise);
>
> (d) requires the franchisee periodically during the period of the franchise to pay to the franchisor sums of money in consideration for the franchise or for goods or services provided by the franchisor to the franchisee; and
>
> (e) which is not a transaction between a holding company and its subsidiary (as defined in section 154 of the Companies Act 1948, now section 736 of the Companies Act 1985 as amended by the Companies Act 1986) or between subsidiaries of the same holding company or between an individual and a company controlled by him.

Reading this definition one can immediately recognise that it is framed to accommodate the business method described above, but it omits the fifth of the basic features, the investment in and ownership by the franchisee of the franchised business. This is a key feature since the franchisee is committed by his investment and expected, as owner, to be better motivated than would be a manager. Although there are references to the business being owned by the franchisee there are two factors which make that ownership different from that enjoyed by a non-franchised businessman.

The franchisee must operate under the franchisor's name, using his system and within the terms of the franchise agreement.

The franchisee's right to operate the franchised business is not infinite but is limited to:

(a) the term of the franchise agreement, or

(b) such lesser period as may be appropriate if the agreement is terminated.

The franchisee thus obtains limited rights to run the business in which he is making his investment. This is important since many franchisees will subsequently assert that they have acquired permanent proprietary rights.

The International Franchise Association (IFA), which is the franchisors' association in the USA, has also adopted a definition. It is similar to but different from the BFA definition:

> A franchise operation is a contractual relationship between the franchisor and franchisee in which the franchisor offers or is obliged to maintain a continuing interest in the business of the franchisee in such areas as know-how and training, wherein the franchisee operates under a common trade name, format and/or procedure owned or controlled by the franchisor, and in which the franchisee has or will make a substantial capital investment in his business from his own resources.

The definitions are close in substance but the IFA text emphasises the investment made in the business by the franchisee.

The European Franchise Federation (EFF), which is a federation of the national franchise associations established in many (but not all) European countries (and not limited to those who are members of the EU), has adopted a common code of ethics to which all members of the national associations subscribe with some national variations. (The EFF code of ethics is discussed in Chapter 18.) This code has a different definition:

> Franchising is a system of marketing goods and/or services and/or technology, which is based upon a close and ongoing collaboration between legally and financially separate and independent undertakings, the franchisor and its individual franchisees, whereby the franchisor grants its individual franchisees the right, and imposes the obligation, to conduct a business in accordance with the franchisor's concept. The right entitles and compels the individual franchisee, in exchange for a direct or indirect financial consideration, to use the franchisor's trade name, and/or trade mark and/or service mark, know-how (*), business and technical methods, procedural system, and other industrial and/or intellectual property rights, supported by continuing provision of commercial and technical assistance, within the framework and for the term of a written franchise agreement, concluded between parties for this purpose.
>
> (*) 'know-how' means a body of nonpatented practical information, resulting from experience and testing by the franchisor, which is secret, substantial and identified;
> — 'secret', means that the know-how, as a body or in the precise configuration and assembly of its components, is not generally known or easily accessible; it is not limited in the narrow sense that each individual component of the know-how should be totally unknown or unobtainable outside the franchisor's business;
> — 'substantial' means that the know-how includes information

which is of importance for the sale of goods or the provision of services to end users, and in particular for the presentation of goods for sale, the processing of goods in connection with the provision of services, methods of dealing with customers, and administration and financial management; the know-how must be useful for the franchisee by being capable, at the date of conclusion of the agreement, of improving the competitive position of the franchisee, in particular by improving the franchisee's performance or helping it to enter a new market;

— 'identified' means that the know-how must be described in a sufficiently comprehensive manner so as to make it possible to verify that it fulfils the criteria of secrecy and substantiality; the description of the know-how can either be set out in the franchise agreement or in a separate document or recorded in any other appropriate form.

This definition is different from those adopted by the IFA and BFA and borrows some of its text from the definition adopted by the European Commission for the purposes of EC competition law. The definition is more limited than the other definitions. This is not intended to limit the effect of the code of ethics but rather to set a standard to which franchisors should aspire.

Although at first sight it may be regretted that the definition in the code does not correspond with the EC definition for the purpose of competition law (*see below*) this would not be fair comment. The EFF code is intended to apply to franchises whether or not the EC regulation applies. The references to end users in the definition of 'substantial' would have been better omitted, although the EFF and BFA would probably take the view that an end user is not necessarily a retail customer, but the purchaser of goods or services at whatever level in the distribution chain.

1.5 Legal definitions

1.5.1 England and Wales

The first formal legal definition to consider is that contained in the Financial Services Act 1986, s 75(6)(f):

Franchise arrangements, that is to say, arrangements under which a person earns profits or income by exploiting a right conferred by the arrangements to use a trade name or design or other intellectual property or the goodwill attached to it.

This definition is intended to prevent franchise arrangements from being regarded as 'collective investment schemes' under the 1986 Act. Since the definition of a collective investment scheme in the Act would not in any event include franchise arrangements, there is no need to exclude them. It is just as well, since the definition of franchise arrangements is far from satisfactory. To qualify as a franchise arrangement the 'person' has to earn profits or income. It is difficult to know what this phrase means. One could differentiate between the words 'profits' and 'income' by taking 'profits' to mean the net proceeds of the business enterprise after deducting expenses, and 'income' to mean gross income regardless of expenses. If this is the correct view the definition would include a business which has not made a profit or which incurs a loss. That would mean that the word 'profit' is superfluous and leaves outstanding the extent to which the word 'earns' controls the word 'income'.

In addition, the use of the disjunctive 'or' would disqualify most if not all genuine franchise arrangements, since a trade name and other intellectual property and goodwill will always be present together. The reference to goodwill is also vague since it is not clear to what goodwill is to be attached. As a definition this contributes little to explaining or identifying franchising arrangements.

1.5.2   The European Union

The next definition to consider appears in EC Commission Regulation No 4087/88 of 30 November 1988 on the application of Article 85(3) of the Treaty to categories of franchise agreements. This Regulation is discussed in detail in Chapter 14 but suffice to say at this stage that the Regulation exempts from the EC competition laws agreements within its scope and which comply with its terms.

The Regulation defines a franchise in the following terms:

> 'Franchise' means a package of industrial or intellectual property rights relating to trade marks, trade names, shop signs, utility models, designs, copyrights, know-how or patents to be exploited for the resale of goods or the provision of services to end users.

This definition is limited in its scope and quite technical. While it recognises the role of branding and the franchisor's system (know-how), it does not deal with the other incidental features of a franchise. There are perhaps two reasons for this. First, a number of those features are referred to in the definition of a 'franchise agreement' (*see below*). Second, the European Commission makes it plain in the preamble to the Regulation that some types of franchise are not intended to be governed by the Regulation. In the preamble it is pointed out that:

(a) industrial franchises (those which concern the manufacturing of goods) are not intended to be governed by the Regulation since they consist of

     manufacturing licences based upon patents and/or technical know-how
     combined with trade mark licences; and
(b) franchises involving the sale of goods at wholesale level could not come
     within the Regulation since the Commission lacked the experience of
     such franchises which is a prerequisite to their inclusion in the
     Regulation.

The definition of a franchise agreement introduces some of the elements
already identified:

> The expression 'franchise agreement' means an agreement whereby one
> undertaking, the franchisor, grants the other, the franchisee, in exchange
> for direct or indirect financial consideration, the right to exploit a fran-
> chise for the purposes of marketing specified types of goods and/or
> services; it includes at least obligations relating to:
>
> — the use of a common name or shop sign and a uniform presenta-
>   tion of contract premises and/or means of transport;
> — the communication by the franchisor to the franchisee of know-
>   how;
> — the continuing provision by the franchisor to the franchisee of
>   commercial or technical assistance during the life of the agree-
>   ment.

There are also definitions of some of the words which appear in the definition
of a franchise agreement.

> 'Contract premises' means the premises used for the exploitation of the
> franchise or, when the franchise is exploited outside these premises, the
> base from which the franchisee operates the means of transport used for
> the exploitation of the franchisor (contract means of transport).

These definitions therefore include both franchised businesses which operate
from a fixed base—premises which the customers visit—and those where the
franchisee is mobile, for example van or vehicle-based, when the franchisee
visits the customer.

> 'Know-how' means a package of non-patented practical information
> resulting from experience and testing by the franchisor which is secret,
> substantial and identified.

The value of this definition, coupled with that of the word 'secret' which
follows, is the recognition that the franchisor's know-how will often contain
elements of knowledge within the public domain, but the skill and the confidentiality of the franchisor's know-how is secured by the way in which the
elements are brought together into a package. 'Secret' is thus defined as
meaning:

that the know-how, as a body or in the precise configuration and assembly of its components, is not generally known or easily accessible, it is not limited in the narrow sense that each individual component of the know-how should be totally unknown or unobtainable outside the franchisor's business.

'Substantial' means that the know-how includes information which is of importance for the sale of goods or the provision of services to end users, and in particular for the presentation of goods for sale, the processing of goods in connection with the provision of services, methods of dealing with customers, and administration and financial management; the know-how must be useful for the franchisee by being capable, at the date of conclusion of the agreement, of improving the competitive position of the franchisee, in particular by improving the franchisee's performance or helping it to enter a new market.

Any franchisors whose system is properly pilot-tested and structured should have no difficulty in meeting the criteria for substantiality (but *see* Chapter 14).

'Identified' means that the know-how must be described in a sufficiently comprehensive manner so as to make it possible to verify that it fulfils the criteria of secrecy and substantiality; the description of the know-how can either be set out in the franchise agreement or in a separate document or recorded in any other appropriate form.

This recognises the widespread practice among franchisors of using a manual or manuals which contain details of the franchisor's system, and the operations and methods and standards to be applied.

Overall, this definition provides a useful summary of what comprises a business format franchise, despite the deliberate limitations. In particular it is interesting to note how the definition meets the eight features listed on p 6:

(1) There must be a contract (*see* definition of franchise agreement).
(2) The franchisor must develop a system (*see* definition of know-how).
(3) There must be training (*see* definition of franchise agreement—communication of know-how).
(4) There must be continuing support (*see* definition of franchise agreement—the ongoing provision of commercial or technical assistance).
(5) There must be the grant of the right to operate the business by this system and branding (*see* definition of franchise agreement—'one undertaking grants to the other the right to exploit a franchise' and 'the use of a common name or shop sign').
(6) and (7) These features are not really addressed in the definition. However, the preamble to the Regulation refers to franchisees as 'independent traders setting up outlets more rapidly and with higher chances of success', and the Regulation is conditional upon 'the franchise indi-

cating its status as an independent undertaking' (*see* preamble para 7 and art 4(c)).

(8) There has to be a payment (*see* the definition of 'franchise agreement').

1.5.3   Australia

In Australia there have been various attempts at regulating franchising. Initially, following a decision by a court that the sale of a franchise was the sale of a prescribed interest and thus regulated by the companies' codes, a disclosure regime was introduced by the Securities Commission. The Federal Government introduced two draft bills to regulate franchising but, following universal criticism, both were withdrawn and a regulation which took franchising outside the companies' codes was adopted.

Pressure for action continued, and in December 1990 the Minister for Small Business and Customs announced the appointment of a franchising task force to investigate franchising and to examine and report on the potential for self-regulating codes and other measures for countering market failure. The task force reported in December 1991 and recommended a voluntary code of practice to apply to franchises which met the requirements of the following definition:

'Franchise' means a contract agreement or arrangement, whether express or implied, whether written or oral, between two or more persons (such contract, agreement or arrangement hereinafter called the 'franchise agreement') by which a party to the franchise agreement (hereinafter called the 'franchisor') authorises or permits the other party to the franchise agreement (hereinafter called 'the franchisee') the right to engage in the business of offering or selling or distributing goods or services within Australia and such franchise agreement contains at least the following obligations or provisions:

— the franchisor grants the right to the use of a mark in such a manner that the business carried on by the franchisee is or is capable of being identified by the public as being substantially associated with the mark identifying, commonly connected with or controlled by the franchisor;
— the franchisee is required to conduct the business, or that part of the business subject to the franchise agreement, in accordance with the marketing, business or technical plan or system specified by the franchisor; and
— the franchisor provides ongoing marketing, business or technical assistance during the life of the franchise agreement.

Notwithstanding this, a contract agreement or arrangement which purports to be a franchise contract agreement or arrangement shall be deemed to be a franchise agreement for the purposes of the definition

13

notwithstanding that it may lack any or all of the aforementioned obligations or provisions.

The term 'mark' includes a symbol, design, device, brand heading,
label, ticket, name, signature, word, letter or any combination of these.

This definition is rife with drafting inconsistencies and seems to be an attempt
to draw the definition far too widely, but one can detect that the following features are essential:

(1) There must be a contract, or perhaps even an understanding which does
not amount to a contract. But whether or not it has the characteristics set
out in the definition, it would be within its scope if it 'purports' to be a
franchise contract. How it can purport to be a franchise contract if it
lacks the characteristics set out in the definition will require some creative thinking. It is likely that many arrangements involving licensing
which are not franchises at all could be brought within this definition.

(2) There must be two or more persons as parties to the contract.

(3) There must be the grant of the right to use a mark. Curiously, the definition of 'mark' does not refer specifically to trade marks and trade
names, but since it includes letters, words, devices, symbols or any combination thereof it will be a rare trade mark which is not within the definition.

(4) The franchisee must be required to use the franchisor's system.

(5) The franchisor must provide continuing marketing, business and technical assistance.

What is also curious is that there is no mention of payment by the franchisee to
the franchisor.

What the definition amounts to, basically, is that if the authority adminis-
tering the voluntary code believes a business to be a franchise then it is. This is
scarcely helpful for business people or their advisers who wish to know whether
their business arrangements may properly be effected as franchises.

Following a review of the operation of the voluntary code a number of
changes have been recommended which are being considered by the government.

1.5.4   The USA

No discussion of what franchising is would be complete without considering
the approach adopted by legislatures in the USA. There are three definitions to
which reference will be made. The first is that which appears in the first US
franchising legislation which was introduced in the State of California in 1970:

'Franchise' means a contract or agreement, either express or implied,
whether oral or written, between two or more persons by which:

(1) a franchisee is granted the right to engage in the business of offering, selling or distributing goods or services under a marketing
plan or system prescribed in substantial part by a franchisor;

(2) the operation of the franchisee's business pursuant to such plan
or system is substantially associated with the franchisor's trade
mark, service mark, trade name, logo type, advertising or other
commercial symbol designating the franchisor or its affiliate;
and

(3) the franchisee is required to pay, directly or indirectly, a franchise
fee.

The definition is extended to include contracts to which petroleum dealers are
parties, and there are also definitions of franchisor, franchisee and franchise fee.

This definition of 'franchise' is less extensive than the European
Commission's definition and is typical of those which have been adopted in
statutes in the USA dealing with franchising.

The second US definition which we shall examine appears in the Federal
Trade Commission Franchise Rule. This rule was introduced in 1979 and
defines 'franchise' as follows:

(a) The term 'franchise' means any continuing commercial relationship
created by any arrangement or arrangements whereby:

(1)(i) (A) A person (hereinafter 'franchisee') offers, sells, or distributes
to any person other than a 'franchisor' (as hereinafter defined) goods,
commodities, or services which are:
(1) identified by a trade mark, service mark, trade name, advertising or other commercial symbol designating another person
(hereinafter 'franchisor'); or
(2) indirectly or directly required or advised to meet the quality
standards prescribed by another person (hereinafter 'franchisor')
where the franchisee operates under a name using the trade mark,
service mark, trade name, advertising or other commercial symbol
designating the franchisor; and
(B) (1) The franchisor exerts or has authority to exert a significant
degree of control over the franchisee's method of operation,
including but not limited to the franchisee's business organisation,
promotional activities management, marketing plan or business
affairs; or
(2) The franchisor gives significant assistance to the franchisee
in the latter's method of operation, including, but not limited
to, the franchisee's business organisation, management, marketing plan, promotional activities or business affairs; provided
however that assistance in the franchisee's promotional activities

15

shall not, in the absence of assistance in other areas of the franchisee's method of operation constitute significant assistance; or

(ii)(A) A person (hereinafter 'franchisee') offers, sells or distributes to any person other than a 'franchisor' (as hereinafter defined) goods, commodities or services which are:

(1) Supplied by another person (hereinafter 'franchisor') or

(2) Supplied by a third person (eg supplier) with whom the franchisee is directly or indirectly advised to do business by another person (hereinafter 'franchisor') where such person is affiliated with the franchisor; and

(B) The Franchisor

(1) Secures for the franchisee retail outlets or accounts for said goods, commodities or services; or

(2) Secures for the franchisee locations or sites for vending machines, rack displays, or any other product sales display used by the franchisee in the offering, sale, or distribution of such goods, commodities or services; or

(3) Provides to the franchisee the services of a person able to secure the retail outlets, accounts, sites or locations referred to in paragraph (a)(1)(ii)(B)(1) and (2) *above*; and

(4) The franchisee is required as a condition of obtaining or commencing the franchise operation to make a payment or a commitment to pay to the franchisor or to a person affiliated with the franchisor.

The terms 'franchisor' and 'franchisee', having already been defined three times and twice respectively, are further broadly defined:

The term franchisor means any person who participates in a franchise relationship as a franchisor as denoted in paragraph (a) of this section [the paragraph defining 'franchisor'].

The term franchisee means any person (1) who participates in a franchise relationship as a franchisee as denoted in paragraph (a) of this section or (2) or whom an interest in a franchise is sold.

There are exceptions which, briefly, include:

(a) 'fractional franchises' where the franchisee has another related business and the franchised business does not represent more than 20 per cent of the dollar sales volume of the franchisee;

(b) where the total payments to the franchisor or person affiliated to the franchisor are less than US$500 during the first six months of operations;

(c) employment relationships;

(d) partnership relationships;

(e) membership of a bona fide co-operative association; or

(f) a bare trade mark licence.

It will be appreciated that, while the first part of the definition relates to business format and product distribution franchises, the second part relates to the wider business opportunities field. Good examples of the sorts of opportunity which the definition includes are rack jobbing and vending machine rounds. Some of these opportunities can be structured as business format franchises.

The US definitions are limited to the 'nuts and bolts' and do not add to these basic elements what might be described as the methods of implementing a franchise in practice, which the commercial and European definitions all contain.

The basic elements in these US definitions include many of the eight features listed at p 6:

(1) There must be a contract (but it need not be in writing to be caught by the US statutes).

(2) There must be a system.

(3) There must be branding: a trade mark, trade name, etc.

(4) There must be a grant of rights.

(5) There must be payment of money.

One can detect in these definitions how what is conceptually a simple business technique has become the subject of tortuous and complex legal definitions.

Chapter 2

History and Development

Chapter 2

History and Development

2.1 Introduction

This book is essentially concerned with the business format franchise described in Chapter 1 which in its current form is a relatively recent development. However, the licensing technique which is at the heart of franchising has been with us for many centuries. Throughout history there have been systems under which rights were granted or powers delegated in return for payment.

There was, for example, the baronial system in England, where the King granted rights to barons who collected and accounted for taxes. Indeed it could be said that the first franchisee class action (as the Americans call it) was that which was taken by the barons in their revolt against the rule of King John and whose terms of settlement were enshrined in Magna Carta.

The Guild system which operated in the City of London was also a form of franchise. Franchise rights granted by the Crown include rights to hold markets and fairs, and to provide bridges and fords across rivers and streams. Some of these ancient rights subsist today and are the subject of litigation from time to time.

2.2 Ancient franchises

In *Blackstone's Commentaries* (Vol II p 37), dealing with 'The Rights of Things', franchises are identified:

> franchise and liberty are used as synonymous terms and their definition is, a royal privilege, or branch of the King's prerogative, subsisting in the lands of a subject. Being therefore derived from the Crown, they must arise from the King's grant, or in some cases be held by prescription, which, as has been frequently said, presupposes a grant. The kinds of them are various and almost infinite: I will here briefly touch upon some of the principal; promising only, that they may be vested in either natural persons and bodies politic; in one man, or in many; but the same

identical franchise, that has before been granted to one, cannot be bestowed on another, for that would prejudice the former grant.

Blackstone includes in his list of franchises:

(a) to be a county palatine;
(b) to hold a court leet;
(c) to have a manor or lordship, or at least to have a lordship paramount;
(d) to have waifs and wrecks;
(e) treasure trove;
(f) royal fish;
(g) forfeitures and deodands;
(h) a court of one's own or liberty of holding pleas and trying cases;
(i) to have a fair or market;
(j) the right of taking a toll as at bridges, wharfs or the like; which tolls must have a reasonable cause of commencement as in consideration of repairs or the like.

It is also of interest to consider the position of the City of London's livery companies (*see The Livery of the City of London*, published by the City Corporation). Membership of a livery company carried many privileges. The usual method of entry was through apprenticeship which, when successfully completed, conferred the status of a freeman—free to serve any master or to set up on his own. The company protected standards of goods and work and effectively limited competition; in essence membership of the company gave the right to work within the City of London but to a standard which was supervised. Indeed without membership of the livery company one could not 'keep a shop and exercise a trade or handicraft within the City'. It could be said that the livery companies granted a 'franchise' to their members to trade in the City to a standard consistent and associated with membership of the relevant company.

The basic concept of someone granting a licence to another permitting that other to carry out some function can be seen in many relationships of a trading nature over many centuries.

2.3   The emergence of modern franchising

The modern form of franchising in business is widely believed to have first seen the light of day in 1863 when the Singer Sewing Machine Co 'developed what may have been the first commercial application of franchising' (Robert Rosenberg, *Profit from Franchising* (McGraw Hill, 1969)).

It was around the turn of the century in the USA, when three industries adopted franchise marketing methods, that one was able to detect the laying of more substantial foundations for what was to follow. The three industries were automobiles, soft drinks and drug stores.

There were, it appears, something like 77 firms which achieved commercial production of automobiles in the first decade of the century (Charles Mason Hewitt Jr, *Automobile Franchise Agreements*, (Michael D Cowin Inc, 1956) to which the authors are indebted for the information in this chapter relating to the automobile industry). Hewitt summarises the basic distribution needs of the manufacturers as:

> (1) some rapid means of acquiring retail outlets requiring a minimum of attention, outlay and fixed expense; (2) some means of making their cars conveniently available for customer inspection in advance of purchase on a nationwide basis; (3) some means of coping with the repair problems; (4) some means of coping with the off-season storage problem; (5) some means of acquiring a ready market for their goods without having fixed legal commitments for delivery; (6) some means of acquiring cash on delivery or even in advance if possible.

In the early period of development, manufacturers sold direct to the customer by diverse methods ranging from solicitation of orders by mail, travelling salesmen and the sale of total output through a single distributor.

At some point a manufacturer introduced the franchised 'agency' or 'dealer'. At that time, it was apparently common practice in the USA to refer to retailers as agents even when there was a clear buyer-seller relationship with an independent retailer. The contractual provisions appear to have been simple, granting exclusive territorial rights coupled with terms relating to the sale of goods. Franchising petrol filling stations (or as they are called in the USA 'gas stations') by the petrol companies did not commence until around 1930, and between then and 1935 the practice spread to the point where it became the sole method of distributing gasoline. (*See* Rosenberg, *ibid* at p 10.)

At the same time as the infant automobile industry was establishing by experiment the best method of marketing and distributing its products, Coca Cola were introducing the franchising of independent bottlers. The basic arrangement is that the company manufactures the syrup or syrups which form the basis of the drink. The company sells the syrups to the bottlers who mix as directed and place the resulting drink into the appropriate containers for distribution and sale. This method is still employed widely in the soft drinks industry.

The drug store business first experienced franchising in 1902 when Lewis K Leggett invited a group of drug stores proprietors to a meeting to discuss a plan for a 'drug co-operative'. Leggett explained that they could increase profits by paying less for what they purchased and they could also set up their own manufacturing company. The manufacturing company would create its own brand name and only its members or licensees could sell these branded products. From this emerged the *Rexall* brand name, with company-owned and franchised outlets (*See* Rosenberg, *ibid*, pp 3 and 4.)

Ben Franklin Variety Stores began franchising in 1927 and had some 2,400 stores by the early 1960s. (M Mendelsohn (ed), *International Franchising—An Overview* (North Holland, 1983) Chapter 1, An Introduction to Franchising by Lewis G Rudnick, p 4.)

In the early 1930s the Western Auto Supply Company began its franchise operations and set up more than 4,000 establishments within 30 years. (*See* Rudnick, *ibid.*)

Rudnick explains the introduction of franchising to the food service industry in the following way:

> Franchising was introduced to the food service industry in the 1930s when Howard Johnson established his first franchise. Johnson had successfully established two ice cream businesses and a restaurant but lacked the capital to open additional restaurants. However, he agreed to help a former classmate design, furnish, and supervise a restaurant and to sell him ice cream and other supplies under a Howard Johnson's franchise. When the first franchise was successful, Johnson granted other franchises and opened additional restaurants of his own. By 1940, over 100 Howard Johnson's restaurants were in operation. Many of these were owned by franchisees who had no prior experience in the restaurant business. Through franchising the restaurant owners obtained the benefit of the franchisor's expertise and guidance and the opportunity to profit from a proven concept. In return Howard Johnson's made a profit from the supplies it sold to the franchisees.

Many companies which commenced business in the 1930s, did not franchise until much later. Examples include Choice Hotels (commenced business 1939, franchising 1960); Sheraton Hotels (1937/1962); Travelodge (1935/1966). International Dairy Queen commenced business and franchising in 1940. Thus, a number of businesses established in the 1930–1950 period, laid the foundations for the widespread adoption of the franchise method of marketing.

2.4   Rapid growth

From shortly after the end of the Second World War up to 1960 the growth in franchise networks was rapid and spanned a broad range of business categories. Many now well-known franchising names emerged in this period, as this list illustrates:

Company	Year Commenced Business
ServiceMaster	1949
Holiday Inn	1952
Burger King	1954

Dunkin' Donuts	1954
McDonalds	1955
Budget Rent a Car	1958

Growth was so rapid that by 1960 it was reckoned that there were some 700 franchise systems in operation. Many of the early entrants into franchising chose this method of expanding their business in response to demand from customers and friends who, having seen the success which the businesses enjoyed, asked if they could be shown how to run similar businesses. The early pioneers, if one may so describe them, rapidly appreciated that franchising provided two of the most scarce and necessary ingredients for business development. First, franchisees provided the capital resources which were necessary to open a new business; second, franchisees provided the management of the business, and removed from the franchisor the need for costly day to day supervision and control of a 'branch', and the cost of back-up staff.

In the USA the Department of Commerce conducted annual surveys of franchising from a relatively early date. The surveys differentiated between 'product and trade name franchising' and business format franchising. In the former category they included automobile and truck dealers, petrol filling stations and soft drink bottlers. The number of outlets in this category has declined over the years, which is almost wholly attributable to the closure of petrol (gas) stations. The 1972 survey showed a total of 262,100 establishments with annual gross sales of $72bn, while in 1988 there were 140,820 establishments with annual gross sales of $281bn. By contrast, in 1972, business format franchising establishments produced annual gross sales of $17.9bn from a total of 189,640 outlets, which had grown by 1988 to 368,458 outlets producing $118.8bn in annual gross sales.

In the period from 1946 to 1972, almost 190,000 outlets, ranging from small one-man businesses to hotels, were opened using the franchising system, and some 902 franchise systems had by then been identified.

At the time of writing, franchising in the USA accounts for 34 per cent of retail sales; there are over half a million outlets whose annual gross sales are heading for $640bn. Franchise businesses directly employ around 7.5 million workers, while the total impact on employment cannot be fully judged without including those employed in businesses which supply goods and services to franchised businesses.

The production of reliable statistics in countries other than the USA has been slow to develop and range from the professionally prepared to best estimates made by franchise associations. Whichever method of preparing statistics is employed it is certain that no one succeeds in identifying all franchise systems in any marketplace, and that some companies included in the statistics are either not franchisors or are, for one reason or another, only transient. The following table, which excludes sales of petrol, automobiles, trucks and soft drinks, comprises the most recent information available from published sources and/or franchise associations.

		No of Franchises	No of Outlets	Annual Sales
Argentina	(1992)	40	1,300	N/A
Australia	(1991)	500	17,000	A $32bn[1]
Austria	(1991)	80	2,500	N/A
Belgium	(1990)	90	3,200	3,300m ECU
Canada		500	40,000	N/A
Denmark	(1991)	42	500	500m ECU
France	(1993)	500	27,000	US$34bn
Germany	(1991)	265	9,950	DM4,000m
Italy	(1992)	336	15,000	8,500m ECU
Indonesia	(1993)	60+	N/A	N/A
Japan	(1992)	688	141,365	Y10
Netherlands	(1991)	309	11,005	6,300m ECU
Spain	(1990)	117	14,500	2,100m ECU
Sweden	(1991)	200	9,000	6,000m ECU
UK	(1994)	400	22,500	£5.4m
South Africa	(1992)	80	3,000	N/A
Portugal		55		N/A
Greece		35	80+	N/A
Switzerland		200	3,000	N/A
Finland	(1993)	44	1,571	FIM 1,830m
Brazil	(1992)	500	52,652[2]	US $38bn
Hong Kong		59	N/A	N/A
Hungary		150[3]	N/A	N/A
United States	(1991)	2,500+	542,496	$757.8bn

[1] Includes petrol sales.

[2] Includes car and petrol sales outlets.

[3] Estimated by the local franchise association but probably includes many embryonic businesses or distribution systems.

The UK franchise market is still quite small. There are, according to the latest NatWest Bank/BFA survey, some 400 franchises with 22,500 outlets. Pro rata to the respective population of the UK and the USA there would need to be 106,000 additional outlets to reach the same level of penetration of the retail market. In the rest of the European Union, an additional 213,484 outlets would be required to achieve the same level as the USA. This is without allowing for the increased size of the EU from 1 January 1995, when Sweden, Austria and Finland were admitted.

Cross-border franchising has been developing since the early days and in almost all countries in the world (and there are at least 140) where franchising is found, systems have been imported or exported or both. Chapters 19 to 21 of this work deal with international franchising.

2.5   Techniques

The steady growth of franchising has led to the introduction of many new techniques and progress has not been without some difficulties. A number of distribution methods which have developed do not amount to franchising systems, but are happy to borrow the description to gain a respectability for their activities which they do not merit. Many are the offers of distribution rights for single products for which no market exists, but the greedy and gullible pay large sums of money for the exclusive rights to sell them in a given area. Probably the most persistent in this category are those who peddle the pyramid selling schemes, discussed in Chapter 6.

The very success of franchising has led to many techniques having to be devised to deal with the market considerations. The various specialised techniques do not necessarily work everywhere, but the situations in which they arise need to be understood. They are considered where relevant in this work, principally in Chapters 6, 18 and 20.

Franchisors realised at an early stage that the most skilled and talented franchisees were capable of running more than one outlet. In some cases franchisors have permitted franchisees to take up a franchise with another franchisor. As techniques of franchising improve, the advantage of establishing as franchisees those whose intention it is from the outset to open more than one outlet has emerged, and franchisors have had to consider how to create the right framework.

In the USA the device of a development agreement has been widely used to enable franchisors to cope with the vast distances. Under these agreements the developer undertakes to open a predetermined number of outlets in an exclusive territory within a fixed time. It is a form of multiple-unit operation for an allocated territory.

In international franchising, master franchise agreements are usually used to establish the sub-franchisor in the 'shoes' of the franchisor in the target territory in which he operates his own outlets and predominantly sub-franchises. In some countries anti-pyramid selling laws may prohibit or affect this arrangement.

An area franchise agreement will usually be employed where the area franchisee's activities combine the features of a development agreement and a master franchise agreement, but, unlike the latter, the area will be part of a country and the area franchisee's role much more limited. Again, anti-pyramid selling laws may prohibit or affect this arrangement.

Fractional franchising is where the franchised business forms only a part of the franchisee's overall business. A good example of a fractional franchise is a car rental business franchised to a garage.

Conversion franchises are those where an existing business is 'converted' to a franchise in the same line of business, such as an estate agency, a travel agency or a convenience store. This method may be employed from the outset or when a network is relatively mature, when it may be a convenient and rapid way of filling in gaps in the marketplace. This method is not without its practical difficulties.

In recent years a practice known as 'combination franchising' has been introduced. It has grown from the need to cope with high retail rental costs in major cities. The objective is for franchise systems to share premises so that the maximum return can be obtained from the quality of the location, which reduces the overall impact of premises cost. One could therefore find, for example, three different fast food franchises in the same premises, each with its own food preparation and serving areas, but with a common seating area—a mini food hall such as one now finds in shopping centres. There may be one franchise of all three, or there may be a separate franchise for each franchisor.

In some businesses, principally the hotel trade, franchise arrangements have been combined with management contracts under which the franchisor manages the business for the franchisee whose interest is as an investor.

We have by no means seen the end of the techniques which will be employed in franchising. Some ideas will be tried, some will work, some will fail. In the long run it is likely that the principles on which franchising is based, and to which it owes its success, will not change, and that attempts to attack the basic principles will prove counter-productive.

Chapter 3

The Commercial Rationale

Chapter 3

The Commercial Rationale

3.1 Introduction

Franchising as a good idea would not have had the success it has had without the good commercial reasons which make it work to the advantage of the franchisor, the franchisee and the consumer.

The history and development of franchising, which is traced in the previous chapter, explain why manufacturers became involved, the creation of the wholesale co-operative which developed into a franchise, and the horizontal growth which followed the post-war boom. The layers between manufacturer and consumer have interacted with each other in franchise relationships. Manufacturers have used franchising as a method of securing outlets for their products which are sold in defined and controlled systems. Wholesalers have used franchising as a method of securing outlets for products while ensuring full use of their storage and distribution facilities. Horizontal growth at retail level has enabled small businesses to develop into larger, and in some cases significant multinational, companies either more rapidly or extensively than would otherwise have been possible.

Success is based on the ability to develop a successful business and to market that success by persuading others to invest their resources in establishing a similar business. The success of that business will depend on its appeal, or the appeal of its products and/or services. That success will have to be maintained throughout the life of the franchise network, for without it the franchisees will not succeed; if the franchisees are not successful, the franchisor has no business.

From this brief analysis, it is possible to see the commerce which underlies the principles discussed in Chapter 1.

3.2 The risks

3.2.1 For the franchisee

For someone establishing a new business the risks are high; mistakes may be made; money may be wasted; perhaps the wrong equipment is obtained;

perhaps the product mix is not right; staff schedules may be wrong. There is much to learn about customer flows, effective marketing and promotion, control systems, merchandising the optimum range of products and services. The list could be endless. A great number of new businesses fail because the promoter's money runs out before all the problems are solved and the business becomes successful. However, a franchisee in taking up a franchise is eliminating from his business risk the risk of trial and error. He does not eliminate risk entirely; the nature of the risk changes into the risk that the franchisor has not properly learned the lessons or solved all the problems. Indeed, for the franchisee there will be the franchisor risk factor throughout the relationship, including not only the question of how well did the franchiser pilot-test its operation (which is only relevant in the early days of the franchise) but:

(a) will it prove capable of running its own business?
(b) is it sufficiently well capitalised?
(c) will it seek unfairly to take advantage of its franchisees?
(d) will it provide and maintain a high quality level of continuing support services?
(e) will it make mistakes and policy decisions which will hurt its franchisees?

The earlier in the development of the franchisor's business that the franchisee comes in, the more difficult it is to judge the franchisor's qualities. No one should become a franchisee without being prepared to accept the business risk. Anyone who considers that undertaking a franchise business is a guarantee of success is deceiving himself. Whatever degree of investigation is undertaken, a subjective judgment will have to be made. Would-be franchisees who are besotted with the business idea or system, or who are motivated by greed, have no place in franchising. Professional advisers will rarely be able to satisfy themselves that a proposition is safe for the would-be franchisee client. Everything may look right, but the franchisee will fail. Everything may look absolutely wrong; the franchisee may be advised not to proceed, yet he may succeed.

3.2.2   For the franchisor

Despite the good qualities of a franchisor, franchising is full of uncertainties and conflicts. Even those franchisors whose credentials and achievements would be considered beyond question experience franchisee failure from time to time. What the franchisee is provided with is a business 'Do It Yourself' kit. It comes with instructions (training and manuals) and after-sales service (the franchisor's continuing support), but whether or not the kit is made to work depends to a great extent on the effort, commitment and skill contributed by the franchisee.

There is a fundamental conflict between the establishment in business of an independent entrepreneur who is encouraged to think and develop as the owner of his own business, and the fact that at the same time he must work within a controlled system and method. This again points to the need for sound objective appraisals by prospective franchisees, and acceptance of the pro-active role they must play despite the controlled environment.

The statistics and research on franchisee failure are few and far between. In the UK the best information available is the annual NatWest Bank/BFA survey and the experience of the banks who lend extensively to franchisees. The sum of the information available indicates that the new franchisee is eight to ten times less likely to fail than the new non-franchised businessman.

There is a fallacious belief that franchisors are big business and franchisees are small business. While there is undoubtedly a significant number of large businesses engaged in franchising as franchisors, the vast majority of franchisors are small businesses who are able to make a more significant impact in the marketplace than their size would suggest.

3.3   The attractions

3.3.1   For the franchisee

Given these risks, why do people take up franchises? It has already been noted that the business risk inherent in opening a new business is significantly reduced.

Based on experience obtained from the pilot-testing and other trading activities conducted by the franchisor, the franchisee will receive training in how to conduct the business and in related aspects, such as accounting, marketing and promotion. As a result of the franchisor's experience, the franchisee's capital investment will be used in the most cost-effective way.

The franchisee will benefit immediately he commences trading from the franchisor's trade mark or branding and the goodwill associated with it. The franchisee will invariably receive a range of services to assist in opening for business. These are probably not available elsewhere in the marketplace or, if they are, are not so narrowly focused and cost-effective. The franchisee will benefit, as a member of a larger network, from the bulk purchasing power which it will command. The pooling of resources will enable more effective advertising and promotion than an individual trader could secure.

A franchisor who is doing his job properly will provide a range of specialist services to assist the franchisee in coping with day-to-day practical problems. He will also engage in research and development and market testing to ensure that the franchise network maintains its competitive position.

In short, the franchisee will receive a range of services and benefits at a price he can afford, which no individual trader could secure.

3.3.2   For the franchisor

The advantages for a franchisor of using the financial and manpower resources of the franchise, and the benefits which flow to franchisors in various capacities, have already been noted. There are other reasons why business people establish franchising systems. Franchising permits a speed of growth which is otherwise difficult to match. Franchising is geared to reproduce like businesses, and its speed is limited by three factors:

(a) the ability of the franchisor to develop its supporting infrastructure;
(b) the availability of franchisees of suitable quality and ability;
(c) the availability of trading locations of the right type and in the right place.

The scale of the franchisor's operations, and thus its staffing requirements, is smaller than it would be if all outlets were in single ownership. The quality and qualifications of the head office staff will probably be more concentrated.

The franchisor will hope to find that the franchisees who own the franchised businesses will be easier to motivate than employed managers. However, they are likely to be more challenging. By not participating in the day-to-day problems of each outlet, the franchisor is able to devote its attention to strategic issues which confront the network and to concentrate on creating the right atmosphere in its relations with its franchisees, and to enhance the effectiveness of the sales efforts of the network.

The franchisor's biggest problems will be people problems. It has to learn how to handle franchisees who go through many stages, from eager learners to the over-confident who, as their years in the network provide them with success, question whether they need a franchisor at all.

Given the ups and downs and the risks which confront franchisors and franchisees one may wonder why they do it. They do it because for the vast majority it makes sense and they profit from it.

Chapter 4

How the Law Affects Franchising

Chapter 4

How the Law Affects Franchising

4.1 Introduction

There are two separate strands of law which should be considered in the context of franchising:

(a) laws which affect business generally and the industry in which a particular business operates; and

(b) laws which are relevant only because the marketing method which has been chosen is franchising.

So far as the former are concerned, it is clear that any business person would have to identify and comply with all legal requirements which affect his business. In the franchise context there is a difference, since the franchisee relies on the franchisor to have identified correctly and comprehensively all relevant laws which affect the business being franchised. The development of the business for franchising through a pilot operation should enable the franchisor to identify these relevant laws; the franchisee will certainly expect that the franchisor's system reflects and respects all relevant laws.

So far as the second group of laws is concerned, it is convenient to break down the franchise transaction into various stages, identifying the issues which need to be considered at each of these stages. There are seven stages to be considered:

(a) the development of the concept;

(b) structuring the franchise package;

(c) marketing the franchise package;

(d) opening for business;

(e) the long term relationship;

(f) the termination of the contract;

(g) the consequences of termination.

4.2   Contract stage A: development of the concept

Commercial considerations

Legal considerations

Objective: to ascertain the efficacy of the proposed franchise system and the business concept on which it is based.

Objective: to anticipate, consider, protect, control and comply.

The importance of this stage and the next stage is often not recognised. It is at these stages that the main intellectual property rights come into play, and the major decisions with legal implications will be made.

The concept is developed by means of a pilot operation.

Identify special industry laws which may apply to the business.

The pilot operation should:
— explore the validity of the concept in practical opera-tions;
— fine-tune it;
— establish business, operational and accounting systems;
— provide evidence of mar-ketability of the goods and/or services being provided to the consumer;
— provide evidence of success to enable the franchisor to sell the 'successful' business concept to franchisees;
— identify the location, nature and extent of premises, or, if the operation is to be mobile, the optimum method of fitting out and equipping the vehicle;
— enable the franchisor to iden-tify the optimum use of equip-ment;
— develop an operational man-ual with full details of the system to be used in training franchisees and to provide a record (which will be updated from time to time) of opera-tional procedures.

Identify the effects of:
— general and other specific laws applicable to the type of business;
— town and country planning restrictions;
— by-laws and building regula-tions;
— health and safety at work leg-islation;
— Shops Acts;
— Trade Descriptions Act;
— Sale of Goods Act;
— Supply of Goods and Services Act;
— Local by-laws which may affect the business;
— employment laws;
— tax laws;
— Value Added Tax.

While this activity is going on, the pilot operation will result in the franchisor's creating some or all of the following intellectual property rights:

— a trade mark. This may already exist if the franchise and the main product line is already trade marked;
— a trade name;
— goodwill;
— trade secrets;
— confidential information;
— copyright material;
— designs;
— patents (but this is rare);
— processes for manufacture or preparation;
— formulae;
— recipes.

Steps have to be taken to ensure that the names and logos used are registrable as trade marks, and that designs and patentable processes or inventions are properly protected at law. The international prospects should also be considered at some stage since, in the case of patents particularly, delay can be fatal and names do get solen. All the necessary steps to effect such registrations must be taken. It may be appropriate to consider the law of passing off.

4.3   Contract stage B: structuring the package

This is the stage when the franchisor, having decided that, as a result of his pilot operation(s), he has a viable franchisable concept, concerns himself with drawing the elements together into a marketable commodity. Now is the time to make structural decisions which will affect the commercial and legal shape of the transactions which will follow.

Commercial consideration

Does the franchisor wish to become involved in the property chain?
— advantages: control, retention of site;
— disadvantages: financial exposure, security of tenure in jeopardy.

Tied products:
— securing;
— pricing policy;
— sources.

Legal considerations

Landlord and Tenant Act 1954 (as amended).

— EC and UK competition law;
— Treaty of Rome, art 85;
— Restrictive Trade Practices Act 1976;
— Competition Act 1981;
— Resale Prices Act 1976.

Territorial considerations:
— exclusivity;
— size/viability;
— targets.

Length of agreement.

Rights of renewal.

Common law restraint of trade (*see further* under contract stage E).

Establish level of fees:
— initial;
— continuing.

What is the character of the fees and what are the taxation implications for franchisor and franchisee?

Methods of collecting and policing fees.

Consider requirements relating to the payment of fees.

Establish procedures for advertising; usually contributions are collected from franchisees and spent by the franchisor.

What is the nature of the arrangement? Consider:
— tax consequences;
— trust implications.

Establish nature and range of:
— initial services;
— continuing services. These may include a wide range of topics: training; property expertise; site selection; design and layout of premises; updating of manuals; shopfitting; operational procedure; business methods; marketing methods; access to common facilities, eg computer services; central ordering; bulk purchasing; research and development; PR; advertising and marketing.

Consider, in respect of the services to be provided, legal liability:
— to franchisees in contract and tort;
— to third parties in tort;
— under the Data Protection Act.

Consider the character of the franchisee as:
— investor;
— large company;
— small proprietorial company;
— an individual.

Consider how the franchisor's industrial and intellectual property rights (particularly trade secrets and confidential information) may be protected in each of these cases.

Avoid a pyramid structure.

Part XI, Fair Trading Act 1973.

4.4   Contract stage C: marketing the package

The franchisor, having tested his ideas and prepared his package, now embarks on marketing the package to would-be franchisees.

Commercial considerations

Marketing material such as brochures.

Franchisee advertisements.

Other recruitment methods, eg exhibitions, media comment.

Interviews with franchisees and selection procedures.

Arrangements with bankers or other lending institution financing franchisees.

Legal considerations

Misrepresentation.

Unfair Contract Terms Act.

Contract.

Tort.

Sex discrimination legislation.

Racial discrimination legislation.

Protecting secret and confidential information during negotiations.

4.5   Contract stage D: opening for business

The franchisor has recruited his franchisee and the contract is signed. Now there is the task of transforming the new recruit into a fully trained operator ready to open the door for business.

Commercial considerations

Site evaluation:
— suitability as a trading position;
— suitability from physical point of view.

Training.

Specifications and plans for conversion of premises.

Shopfitting.

Equipment:
— nominated source;
— tied supply.

Legal considerations

Town and country planning laws.

By-laws and building regulations.

Possible vicarious liability to suppliers.

Contractual liability.

Treaty of Rome, art 85.

UK Competition Law.

Acquisition of stock.

Arrangements with utilities.

4.6   Contract stage E: the continuing relationship

The franchisee is now open for business. The parties hope that a long-term relationship has started. The franchisor will want to ensure that the franchisee performs and that its system is protected in operation and from unfair competition.

Commercial considerations

The range of the franchisor's services will be specified in the contract.

Protection of the franchisor's system, know-how and operational procedures

Operational system requirements, eg guarantees to consumers.

The commitment of the franchisee:
— to the business;
— not to compete with the system.

Providing for innovation and change.

Sale of business.

Death of franchisee or (if corporate franchisee) the moving force.

Dispute resolution.

Legal considerations

Treaty of Rome, art 85.

Restrictive Trade Practices Act 1976.

Common law on restraint of trade.

Arbitration law and ADR.

Contract liability.

Tortious liability.

Consider boilerplate clauses for contract.

4.7   Contract stage F: termination

Develop strategy which will affect administration of network.

Decide appropriate time for opportunity to cure defaults.

Specify events of default and method of termination.

Consider remedies for franchisee/ franchisor.

Landlord and Tenant Act 1954 (as amended).

4.8   Contract stage G: consequences of termination

Contract termination: develop strategy for the protection of franchisor and network against unfair competition post-termination.

Post-termination restraints against:
— conducting a competing business;
— soliciting or touting for business from another base;
— use of know-how and confidential business.

Requirements to
— change business premises to de-identify;
— return of operational manuals;
— stop use of name;
— grant option for franchisor to purchase lease of premises;
— stop use of copyright material.

Treaty of Rome, art 85.

Common law rules on restraint of trade.

Common law rules on trade secrets.

The issues identified in this chapter are dealt with in the chapters which follow.

Chapter 5

The Relationship of the Parties

Chapter 5

The Relationship of the Parties

5.1   Introduction

As will have been appreciated from Chapter 1, the franchise relationship is created by contract between two independent business people. In many cases the franchise agreement determines at the outset the nature of the franchisee's business.

There are potential dangers for the parties to the agreement if the contracts are not properly structured. This is because franchising, in legal terms, is hybrid. Many elements found in other transactions can be part of a particular franchise arrangement. For example, a product-based franchise is in reality a marketing method of distributing products. Clumsily attempting to disguise employment as a franchise, as has been tried (*Customs and Excise Commissioners* v *Jane Montgomery (Hair Styles) Ltd* [1994] STC 256), will not impress the fiscal authorities. There have been decisions in other jurisdictions where a contract described as a franchise agreement was held on the facts to create the relationship of employer and employee. However, in Italy an attempt by a franchisee of a convenience store to have the relationship characterised as employment failed. The judge pointed out that 'the burdensome terms of a contract are not a strong enough reason to turn an entrepreneurial business (even if it was restricted by a cleverly drawn up agreement to allow the franchisee to have a minimum of independence and income) into a contract of service'. (*Bratti* v *Ges Comm Srl and Cipac Spa* (1987) JIFDL p 38.)

A number of commercial arrangements are capable of existence within any given franchise system. What is crucial is that the differences are recognised and potential traps are avoided. The relationships which are claimed or alleged to exist in franchising fall into three categories and are:

(1)   The traditional relationships which are invariably found in a franchise: those of buyer and seller and of distributorship.
(2)   The relationships which can be confused with franchising: licensing; agency; employer and employee; partnership.
(3)   Relationships which some have sought to assert as existing as a matter of law: shadow directorships; fiduciary relationships.

Generally, the first category includes relationships which are encouraged, the second includes relationships which the parties seek to avoid, and the third includes relationships which are not a part of franchising but might be claimed by those who seek some advantage by asserting that category of relationship.

5.2 Supply relationships

5.2.1 Buyer and seller

The creation of the franchise relationship inevitably involves the sale by the franchisor of the franchise package and its purchase by the franchisee. This buyer/seller relationship continues throughout the term of the franchise agreement and any additional terms. The initial sale will involve a mixed package of products and services. It also includes a licence by the franchisor to the franchisee (*see* p 49, *below*). In a product franchise, the continuing relationship may involve the ongoing sale of the products which are to be sold by the franchisee. In a service franchise, there may be the ongoing sale of products which are to be supplied or used in the course of the provision of services by the franchisee. In both cases the franchisor will continue to provide services to the franchisee at a price.

5.2.2 Distribution

In a product franchise the franchisee will be a distributor of the product but not in the traditional sense. In a traditional distribution agreement, the distributor's business is just that. He may sell competing products; he may sell complementary products. It is most unlikely that he will sell only one supplier's products. He will sell whatever he distributes under his own name, although he may have signs on display representing the products in his range. He will sell his products in his own way using his own business systems and methods, which may bear no resemblance to his suppliers' systems and methods. He will need no special training beyond becoming familiar with the product range, its capabilities and any follow up services which may be appropriate. He will not pay fees.

The franchisee's position is in complete contrast. He will sell only the range of products associated with the franchisor's business, using the franchisor's name and the franchisor's systems. He will invariably not know how to run a business according to the franchisor's system; he may never have run a business before, and will be the subject of training focused on how to run the franchisor's system. He will pay fees.

5.3   Relationships to be distinguished

Invariably, franchise agreements expressly exclude agency and partnership as the basis of the relationship between the parties. The structure of franchise arrangements usually makes it plain that the franchisee is an independent business entity. However, in all cases the way in which obligations, rights and duties are in fact structured, and the way in which third parties are treated, may override the specific contractual provisions.

5.3.1   Licensing

Licensing is often confused with franchising, for the very good reason that at the heart of every franchise there is indeed a licence (in legal terms) to use a trade mark or trade name and other intellectual property rights. However, franchising is not what is intended to be described when the term 'licensing' is used, and although all franchises include licences, to regard franchises as merely licences with extra provisions added is to invite confusion. The confusion is understandable. The commercial distinction is that franchising is a method of marketing goods and services, whereas in practice licensing tends to relate to the manufacturing stage and the production of goods which subsequently enter the marketing chain. The following table illustrates the main differences.

	Franchise	*Licence*
— manufacturing process	Rarely	Yes
— previous experience in performing necessary activities	Rarely	Essential
— uses trading name of franchisor/licensor	Yes	No
— uses business system of franchisor/licensor	Yes	No
— uses premises designed and laid out according to franchisor/licensor requirements	Yes	No
— part of a network of identical operations	Yes	No

5.3.2   Agency

Agency can arise in two ways; by express appointment and by 'holding out'. It is rare to find agency by express appointment in any franchise arrangement, although there can be elements in some arrangements (such as parcels' delivery franchises) where agency is appropriate.

There is a risk that the use of the franchisor's name by the franchisee may lead third parties to believe that they are dealing with the franchisor, or at least its authorised agent. The risk is well documented:

> Where a person, by words or conduct, represents or permits it to be represented that another person is his agent, he will not be permitted to deny

the agency, with respect to any dealing, or the fact of such representations, with the person so held out as agent, even if the relationship of principal and agent has not arisen.

(Bowstead, *Law of Agency*, 15th edn (Sweet and Maxwell, 1985), p 90.)

The increasing popularity and volume of franchising and the level of awareness of its existence will make it more difficult for a third party to sustain a claim of misrepresentation. There are many analogous transactions where common branding has not led to the owner of the brand being held liable to third parties. Examples include motor vehicle distributorships, public houses, petrol filling stations.

The important point for the franchisor is to ensure that whatever is represented by the franchisee to third parties contains the clear message that the franchise is an independent business operated under licence or franchise from the franchisor. The Business Names Act 1985 requires that the true owner of a business trading under a name other than that of the proprietor is identified on notepaper and elsewhere. The European Commission, in the Block Exemption Regulation for categories of franchise agreement (*see* Chapter 16), recognises the importance of this issue by making it a condition of the application of the Regulation that the franchisee is required to be identified as an independent business. The absence of such a statement will not necessarily mean that the liability issue is clear, but it should make it easier for the franchisor to defend itself against third party claims.

5.3.3   Employment

Whether the franchisee is an employee of the franchisor is relevant for a number of purposes including tax, social security benefits and employment protection rights and in the context of business transfers.

The Employment Protection (Consolidation) Act 1978 defines an employee as an individual who has entered into or works under a contract of employment. This definition does not apply universally, however, nor does it help much in identifying whether an individual is working under a contract of employment or is self-employed. Case law must also be examined.

Employee or self-employed

Although in the past the courts have applied a variety of tests to determine employment status, the modern approach is to consider a number of factors (none of which is likely to be conclusive) against the background of the individual circumstances. The main questions the court will ask (see *Ready Mix Concrete (South East) Ltd* v *Minister of Pensions and National Insurance* [1968] QB 497) are:

(1) Is the individual obliged to provide his personal services and skill in return for remuneration?

(2) Is there a sufficient degree of control to indicate an employment relationship?

(3) Are all the other factors consistent with an employment contract?

The court will consider all the relevant factors and make a decision based on a qualitative appraisal of the whole picture. It is not possible to provide an exhaustive list of all the relevant factors (which may depend on which statutory authority is considering the issue—the Inland Revenue, the Department of Social Security, an industrial tribunal or court), but the more important factors include:

(1) *The exercise of control:* for example, who has responsibility for discipline, dismissal, hours of work and the manner of working. If the individual has freedom to determine when and how to provide the services, this suggests an independent contractor rather than an employee. In franchising this has to be considered in the light of the controls which the franchisor imposes in licensing its intellectual property, to ensure uniformity and quality of operations and to protect and secure its intellectual property rights.

(2) *Financial risk:* what are the commercial realities of the relationship and, in particular, does the individual invest his capital in the business and profit by his own management? Again, this is an important factor in franchising since the franchisee will generally bear the entire financial risk involved in the franchise (unless he is directly employed on a type of assisted franchisee scheme). In the case of *McKernan v British School of Motoring* COIT Case No 11300/93, Mr McKernan had entered into a franchise and agency agreement with the British School of Motoring under which he received fees direct from clients. He paid them to BSM, which in turn deducted the franchise fee and returned the balance to Mr McKernan. There was no direct payment by BSM to the franchisee. The Tribunal decided the franchisee was self-employed. It must be emphasised, however, that each case will be decided on its own facts and that the BSM decision is not binding on other tribunals and courts. The avoidance of direct payment between the franchisor and franchisee is not therefore conclusive evidence that a 'franchisee' is self-employed.

(3) *Mutuality of obligation:* the court will consider whether there is a degree of mutual obligation such that the 'employer' is obliged to continue to provide and pay for work, and the 'employee' to continue to do the work.

(4) *Provision of equipment:* if the individual provides his own tools and equipment this will generally indicate self-employed status.

(5) *Remuneration and benefits:* the amount of remuneration and the method of payment can illustrate the type of relationship. Wages, of course, indicate an employee, while a profit share or commission-based remuneration could indicate an independent contractor. Equally the provision of benefits (such as paid holiday, sick pay, insurances, a car) tend to indicate employment.

(6) *Form of agreement:* the form and contents of the agreement can indicate the intention of the parties. The label applied (franchise rather than employment) cannot change the status of the relationship. If all the other facts point toward self-employment, however, then the form of the agreement may be conclusive.

In most cases the franchisor will wish to avoid creating an employment relationship with the franchisee. The franchisor should consider the factors outlined above when the terms of the franchise agreement are being framed. The commercial realities and the precise nature of the franchise will inevitably dictate certain of the terms. The agreement should cover the following points:

(1) The franchisee should be expressly responsible for obtaining and providing fittings and fixtures in any premises, together with any equipment necessary to run the business.

(2) It should be clear that the individual is investing in the business and is able to profit by his own management, as well as bearing the financial risk of failure.

(3) It must be clear that the franchisee has as high a degree of control as commercially feasible over the operation of the business, including the power to delegate to others and to employ staff for whom he will be directly responsible.

Business transfers

The Transfer of Undertakings (Protection of Employment) Regulations 1981 apply in the context of certain business transfers to protect the rights of employees working in a business. The Regulations may be relevant to franchising in a number of situations, including:

(a) on the assignment of the franchise by the franchisee;

(b) on the termination of the franchise by the franchisor, resulting in the operation of the franchise business directly by the franchisor, indefinitely or until a new franchisee is appointed;

(c) on the termination of the franchise by the franchisor and immediate substitution of a new franchisee.

The Regulations have the following main effects:

(1) The contracts of employees engaged in the business, together with all rights and liabilities associated with those contracts (for example arrears of pay, accrued holiday pay, employment protection rights), are transferred to the recipient of the business or transferee (the incoming franchisee or, in certain cases, the franchisor).

(2) Certain dismissals will be automatically unfair if they are made for a reason connected with the transfer.

(3) The transferee will also inherit liability for certain pre-contract dismissals effected by the transferor (the outgoing franchisee).

(4) The parties are obliged to consult representatives of recognised trade unions (or workers' representatives) over the transfer.

Any attempt by the parties to contract out of the unwelcome effects of the Regulations will be void, although there is no restriction on the use of indemnities to determine where the ultimate financial liability will lie.

The meaning of 'transfer'   For the Regulations to apply there must be a transfer from one person to another of an 'undertaking' or part of an undertaking situated in the UK. There must be a change in the legal ownership or in the identity of the legal person responsible for operating the business. A transfer can take place in a single transaction (as in the case of an assignment of a franchise from one franchisee to another), or a series of transactions (for example on the termination of a franchise by the franchisor and subsequent grant to a new franchisee). The definition of 'transfer' has been extended to apply to situations where no property is transferred. This change gives effect to the European Court's decisions in *Landsorganisationen i Danmark* v *Ny'Molle Krø* [1989] IRLR 37 and *P Bork International A/S* v *Foreningen af Arbejdsledere i Danmark* [1990] 3 CMLR 701, and is intended to extend the Regulations to transfers of franchises and sub-contracts.

The tests for identifying transfers to which the Regulations apply have changed considerably in recent years, away from the requirement for a transfer of a business as a going concern, to the approach adopted by the European Court in cases concerning the European directive on which the Regulations are based. The decisive criterion is now whether, having taken account of all the surrounding circumstances, there is (i) a recognisable economic entity which is run or operated or carried on by the transferor (franchisee) which is (ii) continued or resumed by the transferee (incoming franchisee or franchisor) (*Wren and Others* v *Eastbourne Borough Council and UK Waste Control Ltd* [1993] ICR 955 EAT). To determine whether these two conditions are satisfied all the surrounding factual circumstances must be considered, including:

(a) the type of business or undertaking concerned;
(b) whether tangible assets (for example buildings and moveable property) are transferred;

(c) the value of intangible assets at the time of transfer;
(d) whether or not the majority of the employees are taken on by the new owner;
(e) whether or not customers are transferred;
(f) the degree of similarity between the activities carried on before and after the transfer;
(g) the period if any for which those activities are suspended.

The presence, or indeed absence, of any one of these factors is unlikely to be conclusive. The court or tribunal must make an overall assessment (ECJ in *Spijkers* v *Gebroeders Benedik Abattoir CV* [1986] 2 CMLR 296, reaffirmed in *Rask and another* v *ISS Kanteineservice AS* [1993] IRLR 133).

Following recent changes to the Regulations and the test used by tribunals to identify a business transfer, it is more likely than not that, on the assignment of a franchise, the incoming franchisee will inherit the employees of the out-going franchisee, together with liability for pre-assignment dismissal. *See* for example *LMC Drains Ltd and Metro Rods Services Ltd* v *Waugh* [1991] 3 CMLR 172, where the Employment Appeal Tribunal concluded that the Regulations applied on each assignment of a franchise to operate a drain maintenance system. It is also likely that the Regulations will be held to apply on the termination of the franchise where the franchise business is operated for a period by the franchisor, or where a new franchisee takes over from the out-going franchisee. The franchisor or the new franchisee will become responsible for the employees of the out-going franchisee. The extent of the franchisor's liability will depend on the level of its involvement in the franchise operation, and the length of time before any subsequent franchise is granted in the same area.

The franchisor can only protect its position to any degree by including indemnities in the franchise agreement, to apply on termination of the agreement for any reason; similarly indemnities should be obtained on the assignment of a franchise between franchisees.

5.3.4   Partnership

No franchisor would unwittingly wish to be in partnership with its franchisees. In *Body Shop International plc* v *Rawle and Others* (1992) unreported (QBD) Sir Peter Pain stated, in relation to the franchise agreement:

> One sees that this agreement provided for a very close relationship between the franchisee and The Body Shop. It was not a partnership agreement: clause 16 says specifically that it was not so. But in some ways it was similar to a partnership agreement, in that it required co-operation and good faith as between the parties to the agreement if it was to work effectively.

That the relationship between franchisor and franchisee requires co-operation and good faith if it is to work is a practical commercial reality rather than a legal concept, as the judge recognises.

'Partnership' is defined in s 1(1) of the Partnership Act 1890 as 'the relationship which subsists between persons carrying on a business in common with a view of profit'. Section 2 of that Act contains rules for determining the existence of partnership. These rules provide, *inter alia*:

(a) that common ownership of property does not in itself create a partnership in respect of it whether or not the owners share profits made by its use (s 2(1));

(b) the sharing of gross return does not of itself create a partnership (s 2(2));

(c) the receipt by a person of a share of the profits of a business is prima facie evidence that he is a partner in the business, but the receipt of such a share, or of a payment contingent on or varying with the profits of a business, does not in itself make him a partner in the business (s 2(3)).

A franchise relationship does not meet any of the criteria of the definition of a partnership. Whilst there clearly is a business conducted by the franchisee, he is doing so in an arm's length relationship with the franchisor. The franchisee does not carry on business in common with the franchisor, since the franchisee's business is conducted pursuant to the authority given to it by another. The franchisor's income, as will be seen in Chapter 6, may derive from many sources, but not from the profits with a view to which the franchisee's business is established. The franchisor is paid as a supplier of goods and/or services to the franchisee's business. Even if a franchisor is paid a franchise fee as a percentage of the franchisee's net profits that payment is not made in respect of the carrying on of a business in common, but for the services which the franchisor provides. The references to net profits is merely a method of computing the level of the payment to be made.

There are indeed many provisions in a franchise agreement which are totally inconsistent with the features of partnership, not the least of which is the franchisee's ability to sell the business and to retain the proceeds for his own benefit. He may have to pay a transfer fee to secure for the incoming purchaser of his business the benefit of joining the franchise network; he may pay a brokerage fee if the franchisor introduces the purchaser. Both these payments, however, are clearly related to the provision of services from one business to another, and not with the settling of an account between partners. Other factors inconsistent with partnership are the requirement on the franchisee to fund the capital expenditure in establishing his business, and his sole ownership of its assets. Although the franchisor has the right to lay down the franchisee's operating system, this arises out of the franchise agreement as an essential feature of the franchise and licensing package. It has been suggested that franchisees are to be considered partners because of the level of control (Adams and Jones,

Franchising, 3rd edn (Butterworth 1990) p 43), but that is not justified by the definition of a partnership and would lead to the conclusion that all licensing agreements, with their inevitable controls, lead to the creation of partnerships.

Whatever the level of control, one must refer to the definition of a partnership to ascertain whether or not there is being conducted a business in common. Unless there is a deliberate partnership or joint venture, that is unlikely to be the basis of any franchise relationship.

5.4   Shadow directors and fiduciary relationships

5.4.1   Shadow directors

A 'shadow director' is a creation of company and insolvency legislation. The expression is defined in s 251 of the Insolvency Act 1986:

> A 'shadow director' in relation to a company means a person in accordance with whose directions or instructions the directors are accustomed to act (but so that a person is not deemed to be a shadow director by reason only that the directors act on advice given by him in a professional capacity).

The objective was to provide an opportunity to make liable in an insolvency (*see* s 214 of the Insolvency Act 1986) someone who, while not identified as a director, 'pulled the strings' behind nominee or controlled directors. The relevance of this to franchising is that a liquidator may argue that a franchisor is a shadow director.

There are not many reported decisions on the meaning of a 'shadow director'. As far as franchising is concerned, the issue will be whether the nature of the relationship between licensor/franchisor and licensee/franchisee is such as to constitute the franchisor a shadow director. In *Re Hydrodam (Corby) Ltd* [1994] 2 BCLC Millet J said:

> Directors may be of three kinds: *de jure* directors, that is to say, those who have been validly appointed to their office; *de facto* directors, that is to say, directors who assume to act as directors without having been appointed validly or at all; and shadow directors, who are persons falling within the definition I have read . . . Liability for wrongful trading is imposed by the Act on those persons who are responsible for it, that is to say, who were in a position to prevent damage to creditors by taking proper steps to protect their interest. Liability cannot sensibly depend upon the validity of the defendant's appointment. Those who assume to act as directors and who thereby exercise the power and discharge the functions of a director whether validly appointed or not must accept the responsibilities which are attached to the office. Nevertheless, the

statutory liability is imposed exclusively upon directors of one or other of the three kinds I have mentioned. Accordingly the liquidator must plead and prove against each defendant separately that he or it was a director of the company.

Millett J usefully summarised what needs to be established to show that a defendant is a shadow director of a company:

> It is necessary to allege and prove: (1) who are the directors of the company, whether *de facto* or *de jure*; (2) that the defendant directed those directors how to act in relation to the company or that he was one of the persons who did so; (3) that those directors acted in accordance with those instructions; and (4) that they were accustomed so to act. What is needed is, first, a board of directors claiming and purporting to act as such; and secondly, a pattern of behaviour in which the board did not exercise any discretion or judgment of its own, but acted in accordance with the directions of others.

This analysis makes it plain that the directions acted upon should relate to the activities of the board as directors. Arm's length contractual obligations are entered into by companies regularly. Many of them, particularly those involving the family of contractual relationships to which franchising belongs, impose obligations and controls. It is inherent in intellectual property arrangements such as trade mark licences, manufacturing licences and know-how licences, that there will be operational controls on the way in which the licensed activities are carried out. This is also the case with franchising arrangements, with controls on how the franchisor's name and goodwill are presented and its systems operated and controlled. The directors remain free to take whatever decisions should properly be taken by them as directors. Franchisors provide advice and guidance to franchisees in the course of the normal contractual franchise relationship. The decision whether or not to accept the advice is the board's responsibility, as are the consequences. There are also provisions in franchise agreements which impose mandatory requirements on the franchisee. This is not uncommon in many contractual arrangements. The important factor is that the board is, at the outset, free to accept or reject the contractual documentation; the fact of the board's having already contracted the company to the franchisor to perform certain obligations does not constitute the franchisor a shadow director.

5.4.2 Fiduciary relationships

In the USA it has been asserted that there is a fiduciary relationship between the franchisor and franchisee, though without success except in one case where the franchisor's conduct would probably have been better characterised as fraudulent. *See* for example *Thomas Bevilacque et al v Ford Motor Co et al* CCH Business Franchise Guide 8808; *Fashion Boutique of Short Hills Inc v Lewis USA Inc* CCH Business Franchise Guide 10039 and *Hardees of Maumelle Arkansas Inc et al v Hardee's Food Systems Inc* CCH Business Franchise Guide 10322. There does not appear to be any precedent in English law for the suggestion that entry into what is an undoubted commercial contractual relationship, between arm's length parties, creates a fiduciary relationship. Indeed, there are a number of decisions which suggest that it is difficult to support a fiduciary relationship in such circumstances. *See* for example *Matthew v Bothams* (1980) 256 EG 603 (landlord/employer and tenant/employee); *Alec Lobb (Garages) Ltd v Total Oil (Great Britain) Ltd* [1983] 1 WLR 87; affirming [1985] 1 WLR 173 (petrol company and garage proprietor); and *National Westminster Bank plc v Morgan* [1985] Sc 686 (bank and customer). The *Alec Lobb v Total* case is of particular interest for franchising since the court noted that the parties may have had common goals and that the garage owner may have reposed a degree of trust and confidence in the petrol supply company and may have trusted it to deal fairly, but it did not regard this as the same as finding that the company had accepted a fiduciary duty of care towards the garage owner.

It is clear from the decisions that the existence of a fiduciary relationship does not of itself provide a remedy; that relationship has to be such that a presumption of undue influence is raised; see *National Westminster Bank plc v Morgan* (*above*). There are well-established relationships in which the presumption of undue influence exists, unless on the facts the presumption can be displaced. See Snell, *Principles of Equity*, 29th edn (Sweet and Maxwell, 1991) pp 534, 535–6. These include parent and child; guardian and ward; fiancé and fiancée; husband and wife; religious, medical and other advisers; and solicitor and client.

In applying the doctrine, the court appears to be concerned with any undue influence to which one party is subjected by the other at the time of entering into the contract. There does not seem to be any authority for the proposition that the court will import a fiduciary relationship to enable a contracting party to secure a different or better deal if he subsequently changes his view of how good the deal has been for him.

As Lord Scarman, giving the unanimous judgment of the House of Lords, pointed out in *National Westminster Bank plc v Morgan* (*above*):

> This brings me to *Lloyds Bank Ltd v Bundy* [1975] QB 326. It was, as one would expect, conceded by Counsel for the respondent that the relationship between banker and customer is not one which ordinarily gives rise to a presumption of undue influence: and that in the ordinary course of banking business, a banker can explain the nature of the proposed transaction without laying himself open to a charge of undue influence. This

proposition has never been in doubt, although some, it would appear, here thought that the Court of Appeal held otherwise in *Lloyds Bank Ltd* v *Bundy*. If any such view has gained currency, let it be destroyed now once and for all time.

Lord Denning MR believed that the doctrine of undue influence could be under the general principle that English courts will grant relief where there has been 'inequality by bargaining power'. He deliberately avoided influence to the will of one party being dominated or overcome by another. The majority of the court did not follow him: they based their decisions on the orthodox view of the doctrines expended in *Allcard* v *Skinner* (1887) 36 Ch D 145.

Nor has Counsel for the respondent sought to rely on Lord Denning MR's general principle; and in my view he was right not to do so. The doctrine of undue influence has been sufficiently developed not to need the support of a principle which by its formulation in the language of the law of contact is not appropriate to cover transactions of gift where there is no bargain. The fact of unequal bargain will of course be a relevant feature in some cases of undue influence. But it can never become an appropriate basis of principle of an equitable doctrine which is concerned with transactions 'not to be unreasonably accounted for on grounds of friendship, relationship, clients or other ordinary notices on which ordinary men act' (*Allcard* v *Skinner* at p 185). And even in the field of contract I question whether there is any need in modern law to erect a general principle of relief against inequality of bargaining power. Parliament has undertaken the task—and it is essentially a legislation task—of exactly such restrictions upon freedom of contact as are in its judgment necessary to relieve against the mischief: . . . I doubt whether the court should assume the burden of formulating further restrictions.

More recently, in *Re Goldcorp Exchange Ltd* [1994] 2 All ER 806, a Privy Council case, Lord Mustill said:

But the essence of a fiduciary relationship is that it creates obligations of a different character from those deriving from the contract itself. Their Lordships have not heard in argument any submission which went beyond suggesting that by virtue of being a fiduciary [Authors' Note: It was not held in this case that the company was a fiduciary] the company was obliged honestly and conscientiously to do what it had by contract promised to do. Many commercial relationships involve just such a reliance by one party on the other and to introduce the whole new dimension into such relationships which would give them a fiduciary character would (as it seems to their Lordships) have adverse consequences for exceeding those foreseen by Atkin LJ in *Re Wait* [1927] 1 Ch 606. It is possible without misuse of language to say that the customers put faith in the company and that their trust has not been repaid. But the vocabulary is misleading; high expectations do not necessarily lead to equitable remedies.

It is clear that the franchise relationship does not create a fiduciary relationship such as to affect the entry into and performance of the franchise contract and that any claim by a franchisee that the contract was a bad bargain or its performance did not meet his expectations will not be advanced by seeking equitable relief on that ground or on the ground that there has been undue influence.

Chapter 6

The Structure of Franchise Arrangements

Chapter 6

The Structure of Franchise Arrangements

In this chapter we shall be concerned with the ways in which various franchise arrangements, domestic or international, are structured, the issues, and the techniques which are employed for dealing with the particular circumstances involved.

6.1 Types of agreement

It is helpful first to identify the various types of agreement and to indicate their uses. Confusion arises because agreements named in a particular way are understood differently by different people. In an attempt to overcome these difficulties of terminology, the International Franchising Committee of the Section on Business Law of the International Bar Association produced a *Lexicon of Terms Used in International Franchising* (published by the International Bar Association London). The *Lexicon* was written by Alexander Konigsberg QC, and reflects the considered input of members of the Committee with international experience. In this book the terminology recommended in the *Lexicon* will be used. The agreements are described as follows:

6.1.1 Franchise agreements

A franchise agreement is the basic contract for the operation of a franchised unit. The person who grants the franchise rights is described as the 'franchisor'. The person who operates the franchised unit is described as the 'franchisee'. The franchise agreement is used to 'franchise' the operation of the franchised business, and contains the full range of provisions which are relevant for this purpose (*see* Chapter 18).

There may be agreements which are supplemental to the franchise agreement, such as:

(a) a lease of the premises upon which the franchised unit is operated;

(b) a lease or hire arrangement in respect of a vehicle or vehicles used in the operation of the franchised unit. If the franchised business is a mobile franchise (one in which the franchisee visits his customers and conducts his business from his vehicle), the vehicle will be analogous to premises;

(c) supplementary obligations undertaken by the shareholders/directors of the franchisee;

(d) lease or rental arrangements in respect of signage or equipment which is used by the franchisee in the franchised unit;

(e) a software licence.

6.1.2   Master franchise agreements

A master franchise agreement is an agreement granting rights to exploit a territory, invariably by a combination of company-owned and sub-franchised franchise units. The person to whom these rights are granted is the 'sub-franchisor'. The person giving the rights is called the 'franchisor'. The conclusion of the author of the *Lexicon*, following discussion and debate, was that the company with the ownership of the rights should always be called the franchisor, and the operator of the franchised unit should always be called the franchisee. Any other descriptive names required in the family tree between these two 'ends' of the franchise relationship should be different, to avoid the confusion which had hitherto existed. In Chapter 20 there is a description of the master franchise agreement and its provisions.

6.1.3   Development agreements

A development agreement or area development agreement is one under which the franchisor grants rights to a 'developer' which enable the developer to open and operate an agreed number of franchise units in a given area within an agreed time frame (the development schedule). The developer enters into a franchise agreement for each franchise unit which is opened. The development agreement is essentially a form of option agreement permitting the developer to open franchise units, with sanctions if he does not achieve the development schedule. In Chapter 20 there is a description of the development agreement and its provisions.

   In addition to the above three well recognised arrangements are two others, which are considered next.

6.2   Multiple franchise units

The number of franchised units operated by a franchisee can grow to the point that an umbrella agreement may be advisable for the franchisor, to ensure that the franchisee has the right overall mechanisms and central administrative structure in place to ensure the proper management of all the franchised units. Consideration needs to be given to what the consequences should be if the number of franchise units reaches the point where the franchisee cannot ensure the maintenance of the required quality of service. The franchisee may reach that point because the franchisor permits growth beyond the franchisee's capacity to cope. The provisions which one might expect to find in an umbrella agreement will be similar to those described in the development agreement (*see* Chapter 20) other than the development provisions.

6.3   Conversion franchising

A conversion franchise is one where the franchisee already has an established business which is similar to that offered by the franchisor. Examples are convenience stores, estate agencies and travel agencies. There are special considerations since the franchisee already owns a business which he is expected to change so that its identity and systems conform to the franchisor's requirements. For the franchisee, the adoption of the franchise must bring benefits which will improve his profitability after payment of the franchise fees. The franchisor has to face up to the inevitable problems which can arise where it takes on a franchisee who has already developed his own ideas on how to run his business and who perhaps has to unlearn some of his ideas and adopt new ones. The relationship may be put under stress since the franchisee may be more likely to challenge the franchisor's principles and methods with a confidence developed from his earlier experiences.

In addition, the consequences of future termination will have to be considered; someone with an existing business is unlikely to accept that signing a franchise agreement could result, on termination, in his losing his right to continue trading as he did before joining the franchise network.

6.4   Combination franchising

Combination franchising is a technique developed in the USA to cope with the problems of high rental costs in major city centres. The basic idea is that if two or three franchise units each occupy part of premises with a common area, the sharing of occupational costs will increase the ability of the combined operations to become sufficiently profitable to justify occupying a prime position.

There are two possibilities. The first is that each part of the premises is occupied by a different franchisee operating a different franchise. The franchisees clearly will have to agree about the way in which the common areas are fitted out and maintained. They will also have to decide who will be the tenant of the total facility as well as of the common area.

Each franchisor will have to ensure that:

(a) each franchisee operates the franchise properly from his portion of the premises;
(b) there are adequate contractual obligations to ensure that common areas are properly maintained;
(c) the facilities available are consistent with the franchisor's requirements; and
(d) the franchisor is able to enforce its standards.

There are many other practical considerations:

(1) Will one franchisor or franchisee lease the area and sublet to the others?
(2) Will each franchisor and/or franchisee be able to exercise the level of control which they require over the common area?
(3) Will each franchisee operate to a standard which will not detract from the standard imposed by the other franchisors of the other franchisees?
(4) Will the association with the franchise operation in one part of the property harm the others?
(5) What will happen if one of the franchisees fails? With whom should that franchisee be replaced? Who would have responsibility for arranging a replacement and ensuring that the incoming franchisee fits in?
(6) What would be the position if one of the franchisors or his franchisee decides that the location is wrong for them or that they are not doing as well as they should? Should they be able to opt out? If so, on what basis? By whom should they be replaced, on what terms, and whose responsibility should it be to deal with the problem?
(7) If a franchisor and franchisee have an operation which is not doing well and decide that the location and/or conceptual approach is wrong, who will find the replacement? Should the other franchisors and/or franchisees have any say about the replacement and about what their operation should be?
(8) If one of the franchisees runs his operation badly so that the other franchisees suffer, what redress should there be, and who will enforce it?
(9) Similarly, if one franchisee does not meet his obligations to maintain the common area, who will enforce these obligations against him and secure his compliance?
(10) Should there be an overall agreement between all the franchisors to regulate the operations? If there is such an agreement should each of the franchisees also be a party to it so that he can enforce its provisions?

The second possibility is that there will be one franchisee of all the franchises to be conducted from the premises. In such a case there are further issues to consider. The most striking disadvantage for the franchisor appears to be that he risks losing control, with a consequent lowering of standards. It is not difficult to see how this happens since the arrangement has some fundamental features which are likely to give rise to these difficulties:

(1) The franchisee is not under the control of any one franchisor.

(2) The franchisee is entering into the arrangement to maximise the use of space and staff, and minimise expense.

(3) The common area is not under the control of any of the franchisors, so that none of them can impose standards of uniformity, supervision and cleanliness which match those found in a unit wholly dedicated to that particular franchise.

(4) The franchisee is in a position to play off one franchisor against another, and to display a degree of independence (because he has other franchises in the same location) which undermines control and standards.

(5) The franchisee has no incentive to promote all operations if he can achieve the financial result he seeks by concentrating his efforts on the one he considers will produce the best results.

(6) Each franchisor's position in relation to the franchisee is relatively weak, since the franchisee's relationship with other franchisors reduces his dependence on any one of them.

(7) The franchisors are placed in a situation in which conflicts of interest can develop between them; even businesses which appear to be complementary can be or become competitive, and can have overlapping product, service or menu items.

(8) Where such overlapping exists, the temptation for the franchisee to standardise the product, service or menu items—despite the normal differences imposed by the franchisors in terms of quality of product supply and methods of preparation—is considerable, and difficult for each franchisor to monitor on a regular ongoing basis.

(9) The possibility of the sale by the franchisee of each franchise individually is fraught with problems. The criteria for franchisee selection by each franchisor may differ, and a prospective purchaser from the franchisee may not satisfy the approval requirements of all the franchisors. Furthermore, some of the problems of having different franchisees may arise. These have already been discussed.

(10) Each franchisor runs the risk of being associated with another franchisor whose business may fail, suffer a loss of credibility, fall into disrepute, or become heavily involved in litigation with franchisees. It is likely that any of these events could adversely affect the innocent franchisors, not only because consumers may associate them with the franchisor in difficulty, but also because they may become involved in any litigation, particularly on the bankruptcy or liquidation of a franchisor.

(11) Participation by the franchisee in any of the franchised networks' marketing, promotional and advertising campaigns, particularly those involving point-of-sale material, may be in question since the others may resent the promotion of one franchise without the other. Liaison between all the franchises on marketing, promotinal and advertising strategy may be impossible because of the sizes and spreads of their own networks. To try to establish contractual commitments in this area may not be practicable.

(12) Franchisors will probably have used this technique to achieve more rapid growth than would otherwise be available to them, putting themselves under what might be the wrong pressures. Further, it would probably be difficult for them to resist further growth by this method by their common franchisee in the area of the operation in question or the surrounding area.

Anyone considering this method of growth must take considerable care in structuring the arrangements, and should seriously question whether the likely benefits, compared with those of their normal method of expansion, are worth the undoubted risks.

· 6.5   Sub-franchising

Master franchise arrangements involve sub-franchising. Where sub-franchising is involved consideration has to be given to the provisions of Part XI of the Fair Trading Act 1973 ('the Act'), relating to so-called 'pyramid selling' schemes. At the time of writing, the government is considering changing both the primary legislation and the regulations referred to below.

6.5.1   Fair Trading Act 1973, s 118

Section 118 of the Act applies the provisions to a 'trading scheme':

(1) This Part of this Act applies to any trading scheme which includes the following elements, that is to say:

(a) goods or services, or both, are to be provided by the person promoting the scheme (in this Part of this Act referred to as 'the promoter') or, in the case of a scheme promoted by two or more persons acting in concert (in this Part of this Act referred to as 'the promoters'), are to be provided by one or more of those persons;

(b) the goods or services so provided are to be supplied to or for other persons under transactions effected by persons (other than the promoter or any of the promoters) who participate in the scheme (each of whom is in this Part of this Act referred to as a 'participant');

(c) those transactions, or most of them, are to be effected elsewhere than at premises at which the promoter or any of the promoters or the participant effecting the transaction carries on business; and

(d) the prospect is held out to participants of receiving payments or other benefits in respect of any one or more of the matters specified in the next following subsection.

(2) The matters referred to in paragraph (d) of subsection (1) of this section are:

(a) the introduction of other persons who become participants;

(b) the promotion, transfer or other change of status of participants within the trading scheme;

(c) the supply of goods to the other participants;

(d) the supply of training facilities or other services for other participants;

(e) transactions effected by other participants under which goods are to be supplied to, or services are to be supplied for, other persons.

(3) For the purposes of this Part of this Act a trading scheme shall be taken to include the element referred to in paragraph (b) of subsection (1) of this section whether the transactions referred to in that paragraph are to be effected by participants in the capacity of servants or agents of the promoter or of one of the promoters or in any other capacity.

(4) In determining, for the purposes of paragraph (c) of subsection (1) of this section, whether any premises are premises at which a participant in a trading scheme carries on business, no account shall be taken of transactions effected or to be effected by him under that trading scheme.

(5) For the purpose of this part of this Act such a prospect as is mentioned in paragraph (d) of subsection (1) of this section shall be taken to be held out to a participant:

(a) whether it is held out so to confer on him a legally enforceable right or not, and

(b) in so far as it relates to the introduction of new participants, whether it is limited to the introduction of new participants by him or extends to the introduction of new participants by other persons.

(6) In this Part of this Act 'trading scheme' includes any arrangements made in connection with the carrying on of a business, whether those arrangements are made or recorded wholly or partly in writing or not.

(7) In this section any reference to the provision of goods or services by a person shall be construed as including a reference to the provision of goods or services under arrangements to which that person is a party.

6.5.2   Section 118 explained

This section is neither easy to follow nor to understand. The following are its basic features.

This part of the Act applies to 'any trading scheme'. Subsection 6 provides a non-exclusive definition of 'trading scheme' to include 'arrangements' made in connection with the carrying on of a business (s 137(2) of the Act). There are two factors to consider at this stage:

(1) The expression 'scheme' suggests systematic promotion of activities by the 'promoter', rather than isolated transactions which have no linking features or pre-planning. Something spontaneous and unexpected, such as gratuitously making a payment to a franchisee for introducing a new franchisee, would not constitute a 'scheme'.

(2) The expression 'arrangements' is not defined, but is clearly intended to be wider than just a binding contract, particularly in view of s 118(5)(*a*) by way of contrast with the reference in s 119(3)(*a*) to 'an agreement in writing' which must in context mean a binding contract. It would seem therefore that a 'gentlemen's agreement' could be an arrangement, and that any informal non-binding obligations would be included in this expression. 'Arrangements' must mean that there has been some degree of consensus or a common purpose, or at the very least some advance understanding of what each party expects of the other.

For a scheme to be a trading scheme for the purposes of Part XI of the Act, it must include all four elements referred to in s 118(1). It is safe to assume that all basic franchise schemes, as commonly understood, would be schemes. The question which arises in relation to a particular scheme is whether it is a trading scheme to which Part XI of the Act applies—does it include all the elements? As will be seen *below*, however, not all trading schemes which are within the definition of s 118 of the Act, are necessarily affected by its provisions.

The first element to be satisfied requires that goods (s 137(2) of the Act) or services are to be provided by the promoter (the person promoting the scheme). Under subs 7 this includes a reference to the provision of goods or services under arrangements to which that person is a party. The latter provision is obviously an anti-avoidance provision to prevent an informal off-the-record diversion of goods or services through an apparently arm's length third party. All business format franchise schemes would feature this element, with the expression 'promoter' meaning the 'franchisor'.

The second element to be satisfied is that the goods or services provided by the promoter are to be supplied to or for other persons under transactions effected by participants (persons other than the promoters who participate in the scheme). (For the meanings of 'supply of goods' and 'supply of services' *see* s 137(1) and (3).) This is intended to include recruitment by participants of third parties. The promoter is not a party to these transactions, and the other person to whom the supply is made is neither promoter nor participant until the transaction is concluded. The recruiting participant is therefore acting as a conduit through which the goods or services are supplied. Despite the intention to deal with recruitment, this element is drafted sufficiently widely to embrace consumer sales by a participant. It is difficult to understand how these provisions apply to services. The flow of services is not the same as the flow of goods. The goods do not change in character unless a process is applied to them. However, a service is an individual creation by each supplier of each service. The services provided by a franchisor to a sub-franchisor, by a sub-franchisor to a franchisee, and by a franchisee to the consumer, will each be totally different, although the objective is to ensure the delivery by the franchisee to each consumer of a service of consistent quality and character. It is difficult to give the reference to services a practical meaning without stretching the imagination.

The third element relates to the transactions to be effected by the participant who is ascertained under the second element. It is aimed at situations in which such transactions, or most of them, are intended to be carried out elsewhere than on the promoter's or the participant's business premises. When read together, the second and third elements clearly relate to the aspects of the scheme concerned with recruiting participants. Subsection (4) of the section provides that transactions effected by a participant, such as recruitment of other participants or product sales, are to be ignored in determining whether or not any premises are premises at which the participant carries on business. Indeed subs (4) means that if the only business carried on by a participant on any premises is that transacted under the trading scheme, they are not premises at which the participant carries on business. He must therefore carry on some other business from those premises if they are to be considered as premises at which he carries on business. This would rarely be the case in a pyramid-type scheme or even in a franchise system.

The fourth element deals with the motivation of the participants: the holding out to any participant of the prospect of financial or other benefits. Section 118(5) makes clear that the expression 'holding out' includes a legally unenforceable right to benefit by payment or otherwise for the introduction of 'sub-participants' at a lower level in the structure.

The prospect of payment or other benefits must arise in respect of one or more of the matters set out in s 118(2). They include benefits from introducing participants, change of status within the scheme, supply of goods or training facilities and commission on the sale of products or supply of services to other persons.

For this element to have effect it must be a feature of the scheme (although not necessarily a legally enforceable obligation) that the prospect is held out to participants. It would be unusual to find such features in a bona fide franchise scheme which does not involve sub-franchising.

The provision does not concern itself with the question of who pays the money or promotes or provides the benefit. It is enough that a payment or benefit is held out as a prospect in respect of one of the matters referred to.

6.5.3   The pyramid selling regulations

If a system is regarded as a trading scheme under the Act, the scheme must comply with regulations made under the Act. Section 119 of the Act permits the Secretary of State to make regulations with respect to the issue, circulation or distribution of documents, and the regulations may prohibit certain practices. The current Regulations came into force on 1 March 1990: The Pyramid Selling Schemes Regulations 1989 (SI 1989 No 2195), as amended by the Pyramid Selling Schemes (Amendment) Regulations 1990 (SI 1990 No 150) ('the Regulations').

Application

The Regulations apply to trading schemes as defined in the Act, other than a scheme under which the prospect of payments or benefits is held out to only one participant in the United Kingdom, or under which the only prospect of benefit is the receipt of a sum not exceeding £30 in respect of the introduction of other participants.

   The problem for franchising, as will be seen *below*, arises where levels of participants are introduced into a franchise system which may be illustrated as follows:

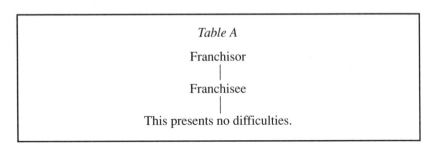

Table A

Franchisor

|

Franchisee

|

This presents no difficulties.

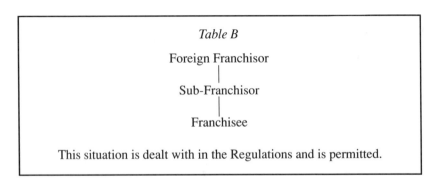

Table B

Foreign Franchisor

|

Sub-Franchisor

|

Franchisee

This situation is dealt with in the Regulations and is permitted.

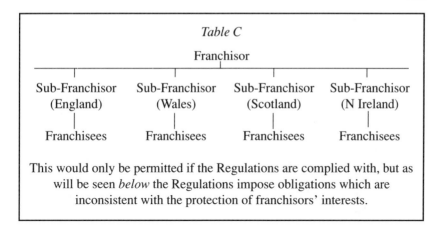

Table C

Franchisor

Sub-Franchisor (England)	Sub-Franchisor (Wales)	Sub-Franchisor (Scotland)	Sub-Franchisor (N Ireland)
Franchisees	Franchisees	Franchisees	Franchisees

This would only be permitted if the Regulations are complied with, but as will be seen *below* the Regulations impose obligations which are inconsistent with the protection of franchisors' interests.

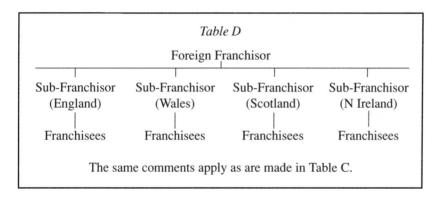

Table D

Foreign Franchisor

Sub-Franchisor (England)	Sub-Franchisor (Wales)	Sub-Franchisor (Scotland)	Sub-Franchisor (N Ireland)
Franchisees	Franchisees	Franchisees	Franchisees

The same comments apply as are made in Table C.

Obligations inconsistent with franchising

The obligations under the Regulations which are inconsistent with franchising are as follows:

(1) The Regulations contain restrictions on the contents of documents, including advertisements:

> Such documents shall not contain any statement which indicates or suggests that a participant will as a result of participation acquire a specified financial benefit or a financial benefit which will be greater than or not less than a specified sum unless the indication or suggestion is justified by actual results. If such an indication or suggestion is given or made there must be a statement published with equal prominence immediately below which states 'The figures shown do not represent any automatic

earnings. Actual earnings will depend on time and effort spent on the business and the total number of participants in the scheme'.

The last sentence is relevant to a pyramid scheme, but is not at all appropriate to a franchise system.

(2) The Regulations also provide that there must be a written contract if goods and services are to be supplied or provided to participants, and that this contract must contain certain information and statutory wording of a set size and format.

(3) The Regulations provide extensive rights to a participant on termination. The most fundamental is the right to terminate at any time without penalty by giving 14 days' written notice. If that notice is given within 14 days after the contract is signed, the participant is entitled to all his money back, less amounts due for goods sold or the amount representing loss in value due to damage or determination, or for goods not returned to the promoter.

(4) The participant also has the right to require the promoter to purchase his inventory (whether or not purchased from the promoter) for not less than 90 per cent of cost price less an allowance for deterioration to the goods.

(5) On termination the participant is discharged from all contractual liabilities to the promoter except liability relating to payments made to him under contracts entered into as agent for the promoter, or liability to pay for goods sold to him by the promoter. Significantly, the promoter does not need to be the supplier of the goods. Moreover, all the usual contractual provisions basic to the protection of a franchisor's legitimate interests post termination are excluded as the contract is discharged, so there will be:
 — no post-term protection of know-how or system,
 — no post-term protection against unfair competition, and
 — no contractual rights on termination to items such as customer lists, de-identification of premises and vehicles, prevention of passing off, transfer of telephones to the franchisor, or return of manuals and other material of the franchisor.

There may also be difficulties in enforcing other rights protecting the franchisor's intellectual property, depending on how the courts interpret the provisions in the Regulations relating to termination.

(6) The promoter is not permitted to accept from a new participant any payment or undertaking to pay a sum exceeding £75 for goods or services until seven days have elapsed from signing the contract. Nor can the promoter require security for payment for goods.

(7) The Regulations require that a participant is given prior notice that he has a free choice whether or not to avail himself of the franchisor's train-

ing facilities, and the cost. No franchisor can operate on the basis that a franchisee can decide not to be trained in the operation of the franchised business.

(8) There are criminal sanctions for the breach of the Regulations. The penalties range from a fine not exceeding £400 or imprisonment for a term not exceeding two years, or both.

(9) It is also an offence, punishable in the same way (s 120(3)):

> If any person who is a participant in a trading scheme to which this Part of this Act applies or who has applied or been invited to become a participant in such trading scheme:
>
> > (a) makes any payment to or for the benefit of the promoter or (if there is more than one) any of the promoters, or to or for the benefit of a participant in the trading scheme, and
> >
> > (b) is induced to make the payment by reason that the prospect is held out to him of receiving payments or other benefit in respect of the introduction of other persons who become participants in the trading scheme any persons to whom or for whose benefit that payment is made shall be guilty of an offence.

And s 120(4):

> If the promoter or any of the promoters of a trading scheme, to which this Part of this Act applies or any other person acting in accordance with such a trading scheme, by holding out to any person such a prospect as is mentioned in subsection (3)(b) of this section, attempts to induce him:
>
> > (a) if he is already in the trading scheme, to make any payment to or for the benefit of the promoter or any of the promoters or to or for the benefit of a participant in the trading scheme, or
> >
> > (b) if he is not already a participant in the trading scheme, to become such a participant and to make any such payment as is mentioned in the preceding paragraph,
>
> the person attempting to induce him to make that payment shall be guilty of an offence.

So, even if a scheme is permissible (*see below*) subject to compliance with Regulations, compliance will be impracticable for a franchisor since:

(a) the franchisee can terminate at any time on 14 days' notice and require the franchisor to purchase all his inventory whether or not supplied by the franchisor;

(b) the franchisor cannot effectively protect his interests post-termination; and

(c) the franchisor cannot compel the franchisee to be trained by the franchisor.

The right for a franchisee to terminate on 14 days' notice would provide the franchisees collectively with immense power to act together and dismantle the network without suffering any penalties or post-termination restraints. It is a charter for breakaway franchisees and introduces an unacceptable level of uncertainty for a franchisor. The government is, at the time of writing, giving consideration to this aspect of the law on which it is inviting observations.

6.6   Foreign franchisors

The Act also potentially affects the contractual documentation for master franchise arrangements. The Act defines 'promoter' as the person providing goods or services, or both, who promotes the scheme. If there are two or more persons acting in concert, resulting in the provision by one or more of them of goods or services, they are defined as 'the promoters'.

6.6.1   Identifying the promoter

The issue to be resolved is who will be the promoter of the scheme in the United Kingdom. Is it the foreign franchisor or the UK-based sub-franchisor? The Regulations seem to assume that it will be the foreign franchisor, since they grant exemption where the prospect of payment or benefits is held out to only one participant in the United Kingdom. If the foreign franchisor is the promoter, the master franchise agreement could be affected by the restrictions in the Regulations, as well as all the other contracts at the lower levels. It would not be affected in the case described in Table B *above* but in the case described in Table D the problem does require to be considered.

6.6.2   The risks

There may be a case for arguing that since a sub-franchisor is in reality the 'franchisor' in the UK, the foreign franchisor and the sub-franchisor are acting in concert and are thus co-promoters. It may be sensible to ensure that they are indeed co-promoters since the contract between them would not then be affected by the provisions of the Act or the Regulations. In such a case the risks which the foreign franchisor would run must be considered:

  (1) There is no requirement in the Act or the Regulations for all promoters to contract with participants. Indeed the definition of 'promoters' envisages that one or more of the promoters will provide goods or services. Those good or services are to be supplied to or for other persons under contracts effected by participants.
  (2) The Regulations make it plain that they apply only to the person who is

acting in the role of participator in promoting the scheme in the UK (*see* Clauses 4 and 5). Therefore the agreement between the foreign franchisor and the sub-franchisor would not be subject to the Regulations.

(3) Since the foreign franchisor does not need to be involved in the contractual arrangements in the UK it would not have contractual liability. The expression 'acting in concert' does not impose a relationship under which joint and several liability could be implied, and since the foreign franchisor would not take part in the business activities of the sub-franchisor, there would not appear to be any greater civil liability risk for the foreign franchisor than might otherwise exist. In any event most franchisors would expect an indemnity, and so long as the sub-franchisor has sufficient financial substance this would suffice.

(4) The greatest risk is that an offence may be committed under s 120 of the Act, but that risk would appear to be manageable:

(a) Section 120(1) refers to 'any person' who issues creates or distributes (or causes him so to do) a document in contravention of the Regulations. If one only of the promoters (the UK or other franchisee) does this and the others do not 'cause' him to do so, those others would not be committing an offence.

(b) Section 120(2) is limited in its scope to 'any person' who contravenes, and focuses on the contravening person.

(c) Section 120(3) refers to payments to or for the benefit of the promoter or any of the promoters. The recipient is guilty of the offence.

(d) Section 120(4) is directed at the promoter or any of the promoters who attempts to induce participants or prospective participants to make payments to or for the benefit of a promoter or participant within the trading scheme.

(e) Section 120(6) provides that all promoters are equally guilty, but affords to an inactive promoter the defence provided for in s 121(2)(*b*), namely that 'the act constituting the offence was committed without his consent or connivance'.

Taken together the effect seems to be that the offences are committed by the person who commits the offending acts; a co-promoter will prima facie have criminal liability; and a co-promoter who neither consented to nor connived in the commission of the offending act has a defence.

One fundamental problem, to which scant attention has been given by the authorities, is that the effect of s 120(3) and (4) is that even the operation of a trading scheme (whether or not it is a franchise) which complies with the Regulations can amount to an offence. The Regulations purport to authorise the payment of inducements referred to in these sections, albeit with safeguards, but the Act does not provide that compliance with the Regulations will cause s 120(3) and/or (4) not to apply.

The effect of these sections would be to render the contracts illegal and thus void.

These provisions make it difficult, and in the case of some franchise systems impossible to divide the UK into marketing areas with area or development agreements involving sub-franchising.

6.7   The techniques of international franchising

A franchisor who intends to expand into foreign territories has a number of strategic business decisions to make, which may be affected by tax-planning considerations. Whichever course of action is chosen, one or more of the following methods or techniques will be appropriate:

(a) company-owned operation;
(b) direct franchising;
(c) master franchising;
(d) area developments;
(e) joint ventures.

In connection with any of these methods the franchisor may establish a branch operation or form a subsidiary company.

We shall consider each of the methods and techniques. The contractual considerations relating to master franchise and area development agreements will be dealt with in Chapter 20.

6.7.1   Company-owned operation

A potential franchisor with substantial manpower and financial resources may decide to establish its own operations and units. A successful company-owned network could later form the basis for introducing franchising should such a change of course be considered desirable.

6.7.2   Direct franchising

In direct franchising, the franchisor enters into a direct franchise agreement with each individual franchisee. The franchisor will provide the basic back-up and continuing support. This technique has limited scope, because the further the franchisor is from the target territory, the more difficult it becomes to service franchisees. Very often direct franchising, combined with the establishment of branches or subsidiaries, can provide tax advantages (*see* Chapter 21). The direct franchising route makes it more difficult for the franchisor to recognise the differences between the territory in which the business originated and the target territory. Pilot operations are advisable to achieve the transition. Some seek to overcome the problem by using area development agreements to keep the numbers of franchisees with whom they have to deal to manageable proportions. Area development agreements provide for direct franchising of multiple unit franchisees.

Those intending to do business with or in the European Union (EU) (as it is now, aspirationally, known following the Maastricht Treaty; it has been formerly and successively known as the European Economic Community and the European Community) will bear in mind that the Single European Act aimed to eliminate the internal barriers within the then-called European Community, by the end of 1992. Considerable uniformity has indeed been achieved by the removal of physical barriers (to the movement of people and goods, for instance); technical barriers (product specifications, professional qualifications) and fiscal barriers (harmonisation of tax rates). Despite these measures, there will remain many differences between the member states of the EU. Each will continue to be a 'foreign country' for the nationals of the other states. This is despite the creation, by the Maastricht Treaty in 1993, of citizenship of the EU. The member states will continue to use their own languages. In some countries, Ireland and Belgium for example, there will be more than one. Local laws which could affect franchising, franchise operations and agreements will continue to be different. Indeed in France there are laws which affect all agreements (including franchise agreements) concerning the licensing of trade marks. Culture, life-style, tastes and habits will continue to be different; national and indeed regional characteristics will not change at all. The need to adapt a franchise system to local conditions will continue to be essential and no franchisor should be lulled into thinking that the political and legal changes reduce that need.

Branch operation

A branch operation may be established for any of the following purposes:

  (a) for the franchisor to operate its own outlets;
  (b) for servicing franchisees by way of support for direct franchising into the target territory;
  (c) as a regional base supporting franchisees in the region.

The business decision whether or not to establish a branch may well be affected or determined by fiscal or legal considerations. These considerations may lead the franchisor as an alternative to establish a subsidiary company.

Subsidiary company

The establishment of a subsidiary company may fulfill any of four functions:

(a) to service franchisees where the franchisor is franchising directly from his domestic territory into the target territory;

(b) to open its own operations or sub-franchise, or both, under the appropriate form of franchise or master franchise agreement;

(c) to act with a joint venture partner;

(d) to serve as a regional base, to provide support services to sub-franchisees or sub-franchisors in the region.

The services which the branch or subsidiary would provide to individual franchisees would be similar to those provided by the franchisor, covering the whole range of franchisor services, including, as the network develops, a training facility.

6.7.3   Master franchising

The sub-franchisor will usually have the exclusive right in a country to open his own outlets and to sub-franchise. The sub-franchisor in essence acts as the franchisor in the territory. As is always the case, there are advantages and pitfalls. There are some basic business issues which all franchisors must bear in mind:

(a) the difficulties identifying and selecting the right person or company as sub-franchisor;

(b) the need for a strong and profitable home base and business to sustain the demands which will be made on the franchisor;

(c) the diversion of manpower and financial resources from domestic operations. To stand the best chance of success the franchisor will have to dedicate resources exclusively to the international operation. It should be emphasised that it will always take more people and cost more than expected;

(d) the time factor: it will also always take much longer than one expects.

Other considerations include:

(1) The appointment of a sub-franchisor will mean that the franchisor has only one entity with which to deal in the target territory, and will not be concerned in day-to-day dealings with the franchisees who operate the outlets.

(2) The quality of the sub-franchisor's selection and training of sub-franchisees, and all the other franchisor services he provides to his sub-franchisees, are crucial. The franchisor has an obvious interest in ensuring the quality of continuing support services and control and supervision of standards by the sub-franchisor. Neglect of these areas will mean that the franchisor may have to terminate the master franchise agreement and then cope with a troublesome, substandard, disgruntled and aggressive network of franchisees.

(3) The franchisor should make some effort to integrate the sub-franchisor and its network into the franchisor's total network of franchises wherever they may be. He should not usurp the functions of the sub-franchisor, but must find the right balance between integration and supervision of quality standards.

(4) Master franchise arrangements follow basic franchising principles in that expansion is achieved using the resources of others. In international master franchises the franchisor manages this at two levels instead of one. At one level, the sub-franchisor will be required to provide the financial resources to establish, exploit and operate the system in the target territory. At the second level, the financial and manpower resources will be contributed by the franchisees.

(5) The sub-franchisor will of course make his own calculations of the financial viability of a proposition. Suffice it to say that decisions will have to be taken, during the course of negotiations, about the nature and extent of pilot operations, as well as the contribution to be made to their establishment and operation by each of the parties.

(6) The master franchise arrangement encourages the blending of the franchisor's developed system with the sub-franchisor's knowledge and experience of local conditions. Local knowledge cannot be acquired sufficiently quickly by a visitor to the target territory, and this is one of the reasons why master franchising arrangements are so popular. Of course the franchisor who has the resources may well (as some have done) open its own outlets, recruiting local staff with the requisite skills.

(7) The franchisor under a master franchise arrangement can generate income only from product sales (if appropriate) or by taking a part of the franchise fee income of the sub-franchisor. The sub-franchisor will therefore have to finance his own operations, and pay the franchisor from the fees it charges the sub-franchisees. What the fee will be, and how it is calculated, will be a matter for negotiation. It is unlikely that the fee charged to franchisees in the target territory will differ much from that charged to franchisees in the franchisor's domestic territory, so the amount available to be shared will be limited.

(8) The problems which arise on termination of a master franchise agreement are many and varied. It is likely that the franchisor will be confronted with difficulties since termination may result from the breach by the sub-franchisor of its obligations either to the franchisor or to the sub-franchisees. Whatever the reason for termination there will be a substantial element of neglect of the network. Franchisees always find a change of ownership of their franchisor troubling. Franchisees may be pleased that a new franchisor has taken over the reins, but there will inevitably be a feeling that perhaps the franchisor should have done more to prevent the problems from occurring. In any event, the

franchisees will feel that they have been let down. Many may be hostile and resentful. This will require careful handling and an outstanding performance by the franchisor before these feelings are overcome.

6.7.4   Joint ventures

It is not the purpose of this work to consider the advantages and disadvantages of joint venture arrangements, but only the issues which are particularly relevant to franchising. Many of the problems which have been outlined will apply even if there is a joint venture. The need to identify and reach agreement with the right person will be the same. But there is more to it than that. The franchisor and the co-venturer will have to negotiate what shares to take up and decide how to finance the venture. In some cases, the franchisor's contribution to the joint venture will take the place of the front-end fee normally payable, and in other cases the front-end fee is paid, but returned in whole or in part by the franchisor to the joint venture as its contribution. Sometimes a value is placed on the services and/or know-how provided by the franchisor and this value is taken as the measure of the franchisor's contributions to the capital of the joint venture.

The joint venture entity will become the sub-franchisor and will enter into a master franchise agreement with the franchisor. The franchisor will bear the risk of operational losses which it would otherwise have avoided. It will also find much scope for disagreement on operational matters with joint venture partners, who may resent the fact that the master franchise agreement gives the franchisor (a joint venture partner) the last word on many issues. This highlights the dual role of the franchisor in this type of arrangement, which creates scope for friction beyond that which normally arises.

A franchisor who is confronted with a buy-out situation, or who needs to terminate the joint venture or the master franchise agreement, will find itself in a difficult position. The joint venture partner will have an established presence in the territory and will invariably be in operational control. Unless the franchisor has a presence in the territory, or the ability rapidly to put the right person in position (which will be rare), it will be at a considerable disadvantage in trying to take over the operation. It is infinitely more difficult to divest oneself of an unsatisfactory joint venture partner than it is to terminate a sub-franchisor (not that the latter is an easy option). To have to face the prospect of coping with both at the same time is something to contemplate long and hard.

Chapter 7

The Financial Aspects

Chapter 7

The Financial Aspects

7.1 Introduction

At its core, a franchise arrangement has three principal financial aspects. First, the cost to the franchisee of joining the network and establishing the business; second, the continuing cost of membership of the network and the provision of the franchisor's goods and/or services; third, the arrangements for advertising made by the network.

The financial implications go beyond these three elements. There are sources of finance, which may be banks, finance houses, leasing companies or franchisors. There are implications for franchisors who re-schedule payment of outstanding debt. There are also insolvency-related legal and practical issues.

7.2 Initial fees

Revenue for a franchisor can arise at two stages only in the relationship: the contract-signing stage and the contract-performance stage.

The nature and structure of the revenue sources will depend on the type of franchise. A franchise which involves the resale of products supplied by the franchisor may well have a product mark-up built in; a service franchise will not provide a comparable source of income even though the franchisor may supply products which are used or which form part of the provision of the service.

Whatever the structure, the franchisor's gross revenue can come only from the activities of the franchisees. This means that the franchisees have to be able to generate sufficient profitable activity so that they make the profits they expect, and to contribute to the gross revenue of the franchisor so that the franchisor makes the profit it expects. In the early stages of the development of the franchise system the franchisor will have little prospect of receiving sufficient gross revenue to cover its expenses. Indeed, until it achieves a critical mass in terms of franchisee numbers, the franchisor cannot become profitable. This will mean that unless its pilot or other operations bridge the gap, the franchisor will need to find the capital resources necessary to sustain its business. It can take up to three or more years, depending on the rate of healthy growth which is achieved for the franchisor to reach a level of profitability from its activities as a franchisor.

There are three approaches which can be adopted in setting up a franchisee in business.

(1) The franchisor will, for a fee, provide a range of services and advice which will enable the franchisee to prepare himself and open for business. The fee will cover the cost of the services provided, including training, site selection, premises fitting-out and the other services which comprise the franchise package. The fee may also involve a price for joining the franchise network, and a mark-up.

(2) The franchisor may sell the franchisee a package which includes not only the services referred to *above*, but also a package of equipment and, if appropriate, an opening inventory of stock. The fee charged will invariably also include a mark-up on the tangible items sold to the franchisee.

(3) The franchisor may, in addition, acquire the proposed trading premises, and fit and equip them so that they are ready for the franchisee to move into and commence trading. The fee chargeable will reflect the fitting-out costs and a profit from them. This technique is commonly referred to as a turnkey operation.

The services which a franchisor provides can also include designs and plans prepared by the franchisor's in-house facility or by an independent designer or architect, together with project management of the works necessary to prepare the proposed trading premises. Similarly where the franchised unit is not premises-based but the franchisee is mobile, the franchisor will have a design for the fitting out of the vehicle which the franchisee must use. In many such cases the franchisor may have arrangements with a vehicle supplier who will sell or lease to the franchisee a fully fitted and equipped vehicle which meets the franchisor's requirements. In most cases the franchisor will be looking for a mark-up to cover its costs of providing the products and services, as well as a network membership fee. The network membership fee may increase as the network becomes better known and the benefits of membership are perceived to have a greater value.

The franchisor may become involved in the property chain by acquiring the freehold or a lease of the proposed trading premises and granting a lease or underlease to the franchisee (*see* Chapter 14). In doing so the franchisor which owns the freehold will be looking for a market rent and, where it holds a lease, a possible profit rent. Depending on the state of the property market there could be premiums or reverse premiums on taking leasehold property. The cost or benefit and the allocation of any such premiums must be structured so as to have them end up where they should reasonably be, and care must be taken to avoid tax problems. The destination of the cost or benefit of such premiums should not be overlooked when considering issues of termination or sale of the business.

7.3   Continuing fees

A franchisor's continuing fee income is important since it will, in the medium to long term, provide it with its principal income. Traditionally franchisors, with some exceptions, have charged fees by reference to the gross sales revenue generated by the franchisee. Gross revenue is chosen because it is more difficult to disguise or distort than a net figure.

These fees are sometimes described as a royalty but this is often a misnomer. Royalties are normally passive income arising in respect of the exploitation of an asset such as a copyright or patent. In franchising, the continuing fee is paid to the franchisor for more than the use of an asset; rather it is a payment to the franchisor which enables the franchisor to finance its activities in providing a wide range of services to its franchisees, and to make a profit. As has already been noted, the franchisor may take three years or more to reach profitability. Until then the franchisor has to fund its activities out of its capital resources or other trading activities. In product franchises the franchisor will probably charge a mark-up on the products which it sells to franchisees, but the viability of this approach may depend on the mark-up which can reasonably and competitively be charged. The products may be subject to low profit margins, relying on high volume sales for success, and there may not be room for an additional mark-up. Some franchisors structure the payments by combining a mix of product mark-up and a separate franchise fee. There are also cases where products are supplied at cost, or at cost plus a reasonable handling charge, in each case with a separate franchise fee.

There are also cases where the fee is calculated by reference to items of work performed where there are high-margin, low-volume transactions in which gross revenue calculations may not be appropriate. The structure of continuing franchise fees must reflect the underlying business, the income flows and the margins which are available. If it is not possible to find a formula which the franchisee can afford, and which will provide the franchisor with sufficient gross revenues to enable it to make a reasonable profit, the proposed franchise will not be viable. This is probably the most common reason for a prospective franchisor deciding not to proceed.

7.4   Advertising

Most franchise systems provide for advertising. The franchisor will wish to retain control of its trade marks or trade names and of any claims made in advertisements about the goods or services sold or promoted by the franchisees.

There are different approaches. A franchisor which manufactures, sells and advertises a range of products in which franchisees deal may provide advertising support within that framework free of charge to the franchisees. This approach is available only in limited circumstances.

The most common approach is for the franchisor to collect contributions, based on a percentage of gross revenues, from franchisees in the same way as continuing franchise fees are invariably calculated and to undertake to spend the aggregate contributions on advertising and promotional activities. It is important from the franchisor's point of view that there is no formal fund constituted in such a way that franchisees could claim that the contributions are held in a trust. It was recently held in Canada that advertising contributions were not trust money (*see* 7.6.2). A trust would be an unmanageable creature. Franchisees join and leave a network at different times during each year; most remain in it from one year to another. Claims from outgoing franchisees that they are entitled to a proportion of unspent funds would be impracticable to deal with. In addition, advertising is spent in limited periods during which campaigns are held; expenditure is rarely spread evenly throughout a year. This would mean that funds could be contractually committed for expenditure which will be incurred after a franchisee leaves the network. The highest degree of flexibility to carry funds forward and to make forward commitments is essential for advertising arrangements to work. The recommended course is for franchisees to have a contractual obligation to make the payments, and for the franchisor to contract for its expenditure for identified purposes. The contractual provision has to be drafted with these issues in mind.

In drafting it is also sensible to consider the issues most frequently raised by franchisees in relation to advertising. These include:

(1) 'The franchisor's advertising and promotional activities are useless.'
(2) 'The franchisor spent money on things it should not have.'
(3) 'The franchisor does not spend any money on me and my outlet.'
(4) 'The network gets no benefit from the franchisor's advertising.'
(5) 'The franchisor did not spend enough.'
(6) 'The franchisor is misusing the funds by charging its expenses to advertising.'

Many franchisors incur expenses in the administration of advertising and promotional activities. Indeed, some franchisors have marketing directors or marketing departments whose functions are to devise, organise and implement the advertising and promotional activities of the network. It is proper that expenses genuinely incurred for the purposes of these activities should be charged to the advertising contributions. Some of these issues can be handled by techniques of management of a network; others by contractual provisions which clearly lay down the parameters.

When preparing its franchise package, the franchisor must decide how the advertising will be best organised. There are three possibilities:

— national advertising
— local advertising
— a combination of local and national advertising.

One then has to decide who will do what and how will it be organised. There are some systems where local advertising will be the most effective promotion of the franchisee's business. Even in such a case, it is likely that some expenditure on a national corporate image will make sense once the network reaches a certain size. This possibility should not be overlooked, and will need to be addressed in the drafting of the provisions in the contract.

The fee charged by some franchisors includes the continuing franchisee fee and an advertising contribution, the franchisor undertaking to provide advertising and promotional expenditure out of the funds received. It is normally in the interests of both franchisor and franchisee in these cases to specify what proportion of the total fee charged will be spent on advertising and promotion. In that way the franchisor's financial commitment is fixed, and the franchisee can identify how much will be allocated for advertising and promotion.

7.5 Sources of finance

Since 1981, when the National Westminster Bank became the first UK bank to examine the potential of providing finance to the franchising community, the number of sources of financial assistance has grown. Most of the major banks now have specialist units or individuals who market the bank's services to franchisors and franchisees. These units and individuals are in frequent contact with existing and prospective franchisors and franchisees, and have accumulated a great deal of information about franchising which equips them rapidly to evaluate applications for financial assistance. Because franchising is a safer method of establishing a new business, the banks offer better terms to new franchisees than they would to non-franchised new businesses. They tend to offer a larger percentage of total setting-up costs (70 per cent rather than 50 per cent), lower interest rates and capital repayment holidays. They are also highly competitive in those areas.

The banks' practices have changed over the years and there is an increasing emphasis on business plans and budgets which have to be prepared and submitted when applications for loans are made. Inevitably franchisors become involved in assisting their prospective franchisees in preparing such business plans and budgets. In such circumstances franchisors need to ensure that the banks appreciate that they are not giving any warranty that the projected income is anything more than a reflection of experience elsewhere, and that it is not a firm commitment of what the particular prospective franchisee can achieve. In view of the difficulty of assessing how well or poorly an individual franchisee will perform when his business is established, no franchisor would wish to risk a claim from a bank, or indeed the franchisee, that gross income projections were firm promises of what would be achieved.

In addition, the banks have to ensure that, in approving an application by a franchisee for a loan, they are not representing the soundness of the franchisor, the proposition or the business plan and budgets presented. Banks do of course, represent themselves as possessing expertise, and offer advice to would-be franchisors and franchisees. Care has to be taken to ensure that claims against them for negligent advice, or breach of a warranty do not arise (*see Esso Petroleum Co Ltd* v *Mardon* [1976] QB 801, [1976] 2 All ER 5); and that the advice they give is sound.

Financial assistance can come from the franchisor (although this is rare unless the franchisee encounters financial problems; *see below*) or from financial institutions other than banks.

7.5.1   The Consumer Credit Act 1974

In some cases franchisors hire or lease, or arrange for the hire or lease of, all equipment to franchisees. Regard must then be had to the provisions of the Consumer Credit Act 1974 (the 'Act'). The Act will apply if a franchisee, who is either a sole trader or a partnership (a limited company is outside the scope of the Act), either takes a loan or leases equipment from anyone, including the franchisor, for a value up to £15,000. Such loan or hire agreements would constitute consumer credit agreements pursuant to s 8 of the Act.

Exempt agreements

Section 16 exempts certain credit agreements, in particular certain agreements relating to land. However, a loan by a franchisor in respect of land would probably not be exempt, because it is unlikely that the franchisor would be one of the exempt bodies defined in s 16. Section 16 also exempts debtor-creditor-supplier agreements for a fixed sum of credit where the credit is repayable within 12 months by four or fewer payments. A debtor-creditor-supplier agreement is one where the creditor/supplier is one and the same person, or where the creditor and supplier have a pre-existing business relationship and the loan is linked to the supply of specific items. An agrement for the hiring of certain equipment from the franchisor, or even a loan to the franchisee to enable him to purchase equipment, would be a debtor-creditor-supplier agreement.

If the loan is a debtor-creditor loan and the total charge for credit is not greater than either 13 per cent, or 1 per cent above the highest of the clearing banks' current base rates, the agreement will be exempt. This may be the case where the franchisor lends money to the franchisee without specifying what the loan is for. However, franchisors are unlikely to do this, preferring to link the loan to the purchase of the equipment package. In such a case the loan would be a debtor-creditor-supplier agreement; the supplier could either be the franchisor (if it owns the equipment) or a third party supplier of the equipment.

Rights of concellation

The Act is principally designed to protect the hirer and the agreement must clearly set out the rights of the hirer as specified in regulations made under the Act.

To protect the hirer, the Act contains strict provisions regarding execution of the agreement, and requiring copies of the agreement to be provided to the hirer before it comes into effect. If the procedures are not followed, or the time limits are not observed, the hirer has the right to cancel the agreement (ss 60–74). If the regulated agreement restricts the use of the credit, there is again a possibility that the franchise agreement could be cancelled, because it could arguably be classified as a linked transaction pursuant to s 19(1)(c)(iii) of the Act, as it stipulates a use for the goods or services acquired under the regulated agreement.

However, the agreement will not be capable of cancellation if it is signed by the debtor or hirer at premises where any of the other parties to the agreement are carrying on a business. The franchisor should therefore ensure that all agreements are signed at its place of business.

The Act requires all consumer credit agreements to contain all the terms of the agreement. This means that if the hire agreement refers to and incorporates any terms of the franchise agreement, the franchise agreement must be annexed to the hire agreement. For example the franchisor would wish to ensure that it can terminate the hire agreement if the franchise agreement is terminated for any reason.

Power to reopen agreements

Sections 137–140 of the Act give the court power to reopen any credit agreement (even if the credit supplied is greater than £15,000 or the agreement is exempted under s 16) and adjust the terms of the agreement and order a refund to the debtor if the court considers it to be 'an extortionate credit bargain'. In determining whether a credit agreement is extortionate the court has regard to factors such as interest rates prevailing at the time the agreement was made; the age, experience and business capacity of the debtor; the degree of financial pressure on the debtor; the degree of risk to the debtor in the light of the value of the security provided; and any other relevant considerations.

91

If a franchisor agrees with a defaulting franchisee to reschedule the debt, this could be a restricted-use regulated loan agreement and therefore, subject to what has been said *above*, the Act would apply.

Credit brokerage

Sections 145–160 of the Act relate to all ancillary credit business (for example, debt-counselling, debt collectors, credit reference agencies), most of which is not applicable to franchisors. However, franchisors could be involved in credit-broking, that is to say, effecting introductions of individuals desiring to obtain credit to other credit sources, no matter what the amount of the credit may be.

Consumer credit licence

If the franchisor is entering into any such agreements with a franchisee, or if the franchisor arranges finance for franchisees with, or refers franchisees to, other institutions for financial assistance, it will be engaging in consumer credit business or credit brokerage and the Act requires the franchisor to obtain a consumer credit licence: category A for consumer credit business; category B for consumer hire business; and category C for credit brokerage. Licences are obtained from the Office of Fair Trading. When applying, the franchisor should ensure that the licence will cover all categories which may be relevant as, apart from any criminal penalties that the franchisor could incur, the licence could be revoked entirely if it does not cover all of the franchisor's activities.

Debtor-creditor-supplier agreements

Sections 56 and 75 of the Act apply solely to debtor-creditor-supplier agreements, and have the effect of making a creditor liable for the actions of the supplier in certain circumstances. Applying this principle to franchising, the franchisor, if supplying the credit for a franchisee to hire or purchase equipment direct from a supplier, could be liable for the actions or defaults of that supplier.

Section 56 provides that any antecedent negotiations by the supplier or credit broker are conducted by him as agent for the creditor. Therefore, the creditor would be bound by the agent's representations. It is not possible to contract out of this provision.

Section 75 provides that a debtor who has a claim against a supplier for misrepresentation or breach of contract has a like claim against the creditor. Section 75 is narrower than s 56 because it (i) covers the supplier only and not a credit broker; (ii) applies to misrepresentation or breach of contract only; and (iii) applies only if the cash price is between £100 and £30,000.

7.6 Insolvency

7.6.1 Introduction

It is necessary to consider the effect on the franchisor and the franchisee of the insolvency of the other. Under the Insolvency Act 1986 financial difficulties of an individual or a company may lead to one of the following four procedures being adopted:

(1) A voluntary arrangement, under which the creditors (and in the case of a company the shareholders) are asked to agree a composition in satisfaction of the individual's or company's debts, or a scheme of arrangement. If agreed to by 75 per cent in value of the creditors, it is binding on all of them.

(2) Receivership, where a secured creditor appoints a receiver to receive income and dispose of the charged assets. In the case of a company which has created a floating charge, a receiver may be appointed as an 'administrative receiver', in which case he will have wider powers than an ordinary (or Law of Property Act) receiver. An administrative receiver has power to carry on and dispose of the company's business as a going concern, whereas a Law of Property Act receiver can dispose of specific charged assets only. Following—or even during—receivership, a company will often go into liquidation.

(3) Administration is a procedure introduced by the Insolvency Act 1986, under which an administrator is appointed by the court to manage the business and assets of a company with a view to achieving a specified purpose. This purpose is usually either the survival of the company or a part of it as a going concern, or a more advantageous realisation of its assets than would be possible in a winding-up. The importance of this procedure is in the creation of a moratorium and the effective freezing of creditors' rights from the date of the presentation of an administration petition. The disadvantage of administration is that it can be prevented by any lender with a floating charge who appoints an administrative receiver instead.

(4) Winding-up/liquidation under which a liquidator is appointed by the shareholders, creditors or the court (depending on the state of the company's solvency), whose duty will be to realise the company's assets and distribute the proceeds to the creditors. The equivalent for an individual is bankruptcy.

The franchisor

The insolvency of a franchisor can undoubtedly lead to major difficulties, including the risk of failure for franchisees. Some of the reasons for failure are:

(a) the franchisor had not properly pilot-tested its concept before franchising;

(b) the franchisor is under-capitalised;

(c) the franchisor makes poor business decisions;

(d) the franchisor has been dishonest;

(e) what was involved was not a franchise but some other, fraudulent,
scheme described wrongly as a franchise; and

(f) the franchisor failed to provide the continuing services properly or at all
through inefficiency or lack of resources.

Any of these factors could lead to the failure of the franchisor and may also
bring down the franchisee. Unless the franchisee has the financial and business resources to seek his own salvation by continuing to trade he will fail.
Franchisees are well advised to pool their resources if a franchisor fails.
They may have lost their franchisor, but they still own businesses and assets
and have business experience. Enlightened attitudes can enable the franchisees to secure a viable alternative by acquiring the intellectual property
assets of the failed franchisor and so re-establish the provision of franchise
services. The word 'enlightened' is used deliberately. There will be anger
and resentment but if there is also a positive and contructive approach the
franchisees can ensure that they do not follow their franchisor into failure.
Where there is a master franchise arrangement the ultimate franchisor may
well provide the support necessary or appoint a new sub-franchisor.

The franchisee

There also are signs if a franchisee is moving towards failure. These will probably first show themselves as a shortage of cash. This does not happen
overnight. Insolvency is a developing situation, and the franchisor's field
support system and monitoring of franchisee performance should reveal the
warning signs. These will include slowness in paying and in doing the many
things necessary to keep the business and staff on their toes. The franchisor
should be aware of the developing insolvency long before the point of no
return is actually reached, so that it can do something to help the franchisee
avoid it.

Identifying why the franchisee is sliding into insolvency is important. There
are many possibilities:

(a) failure to follow the system;

(b) failure or refusal to take advice from the franchisor (which is not
uncommon);

(c) the franchisee not being suited to the type of business;

(d) the franchisee being under-capitalised;

(e) over-spending on non-essentials;

(f) the franchisee not working hard enough or misdirecting his efforts; or

(g) the franchisee drawing too much out of the business.

Selecting a franchisee is a value judgement and however much care is taken, a franchisor may or may not be right. With experience, franchisors are more often right than wrong, but even so, some franchisees selected may prove incapable of running the business. Despite training, a franchisee may fail to appreciate the importance of cash flow management, perhaps drawing more out of the business than the business can afford. The franchisor has little control over matters such as this.

There could well be other reasons contributing to failure, and it is important to identify them. Otherwise it may not be possible to find a cure. The franchisor should ensure that those in its organisation with the right skills are brought in as soon as possible.

The franchisor may decide, long before bankruptcy looms, that it will terminate the franchise contract because however much it tries, it is not able to persuade the franchisee to comply with the contract or the directions given to him. However, the franchisor may decide not to terminate, instead trying to help a franchisee in difficulty to recover as much as possible. Ultimately, if the franchisee is unsuitable, the franchisor should assist him in finding a purchaser of the business on a basis which will recover for him as much as possible of his capital investment. Sometimes a franchisee will not respond to an offer to help, but experience shows that franchisees (with rare exceptions), if sensitively handled, usually do respond, and are relieved that someone is prepared to help them out of their difficulties.

7.6.2 Insolvency of the franchisor

It is unusual, although not unknown, for the franchise agreement to contain provisions dealing with the insolvency of the franchisor. Termination on the franchisor's insolvency is unlikely in practice to benefit either franchisor or franchisee, or the creditors of the franchisor. Indeed, automatic termination is likely to harm the franchisee, who will probably wish to continue to operate his business, while the insolvency practitioner will probably wish to sell the franchisor's business as a going concern, with the franchise continuing to operate, to obtain the best price.

The effect of the insolvency of the franchisor on the franchise network will depend on the type of insolvency procedure into which the franchisor has been placed. The following are therefore considered:

(1) Financial difficulties before an insolvency procedure is adopted: unless the franchisor's insolvency creates a repudiatory breach of contract, the franchisee will be required to perform all his obligations under the

agreement, although he may be in a stronger position to renegotiate some of the terms.

(2)   Voluntary arrangement: unless the franchisee was a creditor at the time of the proposal, he will not be bound by a voluntary arrangement.

(3)   Administration: if the franchise is profitable, the administrator is likely to leave well alone. However, he might be tempted to dispose of any rights or property belonging to the franchisor, which are used by the franchisee under the agreement to a third party, assuming there is no prohibition on assignment. He will have to maintain franchisor services in the meantime.

(4)   Receivership: the receiver could seek to repudiate the franchise contracts (although the franchisee could decline to accept the repudiation because otherwise he would lose all rights to continue to use the franchisor's intellectual property rights) or may seek a sale to a third party.

(5)   Liquidation: the liquidator could maintain the agreement or again seek a sale. However, if the liquidator considers the agreement to be particularly onerous, comprising 'an unprofitable contract', he may seek to exercise his powers under s 178 of the Insolvency Act 1986 to disclaim the agreement. The effect of disclaimer is to determine the rights, interests and liabilities of the franchisor with respect to that contract. If the franchisee suffers any loss as a result of a breach of contract by the franchisor he may prove in the liquidation for the loss. If the liquidator does not disclaim, but nevertheless fails to perform, the franchisee may serve notice requiring the liquidator to disclaim within 28 days beginning with the day on which notice is given. On expiry of this period, the liquidator's right to disclaim is lost.

As has already been noted, in a recent Canadian insolvency case (*Bankruptcy of Factory Carpet Inc* (1994) JIFDL p 17) it was held that in the absence of clear wording or intention of the parties, contributions by a franchisee to an advertising fund administered by a franchisor do not constitute trust funds. For the reasons explained above it is not advisable to constitute a fund for advertising, far less to create a trust.

7.6.3   Insolvency of the franchisee

It is common for the franchise agreement to incorporate a list of events of default on the part of the franchisee which will include the various insolvency procedures referred to above as well as a number of events short of insolvency evidenced by failure to pay debts (Insolvency Act 1986, s 122(1)(f)). However, it may not always suit the franchisor to enforce its rights immediately. For example, a receiver or liquidator of the franchisee may be able to sell the business, and the franchisor may wish to wait and see what is proposed before enforcing its rights. A franchisor may be able to introduce a purchaser, but much will depend on the reason for the insolvency.

An important issue is whether the franchisor can enforce its rights following the presentation of a petition for an administration order. In particular, s 10 of the Insolvency Act 1986 provides, *inter alia*, that during the period beginning with the presentation of a petition for an administration order and ending with the making of an order, or the petition's being dismissed:

> no steps may be taken to enforce any security over the company's property, or to repossess goods in the company's possession under any hire-purchase agreement except with the leave of the court and subject to such terms as the court may impose; and
>
> no other proceedings and no execution or other legal process may be commenced or continued and no distress may be levied against the company or its property except with leave of the court and subject to such terms as aforesaid.

Section 11 imposes similar restrictions during the period for which an order is in force, save that the consent of the administrator may be sought as an alternative to seeking leave of the court.

If a franchisor has not exercised any powers which were available to it before the presentation of a petition, then it must carefully analyse the position to see whether the exercise of its rights under the agreement may be prohibited under s 10 or 11. It has been held that the administration 'moratorium' does not prevent one party to a contract from terminating its contract with the company in administration in reliance on an express provision entitling that party to do so (*Re Olympia & York Canary Wharf Ltd* [1993] BCC 154). However, there is sufficient other authority and dicta to make it clear that the franchisor must be sure that it exercises only those rights which come within the scope of the right to terminate the contract in response to a repudiatory breach by the franchisee or pursuant to an express provision in the contract, rather than rights to enforce security, commence proceedings or any other action caught by ss 10 and 11 of the Insolvency Act 1986.

In the unlikely event that the franchise agreement does not contain the usual events of default, general contract and insolvency law principles will apply. The effect will be that the insolvency of the franchisee will not itself constitute a repudiation or breach of the franchise agreement such as to permit its termination, although there are likely to be other defaults (including non-payment of fees) caused by insolvency which could amount to such repudiation or breach.

If one of the four insolvency procedures is followed, it will be for the insolvency practitioner in each case to decide whether or not he will use the assets under his control to maintain the agreement. This in turn will depend on the profitability of the franchise operation. It may be that the insolvency has been caused by some element of the franchisee's business activities other than the franchise. However, unless the agreement has only a short time to run, in which even the insolvency practitioner may merely wish to run the franchise to the end of its term, the insolvency practitioner will be trading with a view to selling the franchise operation. His ability to do so will depend on the terms of the agreement. The position of the franchisor in these circumstances needs to be considered:

(1) In the case of a voluntary arrangement, if the franchisor was properly served with notice of the creditors' meeting, then even if it voted against the proposal, if 75 per cent or more of other disinterested creditors voted for it, the franchisor will be bound by it in respect of debts owed to it by the franchisee. This is subject to one qualification, that if the franchisor has grounds for claiming that the proposal 'unfairly prejudices' its interests it may apply to the court for relief (s 6). Unlike in the case of an administration, where the moratorium applies from the presentation of the petition, the proposal in a voluntary arrangement becomes binding only when it is adopted. It would therefore be open to a franchisor to enforce any rights to recover fees or other sums due to it before the meeting is held.

(2) On receivership, an administrative receiver, and (if the instrument under which he is appointed contains an appropriate express power) an ordinary receiver, may repudiate or otherwise frustrate the agreement and, provided that this power is exercised in good faith, he is immune from a tortious action for inducing a breach of contract. The franchisor's only remedy in such an event would be an unsecured claim against the franchisee. However, this is a specific immunity and would not apply to other torts. If the receiver, notwithstanding repudiation of the agreement, purported to use or sell the intellectual property of the franchisor, he may be liable to the franchisor for trespass or conversion.

(3) If the franchisee goes into administration, in the absence of any contractual rights to the contrary, the franchisor will have to await notice of a meeting of the creditors and then vote on the proposal. Moreover, if at the meeting the resolution in favour of the proposal is passed by a simple majority in value of those creditors present and voting, the administration will proceed in order to implement the proposals. In particular, while all debts and liabilities incurred by the administrator under contracts entered into by him are, like his remuneration and any expenses properly incurred by him, charged on and to be paid out of any property of the company under his control (Insolvency Act 1986, s 19(5)), this does not extend to contracts entered into before the administration order was made which are performed or 'adopted' by the administrator. Therefore, in the absence of any other contractual provision, the franchisor would have no automatic preference or priority. However, as

mentioned above, it appears that, notwithstanding the moratorium, the franchisor would be able to accept the franchisee's repudiatory breach and terminate the franchise agreement if the agreement contained an express provision entitling him so to do.

(4) In a liquidation, the liquidator could continue to maintain the agreement but he could not demand performance by the franchisee without effective performance on the part of the franchisor. It is equally open to the liquidator simply not to perform. If there are several franchise agreements he may choose to perform some but repudiate others, unless this is prohibited by cross-default provisions, or all the franchise agreements are governed by a head agreement. If the liquidator believes the agreement represents an unprofitable contract and is therefore onerous property of the franchisee, it is likely that he will seek to exercise his powers under s 178 to disclaim it.

The court has a wide discretion in most of the insolvency procedures, and in particular in a liquidation. As well as this general discretion, there are specific provisions which allow the court to interfere with contractual arrangements. For example, under s 186 the court may, on the application of a person who is, as against the liquidator, entitled to the benefit or subject to the burden of a contract made with the company, make an order rescinding the contract on such terms as to payment by or to either party of damages for the non-performance of the contract, or otherwise as the court thinks just. Moreover, any damages payable under the order to such person may be proved by him as a debt in the winding-up.

Chapter 8

The Franchisor's Liabilities

Chapter 8

The Franchisor's Liabilities

8.1 Introduction

There are many issues which arise in or in relation to franchise transactions which have the potential to create liability claims against a franchisor. Some of these issues have already been addressed in Chapter 5 where the nature of the relationship is discussed; some are addressed in Chapter 17 where remedies are discussed.

This chapter will, as appropriate, expand those discussions and deal with other issues not dealt with in those or other chapters. It is essential that a franchisor is conscious of these issues when structuring its franchise system and contractual documentation.

There are two categories of persons to whom a franchisor may have a potential liability. The first category is the franchisees; the second is third parties with whom the franchisee has dealings. We shall consider each in turn.

These liabilities tend to arise under two headings:

— pre-contract;
— contractual.

8.2 Liabilities arising out of pre-contract negotiations

The principal pre-contractual issue which can provide the foundation for claims by franchisees is the discussions between a franchisor and its prospective franchisees. The larger the franchisor's organisation, the greater the risk that someone dealing with the prospective franchisee may make an inaccurate statement. Even before the parties have met, a franchisor can create the circumstances out of which a claim could arise, by its recruitment activities. Franchisors make contact with prospective franchisees in a variety of ways, but whichever method a franchisor uses, it must be aware of its exposure to risk.

8.2.1   Misrepresentation

Written communications

A franchisor may be brought into contact with a prospective franchisee by an advertisement. The advertisement will provide some information about the franchise proposition. While the contents of the advertisement may not in themselves support a claim for misrepresentation, given subsequent discussions the contents may, in the event of a dispute about recollection, confirm what the franchisee asserts that he was told. The usual response by a franchisor to a request in reply to an advertisement will be to send a brochure or other literature descriptive of the franchisor, the franchise proposition and in particular what services the franchisor offers franchisees, both in assisting the franchisee to establish his business, and by way of continuing support for the franchisee. Care must be taken in presenting this information to ensure that what is offered is actually to be delivered and will be reflected in the contractual documentation. Frequently franchisors' brochures include sample figures which illustrate what net profit performance may be achieved, given the realisation of stated turnover levels. Any such sample figures must be correctly described so that the franchisee may know whether they reflect the reality of actual achievements, or are merely indications of the percentage breakdown of gross and net margins at arbitrarily selected turnover levels.

So far as the presentation of possible gross revenue and profit figures is concerned, one must not lose sight of the fact that even if the figures presented reflect actual audited performance by one or more franchisees, there can be no guarantee, or perhaps even a suggestion, that the prospective franchisee will achieve the indicated level of performance. All franchise networks have franchisees with different levels of performance and success. Various factors can have an effect on performance. Some do not necessarily arise from any act or default on the part of the franchisor or the franchisee, because franchising does not insulate any franchisee from the pressures to which other businesses are subjected. It seeks to reduce the impact of those pressures by the application of accumulated know-how and experience. Factors which can adversely affect performance include the following:

(1) The location or territorial catchment area may not produce the levels of business which, given the application of normally successful selection criteria, appeared likely.
(2) The location may be affected by local developments, such as the establishment of a shopping mall which draws customers away from that part of the shopping area where the franchisee's business is established.
(3) A competitive business may move into the area and adversely affect the franchisee's business.

There are cases where the franchisor may be at fault, for instance, where a location is selected without proper regard to its established criteria.

There are cases where the franchisee may be at fault, for instance:

(a) where the franchisee does not operate the franchisor's system properly;
(b) where the franchisee does not make the appropriate commitment or does not put in the necessary effort;
(c) where the franchisee believes that the franchisor should deliver customers and success to him.

Another factor which is perhaps more a joint failure is where, with the benefit of hindsight, it becomes clear that a franchisee is not suited to self-employment or franchising.

There are other factors, but it is crucial that franchisors do not raise hopes to the level where a franchisee believes that success is an inevitable conclusion of signing a franchise agreement. All who enter self-employment through franchising need to make a considerable commitment. A franchisor's potential liability will be reduced or eliminated by a frank and realistic presentation of the relevant facts to its prospective franchisees. The Code of Ethics of the British Franchise Association, supplemented by the BFA's Best Practice Guide to Ethical Conduct, should be used as a benchmark.

Business plans

In more recent years the requirements of the banks to be provided with business plans by prospective franchisees who wish to borrow has increased the risk for those franchisors who participate in their preparation or produce business plans for franchisees. If any franchisor undertakes such participation or production it should ensure that both the prospective franchisee and the bank understand the assumptions and criteria applied, and the plan should include appropriate caveats.

As pointed out in Chapter 17, a franchisee who wishes to pursue a claim will invariably base it on all possible grounds; almost certainly, whatever the real root of the problem, there will be a misrepresentation claim. This is why franchisors must be certain of what they say and aware of the risks.

Remedies

The law provides remedies not only for fraudulent misrepresentations but also for innocent or negligent misrepresentations, unless the person making the statement complained of can prove that he had reasonable ground to believe, and did believe up to the time the contract was made, that the facts represented were true (Misrepresentation Act 1967, s 2(1)). This means that an innocent misrepresentation can provide the franchisee with a right to rescind the contract. The same rule applies in the case of negligent misrepresentation.

The basic rule at common law was that to make a representation there had to be a statement of fact rather than an expression of an opinion. This was the problem with which the court was faced in *Esso Petroleum Co Ltd* v *Mardon* [1976] QB 801; [1976] 2 All ER 5, CA. In this case, which is analogous to franchising, Esso were negotiating a tenancy and supply agreement for a petrol filling station with Mr Mardon. While the station was in the planning stage, Esso's representative (a man with 40 years' experience in this field) estimated that the annual gallonage would be 200,000 gallons. This was on the assumption that the station had its entrance on a main road. The planning authority had other ideas, and required that the entrance should be on the other side of the site which fronted a minor road. Mr Mardon quite properly challenged the Esso representative's gallonage estimate, suggesting it should be reduced. The representative stuck by his original estimate and Mr Mardon, impressed by his superior expertise and knowledge, was persuaded to accept those views. Mr Mardon was proved correct after some time in business; the deal was restructured, but Mr Mardon was still on a fast track to oblivion. Esso sued him for arrears of rent and Mr Mardon counterclaimed for misrepresentation, breach of collateral warranty, and negligence.

This case preceded the Misrepresentation Act; there being no suggestion that the misrepresentation was other than innocent and not fraudulent, it was clear that the law then offered no remedy on that ground. The court also dismissed the claim for breach of collateral warranty, since, in the words of Lawson J, the representation did not amount to a guarantee that the estimated gallonage would be achieved.

The Court of Appeal concluded that where a person professing particular skills gives advice to another, there is a warranty that the advice given is sound. Esso was such a person, the advice given was negligent and there was a breach of the warranty for which Esso was liable.

Had the Misrepresentation Act 1967 been in force, its extension to negligent representation would have provided Mr Mardon with his remedy and a tortious claim in negligence is probably no longer necessary. The principle that the person professing skills has a duty to exercise those skills with care is one which clearly applies to franchisors.

8.2.2   Exclusion clauses and entire terms clauses

Franchisors have long sought to protect themselves from claims by exclusion clauses and entire terms clauses. The efficacy of such clauses is under challenge, particularly by virtue of the Unfair Contract Terms Act 1977, which provides in s 8:

> If a contract contains a term which would exclude or restrict—
>> (a) a liability to which a party to a contract may be subject by reason of any misrepresentation made by him before the contract was made; or

(b) a remedy available to another party to the contract by reason of such misrepresentation;

that term shall be of no effect except insofar as it satisfied the requirement of reasonableness as stated in Section 11(1) . . . and it is for those claiming that the term satisfies that requirement to show that it does.

Section 11(1) provides that 'the term must be a fair and reasonable one to be included, having regard to the circumstances which were, or ought reasonably to have been, known or in the contemplation of the parties when the contract was made'.

The effect of clause 1(c) of Sched 1 to the Unfair Contract Terms Act 1977 has yet to be decided by the courts. The extent to which this exclusion from the 1977 Act will apply to franchise agreements is unclear. The wording refers to the 'creation or transfer of rights or interests' or the 'termination of any such right or interest', which raises the question whether it was intended to create a hiatus about what happens between the two events. It must surely refer to the sort of contractual provisions which are commonly found in such transactions; otherwise the exception would be difficult to understand.

As discussed above, many failures have nothing to do with any statement made by a franchisor, and this must have an influence on the reasonableness test. So must the fact that what the franchisor is essentially providing to the franchisee is a 'DIY' kit, and that if the franchisee does not properly exploit it, it may come to nothing.

There have been some cases where such clauses have been held unenforceable. The most recent is *Thomas Witter Ltd* v *TBP Industries Ltd* [1995] Tr Law 145 (Ch D), where an entire terms clause was struck out under s 8 (which was enacted in substitution for s 3 of the Misrepresentation Act 1967). For an exclusion clause to have a clause to escape the consequences of s 8, it would be wise for it to deal with certain issues:

(1) The clause should not seek to exclude liability for fraudulent statements.
(2) The parties should confirm in the contract that they have addressed the reasonableness test in the context of the transaction.
(3) A party to whom representations have been made which he considers induced him to enter into the contract should be encouraged to identify them, so that they can be incorporated in the contract, or so that the party alleged to have made the representations can have an opportunity to make the position clear.

Lastly, it should be remembered that the court can use s 8 to right what it considers to be unreasonable, and that it will have the benefit of hindsight to guide it.

8.2.3   Sale of Goods Act 1979

A franchisor should also be aware of the term implied into contracts by the Supply of Goods and Services Act 1982, that 'where a supplier of services is acting in the course of business the supplier will carry out the service with reasonable care and skill'. A franchisor is supplying a service not only when entering into a franchise agreement, but also throughout the term of that agreement. Quite apart from any express contractual obligation, the franchisor must be mindful of this overriding duty.

8.2.4 Trade descriptions

Although there do not appear to have been any reported decisions affecting franchisors under the Trade Descriptions Act 1968, it should nevertheless be considered. Liability to prosecution under that Act would arise if a franchisor applied a false trade description to any goods or services or to any offers to supply goods or services. A 'trade description' would relate to matters such as quantity, size, method of manufacture or production, processing, composition, fitness for purpose, testing and the results thereof and approval by any person. Such trade description relating to goods could be made either in writing or orally.

Section 14 of the Trade Descriptions Act 1968 contains equivalent provisions regarding the supply of services, and gives rise to liability if a false statement is made 'knowingly' or 'recklessly'. There seems to be scope for asserting that those who make offers of spurious business opportunities or distribution schemes which are not franchises, but who seek respectability by so describing them, could be liable to prosecution under the Act. False forecasts or promises, which in practice are more likely to be given than false statements to potential franchisees, are outside the provisions of the Act, except where they relate to the effect of treatments, processes or repairs (s 14(3) of the Act).

There are defences available. Broadly speaking, it may be a defence for a person such as a franchisor to show that the alleged offence was due to a mistake or was a result of reliance on information or an act or default of another person, an accident or some other cause beyond his control, and that he took all reasonable precautions and exercised care to avoid the commission of an offence. It is also a defence that a person did not know and could not with reasonable diligence have ascertained that words did not conform to the description. The same defence would be available where proceedings resulted from the activities of a franchisee in dealing with customers.

The penalty for breach of the provisions of the Trade Descriptions Act 1968, on summary conviction, is a fine not exceeding £2,000. On conviction on indictment a fine or imprisonment for a term not exceeding two years, or both, could be imposed. In addition a court can make a 'compensation order' requiring the defendant to pay compensation for any personal injury, loss or damage resulting from the offence.

A franchisor's civil liability for false trade descriptions and liability in contract may overlap. Consequently economic loss suffered by a franchisee as a result of a franchisor's breach of the franchise agreement could be recoverable so long as it was not too remote. In negligent mis-statement cases, economic loss is also recoverable, provided that the franchisee, as plaintiff, can prove that the franchisor defendant owed him a duty of care and that the loss is not too remote: *Hedley Byrne & Co Ltd* v *Heller & Partners Ltd* [1964] AC 465; [1963] 2 All ER 575.

8.3   Contractual liabilities

The nature and extent of the franchisor's obligations under the franchise contract will vary from case to case depending on the franchisor's system, the nature of the business and the levels of support which the franchisor considers appropriate. Some constraints and obligations will arise at the very beginning of the relationship; some will continue throughout its life. These obligations are detailed in Chapter 4. One set of objective criteria can be applied to many of these obligations. There will be many instances where the franchisor is required to make subjective judgments in the course of providing advice and guidance to its franchisees. There will undoubtedly be circumstances for which there is no precedent, and others where previous experience may point in a direction which may prove not to be right. A franchisor will be expected to exercise skill and care (*see* the Supply of Goods and Services Act 1982 referred to *above*), and will be regarded as having special knowledge and skill albeit narrowly focused (*see Esso Petroleum Co Ltd* v *Mardon, above*). Experience shows that when pursuing claims franchisees allege every conceivable deficiency. For instance, a frequent complaint is that no training was provided. In many cases franchisors can prove that training did take place by producing evaluations and other records, as well as written franchisee evaluations of the training course attended. Franchisors must therefore keep careful records of all contacts with franchisees and of services provided so that they can be invoked if there is a dispute.

8.4   Liability to third parties

8.4.1   Vicarious liability

A number of the issues which arise in connection with third parties have been dealt with in Chapter 5. There are other issues. The first is that of vicarious liability. The relationship between franchisor and franchisee will almost always involve the franchisor's imposing on the franchisee a system and method of operation, accompanied by controls over the franchisee. The conduct of the franchisee in carrying out his obligations in accordance with the requirements of the franchisor might well be correct, yet result in damage being suffered by a customer of the franchisee or by a stranger who had no contractual relationship with the franchisee. This could lead to a finding by a court that the franchisor was vicariously liable for the acts or omissions of the franchisee. Issues such as whether a duty of care was owed, and whether the loss suffered by the third party was foreseeable, would need to be examined by the court. If the customer or stranger concerned realises that the damages would be substantial, that the franchisee was relatively impecunious, and that the franchisor had a deep pocket, he might be tempted to sue the franchisor on principal/agency grounds, or on the basis of vicarious liability.

If it is alleged that the franchisee's method of operation was not in accordance with the franchisor's requirements, matters such as the extent and conduct of the franchisor's method of monitoring and regulating the franchisee's business would need to be examined by the court to determine whether the franchisor could escape liability on the grounds that the franchisee had failed to observe the franchisor's requirements. A franchisor may also be a victim of the franchisee's defaults. A court might also need to investigate whether the franchisee had resisted pressure from his franchisor with regard to his conduct of the franchised business, and whether the franchisor had acted reasonably in the enforcement or non-enforcement of its requirements under the terms of the franchise agreement. This could subject the franchise relationship to stress, since the franchisee might resent what he regarded as over-regulation by the franchisor. A franchisor may also feel that, to satisfy a court, it would need to take strict legal enforcement measures rather than use less formal techniques to persuade the franchisee to comply.

All these matters point to the need for a franchisor to be circumspect, not only with regard to the drafting of franchise agreements, but also in the way in which it conducts the continuing relationship with its franchisee. While a franchisor has an important interest in ensuring that its franchisee adheres to the franchisor's system for the purpose of achieving consistency and the protection of goodwill arising from the franchisor's trade mark or trade name, excessive control over the franchisee could result in franchisors having increased exposure for the acts or omissions of its franchisees.

A franchisor will therefore need to be alert to avoid controlling day-to-day operations. It is unlikely it would want to do so, since that would negate the principles on which franchising is based and might create other problems. However, where a franchisee is experiencing difficulties, the franchisor may well provide day-to-day operational back up to help overcome the problems.

8.4.2   Product liability

Where the franchisor supplies or approves products it must ensure that the terms of the supply or approval are clearly agreed. The Consumer Protection

Act 1987 contains provisions relating to product liability, consumer safety and misleading price information.

With regard to product liability, the legislation provides for strict liability for defective products in that manufacturers can be held liable without proof of negligence. The 1987 Act imposes civil liability for damage caused by a defective product. Liability falls not just on the manufacturer, but also on anyone who holds himself out as being the producer by putting his name or mark on the product, on anyone who imports a product into the European Union, and on the supplier of a product if he is unable to identify the producer or importer or his own supplier.

A franchisor, who may have nothing to do with the manufacture of a product, is clearly at risk of being regarded as 'any person who, by putting his name on the product or using a trade mark or other distinguishing mark in relation to the product, has held himself out to be the producer of the product'. There is a statutory defence, however, if the franchisor could show that he 'did not at any time supply the product to another'. Consequently, a franchisor who was not in the chain of supply of products to a franchisee would be able to utilise this defence. However, a franchisor who organises global purchasing for its franchisees might well not have the benefit of the statutory defence.

8.4.3   Safety requirements

In relation to consumer safety, the Consumer Protection Act 1987 introduces a criminal offence of supplying consumer goods which fail to comply with certain safety requirements. Goods fail to comply if they are not reasonably safe. The Act imposes criminal liability on the person whose act or default is responsible for the commission of an offence. Thus, a franchisor will potentially be liable where it specifies products, supplies them or nominates or approves sources of supply. A franchisee against whom proceedings are taken could put forward as a defence evidence that he took all reasonable steps, alleging that the offence was due to the act or default of the franchisor or was done in reliance on information given to him by the franchisor.

As regards misleading price information, the 1987 Act creates a criminal offence if, in the course of business, a person gives to a customer an indication which is misleading as to the price at which any goods, services, accommodation or facilities are available. Franchisors will need to be careful when advertising, either at national or local level, and in their marketing and promotional endeavours on behalf of their network of franchisees.

Apart from potential criminal liability, the Act also provides a civil remedy for those who may be affected by contravention of the obligations imposed by safety regulations. This could extend to franchisors.

8.4.4   Defective services

The Consumer Protection Act 1987 resulted from a European Community directive. A further directive has been proposed, to impose liability for the provision of defective services. This met opposition on the grounds that a blanket law for services would be inappropriate, given their diverse nature. The draft directive was withdrawn following the European Council's discussion on subsidiarity. The draft caused concern in the context of franchising because it included a proposal to make franchisors, master-franchisees and franchisees jointly and severally liable for each other's supply of defective services. This approach is clearly flawed, since there is no reason for a franchisee to be jointly and severally liable for his franchisor's defaults. But the issue ran deeper. The suggested justification for imposing such a liability was the common use of a name. Taken to its logical conclusion, the provision should have been extended to all cases where others' names are used, such as trade mark, patent, know-how and manufacturing licences.

The issue was addressed by the European Commission in the Block Exemption Regulation for categories of franchise agreements, where exemption is conditional on franchisees being obliged to indicate their independent status. Providing notice that a product is produced under licence is common in relation to the other transactions referred to above, and would solve the issue which was causing concern without imposing liabilities. In England, the Business Names Act 1985 deals with the matter, and the French Government introduced a new law giving effect to the requirement in the Block Exemption Regulation following its adoption.

The proposal for action in relation to the supply of defective services has not been abandoned. In June 1994 the Commission published a discussion paper on the subject, and while there is no reference to franchising, at this stage nothing can be assumed.

8.4.5   Premises

Statutory liability may also arise in connection with the use of premises. Under the Health & Safety at Work Act 1974, any person who has, to any extent, control of premises, is under a duty to take all reasonable practical steps to ensure that the premises are safe. Thus, where a franchisee is required to fit out and maintain premises to the franchisor's specifications, this may be sufficient for liability to arise if the specification falls foul of the legislation. Section 4(3) of the 1974 Act provides that a person exercising control includes a person who has, by virtue of any contract or tenancy, an obligation of any extent in relation to:

(a) the maintenance or repair of any premises or any means of access or egress to and from the premises; or

(b) the safety of or the absence of risks to health arising from plant or substances in any such premises.

Section 4(4) of the 1974 Act provides that references to a person having control include a person having control of premises or matters in connection with the carrying on by him of a trade, business or other undertaking. If, therefore, a franchisor is also its franchisee's landlord, the franchisor can avoid liability by including in the lease terms which require the tenant franchisee to carry out repairs and maintenance to the premises.

The Offices, Shops & Railways Premises Act 1963 imposes similar specific duties on an occupier of premises and while, generally speaking, any liability for breach of the Act would fall on a franchisee as the occupier of the premises, the franchisor may be liable if it retains any degree of control of the premises such that it would be deemed to be an occupier. While the terms of a lease might seek to ensure that the franchisor/landlord had no control of the use of the premises, it would be a matter of interpretation of the facts whether or not control was naturally exercised by the franchisor and, if so, whether it was sufficient to make the franchisor potentially liable under either the 1963 or the 1974 statute.

Similar considerations will apply in the context of third party liability arising pursuant to the Occupiers' Liability Act 1957 which lays down a statutory duty of care to all visitors to premises. Whether a franchisor or landlord franchisor may be said to be an occupier will be a question of fact in every case. The test laid down by the courts is whether a person has some degree of control associated with and arising from his presence in and use of or activity in the premises.

One further example of a statute relating to the use of premises is the Defective Premises Act 1972, which imposes a duty on a landlord where the premises let to the tenant are defective, and the landlord is, by the terms of the tenancy agreement, either under an obligation to repair, or has the right to enter and carry out repairs, and the landlord is aware of the defect. In these circumstances, a landlord is liable for any damages or injury caused to third parties as a result of the defect. Therefore, a franchisor/landlord which is itself the tenant of a superior landlord, and is under obligations under the superior lease to the head landlord, might well fall within the ambit of the Defective Premises Act 1972.

It must be emphasised, both in relation to possible strict liability under statute and more generally, that in the absence of authoritative court decisions on the principal/agent and master/servant issues in the context of a franchisor/franchisee relationship, it is not possible to make definitive statements about a franchisor's potential liability to third parties. Until the courts provide guidance, franchisors and their advisers must proceed with circumspection.

113

8.5   Indemnity clauses and insurance

Another means for the franchisor to protect itself, or at least mitigate its liability, is to ensure that the franchise agreement includes wording requiring the franchisee to comply with all statutes, statutory instruments and regulations. Failure by a franchisee to comply with this obligation would constitute a breach of the agreement and permit the franchisor to terminate the relationship. However, such a provision would not allow the franchisor to avoid liability imposed by statute; to overcome this, the franchisor may well wish to include a clause requiring the franchisee to indemnify it should a claim be successfully made against it.

Franchisors should also consider requiring franchisees to provide an indemnity against claims arising from the franchisees' activities.

Insurance may also be a suitable means of mitigating loss arising from liability to third parties, whether they be customers or strangers. If the franchisor takes out insurance against public liability on behalf of itself and its franchisees, this may give some measure of protection, although it should be noted that franchisees would not be able to recover under such a policy if held liable to third parties, since they would have no direct contractual relationship with the insurance company. It is usually best for both parties to carry insurance. A franchisor may well be in a position to effect a 'master' insurance scheme in which each franchisee can participate. Clearly, in accordance with the ordinary principles of insurance law, a franchisor will be liable to the insurer to make full disclosure of all material facts concerning the franchise arrangements to overcome any possibility that, if a claim is made, the insurer will avoid the policy on the grounds of material non-disclosure.

Chapter 9

UK Taxation

Chapter 9

UK Taxation

9.1 Introduction

UK tax legislation does not deal with franchising as a discrete topic. Accordingly, the parties to a franchise contract will have to consider the effect of taxation on their proposed operations in the same way as any person establishing a new business activity. This chapter seeks to focus on issues which are relevant in the context of franchise operations; it is not intended to provide a comprehensive guide to the UK tax system.

The chapter deals first with the tax issues associated with the structuring of a new franchise operation, bearing in mind that many franchisees will be starting a new business venture. The commentary could therefore apply equally to many types of new business. Franchisees and their advisers will, for example, have to make an immediate decision on the appropriate business entity to adopt, as would any person starting a new business. The chapter moves on to consider some of the more specific tax issues which commonly arise in connection with franchising transactions and the content of franchise agreements. The chapter explains how certain taxes and reliefs apply in specific situations and points to possible tax planning steps relevant to many franchisors and franchisees; it does not provide a comprehensive explanation of the underlying principles behind the taxes and reliefs and the reader should refer to specialist tax text books for a more detailed explanation.

9.2 General principles

9.2.1 Choice of business entity

The relevant factors

Before commencing a new business, a decision must be taken on the appropriate form of trading entity through which to undertake the business. The choice will be between, on the one hand incorporating a company, and, on the other hand, trading as a sole trader or in partnership.

In the case of franchisees operating as sole traders (ie otherwise than through a company) it will be assumed in this chapter that the franchisee is genuinely self-employed and is not at risk of being treated as an employee of the franchisor. In genuine franchising situations (as opposed to cases where a 'franchise label' is attached to a business relationship which does not have the normal hallmarks of a franchise relationship), it will invariably be clear that the franchisee is operating a business on his own account and there should be sufficient factors pointing to self-employment to rebut any suggestion of an employment relationship (*see* the Inland Revenue's own guide IR 56 for a useful starting point on the employee/self-employed issue).

The decision between using a company and operating as an unincorporated business will often be based on non-tax factors. As far as the franchisor is concerned, commercial considerations, such as the need to attract outside investment and the need for limited liability, may determine that the business will be conducted by a company. So far as the franchisee is concerned, he will often be operating on his own on a relatively small scale; he may not feel the need for limited liability and may not wish to incur the expense of setting up and running a company. The franchisee may find that the only assets available to provide security for the finance required to set up the franchise business are his personal assets so that limited liability would be of little real benefit to him in any event.

Although non-tax considerations will often predominate when deciding whether or not to set up a company, any balanced decision must also take into account the tax implications.

The tax comparison in brief

A brief comparison of some of the tax implications of operating as a sole trader/partner or through a company is set out in the table *below*:

Sole trader/partnership	*Limited company*
(1) Liable for income tax at 20%, 25% or 40%. If taxable income exceeds £24,300, taxed at 40%.	(1) Liable for corporation tax at 25% or 33%. Provided profits do not exceed £300,000, likely to be taxed at 25%. Shareholders liable for income tax on income distributed to them and salary paid to them.
(2) Liable for Class 4 NICs at 7.3% on income between £6,640 and £22,880 regardless of whether income distributed.	(2) No liability to NICs if profits retained in company or distributed by way of dividend. If shareholder receives a salary there will

118

(3) Taxpayer entitled to personal reliefs (including annual exemption for capital gains tax purposes).

(4) Can carry first four years' losses back against income of taxpayer in previous three years (whether or not the income is trading income).

(5) Trading losses can be set against other income or capital gains for year of loss and following year (or preceding year if current year basis of assessment applies (*see* 6 *below*)). Can be carried forward against future income of same trade.

(6) Tax assessed on a current year basis for new businesses (ie businesses commencing after 5 April 1994). Businesses established before 6 April 1994 are currently assessed on a preceding year basis (except for first two/three years and final one/three years). Change to current year basis of assessment for existing businesses to take place with effect from 1997/98 (with transitional rules for 1996/97). For years of assessment up to and including 1995/96, tax is payable in two instalments on 1 January in the year of assessment and 1 July in the following year. From 1996/97 tax will be payable in two instalments on 31 January in year of assessment and 31 July in the following year.

be primary and secondary Class 1 NICs of up to 20.2%.

(3) Company not entitled to any personal reliefs (but can distribute income to shareholders to utilise their reliefs).

(4) First year losses of company cannot be carried back to other income of shareholders.

(5) Trading losses can be set against the company's other income or capital gains of current accounting period or carried back for three years. Can be carried forward against future income of same trade.

(6) Tax assessed on profits on a current year basis and payable nine months after end of accounting period.

(7) Taxpayer fully taxable on profits of business regardless of whether retained in business or withdrawn for personal use.

(7) Shareholders able to take earnings as a mixture of salary and/or dividends, and may also be able to receive repayments of loans. The company will be subject to tax on all profits but will be able to deduct salary and secondary NICs as an allowable expense. The shareholder will be taxed only on his income entitlement (eg salary and dividends).

(8) Trading income constitutes 'earned income' and can be used to make contributions to a personal pension scheme.

(8) Salary will constitute 'earned income' and can be used to make contributions to personal pension scheme. Dividends and profits retained in a company do not count towards pensionable earnings. As an alternative, a company may set up an occupational pension scheme.

(9) Relief generally only available for interest incurred on revenue account if it is a trading expense within s 74(1)(*a*) ICTA 1988 (interest charged to capital may not qualify)

(9) Relief available for interest incurred as a trading expense or as a charge on income and may still qualify for relief as a charge on income where the interest paid has been charged to capital (s 338(3) and (5)(*a*) ICTA 1988).

Some of the points mentioned in the table are dealt with in more detail *below*.

Taxation of profits—comparative tax rates

Since April 1988 the differential in tax rates between a company and an individual/partnership has been greatly reduced. However, as the maximum rate of income tax is 40 per cent (where taxable income exceeds £24,300), while the small companies rate (the lowest rate of corporation tax) is only 25 per cent, there may still be some cases when it is advantageous to use a company, particularly where profits can be retained in the company. The small companies rate of taxation is available for a company which has no 'associated companies' (as defined in s 13(5) of the Income and Corporation Taxes Act 1988 ('ICTA 1988')) where its profits do not exceed £300,000 (the definition of associated companies basically catches all companies which are under common control). An effective tax rate of between 25 per cent and 33 per cent applies where profits exceed £300,000 but do not exceed £1,500,000 (ICTA 1988, s 13). Where such a company has associated companies, the £300,000 and £1,500,000 thresholds will be divided by the number of associated companies (including the company itself). A company with two subsidiaries will therefore pay tax at 25 per cent if its profits do not exceed £100,000 (one-third of £300,000) (ICTA 1988, s 13(3)).

If the profits of a company are such that the lower tax rate will apply, the shareholders may be able to structure their capital contributions so as to mitigate tax liabilities. The shareholders can invest money in the company by subscribing for shares and/or by making a loan to the company. If a loan is made and the company becomes profitable, the company will then be able to repay the loan with no tax cost for the shareholder. The company will have paid corporation tax on the profits but no further tax liability will arise when it repays the loan. A sole trader/partner will, however, be liable to income tax (possibly at the 40 per cent rate), regardless of whether profits are distributed or retained in the business.

National Insurance Contributions

In addition to the income tax/corporation tax liabilities referred to above, the taxpayer will also have to consider his liability to pay National Insurance Contributions (NICs).

Sole trader/partner   A sole trader/partner will be subject to Class 4 NICs at 7.3 per cent of his relevant profits regardless of whether those profits are retained in the business or withdrawn by him for his own use (Social Security Act 1975, s 9). His relevant profits are those profits or gains between £6,640 and £22,880 per year (ie his maximum relevant profits will be £16,240 even if his taxable income exceeds £22,880). A sole trader/partner will also be liable to pay Class 2 NICs at a flat rate of £5.75 per week (Social Security Act 1975, s 7).

A sole trader/partner is able to set half of his Class 4 NIC liability (but not his Class 2 liability) against total income when calculating his income tax liability (ICTA 1988, s 617(5)).

Company   Where profits are generated in a company, liability to NICs will arise only where the company's profits are withdrawn in the form of remuneration paid to directors or employees. There will be no liability to NICs where the profits are retained in the company or where profits are distributed to shareholders by way of dividend. If a salary is paid to the shareholders (or, indeed, to any other employee) the company (as employer) will be liable to pay employer's NICs (secondary Class 1 contributions) on any earnings over £58 per week. Unlike Class 4 contributions, there is no earnings cap on the liability to pay employer's NICs (which are payable at a rate of up to 10.2 per cent, depending on the level of the employee's earnings). The employee will also be required to pay employee's NICs (primary Class 1 contributions) on his relevant earnings up to an earnings cap of £440 per week (at a rate of 2 per cent on the first £58 per week and 10 per cent on the remainder) (Social Security Act 1975, s 4). The Class 1 rates are reduced if the employee contracts out of the state earnings related pension scheme (SERPS). The reduced rate for primary Class 1 contributions on relevant earnings between £68 per week and £440 per week is 8.2 per cent, and the reduced rates for secondary Class 1 contributions is up to 7.2 per cent of relevant earnings between £58 per week and £440 per week, although the standard rate of 10.2 per cent may still be due on the first £58 of relevant earnings and on any excess over £440.

Thus a sole trader/partner will pay NICs at only 7.3 per cent whereas the salary of an employed person may bear NICs at 20.2 per cent.

Shareholders When a company pays a salary to a shareholder, the salary (plus any employer's NICs) will form part of the deductible trading expenses of the company provided it is incurred 'wholly and exclusively' in the course of its trade (ICTA 1988, s 74(1)(*a*)). This will reduce the company's taxable profits and, accordingly, its corporation tax liability. When a company pays a dividend to its shareholders, it is paid from its after-tax profits (and does not reduce taxable profits) (ICTA 1988, s 337(2)(*a*)). When the dividend is paid, advance corporation tax (ACT) at the rate of 20 per cent on the sum of the dividend and the ACT will be payable (ICTA 1988, s 14(1) and Finance Act 1993, s 78). The ACT is available for off-set against both the company's corporation tax liability and the shareholders' tax liability on dividends (by utilisation of the tax credit, as described *below*) (ICTA 1988, s 239).

A shareholder is liable to pay tax on his dividend income but will not have any NIC exposure. A basic rate taxpayer pays income tax on his dividend income at 20 per cent only, and this liability will be extinguished by the tax credit which attaches to a dividend paid by a UK-resident company. A higher rate taxpayer is liable to pay tax at 40 per cent (although he receives a 20 per cent tax credit with the dividend). When a company pays a dividend of £80, the shareholder receives, with the dividend, a tax credit for £20 (20 per cent of £100) and will have a tax liability of £40 (40 per cent of £100). He can set the tax credit of £20 against this tax liability, so that he is liable to pay tax of £20 out of the cash dividend of £80 (Finance Act 1993, s 78(3)).

Pension contributions When comparing the tax treatment of dividends with salary or bonuses it should be noted that contributions paid to a pension scheme out of earned income attract tax relief (ICTA 1988, ss 619 and 639), whereas unearned income (eg dividend income) cannot be used to make such contributions.

Utilisation of losses

Carrying back When considering the sole trader/partner or company issue, s 381 of ICTA 1988, which provides for carry back of losses, may be of particular relevance. In many cases, the franchised business will be the franchisee's first excursion into business on his own account. He may have been in employment in the past and have received Schedule E income over a period of years, paying income tax on that income. If the franchised business is likely to make losses in its opening years, then a sole trader/partner can set any trading losses he makes in the first four years of assessment of the new trade against his general income for the three years of assessment preceding the year of assessment in which the loss arose. Accordingly, if a sole trader setting up business in the tax year 1995/96 makes a trading loss in his first year, he can set this against his other income (eg salary) for the tax years 1992/93 onwards. At a time when the franchisee is likely to be under considerable cash flow constraints, his ability to obtain a repayment of income tax paid in previous years may be of considerable value. If the business is conducted through a company, the trading loss will be made by the company and not by its shareholders. Accordingly, s 381 relief will not be available; normally the loss can be carried forward for set-off only against future trading profits of the company (ICTA 1988, s 393).

Set-off by companies A company, being a separate legal person, can offset its trading losses only against other income of the company. Its trading losses can be set off against:

(a) the company's non-trading income and chargeable gains arising in the same accounting period (ICTA 1988, s 393A(1)(*a*)); or
(b) general income and gains of accounting periods falling wholly or partly within the three years immediately preceding the loss making period to the extent that the losses cannot be utilised under (a); or
(c) trading income from the same trade in future accounting periods, taking earlier income before later income (ICTA 1988, s 393(1)).

If a company forms part of a group (basically 75 per cent common ownership) (as defined in ICTA 1988, s 402), it will also be possible to offset one company's trading losses against another group company's profits for the current period.

Set-off by sole traders/partners Apart from the loss relief available on the commencement of a trade, a sole trader/partner can offset his trading losses as follows:

(1) In the case of a trade which is taxed on a current year basis (ie a trade which commenced on or after 6 April 1994 and, from the tax year

1997/98, all trades which commenced before 6 April 1994), the losses can be set against:

(a) his general income (but not his capital gains) for the year in which the loss arose and/or for the preceding year (there is no requirement that the trade was being carried on in the preceding year) (Finance Act (FA) 1994, s 209(1)); or

(b) capital gains for the year in which the loss arose or for the preceding year, to the extent that the trading loss exceeds the trader's total income (FA 1991, s 72); or

(c) the first available trading income of the same trade (ICTA 1988, s 385 as amended by FA 1994, s 209(4)).

(2) In the case of a trade which is taxed on the preceding year basis (ie trades which commenced before 6 April 1994 until the 1997/98 tax year), the losses can be set against:

(a) his general income (but not his capital gains) for the year the loss arose and/or for the following year provided the same trade is still being carried on in that following year (ICTA 1988, s 380); or

(b) capital gains for the year of the loss or the following year to the extent that the trading loss exceeds the trader's total income (FA 1991, s 72); or

(c) the first available trading income of the same trade (ICTA 1988, s 385).

Conclusion

In any particular case it will be necessary to undertake detailed calculations to determine whether the overall tax liability will be smaller if profits are generated by a sole trader/partner or through a company (which may distribute those profits by a combination of repayment of loans, salaries and dividends). Whether to operate a business through a company or as a sole trader/partner need not, however, be a decision which is made once and for all in setting up the business. A franchisee may sometimes decide that it is appropriate to operate initially as a sole trader/partner (eg to claim s 381 relief) and to incorporate in a later year when sufficient profits are being earned to enable a significant part of the profits to be retained in the company to finance further expansion. A franchisor may often decide that commercial considerations require use of a company from the outset.

9.2.2   Relief for expenditure

In general the rules relating to the deductibility of expenditure incurred in a trade are the same for sole traders/partners and companies. The following basic principles apply:

(1) Revenue expenditure will be deductible if expended 'wholly and exclusively for the purposes of the trade' (ICTA 1988, s 74) subject to a list of exceptions set out in s 74.

(2) A brief discussion of the distinction between revenue and capital expenditure appears *below*, and further comments specific to franchise transactions are made in 9.3.1 *below*.

(3) One of the exceptions set out in s 74 concerns 'annual payments', the meaning of which is discussed in 9.3.2 *below*. Royalties payable by a franchisee may in certain circumstances constitute 'annual payments'. However, a deduction for tax purposes should nevertheless be available subject to compliance with the provisions of s 338 of ICTA 1988 in the case of a company, and s 347A of ICTA 1988 in the case of a sole trader/partner (*see* pp 144 to 145 *below*). The recipient will receive the income after deduction of basic rate income tax; this will be a cash flow cost rather than an actual cost as the recipient will receive a tax credit equal to the tax deducted which can be set against its own tax liability.

(4) A further exception concerns interest, to which the special rules set out at 9.2.4 apply. Differences do arise here in the treatment of sole traders/partners and companies.

(5) To obtain a deduction for an expense, it is necessary to show that the expense is incurred 'for the purposes of the trade' and not merely to put the taxpayer in a position to commence trading (*Birmingham & District Cattle By-Products Co* v *IRC* (1919) 12 TC 92). This general principle creates particular difficulties in respect of the costs of setting up a business (ie pre-trading expenditure). However, legislation now provides that a sole trader/partner can treat any expenditure incurred before the commencement of trading as a loss arising in his first year of assessment for the trade, if that expenditure would have been allowable if it had been incurred after the trade had commenced and was incurred within seven years of the commencement of the trade (ICTA 1988, s 401 as amended by FA 1993, s 109). A company which incurs pre-trading expenditure in these circumstances will be deemed to have incurred the expenditure on the day it commenced trading (ICTA 1988, s 401).

(6) If the expenditure is capital in nature (*see below*), a deduction in computing trading profits will be recoverable only to the extent permitted by the capital allowances regime (*see* 9.2.5 *below*). In other circumstances, the expenditure may sometimes be available as part of the base cost of an asset of the business, available to be brought into account in computing any capital gain realised on the disposal of the asset. This is the basis on which relief will generally be available for expenditure incurred in subscribing for share capital in a company, subject to the special rules discussed at 9.2.6 *below*.

9.2.3 Capital or revenue expenditure?

There is a large volume of case law on the distinction between capital expenditure (which cannot be deducted in computing taxable profits) and revenue expenditure (which can normally be deducted subject to consideration of the rules referred to above). A number of tests can be discerned from these cases and it is often a matter of judgment to select the appropriate test for the particular circumstances.

Fixed or circulating capital

One test focuses on whether the expenditure is applied in respect of fixed capital (capital expenditure) or circulating capital (revenue expenditure). Fixed capital would be regarded as consisting of assets which produce, or are used to produce, income such as shares or property held as investments and machinery or plant in a manufacturing business. Circulating capital refers to capital which may leave the business temporarily, returning to the business with the objective of thereby earning a profit (for example monies spent in acquiring stock). *See* for example *Ammonia Soda Co* v *Chamberlain* [1918] 1 Ch 266 and *Patterson* v *Marine Midland Ltd* [1981] STC 540.

The 'enduring benefit' test

A test often cited is the 'enduring benefit' test. Viscount Cave in *Atherton* v *British Insulated & Helsby Cables Ltd* [1926] AC 205 at p 213 said that:

> When an expenditure is made not only once for all, but with a view to bringing into existence an asset or advantage for the enduring benefit of a trade, I think there is very good reason (in the absence of special circumstances) leading to an opposite conclusion for treating such an expenditure as properly attributable not to revenue but to capital.

To some extent this test must be treated with caution since there certainly are expenses which might be regarded as having an enduring effect but which are properly treated as revenue expenses. An interesting case in this context is *Lawson* v *Johnson Matthey plc* [1992] STC 466. In this case Johnson Matthey plc injected £50m into an insolvent subsidiary as the price for the Bank of England to agree to buy the shares of the subsidiary for £1.00. The board of Johnson Matthey plc had concluded that if the subsidiary had been wound up this would have repercussions for Johnson Matthey plc itself, leading to demands which would have resulted in Johnson Matthey plc, having to cease trading. The House of Lords held that the £50m had been paid, not to divest Johnson Matthey of its shares in the subsidiary, but in the expectation that only if it paid the sum would the bank come to the rescue of the subsidiary thereby enabling Johnson Matthey plc to continue business. The payments did not

126

bring a new asset into existence or produce an advantage for the enduring benefit of the trade; it removed a threat to the trade of Johnson Matthey plc resulting from the subsidiary's insolvency. The sum was expenditure of a revenue nature.

Identity of the asset

Another test focuses on the identity of the asset on which the sum is spent. If money is spent on a capital asset, the expenditure may be capital, otherwise it should be revenue. If it relates to a capital asset and is spent in acquiring that asset, the expenditure will be capital. If the expenditure relates to the repair or maintenance of the capital asset it should be revenue. *See Tucker* v *Granada Motorway Services Ltd* [1979] STC 393.

Non-recurrence of expense

If money is expended once and for all rather than recurring every year it is more likely to be capital: *Vallambrosa Rubber Co Ltd* v *Farmer* (1910) 5 TC 529.

Permanent structure

A more broadly based test, but perhaps one which can be of particular help, was expressed in *Commissioner of Taxes* v *Nchanga Consolidated Copper Mines Ltd* [1964] 1 All ER 208. The cost of creating, acquiring or enlarging the permanent structure which produces the income (the tree from which the fruit is borne) will be capital. The cost of earning that income itself or performing the income earning operations will be income.

9.2.4   Borrowings—deductibility of interest

The somewhat complex rules relevant to the deductibility of interest on borrowings are considered in this section.

As a trading expense

If the borrower is a company carrying on a trade, any yearly interest paid on a loan from a bank carrying on a bona fide banking business in the UK will be deductible as a trading expense provided the interest is incurred wholly and exclusively for the purposes of the trade (ICTA 1988, s 337 applying ICTA 1988, s 74). Interest on a loan will normally constitute yearly interest if the loan is for a period capable of exceeding a year (*Corinthion Securities Ltd* v *Cato* (1969) 46 TC 93 and *Cairns* v *MacDiarmid* (1982) 56 TC 556). If short (ie non-yearly) interest is paid by a company (whether or not to a bank), it should be deductible as a trading expense if it is incurred wholly and exclusively for the purposes of the trade (ICTA 1988, s 74).

As a charge on income

If interest payments made by a company are not deductible as a trading expense (for example, because yearly interest is payable on a non-bank loan), they may be relieved as a charge on income (ICTA 1988, s 338). Relief as a charge on income is given only in respect of interest which is actually paid, whereas a trading expense is generally allowable on an accruals basis. For an interest payment to qualify as a charge on income the following conditions must be satisfied:

(a) it must be paid out of profits chargeable to corporation tax and must ulti-
    mately be borne by the company (ICTA 1988, s 338(1));
(b) it must be yearly interest or, if short interest, be payable in the UK on
    an advance from a bank carrying on a bona fide banking business in the
    UK (ICTA 1988, s 338(3));
(c) it must be made under a liability incurred for a valuable and sufficient
    consideration (ICTA 1988, s 338(5)(*b*); and
(d) it must be either:
    (i) paid by a trading company; or
    (ii) wholly and exclusively incurred for the purposes of trade; or
    (iii) paid by an investment company (as defined in s 130 of ICTA
          1988); or
    (iv) paid in connection with the purchase or improvement of land
         (ICTA 1988, s 338(6)).

If yearly interest is paid to an overseas person it must generally be paid net of basic rate income tax before it can be treated as a charge on income. Further, where yearly interest is paid by a company otherwise than to a person carrying on a bona fide banking business in the UK, it must deduct basic rate income tax (ICTA 1988, s 349).

Effects of treatment as trading expense or charge on income

If the interest is treated as a trading expense, it will reduce the company's trading income (or create a trading loss) and will be eligible for relief in the same way as any other trading expense. If the interest is treated as a charge on income, it may be set against the total profits of the company for the account-ing period in which the interest is paid (ICTA 1988, s 338(1)). Interest relieved as a charge on income cannot be carried back against profits of a previous accounting period and can be carried forward against future trading income of the same trade in succeeding accounting periods only if the interest is incurred wholly and exclusively for the purposes of the trade (ICTA 1988, s 393(9)). If the interest is not so incurred, the relief will be lost if there are insufficient total profits in the current accounting period to utilise the relief.

Sole traders/partners

If the borrower is a sole trader/partner, both yearly and short interest may qualify as a trading expense if incurred wholly and exclusively for the purposes of the trade (ICTA 1988, s 74). Unlike a company, a sole trader/partner does not qualify for charges on income under s 338 of ICTA 1988 and will obtain a deduction only if the interest qualifies as a trading expense or if it is paid in respect of one of the qualifying loans on which interest relief is specifically given (ICTA 1988, s 353). Relief is available in respect of certain specific loans, eg to buy an interest in a partnership or to lend money to a partnership for use in its business (ICTA 1988, s 362), or for a partner to buy plant or machinery for use in the partnership business (ICTA 1988, s 359(1) and (2)).

Companies

Where the business is conducted by a company, the shareholders may borrow funds which they invest in the company either by way of loan or in return for shares. Various provisions determine whether interest on these loans will be allowable for tax purposes. If the shareholder is an individual, s 360 of ICTA 1988 provides that interest paid on a loan used to purchase ordinary shares in a close company or to lend money to such a company for use in its business will qualify for relief as a deduction against the taxpayer's taxable income if he has a 'material interest' therein, or if he spends the greater part of his time in the management or conduct of the company. This relief is available only where the company is a close company when the loan is taken out. 'Close company' is defined as a company under the control of five or fewer participators (basically shareholders) or any number of participators who are also directors in the business (ICTA 1988, s 832(1)). Many franchisee companies will therefore fall within the definition of a close company. The taxpayer will have a material interest if he is the beneficial owner of more than 5 per cent of the ordinary share capital of the company or is entitled to receive more than 5 per cent of the assets of the company on a winding-up or will be so entitled after making the relevant investment (ICTA 1988, s 360A)). The taxpayer will satisfy the 'management or conduct' of the company condition only if he actually devotes the greater part of his time (in practice his normal working time) to the management or conduct of the company. It will be insufficient for him to work full time for the company if he does not do so in a management capacity. The test will be more easily satisfied if he is a director of the company.

Partners

Section 361 of ICTA 1988 provides for relief where a partner pays interest on a loan applied in acquiring an interest in the partnership, or in contributing capital to the partnership, or in making a loan to the partnership where the money so contributed or lent is used wholly for the purposes of the partnership's trade.

Franchisors investing in franchisee companies

Very occasionally, a franchisor may take an equity stake in the franchisee's business. If the franchisor subscribes for shares in the franchisee's company, this is likely to be capital expenditure for which the franchisor is not immediately entitled to any tax relief. However, if the franchisor is a company and the acquisition is funded through bank borrowing, interest relief should be available as a charge on income (ICTA 1988, s 338)).

9.2.5   Capital allowances

Plant and machinery

The Capital Allowances Act 1990 (CAA 1990) provides for tax relief to be given in respect of certain specific types of capital expenditure. In the franchising context, the type of expenditure which will most commonly qualify for capital allowances is expenditure on the acquisition of plant or machinery (CAA 1990, s 24).

Capital allowances will, in principle, be available on a reducing balance basis (effectively depreciation allowances) where a taxpayer carrying on a trade incurs capital expenditure on the provision of plant or machinery wholly and exclusively for the purpose of his trade and, in consequence, that plant or machinery belongs to him (CAA 1990, s 24(1)).

Meaning of 'plant or machinery'   The term 'plant or machinery' is not defined in the legislation and there have been numerous cases on whether an asset qualifies. A number of these cases have concerned restaurants and cafeteria and involve items of expenditure which may well be relevant to a franchised business.

Where expenditure has been incurred on or after 30 November 1993, the starting point in determining whether the expenditure is on plant or machinery is CAA 1990, Sched AA1. This schedule provides that expenditure on the provision of a building cannot constitute expenditure on plant or machinery (para 1 of the Schedule). The schedule includes a list of rather general items which are deemed to comprise part of the building for this purpose (including walls, floors, ceilings, mains services) (column 1 of Table 1). However a list of more specific items qualifies the more general list (column 2 of Table 1). Items in the more specific list are capable of constituting plant or machinery depending on the circumstances. The schedule does not provide whether or not these items will comprise plant or machinery; the conclusion depends on an analysis of relevant case law. By way of example, while electricity systems comprise part of the building (item B of column 1) they are not automatically excluded from comprising plant or machinery if provided 'mainly to meet the particular requirements of the trade' (item 1 of column 2). If this test is satisfied, it is then necessary to turn to case law to establish whether the system in question, or components of it, qualify as plant or machinery. In any particular case, the terms of the schedule will need to be considered in detail.

The case law   Where CAA 1990, Sched AA1 does not prevent a particular item of expenditure from qualifying as plant or machinery, the starting point in analysing the case law will be the classic definition of plant given in the Victorian case of *Yarmouth* v *France* (1887) 19 QBD 647, where it was said that plant:

> in its ordinary sense includes whatever apparatus is used by a business-man for carrying on his business—not his stock in trade which he buys or makes for sales; but all goods and chattels fixed or moveable, live or dead, which he keeps for permanent employment in his business.

This definition has been substantially refined by subsequent cases. These cases are not entirely consistent and a careful presentation of a claim for allowances to the Inland Revenue, justifying the claimant's treatment of particular assets as plant or machinery, can be crucial. The courts have at various times applied a number of tests which can perhaps be reduced to two fundamental issues:

(1) Does the asset perform a function in the conduct of the business; is the item of apparatus used by the business for carrying on the business? Tests of this type are often referred to as the 'functional test' or the 'business use test' (*see*, for example, *Cooke* v *Beach Station Caravans Ltd* [1974] STC 402). Satisfaction of this test suggests that the item may constitute plant or machinery.

(2) Does the asset form part of the premises or the setting in which the business is carried on; does it simply make the premises complete as a habitable structure? Tests of this type are often referred to as the 'premises test', the 'setting test' or the 'completeness test' (*see*, for example, *Commissioners of Inland Revenue* v *Scottish & Newcastle Breweries Ltd* [1982] STC 246 (the setting test), and *Imperial Chemical Industries of New Zealand* v *Federal Commissioners of Taxation* [1970] 1 ATR 450 (the completeness test)). If an asset satisfies one of these tests, this

will suggest that it does not qualify as plant or machinery. CAA 1990, Sched AA1 is intended to place this test on a statutory footing and is probably designed to stop a combination of clever design work and clever presentation of arguments by taxpayers from drawing the teeth of the premises test.

Of particular interest to franchises in the catering industry will be the cases of *Commissioners of Inland Revenue* v *Scottish & Newcastle Breweries Ltd* (*above*) and *Wimpy International* v *Warland* [1989] STC 273. In the *Scottish & Newcastle* case, it was established as a fact that the company's trade included the provision of ambience or atmosphere in its hotels. Accordingly, something which might in another case merely constitute the setting in which the trade was carried on, in this case actually fulfilled a function as it contributed to that ambience or atmosphere. It is understood that the Inland Revenue is reluctant to extend the concept of a trade including 'ambience or atmosphere' to trades outside the hotel and catering sectors; there is no reported decision where a trade outside these sectors has been held to include ambience or atmosphere. CAA 1990, Sched AA1 strengthens the position by seeking to prevent a person in a trade outside these sectors from arguing that decorative items constitute plant or machinery where they fall within the new definition of premises (item 14 in Column 2 of Table 1).

In the *Scottish & Newcastle* case, items such as pictures, plaques, wall plates, light fittings, lamps and lampshades (and even a metal sculpture of seagulls) were found to constitute plant or machinery. In the *Wimpy* case, decorative items such as murals, decorative brickwork, wall panels and a false ceiling were held to be plant by the Special Commissioners, while they found that shop-fronts, floor and wall tiles, a further false ceiling, floors and stairs and light fittings were not plant because they formed part of the premises. Hoffman J upheld the Commissioners' findings, subject to finding that the light fittings also constituted plant on the basis that they also added to the atmosphere of the business. The Commissioners found on the particular facts that one false ceiling qualified as plant as it attracted customers to a particular part of the building, while the other false ceiling did not qualify as plant as it merely formed part of the premises. This illustrates the fine distinction between plant used in a business and the premises where the business is conducted. It is unclear whether a false ceiling can still qualify as plant (Note 1 to Table 1, CAA 1990, Sched AA1).

Although each case will have to be determined upon its own particular facts, *Cole Brothers Ltd* v *Phillips* [1982] STC 307 provides a useful review relating to items of electrical systems. This case upheld the Inland Revenue's view that the constituent parts of an electrical system should be viewed separately to determine whether they qualify as plant or machinery. The general electrical wiring was held to be part of the building and not plant, but specific wiring to lifts and escalators, heating and ventilation systems, smoke detectors, compactor rooms etc qualified as plant. This is consistent with CAA 1990, Sched AA1.

Writing-down allowances   If an asset qualifies as plant or machinery then the taxpayer will be entitled to writing-down allowances (CAA 1990, s 24). Allowances are available in respect of relevant capital expenditure on a reducing-balance basis at a rate of 25 per cent in the first and all subsequent years (CAA 1990, s 24(2)). In the first year 25 per cent of the qualifying expenditure attracts tax relief; in the second year 25 per cent of the balance of the expenditure which has not previously attracted tax relief (75 per cent of the original amount) attracts tax relief; and so on. Subject to some exceptions, writing-down allowances are generally calculated on the written-down value of all plant on a pool basis. This means that all the assets qualifying for capital assets are grouped together, with capital allowances being claimed on the written-down value of all the assets in aggregate rather than on each asset individually. The allowances become available once the expenditure has been incurred (generally where the purchaser's obligation to pay for the asset becomes unconditional, regardless of whether the asset has actually been brought into use during that accounting period (CAA 1990, s 159(3)), but subject to certain anti-avoidance provisions (CAA 1990, s 159(4), (5) or (6)). A taxpayer may choose to claim only part of his writing-down allowances in a particular year, eg if he does not have sufficient taxable income to utilise the allowances in that year (CAA 1990, s 24(3)).

Any expenditure incurred between 1 November 1992 and 31 October 1993 was entitled to a first year allowance of 40 per cent of the expenditure. Where this allowance was claimed, the normal 25 per cent writing-down allowances will be available for subsequent years.

Writing-down allowances are not restricted because an asset is acquired part way through an accounting period. However, if a company's accounting period is less than 12 months, its writing-down allowance will be restricted (CAA 1990, s 24(2)). This will result in a delay in claiming writing-down allowances (rather than a loss of writing down allowances) as the written-down value will be correspondingly higher in subsequent years. In the case of a sole trader/partner, writing-down allowances will be restricted where his basis period is less than 12 months (this will only occur in the first year of assessment of the new trade (CAA 1990, s 24(2)).

The writing-down allowances available are, in effect, a form of depreciation to enable a taxpayer to offset the cost of an item against his trading income during the life of the asset. If the taxpayer could claim capital allowances and subsequently sell the asset at a price in excess of the depreciated value, he would obtain tax relief for depreciation which had not, in fact, occurred. Accordingly, when the taxpayer disposes of the plant an amount will be deducted from the pool of qualifying expenditure (CAA 1990, s 24(6)). In subsequent accounting periods, writing-down allowances can then be claimed on the balance remaining (ie after the deduction of this amount). If the deduction from the pool exceeds the whole of the pool of qualifying expenditure, there will be a balancing charge (an additional tax charge) which will form part of the taxpayer's taxable income (CAA 1990, s 24(5)). Where plant is disposed of to an unconnected person, the deduction from the pool will be the lower of the actual proceeds of sale and original cost (CAA 1990, s 26(2)).

No writing-down allowances are available in the final year of assessment when a trade ceases. Any additions during that period are added to the pool and the final disposal proceeds are deducted from the pool. If the proceeds exceed the pool, there will be a balancing charge. If the pool exceeds the proceeds then there will be a balancing allowance (ie additional allowances can be claimed) (CAA 1990, s 24(2)(*b*)).

Hotels

Of particular interest to persons involved in hotel franchise businesses will be the special allowances available on hotels. Industrial buildings allowances (relating to capital expenditure incurred in constructing a building or in acquiring a newly constructed building) are generally available only for buildings used in productive, as opposed to distributive, industries or other commercial buildings located in enterprise zones. However, legislation provides that capital expenditure incurred in constructing a hotel or in buying an unused hotel will qualify for industrial buildings allowances if it has at least ten letting bedrooms, is open for at least four months between April and October, provides the service of making beds and cleaning rooms, and offers breakfast and dinner as a normal part of its business (CAA 1990, s 19).

If a hotel qualifies for industrial buildings allowances, it will qualify for allowances of 4 per cent of the cost of the building calculated on a straight line basis for 25 years (ie remaining constant) (CAA 1990, s 3). As with allowances on plant and machinery, there may be a balancing allowance or charge on the disposal of the hotel if the disposal proceeds are different from the tax written-down value (CAA 1990, s 4).

Any expenditure incurred between 1 November 1992 and 31 October 1993 on constructing an industrial building (including a hotel) which is brought into use by 31 December 1994 will be entitled to a first year allowance of 20 per cent of the expenditure.

9.2.6   Relief for subscribing for shares in a company

On subscribing for shares in a company, an investor does not generally obtain any immediate tax relief. The money subscribed will be capital expenditure and will be taken into account as part of the shareholder's base cost (for capital gains tax purposes) on a subsequent disposal of the shares. However, an investor may obtain income tax relief under one or two schemes dealt with *below.* If an individual investor has made or will make a capital gain on the disposal of any asset and the new investment is made within one year before and three years after the disposal, the possible availability of reinvestment relief should be considered as a means of deferring the tax liability on the gain in question (TCGA 1992, ss 164A–164N).

Relief on the failure of a company

It may be possible to obtain tax relief if the shares become worthless. This relief will be available under the 'venture capital scheme' (ICTA 1988, s 574). This provides that an investor who subscribes for shares (rather than acquires existing shares) which form part of the ordinary share capital of a qualifying trading company or holding company of a trading group which is, and always has been, UK resident, may treat any capital loss arising on the disposal of the shares (or on the shares becoming of negligible value or the company being wound up) as an income expense available for offset against the investor's general income in the year of loss or the preceding year (ICTA 1988, s 574(2) as amended by FA 1994, s 210). A company will be a qualifying trading company only if it is not quoted on any stock exchange (ICTA 1988, s 574(6)). This relief will be available to an individual shareholder regardless of the size of his shareholding.

This relief may also be available where the shareholder is a company (ICTA 1988, s 573), but this will only be the case where the shareholder is an investment company (and not a trading company). Accordingly, this is unlikely to be of assistance in the case of any investment by the franchisor.

Relief for subscribing for shares in a business

Subject to certain limits and to compliance with very detailed conditions relating to the business and the investor in question, an individual (but not a corporate) investor can sometimes obtain immediate income tax relief for the cost of subscribing for new shares in a trading company. This relief was available under the Business Expansion Scheme (BES) for shares issued up to 31 December 1993 and is available under the Enterprise Investment Scheme (EIS) for shares issued thereafter. It is beyond the scope of this work to comment on the detailed requirements to be satisfied to obtain EIS relief, but the following comments will give some indication of the circumstances in which it may be worth investigating the availability of the relief further (the basic conditions are very similar to those applying to the old BES relief).

Qualifying investments   EIS relief is available only on a subscription for shares in an unquoted company carrying on a 'qualifying trade' in the UK (ICTA 1988, s 289). The relief will be withdrawn if the shares are not retained for five years or, subject to detailed provisions, if the investor receives any remuneration from the company (other than a commercial dividend). Broadly, the company must be a trading company not carrying on one or more of the prohibited activities (which include trading in land and commodities) (ICTA 1988, s 297(1)). One of the prohibited activities is receiving royalties or licence fees. The Inland Revenue originally contended that this prevented the old BES relief from being claimed by investors in a franchisor company. However, in appropriate cases it should be possible to persuade the Inland Revenue that a franchisor is conducting an active trade, providing continuing services rather than the mere receipt of passive income. On this basis, it should be possible to set up an EIS for a franchisor. The franchisee's business should in many cases be capable of satisfying the requirements of a 'qualifying trade'.

The maximum that a company can raise in any tax year is £1,000,000 and the maximum any one individual can subscribe (and obtain tax relief) is £100,000 (ICTA 1988, ss 290 and 290A).

Status of investor   Finally, it is necessary to bear in mind that EIS relief is available only to an investor who is not 'connected' with the company (ICTA 1988, s 291). This means that the investor must not be (nor must an associate of his be) an employee/director of the company, nor possess or be entitled to acquire more than 30 per cent of:

(a)   the issued ordinary share capital of the company; or
(b)   the loan capital and issued share capital of the company; or
(c)   the voting power in the company.

For these purposes, an 'associate' will include a business partner, trustee of a family trust, a parent, grandparent, child and grandchild but not a brother, sister, uncle or aunt. An investor will not, however, be regarded as being connected with the company solely by reason of his becoming a director after having subscribed for the shares where (broadly) any remuneration received by him is reasonable, having regard to the services provided by him in his capacity as a director (ICTA 1988, s 291A(e)(*f*)).

Where the conditions are satisfied, income tax relief at the lower rate of 20 per cent is available on investments of up to £100,000 a year. An exemption from capital gains tax applies to the sale of EIS shares in respect of which the original income tax relief has not been withdrawn and relief against either income tax or capital gains tax is available for a loss arising on the disposal of such shares (Taxation of Chargeable Gains Act 1992, s 150A and ICTA 1988, s 305A). As indicated above, these tax reliefs are available only if the shares are retained for five years.

If an EIS may be of interest in a particular case, the reader should refer to specialist tax textbooks.

9.3   Taxation of franchise transactions

9.3.1   The initial fee

The franchisee will usually pay the franchisor an initial fee on the grant of the franchise. The tax treatment of this payment will depend on whether the payment is considered to be income or capital in nature. If the initial fee is a payment for the grant of the franchise, it may be capital. If it is consideration for services provided to the franchisee by the franchisor it may be treated as income. These are broad generalisations and a more detailed analysis, including consideration of the implications of capital or income treatment for the franchisor and the franchisee, are considered further *below*.

Does it follow that the characterisation of the initial fee will be the same for both the franchisor and the franchisee? If it is a capital expense for the franchisee must it be a capital receipt of the franchisor? Symmetry of treatment is not inevitable. If a desk manufacturer sells a desk to a firm of solicitors, it will receive a revenue receipt, although the solicitors are incurring a capital expense (acquiring a capital asset). The correct approach is to consider the nature of the transaction separately from the perspective of each of the franchisor and the franchisee.

The franchisor's position

It will often be strongly arguable that the initial fee constitutes trading income in the franchisor's hands. If the franchise agreement states that the fee is paid in return for the services provided by the franchisor under the agreement, and real services are provided under the agreement, it is difficult to see how the fee can properly be characterised as anything other than trading income. Even where the franchise agreement does not state that the fee is being paid in return for services, but expresses it as being paid in consideration for the grant of the franchise to a franchisee, the franchisor should still often be treated as receiving trading income. In such a situation the franchisor will receive the fee in the course of its trade (which includes the process of granting franchises). The receipt of front-end fees by the franchisor may well be part of the franchisors' normal trading pattern, with the fee being received as part of the profits of the trade.

Initial fee treated as trading income   If the fee is treated as trading income, all normal trading expenditure can be taken into account in computing the taxable profit. Any trading losses incurred in previous accounting periods will also be available to off-set against those fees (ICTA 1988, ss 385 and 393(1)). In practice, this can be very important for a new franchisor, as it may carry forward trading losses for a number of years until it is able to exploit its franchise network profitably.

Initial fee treated as capital receipt   If the fee is a capital receipt it will have to be brought into account as a capital gain if there is a disposal, or part disposal, of a chargeable asset, or if the capital received is derived from an asset (Taxation of Chargeable Gains Act (TCGA) 1992, s 22). The case of *Kirby* v *Thorne-EMI plc* [1987] STC 621 indicates that the freedom to trade should not of itself be regarded as a capital asset for s 22 purposes, but receipts for restrictive covenants may be derived from goodwill (a capital asset). On the grant of a franchise, there may be a number of intangible rights to which a lump sum could relate, and which could bring s 22 into play (assuming the receipt is capital in nature). Deductions may be available in computing the gain (principally those permitted by s 38 of TCGA 1992), but in practice these deductions may not reduce the taxable gain significantly unless the asset in question has been purchased by the franchisor.

The case law   An appropriate test on the capital/revenue distinction, so far as the franchisor is concerned, was stated by Banks LJ in *British Dyestuffs Corporation (Blackley) Ltd* v *IRC* (1924) 12 TC 586, where he said:

> I do not myself think that the method of payment adopted in carrying through a transaction between a company, such as this, and a licensee is very much guide to the true nature of the transaction. The real question is, looking at this matter, is the transaction in substance a parting by the Company with part of its property for a purchase price, or is it a method of trading by which it acquires this particular sum of money as part of the profit and gains of that trade?

Subject to the comments about exclusivity *below*, the essence of the franchise agreement is that the franchisee is permitted to use the franchisor's assets to enable the franchisor to exploit its ownership; it is not a dissipation of that ownership.

   The franchisor's arguments against capital treatment may also be supported by the case of *Body Shop International plc* v *Rawle and Others* (1992) *unreported*. In this case, the High Court confirmed that the goodwill in a franchised business remains the property of the franchisor and is not transferred to the franchisee. Although this was a non-tax case, it should support the view that an initial fee is not paid as a capital item (eg as consideration for goodwill). Case law also assists in rebutting any suggestion that a receipt which might be regarded as paid in respect of the provision of know-how should be treated as a capital sum. Such receipts should be revenue in nature unless either the specific statutory rules referred to *below* apply, or there is a substantial diminution in the franchisor's trade or trading capacity (*Evans Medical Supplies Ltd* v *Moriarty* (1956) 37 TC 540, *Jeffrey* v *Rolls Royce Ltd* (1960) 40 TC 443 and *Coalite & Chemical Products* v *Treeby* (1971) 48 TC 171).

Grant of exclusivity   An area of possible difficulty concerns the grant of franchises giving the franchisee an exclusive licence to conduct the franchised business in a specified territory, the franchisor agreeing not to conduct any similar business operations in that area (and to seek to prevent others from so doing). In such circumstances it may be arguable that the franchisor is making a part disposal of its existing property or rights in return for a capital sum. In *IRC* v *British Salmson Aero Engines Ltd* (1938) 22 TC 29, the distinction was drawn between sums payable under a licence which simply stops a licensor complaining about action which would otherwise be an infringement (revenue receipts), and a licence under which the grantor agrees not to exercise its own rights and to stop others using the rights (sums received were instalments of capital). (*See also Murray* v *Imperial Chemical Industries Ltd* (1967) 44 TC 175. Payments for undertakings not to carry on specified business activities in a certain territory can often be regarded as capital (particularly if there is a substantial restraint of trade involved); *see Margerison* v *Tyresoles Ltd* (1942) 25 TC 59. However *Rees Roturbo Development Syndicate* v *Ducker* (1928) 13 TC 366 was a case where there was an outright sale of patents for a lump sum. On the facts, the Commissioners decided that the company's sole business was the exploitation of patents as part of its trade and the profits arising from sales arose in the course of that trade. The House of Lords agreed.

In most cases, even where exclusivity is involved, the better view with most franchise transactions (applying the Banks LJ test quoted *above*) is likely to be that the franchisor is not in substance parting with its property, but is adopting a method of trading by which it acquires up-front fees as part of the profits of the trade. In practice care should be taken (if income treatment is sought) to avoid the initial fee being specifically characterised in the franchise agreement as consideration for the grant of an exclusive franchise.

Finally, reference should be made to certain specific statutory provisions relating to disposals of know-how, patents and design rights.

Know-how   Special rules apply to a disposal of know-how. The Inland Revenue may seek to treat the fee as consideration for a part disposal. 'Know-how' is defined as 'any industrial information and techniques likely to assist in the manufacture or processing of goods or materials' (ICTA 1988, s 533(7)) and knowledge must, therefore, have some practical industrial use before it comes within the definition. If the know-how disposed of had previously been used by the franchisor in its trade, and the franchisor continues to carry on that trade after the disposal, the receipt will be taxed as trading income (if it would not otherwise be treated as such) (ICTA 1988, s 531(1)). If the know-how is disposed of together with the franchisor's trade or part of that trade, it will be taxed as capital (being treated as a disposal of goodwill) subject to the availability of a joint election to treat it as schedule D(VI) income (ICTA 1988, s 531(2)). There should, however, be a disposal of part of the franchisor's trade only if it is disposing of an existing business, rather than merely granting to the franchisee permission to set up a franchised business. This will generally only be the case where the franchisor is selling an established outlet (eg a pilot operation). In other circumstances, a disposal of know-how will be taxed under Schedule D (VI) (ICTA 1988, s 531(4)) against which previous years' trading losses will not be available for set-off. In most cases if there is arguably a disposal of know-how (eg by virtue of a payment being made for the provision of the franchisor's manual) any sum received will be trading income, either by applying normal principles for computing trading profits or by virtue of s 531(1).

Patent rights   It is most unlikely that a franchisor would have any patent rights that could be treated as being sold to a franchisee but, for completeness, the sale of patent rights for a capital sum will be treated as a revenue receipt taxable under Schedule D(VI) (ICTA 1988, s 524). This income will be assessed over six years, commencing with the year of sale, unless the franchisor elects for the sum to be taxed wholly in the year of receipt.

If the franchisor sells design rights and the franchisor created those rights, the capital receipt will be treated as an income receipt, and the franchisor may have this income assessed over either two or three years (being the year in which the capital sum was received and the previous one or two years, as the case may be). The number of years over which the franchisor may have the sum assessed will depend on whether or not he was engaged in creating the design rights for over two years (ICTA 1988, s 537A).

The franchisee's position

Income expense or capital expenditure   The issue will be whether the initial fee should properly be regarded as an income expense (with the possibility of immediate tax relief being available) or whether it constitutes non-deductible capital expenditure. This will depend on what is being received for the fee. If the fee is being paid for the provision of services then it should be an income expense, whereas if it is being paid for the grant of the franchise it is likely to be capital expenditure. Although the correct tax treatment will depend on the reality of the situation and not solely on the form of the documentation, the terms of the franchise agreement should give a clear indication of how the fee should be treated. If the franchise agreement provides that the fee is paid in consideration of the grant of the franchise, rather than for the provision of services, it will certainly be difficult to establish that the fee can properly be regarded as a revenue trading expense. One possibility to consider will be an apportionment of the fee between the items the franchisee 'acquires', so that relief is obtained for at least some of the expenditure. The general principles outlined in 9.2.3 *above* should be considered.

The classic definition of capital expenditure is the enduring benefit test in Viscount Cave's judgment in *British Insulated & Helsby Cables Ltd v Atherton* [1926] AC 205 (*see* 9.2.3 *above*). If the initial payment is consideration for the grant of the franchise it is likely to fall within Viscount Cave's criteria for a capital payment. By its very nature, there will only be one initial fee and it may be said to 'bring into existence' the franchisee's trade; the fee may be regarded as a payment which acquires for the franchisee the necessary licence or rights to undertake the franchised trade. Alternatively, it may be regarded as a payment to acquire the necessary know-how; as discussed in 9.2.3, a payment made to acquire a capital asset will be a capital payment. Furthermore, the quality of recurrence is missing.

The services provided   However, it can often be contended that the fee should properly be considered, at least in part, as a payment for, or a contribution towards, training and the other initial services provided to the franchisee rather than for the acquisition of the franchised business. The franchisor will invariably perform services in relation to the establishment of the franchisee's business. The franchise agreement will generally require that some or all of the following services be provided by the franchisor:

(a) consultation and advice regarding choice of premises, altering and refurbishing those premises and the installation of fixtures and fittings;

(b) consultation and advice to put the franchisee in a position to commence trading, including the selection, supervision and training of staff, training in accounting and book-keeping and the day-to-day operation of the business and the franchise system;

(c) the loan of the franchisor's plans to assist in any alterations and refurbishments;

(d) advice on any initial advertising campaign.

To determine the tax treatment, it will be necessary to consider each service being provided to the franchisee. Services directly linked to capital expenditure, eg advice on acquisition of premises, may be part of the capital cost of acquiring the asset, while services more generally related to the trading activities may be revenue expenses (*see* 9.2.3 *above*).

Expenditure before commencing trading   The franchisee should not be prevented from obtaining relief on the expenditure merely because it was incurred before trading commenced (*see* 9.2.2(5) *above*).

Reasonableness   To satisfy the Inland Revenue that the expenditure is an income expense, the franchisee may be required to prove that the fee paid is reasonable, given the services provided to him. If the fee were to be excessive for the services performed, the Inland Revenue might seek to disallow it on the basis that part must be a payment for the grant of the franchise and therefore be capital in nature.

Know-how   The fee may include expenditure incurred in acquiring the franchisor's know-how. If this falls to be treated as capital expenditure on general principles, and if the know-how in question falls within the s 533(7) definition (*see* p 139 *above*), expenditure will qualify for capital allowances of 25 per cent on a reducing balance basis (ICTA 1988, s 530). This assumes that there is no disposal or part disposal of the franchisor's trade which includes the know-how; in such circumstances s 531(2) of ICTA 1988 applies, resulting in capital treatment unless the election referred to on p 139 *above* is made.

Turnkey operations

The franchisor may fit out the franchisee's business premises under a 'turnkey operation'. The franchisor fits out the premises and transfers them to the franchisee or grants a lease to the franchisee. A franchisor generally charges the franchisee a fee for the fitting-out services, possibly including a mark-up on the franchisor's costs in the provision of the package. Under a further variation, the franchisor sells the franchisee a package of equipment comprising all or most of the initial equipment requirements of the franchisee, as well as providing a range of services to the franchisee. In such cases, the sale price for the equipment may include a mark-up element.

The tax implications for the franchisor who sells premises to the franchisee, or equips premises on the franchisee's behalf, or sells equipment to the franchisee in the course of the franchisor's trade, is dealt with at 9.3.4 *below*. Where the franchisee buys a turnkey operation, or otherwise buys equipment from the franchisor, there is no universal practice as to whether a separate initial fee should be charged in respect of the initial services provided by the franchisor. The particular circumstances will have to be considered to determine whether the total charge made to the franchisee should be treated as a receipt from the sale of the premises or the goods, or whether part of the charge should be treated as being a fee for the franchisor's services or for the grant of the franchise to the franchisee. If the charge (or part of it) is not to be brought into account as a receipt on the sale of premises or equipment, the tax implications will be determined according to the principles discussed *above*.

9.3.2   Continuing fees

The continuing fees paid under a franchise agreement are commonly called 'management services fees' or 'royalties'. Most franchise agreements will provide for a fee of a specified percentage of the franchisee's gross revenue.

Occasionally a franchise agreement may provide for a fixed fee to be paid peri-odically. Although treatment of the fee for tax purposes will depend on its true nature rather than on the name used to describe it, the commentary that follows indicates that it will often be desirable to avoid characterising the fee as a royalty. Instead, the franchisor and franchisee may wish to ensure that the fee is expressed to be paid as consideration for services provided (assuming, of course, that real services will be provided).

The services provided

The continuing fee will generally be expressed to be payable in respect of some or all of the following services:

(a) the provision of know-how and guidance on the running of the franch-ised business and continuing services in connection with the develop-ment of the franchised business;

(b) the provision of staff whom the franchisee is able to consult regarding the running of the franchised business;

(c) the provision of an operations manual, together with periodic updates, which explain how the franchisee should carry on the franchised busi-ness;

(d) permission to use the franchisor's trade marks.

Trading income/expense

If the fee is regarded as trading income of the franchisor and a trading expense of the franchisee, the income or expenses respectively will be taken into account in calculating their trading profits for tax purposes. The franchisor will also be able to set against the income any trading losses carried forward from previous years (which are available for offset only against future years' income of the same trade and not against annual payments received in future years) (ICTA 1988, ss 385 and 393(1)). The other principal advantage of receiving trading income is that the franchisee can pay the income without deduction of basic rate tax. As far as the franchisee is concerned, he should be able to obtain a deduction for the fee as a trading expense provided the conditions in s 74 of ICTA 1988 are met (*see 9.2.2 above*).

Tax treatment of annual payments

Royalties and other annual payments paid in respect of rights granted may, however, be treated as 'annual payments' taxable under Schedule D (III) (ss 348 and 349(2) of ICTA 1988). The meaning of 'annual payments' is described on pp 145 and 146 *below*. If the payments are so treated, they will constitute 'pure income profit' of the franchisor, taxable in full without expenses being deducted in computing the taxable income (*Essex County Council* v *Ellam* [1988] STC 370). The franchisee will normally deduct basic rate income tax from such payments (*see below*) and pay the franchisor the net sum, giving rise to cash flow disadvantages for the franchisor (the same applies to payments in respect of patents). The franchisee will also have to consider whether such payments can be treated as trading expenses. There is an absolute bar on deducting patent royalties as a trading expense (ICTA 1988, s 74(1)(*p*)). There is also a prohibition against deducting other types of annual payment if the annual payment is 'payable out of profits or gains' (ICTA 1988, s 74(1)(*m*)). Annual payments may therefore be deductible as a trading expense if they can properly be regarded as items of expenditure to be taken into account in computing the profit, rather than a payment out of the profits (*Paterson Engineering Co Ltd* v *Duff* (1943) 25 TC 43, applying *Gresham Life Assurance Society* v *Styles* (1892) 3 TC 185). In the franchising context royalty payments may sometimes constitute 'annual payments', whereas fees paid for services provided will not constitute 'annual payments' (*see further below*). The nature of a royalty is such that there may be a danger that the Inland Revenue will seek to argue that s 74(1)(*m*) of ICTA 1988 applies to prevent the deduction of the payments from the franchisee's trading income as a trading expense, and it may be prudent for the franchisee to assume that this is the case.

Where a franchisee pays an annual payment which is not deductible as a trading expense by virtue of s 74(1)(*m*) of ICTA 1988, the method of obtaining relief for the annual payment will depend on whether the franchisee is a sole trader/partner or a company.

Sole trader or partner making annual payments   In general terms, relief for a sole trader/partner against basic rate and higher rate tax is obtained under separate provisions. Relief at the basic rate is obtained through the deduction of tax machinery (ICTA 1988, ss 348, 349; *see below*). Higher rate tax relief is obtained by permitting the payer to deduct the gross amount of the payment when determining his total income for tax purposes (ICTA 1988, ss 347A and 835(6)). The relief operates to reduce the payer's income in the year the payment is made; if the payment exceeds the payer's taxable income, tax relief may be lost in respect of the excess.

As previously indicated an annual payment is generally made net of basic rate tax. Sections 348 and 349 of ICTA 1988 contain the relevant provisions relating to deduction of basic rate tax from annual payments. Section 348 applies where an unincorporated franchisee makes the whole payment out of profits or gains brought into the charge to income tax. In this situation the franchisee is not *required* to deduct tax and account to the Inland Revenue in respect of such tax. The franchisee is, however, *entitled* to deduct basic rate tax and retain this for himself (ICTA 1988, s 348(1)(*b*)). The tax retained by the franchise will effectively give him tax relief at the basic rate, as mentioned *above* and ICTA 1988, s 3 ensures that there is no double deduction.

If the payment is not made wholly out of profits or gains charged to income tax, the franchisee will be obliged to deduct basic rate tax and account for this to the Inland Revenue (ICTA 1988, s 349(1)).

Corporate franchisee making annual payments   In the case of a corporate franchisee, the annual payment may be treated as a charge on income which can be offset against the current year's profits (ICTA 1988, s 338(2)). The charge on income can be carried forward against future trading income only if it was incurred wholly and exclusively for the purposes of the franchisee's trade (s 393(9)).

A company which is within the charge to corporation tax will always be obliged to deduct basic rate tax from any annual payments (its profits are charged to corporation tax and the payment cannot therefore be made out of profits charged to income tax) (ICTA 1988, ss 349 and 7(1)).

Meaning of annual payment

It is, therefore, essential that payments required to be made under a franchise agreement be analysed to establish whether they may fall within the provisions of ss 348 or 349, and this will in turn require a determination as to whether or not the fee is an 'annual payment'.

A payment will be an 'annual payment' if it has the following characteristics:

(1)   The payment is an income and not a capital payment.
(2)   The income is 'pure income profit' (*Re Hanbury* (1939) 38 TC 588; (*see below*).
(3)   The payment is payable under a legal obligation (*IRC* v *Whitworth Park Coal Co Ltd* [1958] Ch 792).
(4)   The payment is recurring or capable of recurrence (*Westminster Bank Executor and Trustee Co (Channel Islands) Ltd* v *National Bank of Greece* [1971] AC 945).

Income will only be regarded as 'pure income profit' if the whole of it will be 'a taxable receipt in the hands of the recipient without any deduction for expenses or the like'; it will not be 'pure income profit' if it 'is simply gross revenue in the recipient's hands, out of which a taxable income will emerge only after his outgoings have been deducted' (*per* Lord Donovan in *Campbell* v *IRC* (1968) 45 TC 427). In *Re Hanbury* (1939) 38 TC 588, payments made annually were not pure income profit as they were consideration for the use of certain chattels, so the recipient was entitled to deduct any income expenditure incurred in respect of the provision of the chattels in calculating his taxable profits. Essentially, if the recipient is required to do something in return for the payment and, accordingly, incurs expenditure to obtain the payment, it will not be 'pure income profit'. There will be a greater risk of annual payment treatment applying where the consideration (eg the grant of certain rights) is fully provided before the payments begin (passive exploitation of assets or rights by the owner of such assets or rights), as opposed to a situation in which fees are paid annually for continuing backup and services provided by a franchisor.

Where the payment cannot properly be regarded as consideration for services being provided, the possibility of annual payment treatment should be considered. There may be certain rights being granted including, for example, rights to use the franchisor's name, trade marks, know-how and so on. It may therefore be arguable that the recurring 'fee' should be characterised as an annual payment (having the nature of a passive royalty) in respect of such rights. Ordinarily it is considered that the better argument should be that the franchisor is carrying on a franchise trade, actively exploiting its trade marks, know-how etc in the course of that trade and incurring expenses in order to earn the income, so that all receipts should be regarded as trading receipts rather than as pure income profit. The continual support and supervision of the franchise network is an important feature of a franchising business and will help justify this treatment. The franchisor will normally be carrying on an active trade and the income received under the franchise agreement will not be received as pure profit. However, it will nevertheless be desirable to avoid using terminology such as 'royalties' when referring to the continuing fees in a franchise agreement.

Patent income

If the franchisor receives any patent income this will always be paid after deduction of basic rate tax (ICTA 1988, ss 348(2)(*b*) and 349(1)(*b*)). The above analysis, however, is still relevant to determine whether the income should be regarded as trading income of the franchisor taxable under Schedule D(I) (with expenses being deducted in arriving at the taxable profit and greater loss relief being available) or as an annual payment taxable under Schedule D(III).

Apportionment of fee

In some franchise agreements, the agreement provides for a separate, relatively small, amount to be paid as a royalty independently of the management service fee. The royalty may be expressed to be payable for the use of the franchisor's trade mark, know-how, copyright, etc. Inclusion of such a clause may help to ensure that the balance of the fee, the part which is expressed to be payable for services to be provided, is treated as a trading item in any event.

9.3.3 Advertising fees

In some franchise agreements, a separate fee may be payable in respect of advertising, while in other agreements the provision of advertising services will be charged as an integral part of a general services fee. If a separate fee is payable in respect of advertising, it will often be a fixed percentage of the franchisee's gross revenue. The franchise agreement may require this to be dealt with separately from the franchisor's other income; together with contributions from other franchisees it will constitute an 'advertising pool' to be applied in discharging advertising and promotional expenditure incurred by the franchisor. It will be undesirable for legal reasons for a trust to be established in respect of the advertising pool (*see* 7.4). If the pool were regarded as a trust, this would also complicate the tax treatment (the tax treatment of trusts is not considered in this work).

So far as the franchisor is concerned, the receipt of advertising fees from its franchisees is likely to be treated as trading income and any expenditure incurred in respect of advertising should give rise to a deductible trading expense. As the franchisor will receive the advertising income on a relatively constant basis, but will incur expenditure on an irregular basis (when it undertakes an advertising campaign), the franchisor may incur the expenditure in a year later than that in which the income is received. This could give rise to a taxable profit in one year followed by a loss in a later year while, on a year-to-year basis, no overall profit should arise. Much will depend on how the profit is required to be computed for accounting purposes (*Gallagher* v *Jones* [1993] STC 537), and this may in turn depend on the content of the franchise agreement. The franchisor should in practice be able to avoid any liability to tax arising in respect of advertising fees if the franchise agreement provides:

(a) for the franchisees to pay the advertising contributions to the franchisor on the basis that the franchisor will spend the sums it receives on advertising in its discretion;

(b) for the franchisor to provide accounts detailing its expenditure to the franchisees;

(c) for any excess to be deducted from future contributions due from the franchisees where the franchisees have paid more than the actual expenditure incurred by the franchisor; and

(d) for any deficit to be recovered by means of additional future payments due from the franchisees where the franchisor incurs expenditure in excess of the contributions received from the franchisees.

If the franchise agreement provides that the fee is payable on this basis, it should be possible to leave any fees received surplus to advertising expenditure incurred out of the profit and loss account, and merely to record the surplus as a prepayment in the balance sheet. In practice, the prepayment will only be recorded in the profit and loss account when it is spent on advertising expenditure. It is understood that the Inland Revenue accepts this method of recording advertising fees.

9.3.4 Turnkey operations

As discussed at p 142, the franchisor may fit out the premises to be used by the franchisee and then either sell its interest in those premises to the franchisee or grant the franchisee a lease of those premises. If the franchisor sells its interest in the premises to the franchisee, it will generally recover all its costs in relation the premises (its acquisition cost and the cost of fitting out) either with or without a mark-up. If the franchisor grants a lease of the premises to the franchisee, it will generally recover the cost of fitting out, either with or without a mark-up, and will receive a rent for the use of the premises (although the rent may only be a nominal amount).

With any transactions relating to property, the VAT implications should be considered; *see further* 9.4 and 9.5.3 *below*.

The franchisor's position

It is necessary to consider how receipts generated by a turnkey operation should be brought into account for tax purposes, particularly if a mark-up is being charged.

If the turnkey fee is received in the course of the franchisor's trade, it will form part of the franchisor's trading income and the costs of fitting out will be deductible as trading expenses. This is likely to be the case where the franchisor sells its interest in the premises to the franchisee or grants a long lease at a premium (with no rent or a nominal rent). In such cases the franchisor should be regarded as carrying on one trade comprising not only the main franchising activity, but also the turnkey activity. It is considered unlikely that the turnkey operation would be regarded as a separate trade carried on by the franchisor (rather than forming an integral part of the trade of franchising) or as a capital transaction.

If the franchisor plans to retain an interest in the property after fitting out the premises in order to receive a rental income (ie to hold the property as an investment), the franchisor will be incurring capital expenditure in acquiring the property and most expenses incurred in fitting out the property will be capital in nature. In such circumstances, the franchisor should consider whether some of the expenditure will qualify for capital allowances—*see* 9.5.2 *below*. If a profit is made from charging a mark-up on the turnkey (eg by way of an additional premium charged on granting a lease), and the turnkey operation is not regarded as a trade, the receipt is likely to constitute consideration from a disposal or post-disposal for capital gains purposes subject to the tax treatment of premiums on the sale of leases (ICTA 1988, s 34; *see* 9.5.1 *below*).

The franchisee's position

Where the franchisee pays the costs incurred by the franchisor in fitting out the premises, this will be a capital expense for the franchisee. He will not be able to deduct this expense against his trading income but may be entitled to capital allowances (*see* 9.5.2 *below*). A payment of rent by a franchisee will be a trading expense deductible in the normal way.

9.3.5   Sale of goods by franchisor to franchisee

The franchisor's position

In some franchising transactions, the franchisor will sell goods to the franchisee as an additional profit earning activity. Occasionally, the franchise agreement will not provide for the payment of a separate management services fee (or other continuing fee); and the mark-up on the sale of the goods will instead be the sole source of profit for the franchisor. Ordinarily the tax treatment of receipts from the sale of goods will be straightforward for the franchisor. They will simply be brought into account as receipts of the trade. Similarly, if the franchisor requires the franchisee to acquire the goods from specific third parties nominated in the franchise agreement, these third parties may pay a commission to the franchisor; this should also be treated as part of the Schedule D(I) trading income of the franchisor.

In exceptional circumstances the franchisor may sell the goods at a price in excess of a normal arm's length price. Here the Inland Revenue could seek to argue (especially if no separate continuing fee is payable) that the sale price of the goods includes an element which should be treated as consideration for something other than the goods supplied. This will not be important in practice if the amount in question would in any event be treated as trading income of the franchisor and a trading expense of the franchisee. However, it may be necessary to consider whether any part of the payments should be treated as annual payments, eg royalty income for the use of know-how (*see* 9.3.2 *above*).

The franchisee's position

So far as the franchisee is concerned, the tax treatment of the price paid for goods supplied will primarily depend on whether the expenditure is revenue or capital in nature. If stock is being acquired for the franchised trade, the expenditure will be brought into account in computing the profit. If a capital asset is being acquired, no immediate tax deduction will be available unless there is an entitlement to capital allowances (*see* 9.2.5 *above*).

In some franchising transactions, the franchisor may pass on to franchisees benefits it receives by way of commission from third parties, eg by way of a retrospective rebate which forms a credit against future payments due from the franchisee. This will occur as part of the normal trading relationship between the franchisor and the franchisee and the rebates should be allowable as trading expenses of the franchisor, and will either form part of the trading income of the franchisee or will be treated as retrospectively reducing the franchisee's trading expenses. This distinction is unlikely to be material in practice.

9.4   Value Added Tax (VAT)

9.4.1   Introduction

VAT is a European tax. The common system of VAT adopted by the European Community is set out in a number of EC directives, and the framework provided for in the directives is enacted in the UK principally in the Value Added Tax Act 1994 ('VATA 1994') and regulations made thereunder. However, the provisions of a directive can have 'direct effect' (if the directive is sufficiently clear and precise, clear and unconditional, and does not allow member states any substantial latitude or discretion concerning implementation), in which case taxpayers can rely on the directive in national courts. This is not the place for a discussion of European law principles and readers who wish to investigate the European law underlying UK statutory provisions referred to *below* should refer to more specialist publications on VAT.

9.4.2   Chargeable supplies

VAT is charged on a supply of goods or services made in the UK where the supply is made by a taxable person in the course of a business and is not an exempt supply (VATA 1994, s 4). It is clear that 'supply' is to be construed very widely and, as a general rule of thumb, wherever, in an arm's length situation, one person provides consideration to another, the person receiving the consideration will be making a supply of goods or services. Anything which is not a supply of goods but is done for a consideration is deemed to be a supply of services (VATA 1994, s 5(2)(*b*)). Where parties are at arm's length, the rebuttable presumption will be that one person will not provide consideration to the other unless he is to receive something in return. Most payments under a typical franchise agreement will ordinarily be subject to VAT, unless the particular payment falls within a specific exemption or the legislation specifically takes it outside the scope of VAT.

9.4.3   Taxable persons

A taxable person is a person who is registered for VAT or who is required to be registered for VAT (VATA 1994, s 3(1)). There is no obligation to register for VAT unless the value of supplies which are subject to VAT exceed a registration threshold (currently £46,000 per annum) (VATA 1994, Sched 1, para 1). A business which does not exceed the registration threshold may nevertheless apply to be registered on a voluntary basis (VATA 1994, Sched 1, para 9). This will be advantageous where the business incurs VAT on supplies made to it and wishes to recover the VAT (*see further below*).

9.4.4 Liability of taxable persons

A taxable person must charge VAT at 17.5 per cent on all supplies, unless the supply falls within a category which is exempt (so that no charge to VAT arises) (VATA 1994, s 4 and Sched 9) or which is zero-rated (strictly, VAT is charged but at a rate of 0 per cent) (VATA 1994, s 30 and Sched 8).

The most common situation in which exempt supplies will arise in the franchising context is where the franchisor grants a lease to its franchisee. Land supplies are exempt from VAT, although important exceptions are sales of the freehold in a 'new building' and land supplies where the supplier has made an election to waive exemption from VAT in respect of the property (*see* 9.5.3 *below*) (VATA 1994, Sched 10). Certain types of business will make zero-rated supplies. A common example in the franchising context is a catering franchise; the franchisor's supplies of food to the franchisee will often be zero-rated (VATA 1994, Sched 8, Group 1).

9.4.5 Payment and recovery of VAT

A VAT registered person will generally have to account to Customs and Excise on a quarterly basis for any VAT it charges (output tax). It can normally set against the amount due to Customs and Excise the VAT paid on supplies made to it (input tax) (VATA 1994, s 25). If output tax exceeds input tax in any quarter then the VAT registered person will pay the excess to Customs and Excise. If input tax exceeds output tax, the registered person will be entitled to a refund from Customs and Excise equal to the amount by which the input tax exceeds the output tax. If a registered person makes only exempt supplies, or makes both exempt supplies and taxable supplies (ie supplies which are either subject to VAT or which are zero-rated), all or part of the VAT incurred by the business may not be recoverable (VATA 1994, s 26). The fact that exempt supplies are being made will not lead to a restriction in recovery of VAT paid where the tax otherwise attributable to exempt supplies falls within *de minimis* limits (currently £7,500 per year) and does not represent more than 50 per cent of all VAT incurred (VAT (General) Regulations 1985 (SI 1985 No 886), reg 33A(1)).

9.4.6 Penalties

Strict compliance with VAT obligations is important. If a business fails to register at the due time or makes any errors in its quarterly returns, it is exposed to penalties. If the taxpayer submits a return which is inaccurate to the extent of the lesser of £1,000,000 and 30 per cent of the true VAT, he will be liable to a serious misdeclaration penalty of 15 per cent (VATA 1994, s 63). There are other penalties for failing to submit returns (default surcharges) (VATA 1994, s 59); persistent misdeclarations (VATA 1994, s 64); dishonest conduct (VATA 1994, s 60); and criminal prosecution is possible in cases involving fraud or dishonesty. Penalties will not generally be imposed if a taxpayer has 'a reasonable excuse' for being in breach of the VAT rules (*see* eg VATA 1994, s 63(10)) in relation to the serious misdeclaration penalty). There is a vast body of reported VAT tribunal decisions on the question of what amounts to a 'reasonable excuse', and it is not always easy to discern a consistent approach from these decisions. Customs also have a general discretion to mitigate penalties. (VATA 1994, s 70).

9.4.7 The tax point

Taxpayers must not only identify whether VAT is chargeable, but must also account for VAT at the correct time. This will be determined by reference to the date on which the supply will be treated as being made. In the case of a supply of goods, the supply is made when the goods are removed or made available to the customer (VATA 1994, s 6(2)). In the case of a supply of services, the services are treated as being supplied at the time they are performed (VATA 1994, s 6(3)). These rules determine when the 'basic tax point' arises. However, the supply will be treated as taking place on the earlier of the date a tax invoice is issued or the date on which payment is received if either of these takes place before the basic tax point (VATA 1994, s 6(4)). If a tax invoice is issued within 14 days after the basic tax point, and no payment has been received, the invoice date will be treated as the tax point unless the supplier elects in writing for the basic tax point rule to apply (VATA 1994, s 6(5)). There is also a number of special rules fixing the tax point in the case of particular types of supply.

One particular situation worthy of comment is that of a lump sum for the grant of a franchise which is payable in instalments. One might have thought that VAT in respect of each instalment would be collected and accounted for as each instalment becomes due. However, generally the tax point for the supply will arise on the grant of the franchise. VAT would therefore be accounted for in respect of all the instalments when the franchise is granted, even though not all the instalments will have been paid.

Continuous supplies of services (eg management services supplied under a franchise agreement) have no natural tax point and special rules are therefore required. In the case of such supplies, VAT must be accounted for in respect of a particular payment on the earlier of the date on which the payment is received and the date on which the invoice is issued (VAT (General) Regulations 1985 (SI 1985 No 886), reg 23). There are special rules for determining the tax point for certain types of supply (*see* for example VAT (General) Regulations (SI 1985 No 886), reg 19 in respect of leases).

9.4.8 VAT inclusive or exclusive

The VAT legislation provides, in effect, that the consideration payable for a supply will be deemed to be VAT-inclusive unless the contract dealing with the supply provides to the contrary (VATA 1994, s 9(2)). If the consideration is deemed to be VAT-inclusive, the franchisor will have to account for VAT out of the sum received. The franchisor will therefore usually wish to ensure that the franchise agreement will allow him to add VAT where VAT is payable. This will be relevant not only in determining the amount of net income received by the franchisor, but also in determining who bears the risk of any variation in the rate of VAT or in the categories of supply which are subject to VAT. If the franchise agreement does not provide what should happen in the event of a variation in the rate of VAT or in the categories of supply which are subject to VAT, the fees payable under the agreement will change to take account of any such variation (VATA 1994, s 89). However, if the agreement specifically provides that the amount payable is inclusive of any VAT chargeable, then the amount due will not vary to take account of any changes in the VAT legislation. When entering into a franchise agreement, the parties must therefore consider the incidence of VAT, and whether it may give rise to a real cost, and ensure that the franchise agreement reflects the intentions of the franchisor and franchisee.

9.4.9 Exempt and zero-rated supplies

The above represents a very brief summary of some of the importance features of the VAT system. There follows a list of some of the more important categories of exempt and zero-rated supplies:

Exempt

(1) Land (but subject to a number of exceptions—*see* 9.4.4 and 9.5.3) (VATA 1994, Sched 10).
(2) Insurance and finance activities (VATA 1994, Sched 9, Groups 2 and 5).
(3) Education (including private tuition by an individual teacher but not education provided by a profit-making institution) (VATA 1994, Sched 9, Group 6).
(4) Medical services (VATA 1994, Sched 9, Group 7).

Zero-rated

(1) Food provided otherwise than in the course of catering (VATA 1994, Sched 8, Group 1).

(2) Books, newspapers, pamphlets and leaflets (VATA 1994, Sched 8, Group 3).

(3) International services (*see further* Chapter 21 at 21.3 *below*) (VATA 1994, Sched 8, Group 7).

(4) Children's clothing (VATA 1994, Sched 8, Group 16).

When considering whether a particular supply may be exempt or zero-rated, the legislation must be considered in detail.

9.5 Land taxation

Chapter 14 deals with the commercial aspects of why a franchisor may wish, or be required, to take an interest in the franchisee's premises. This section sets out some of the main tax consequences when the franchisor takes an interest in the franchisee's premises.

9.5.1 Taxation of premiums and rents

Schedule A

If the franchisor acquires a freehold or a leasehold interest in the outlet with a view to letting or sub-letting it to the franchisee, the franchisor will be assessed to tax under Schedule A in respect of any rents to which it is entitled (ICTA 1988, s 15). The franchisor will be entitled to deduct its expenses of maintaining, repairing, insuring and managing the premises, any rates it incurs or rent paid to a superior landlord, and the cost of providing any services included in the rent (ICTA 1988, s 25). Interest cannot be deducted in computing the Schedule A liability, but can be deducted from the net Schedule A income. To obtain an interest deduction the interest must arise from a loan applied in acquiring the franchisor's interest in the outlet or improving or developing the outlet (ICTA 1988, s 354(1)). The loan must be a fixed loan capable of lasting at least one year (ICTA 1988, s 353). In addition, the outlet must be let at a commercial rent for more than 26 weeks in any period of 52 weeks, and when not so let must either be available for letting at a commercial rent or prevented from being available for letting by works of construction or repair (ICTA 1988, s 355(1)(*b*)). Particular considerations arise where the franchisor is non-UK resident.

The Finance Act 1995 establishes a new income tax regime for taxing income from property (ss 39–42 and Sched 6). These provisions apply only to income tax and will not therefore affect the existing rules for companies with Schedule A income. Under the new rules, profits arising from UK property are computed by applying most of the rules applicable to the calculation of trading profits under Schedule D. Interest is allowed as a deduction in calculating the profits arising from UK property if it falls within the normal rules for Schedule D, Case I. Essentially, the interest should be allowable if it is expended wholly and exclusively for the purpose of the business (ICTA 1988, s 74(1)(*a*) as applied for Sched A).

Lump sums paid to acquire property interests

Where the franchisor has paid a lump sum on the acquisition of a freehold or a leasehold interest in an outlet with a view to letting the property to the franchisee, the franchisor will not in general obtain a revenue deduction for the lump sum paid. Instead the capital sum paid will represent the base cost of the franchisor's land interest for capital gains tax purposes. On any subsequent disposal of the freehold or leasehold interest a capital gain or loss will arise, and only at that point does the franchisor obtain a tax deduction for the original lump sum payment. This basic position is modified where a premium is paid on the grant of a lease for a term of 50 years or less. In these circumstances part of the premium will be treated as rent assessable under Schedule A. The amount treated as rent will be the premium less 2 per cent of the premium for each complete year of the term of the lease other than the first (ICTA 1988, s 34)). The franchisor will be entitled to a deduction based on the sum treated as rent assessable under Schedule A (ICTA 1988, s 87(1)). For example, if a five year lease is granted at a premium of £20,000 the amount treated as rent would be £18,400 (£20,000 – [8% × 20,000]). In this example, the franchisor would be entitled to a tax deduction of one-fifth of £18,400 for each of the five years of the term of the lease (ICTA 1988, s 87(2)).

Where the franchisee pays a premium on the grant of a lease or sub-lease to the franchisor this will result in a part disposal of the franchisor's interest in the property for capital gains tax purposes (TCGA 1992, Sched 8, para 2). A chargeable gain will arise if the premium exceeds the base cost (and any indexation allowance), applying the part disposal rules in TCGA 1992, s 42 and Sched 8, para 2(2). Special rules apply where the franchisor's interest out of which the sub-lease to the franchisee is granted is a lease which is a wasting asset (ie one with an unexpired term of 50 years or less) (TCGA 1992, Sched 8, para 4).

9.5.2   Capital allowances

The general position regarding eligibility for capital allowances is dealt with at 9.2.5 *above*.

Capital allowances are available only if the expenditure incurred in acquiring the asset is capital in nature. If the franchisor's trade involves the fitting out and disposal of interests in premises, the expenditure will be treated as a trading expense and the franchisor will, therefore, automatically obtain relief in respect of that expenditure. The franchisor will not, in addition, be entitled to claim capital allowances. Whether the franchisor's expenditure should be regarded as capital or revenue in nature is considered at 9.2.3 *above*.

Plant and machinery

While capital allowances are not ordinarily available on the expenditure incurred in acquiring the building itself, they are available for the plant and machinery within the building. Therefore, a franchisor, on acquiring the freehold in an outlet, will often be entitled to claim capital allowances on that part of the price that is referable to the plant and machinery which has become part of the building or which is otherwise affixed to the building.

If a franchisee acquires the freehold in or takes a lease of premises and subsequently incurs expenditure of a capital rather than revenue nature in fitting out the premises, he will be entitled to capital allowances on any expenditure incurred in respect of plant and machinery. However, if the franchisor operates a 'turnkey operation', it will incur the expenditure on fitting out the premises and will then recover this expenditure from the franchisee. It is necessary to consider who will be entitled to capital allowances on any plant and machinery in these circumstances. The following analysis will be equally applicable if the franchisee takes a lease from a third party and that third party has incurred expenditure on plant and machinery.

A potential problem for the franchisee as a tenant of property is the requirement that capital allowances can be claimed only where expenditure is incurred on plant or machinery which 'belongs to him' (CAA 1990, s 21(1)(*b*)). When an item of plant or machinery becomes affixed to land as a fixture, it forms part of the land and ceases to belong to the franchisee. The Court of Appeal, in *Stokes* v *Costain Property Investments Ltd* (1983) 57 TC 688, held that capital allowances could not be claimed by either the landlord (who had not incurred the expenditure) nor the tenant (as the fixture did not 'belong' to him). This case has now been superseded by s 52 of CAA 1990, which allows tenants to claim capital allowances in these circumstances.

A franchisor, having granted a lease or sub-lease to the franchisee, may make a contribution towards the franchisee's fitting out costs. If this route is taken the franchisor may be entitled to claim capital allowances under CAA 1990, s 154. In practice where the fitting out costs are to be borne partly by the franchisor and partly by the franchisee it will be important to address the issue of capital allowances in the documentation. It may be that the franchisor's contribution is to be treated as a contribution towards those items qualifying for capital allowances (to the maximum extent possible). Alternatively, the franchisor and franchisee may seek to apportion their respective contributions pro rata between qualifying and non-qualifying items.

If the franchisor holds the freehold and sells it to the franchisee, part of the price will be referable to plant and machinery and the franchisee will be entitled to claim capital allowances in respect of that part of the expenditure properly attributable to the plant and machinery. If the franchisor holds a leasehold interest and sells it to the franchisee, and the consideration given by the franchisee includes a capital sum which falls wholly or partly to be treated as expenditure on the provision of a fixture, and at the time of the franchisee's acquisition no one has become entitled to allowances for the fixture (or if the franchisor has become so entitled, the sale causes the disposal value to be brought into account by it for capital allowances purposes), then the fixture will be treated as belonging to the franchisee for capital allowance purposes and the franchisee will be entitled to claim capital allowances (CAA 1990, s 54).

If the franchisor grants a lease (or sub-lease) to the franchisee, the franchisor and franchisee can jointly elect for the fixture to be treated as belonging to the franchisee for capital allowances purposes where the franchisee has paid a premium for the grant of the lease (or sub-lease) (CAA 1990, s 55). If the election is not made, the franchisor would be entitled to continue claiming allowances in respect of the fixtures which qualify as plant or machinery.

If the franchisor ceases to be treated as holding the relevant interest in the premises after having previously claimed capital allowances thereon, it will be deemed to dispose of the fixtures qualifying for capital allowances and will incur a balancing charge or allowance (CAA 1990, s 57).

9.5.3 Value Added Tax

The option to tax

If the franchisor is the franchisee's landlord, the franchisor must consider whether to elect to waive the exemption from VAT. The VAT legislation provides that the grant of an interest in property is generally exempt from VAT. Accordingly, VAT will not be chargeable on any premium paid on the grant of a lease or on the rents payable under a lease, and the franchisor will not be able to recover any VAT it incurs on expenditure relating to the property. However, the legislation provides that the owner of an interest in land (eg a landlord) may elect to waive the exemption (otherwise known as the 'option to tax'), so that the franchisor will be required to charge VAT on any premium, rents or other sums received in respect of the property (VATA 1994, Sched 10). The advantage of making the election is that the franchisor will be able to reclaim as input tax the VAT it incurs in relation to the property. This will be particularly important if the franchisor owns a leasehold interest and has to pay VAT on any rent it pays to its own landlord. Even if the franchisor owns the freehold, it may still incur VAT on expenditure relating to the property and may therefore wish to consider exercising its 'option to tax'. Provided the tenant is able to recover all the VAT it incurs (ie it is not 'partially exempt'), the tenant will suffer only a short term cash flow disadvantage as a result of being charged VAT.

'Connected persons'

With effect from 30 November 1994 any election to waive exemption from VAT made by a taxpayer ceases to have effect where the taxpayer makes a 'grant', in relation to land in respect of which the election has been made, to a 'connected person', and either the taxpayer or the connected person is exempt or partially exempt for the purposes of VAT (Value Added Tax (Buildings and Land) Order 1994 (SI 1994 No 3013)). Where this provision applies, the sale or letting of property to a connected person will constitute exempt supplies. This may have serious input tax consequences for the supplier. The definition of a 'connected person' in s 839 of ICTA 1988 is imported. Property transactions between a franchisor and a franchisee should not normally be caught by these provisions. In certain cases, however, franchisor and franchisee may be 'connected', in which case the application of these rules must be considered.

Revoking an election

When considering whether to waive the exemption, the landlord should bear in mind that once the election has been made, it cannot be revoked until 20 years have elapsed from the date of the making of the election and Customs and Excise give their written consent to the revocation. Exceptionally, an election can be revoked within three months of making it, provided that no VAT has been charged on supplies made in relation to the property, no credit for input tax has been claimed by virtue of the election and the written consent of Customs and Excise is first obtained (VATA 1994, Sched 10, paras 4 and 5). Subject to these rules, once the election has been made, VAT will have to be charged on rents received from all future lettings of the property and on any consideration received from the eventual sale of the property. In certain circumstances this may affect the marketability of the property and may reduce its value. This is, however, only likely to be the case only where the location of the property is likely to attract purchasers or lessees unable to recover VAT (eg banks and others in the financial sector). Before waiving the exemption, the landlord must, therefore, consider the relative merits of recovering VAT incurred in respect of the property and the obligation to charge VAT on all future supplies made in respect of it.

Turnkey operations

A situation in which it may be particularly advantageous for the franchisor to waive the exemption is where the franchisor operates a 'turnkey operation' (*see* p 142 *above*). In this situation the landlord will fit out the property before granting a lease or conveying the freehold to the franchisee. The franchisor will contract with the builders and will incur the VAT on the fitting-out expenses but will generally recover these expenses from the franchisee, for example, by way of the amount charged as a lump sum for the sale or the grant of the lease of the property to the franchisee. In this situation the franchisor will be able to recover VAT on its fitting out costs only if it waives the exemption from VAT and charges the franchisee VAT on the rents and any premium payable.

9.5.4   Stamp duty

The principal heads of stamp duty likely to be met in a franchising context are the duty on conveyances or transfers on sale, and lease or tack duty. Conveyance or transfer on sale duty is charged on any instrument effecting the conveyance or transfer or sale of any property (Stamp Act 1981, s 1, Sched 1). It is chargeable at the rate of 1 per cent of the consideration paid on the sale. No duty is chargeable if the consideration is £60,000 or less provided that an appropriate certificate is given (FA 1963, s 55(1)(*a*) (as amended); FA 1958, s 34). Sales of freehold and leasehold interests will fall within this head.

The rate of lease or tack duty payable on the grant of a lease depends on the premium, the rents payable and the length of the term of the lease.

In the case of fixed term leases of less than a year, duty is payable at the rate of 0.5 per cent of the rent for a full year (even if the term is less than a year), together with 1 per cent of the amount of any premium paid.

In the case of leases for a fixed term exceeding one year (or for an indefinite term) stamp duty at the rate of 1 per cent is payable on any premium, together with an amount of duty calculated by reference to the average rent, and at a rate dependent on the length of term of the lease. Where the term of the lease is indefinite or does not exceed seven years, duty at the rate of 1 per cent on the average annual rent will be chargeable. Leases for a term of between seven and 35 years will be liable to stamp duty at the rate of 2 per cent; leases for a term between 35 and 100 years will be chargeable at the rate of 12 per cent; and leases for a term exceeding 100 years will be chargeable to duty at the rate of 24 per cent.

Chapter 10

Intellectual Property: an Overview

Chapter 10

Intellectual Property: an Overview

10.1 The nature of intellectual property

An essential part of the package which a franchisor provides to a franchisee comprises intellectual property. The franchisor owns certain intellectual property which it permits the franchisee to use. The franchisor is concerned to retain ownership of its intellectual property, not to lose it to the franchisee as a consequence of the transaction between them, and to recover it intact when the franchise comes to an end. The franchisee is concerned to identify the intellectual property rights he requires to enable him to operate under the franchise, and to ensure that he acquires them.

Practically, rather than legally, speaking, the intellectual property in a franchise is most likely to relate to logos, signs, brand names, designs, the way of carrying on the business and the other contents of operating manuals, and computer software, but many other instances could readily be found.

The phrase 'intellectual property' covers a number of quite different rights under different legal regimes. Some are more important than others in the context of franchising. The most significant are considered separately in Chapters 11–13. This chapter comprises a general introduction to intellectual property.

'Intellectual property' is not a new expression. In 1847 a court in the USA in *Woodbury* v *Minot* used the term. It has, however, only recently achieved general currency. The phrase 'industrial property', which is roughly equivalent, possibly not extending to copyright, is now less frequently found. Use of the phrase, and its 1980s acronym 'IP', suggests a unified system of law, but, even with the initiatives emanating from the EU, that is far from the case. As the Australian judge Dixon J put it in the case of *Victoria Park Racing* v *Taylor* (1937) 58 CLR 479 at p 509): '. . . the exclusive right to invention, trade marks, designs, trade names and reputation are dealt with in English law as special heads of protected interests and not under a wide generalisation'.

Intellectual property comprises a selection of rights. All rights are intangible, but some are more intangible than others. The rights of a freeholder in relation to a piece of land are anchored to the land in a way in which the rights of the author of a book, which may be reproduced worldwide, filmed or adapted as a video game, are not.

Intellectual property rights relate to the products of peoples' minds, or at any rate such of them as have potential commercial value; hence 'intellectual'. The phrase has no connotations of cleverness. 'Property' indicates how the rights have been treated in English law. The common law tradition has been to treat intellectual property rights as equivalent to other property rights. They may therefore, in principle, be freely transferred and licensed. Such an approach was not inevitable.

10.2   Alternatives to intellectual property

10.2.1   The common law countries

The approach of the common law countries has been to allow a creator or inventor a property right in the results of his or her work; the extent of the property right might be limited both as to the degree of exclusivity and as to the period for which it would subsist. The intention has been to foster creativity and invention by guaranteeing to the owner of the property right a free run (subject to the limits inherent in the right itself) with the resulting work or invention. Since intellectual rights were transferable, the structure also favoured persons funding creations or inventions. The individual creator or inventor might be required to assign his or her intellectual property rights to the person funding the work as the quid pro quo for the funding. Indeed, in relation to a complicated work having a large number of individual contributors, such as a feature film, it would be routine that practically all the relevant intellectual property rights would be assigned to the person organising the creation of the work—in the case of the film, the production company. (In the case of films, restrictions have recently been imposed on a producer's ability to secure all relevant rights following the introduction of the EU's Rental Rights Directive. A statutory instrument to give it effect in English law is, at the time of writing (March 1995), shortly to be issued.

10.2.2   Other jurisdictions

In other jurisdictions, the emphasis is markedly different. Copyright regimes in civil law systems are significantly concerned, in relation to artistic works, with the artistic rights of the creator. In French law, the creator of an artistic work has certain inalienable, non-commercial rights designed to protect him or her, not only against actions by completely independent copiers of the work, but also by those to whom the creator of the work has delivered it for exploitation, for example book publishing companies, film producers, or franchisors commissioning design work.

There is also in certain countries a fundamentally different approach to the actions which should properly be preventable under an intellectual property regime. In English law, the approach is to identify first the intellectual property right owned by the plaintiff, then the actions of the defendant, finally identifying whether the latter infringe the former. Other jurisdictions, particularly civil law ones, approach the issue at least in part as a question of unfair competition. The question is then whether the actions of the defendant are fair, taking into account the relative businesses of the plaintiff and the defendant.

The US, although having a common law system, also has a more developed concept of unfair competition than has the UK.

10.2.3   The example of comparative advertising

For the purposes of this chapter, one example suffices to illustrate the different approaches, and that is comparative advertising. English law, with little or no concept of unfair competition, is ill-adapted to deal directly with questions of comparative advertising. To a non-lawyer the issue is whether use by an advertiser of material concerning a competitor is fair or not. In English law, a company wishing to prevent references to its name and products in advertising by a competitor will rely mainly on trade mark law. Civil lawyers would point out that trade mark law is singularly ill-suited for the purpose, since it is designed to stop one party benefiting from the goodwill generated by another in its name and marks, whereas comparative advertising is designed to do precisely the opposite.

The Trade Marks Act 1994 qualifies, rather uneasily, the traditional English approach to comparative advertising. Section 10 permits comparative advertising which would otherwise constitute trade mark infringement, provided it is in accordance with honest practices in industrial and commercial matters and that it does not, without due cause, take unfair advantage of, or is not detrimental to, the distinctive character or control of the trade mark. How the courts will interpret this rather un-English wording remains to be seen.

Since English law rubs shoulders with non-common law systems in the EU, and the EU is a major source of new law, particularly in relation to intellectual property, concepts such as these, although historically foreign to English law, are finding their way in.

10.3   Types of intellectual property

At this point, it may be helpful to list the main species of intellectual property:

— copyright;
— moral rights;
— performers' rights;

— registered trade marks;
— unregistered trade marks and rights in relation to passing off;
— design right;
— registered designs;
— patents;
— confidentiality.

There are in addition sub-species of rights, such as plant breeders' rights, and topography rights (which relate to printed circuit boards), which are outside the scope of this work; the list is in any event not exhaustive. Of particular concern to franchisors and franchisees are elements of copyright, trade marks both registered and unregistered, and confidentiality. Trade marks are discussed in Chapter 11, confidentiality in Chapter 12 and copyright in Chapter 13. The law relating to patents, which is a significant part of intellectual property, is of little concern to franchisors and franchisees and will not be dealt with in detail.

10.4   The origin of intellectual property rights

The various rights arise in different ways. Most, now, are conferred by statute. Some, for example, registered trade marks and patents, depend on a formal system of registration, whereas others, like copyright, vest in their owners automatically. Some rights comprise true monopolies whereas others confer only relative monopolies. Some rights, in particular rights of confidentiality, arise, if at all, through contract or other dealings between parties.

Even when rights are derived from modern statutes, the law sometimes survives uneasily in circumstances very different from those in which it was first developed. The fundamentals of the law of copyright, for example, were designed to protect the creators of literary works and pictures. The basic principles were developed in the pre-electronic age and have been adapted, sometimes with more elegance than others, to cater for such unexpected phenomena as computer programs (treated as literary works), and exploitation by means of satellite and cable television. The Trade Marks Act 1938, repealed only in 1994, passed into law long before anybody had considered the possibility of character merchandising, or even of the aggressive use of branding which is fundamental to the modern franchise industry. Trade mark law is now governed by the Trade Marks Act 1994, which is discussed in detail in Chapter 11.

10.5   Possible intellectual property rights which failed to be created

If only because of the tendency on the part of business people to treat intellectual property law as a single unified system, and the intention on the part of legislators, particularly in the EU, to turn it into a single unified system, it is worthwhile examining areas where a non-lawyer would expect intellectual property rights to exist, but where they do so fitfully, if at all.

10.5.1 Ideas

It is, as we shall see in Chapter 13, fundamental to copyright law that there is no legal protection for ideas or concepts, but only in their physical expression. The position is different in relation to other intellectual property rights; the protection afforded by patent law to an invention relates to the idea as described in the patent claim submitted for registration, rather than the form of the claim itself. There are also, as we shall see in Chapter 12, possibilities in the law of confidentiality of protecting material which cannot (or in ways which cannot) be protected by copyright. However, in relation to franchising and the part of the franchising package (apart from trade marks) which a franchisor would want to protect, copyright is the most significant area.

To illustrate the point of principle simply, Robert Louis Stephenson's copyright in *Treasure Island* (if it still subsisted) would entitle him to prevent others from copying the whole or sections of the text of the book, but not writing works of their own about islands, treasure and pirates with one leg; William Frith would be entitled to prevent people copying *Derby Day* or sections of it, photographically or by means of prints, but he would not be entitled to stop others making their own pictures of race meetings.

Marketing concepts and systems, which are at the centre of many franchises, may not be capable of protection under copyright law.

10.5.2 Formats

An extension of the rule in relation to ideas or concepts applies to formats. Most experience and litigation relating to formats is in the context of television programmes, but the principle can be applied to franchising. Business people and even lawyers assume that the creator of a format for a programme owns rights in the format which enable him or her to prevent others using the format, or to require them to pay a royalty. Indeed, it is not unusual to find legal documents which refer, without further definition, to the 'format rights' in relation to a programme. However, the creator of the format will in fact have no protection unless there is a physical expression of the format (for example, the central elements are written down) and the elements are described in sufficient detail that misappropriation by somebody else would count as copying for the purposes of copyright law. In *Green v Broadcasting Corp of New Zealand* [1989] 2 All ER 1056, Hughie Green argued there were format rights in the television programme *Opportunity Knocks*, even though no scripts had been written. Lord Bridge stated 'It is stretching the original use of the word

"format" a long way to use it metaphorically to describe the features of a television series such as a talent, quiz or game show which is presented in a particular way, with repeated but unconnected use of set phrases.' That is of
limited use where the concept is such that the competitor can paraphrase it,
getting the same effect but copying nothing. Again, the implications for franchising are obvious.

The government is considering amending the law as it affects formats for
television programmes. Any new law is, it is understood, unlikely to extend to,
for example, restaurant and other formats, which are licensed by franchisors to
the same extent, and on the same insecure legal basis.

10.5.3   Faces

Business people often assume that individuals, and particularly the famous,
have some property right in their own names and appearance. In English law,
an individual has no such right. The position is a little different in other countries. In the USA and some European countries, for example, there is a right of
privacy under which an individual can forbid, or license, commercial use of his
or her name or image. In the USA, the right of privacy has been extended in
certain ways into what is effectively the converse—a right of publicity
accorded to individuals whose name and likeness is valuable. This is clearly
important in relation to character merchandising and to franchising promoted
through the use of individuals.

Where the individual is fictional and his appearance is derived from a
drawing, such as Mickey Mouse, or Ronald McDonald, there will be copyright
in the drawing, and that can be exploited, licensed and so forth, for the purposes of franchising. Furthermore, the drawings can be registered as trade
marks and exploited and protected under trade mark law. Where a human
individual is involved, precisely the same principles, surprisingly, govern the
situation. If one wished to promote a food franchise by using the name and
likeness of a living individual called, say, Colonel Sanders, it would not be
sufficient merely to secure the licence of the individual to make his name and
likeness available; it would also be necessary to secure copyright, or a copyright licence, in the photographs or drawings actually used, to cover the
representations used by trade mark registrations, and to arrange that there was
no practical risk that independent representations of Colonel Sanders would be
created and made available to competitors. The effect is to apotheosise Colonel
Sanders so far as possible to the status of Mickey Mouse, so that the man's
human characteristics become commercially irrelevant. This is more feasible
in franchising than character merchandising, where the occasional live appearance may be unavoidable. All of this, as we shall see, can readily be achieved.
The point is that the means of doing so are not those which might immediately
be expected.

10.6   Software

We will deal in more detail in Chapter 13 with the basis on which software is protected by copyright law. It is however, instructive to consider here how that position came about.

Copyright law was evolved to protect the creators of, among other things, literary works, and to encourage people to create literary works without fear that the results of their labours might be appropriated by others. Copyright law was well established before the first computer was invented and long before the rapid expansion in information technology of the second half of this century. Clearly, software merits protection by intellectual property law if anything does. However, the legislature, as is its way, lagged behind commercial and technical developments and for a long time statute law in England was silent on the protection of software.

If a new intellectual property code were being prepared now without any preconceptions at all, there is more than one way in which software might be treated. Innovative software might be protected, for example, by an extension of the present law of patents; indeed, there are limited possibilities of obtaining patent protection even under the present law. Software might merit a set of rules and rights of its own; some, for example, have suggested a system of registration which would run parallel to the copyright regime. Developers of software might be entitled to protect themselves against competitors under a law of unfair competition rather than by reference to a law based on the ownership of property in the software. What in fact happened, in the absence of statute, was that software became treated as a 'literary work' and therefore protected by the law of copyright. From 1957 until 1989 the law of copyright in England was governed by the Copyright Act 1956, which makes no specific reference to software. During the early part of that period, business was conducted on the assumption that software was protected as a 'literary work'. A consensus grew up based partly on the appalling consequences that would follow if software were not in fact protected at all. The position was regularised in 1985, when the Copyright (Computer Software) Amendment Act 1985 was passed to the effect that software was capable of protection as a literary work, and the position is confirmed in the Copyright, Designs and Patents Act 1988. In the Directive of 1991 on the legal protection of computer programs, the EC required member states to adopt (or, in the case of the UK, maintain) legal systems which protect software under copyright law as a literary work.

Although this is very convenient, it remains undeniable that software is not in fact a 'literary work', and there are still problems in applying law developed by reference to genuine literary works. As we shall see, for a literary work to be protected by copyright it must be both original and a product of human endeavour; a random sequence of letters and numbers or the results of a session of automatic writing would probably not be protected by copyright. However, frequently the preparation of software involves the inclusion of random sequences of digits. These might form part of a security code and would be precisely the material which the owner of the software would not want copied by a competitor. Copyright law then requires the creator of the software to attempt to protect material, the essence of which is that it is meaningless and therefore unpredictable, under law designed to protect written material precisely because it is meaningful.

This instance can for present purposes serve as an example of the strains which arise from applying pre-electronic copyright law to the rapidly developing area of information technology. The USA applies its patent law in certain circumstances to developments in software. Even the EC directive which required member states to protect software as a literary work under copyright law at the same time required member states to permit users to 'reverse engineer' software in certain circumstances which conventional copyright law would not permit, but which the European Commission required in order to maintain the possibility of fair competition.

10.7   Databases

There are parallel problems in the case of databases. Databases are valuable, or people would not pay to have access to them. It has, however, always been doubtful whether particular databases were protected by copyright, given the requirements for originality and skill in the preparation of the database as a putative literary work. In particular cases there might or might not be originality and skill and the database might or might not qualify for copyright protection. However, the compiler's originality and skill would be largely irrelevant to the user and the effect would therefore be random. The EC has now decreed (OJ 1992 C156/4) that databases should be protected under rules all their own.

If there is a connecting principle to be drawn from all this, it is that, in commercial dealings with what appears to be intellectual property, principles are important, but analysis and conveyancing are more so.

10.8   Common denominators

Nevertheless, common denominators of more or less universal application can be identified. Intellectual property comprises property rights which:

(a) give their owners monopolies (more or less); and
(b) are valuable, vulnerable and disposable; and
(c) are in direct conflict with the principles of competition law.

The reference to 'monopolies' requires most qualification. Some intellectual property rights, for example in relation to patents, grant a monopoly which is valid against all others within the jurisdiction. The owners of other rights have more limited protection. A copyright owner is entitled to prevent copying of his work, but not its independent creation by another. The owner of a trade mark is not entitled to protection against a competitor who has a history, before registration of the mark, of innocent use of the same or a similar mark. Where one person imposes an obligation of confidentiality on another, the originator of the confidential information will be entitled to protect it only as against those with whom he has a binding contract, or those who acquire the information knowing it to be confidential. Nevertheless, it is of the essence of intellectual property rights that they entitle their proprietors to stop others doing certain things, or to make them pay for the privilege of doing so.

The reference to competition law is most conveniently picked up in 10.10 *below* on the EU.

10.9 International rights

Intellectual property, like franchising, is essentially international in its application, although intellectual property law varies from country to country. The regime applying in the franchisor's territory, where the rights will normally have originated, may not apply at all in the franchisee's country. In some cases the relevant law may vary fundamentally. To take just one example, as a general rule effective copyright protection in the USA may require registration with the appropriate authority, whereas in the UK no such registration is required, or even possible. In the UK it is therefore necessary to show ownership of the copyright work before the owner is able to enforce its rights.

Because of the international importance of intellectual property, there are international conventions dealing, among other things, with trade marks and copyright. One of the most important of these is the GATT Agreement which requires the harmonisation and strengthening of all forms of intellectual property in all signatory states. Trade mark conventions facilitate registration in more than one country at a time, but the enforcement of trade mark rights remains a matter of national law. The essential effect of the copyright conventions, the most important being the Berne Convention, to which most countries in the developed world are now parties, is to require states which are party to the treaty to give copyright protection under their own law to works originating in other states which are also party to the treaty. It is important to underline that protection is given under national law. The result is not that a work which is protected in one state is protected in exactly the same way throughout all the states which are party to the Berne Convention. It is often the case that, because of variations in the period of copyright, or because registration requirements have not been complied with in particular states, works may be in copyright in some states and not in others.

10.10   The European Union

The area of most significance as far as international rights are concerned is the European Union. Membership of the EU by the UK has led to changes in the law as it affects franchising, and as it affects intellectual property in particular. Chapter 16 is devoted specifically to this issue, and this chapter will be confined to some remarks about the underlying principles. The EU is relevant in three distinct areas:

(a) creation of new intellectual property rights;
(b) harmonisation proposals;
(c) competiton law.

Each will briefly be examined in turn.

10.10.1   New intellectual property rights

It is the long-term aim of the European Commission that, in distinct areas of intellectual property, rights should be available which are supranational. There is, for example, to be a European trade mark regime under which companies would be entitled to apply for a single registration of a trade mark, a Community Trade Mark, which would be valid throughout the European Community. The regime would apply alongside national trade mark regimes. Where trade marks have commercial application within a single member state only, registration for the whole of the Community would be inappropriate and would not be available. When the regime is in place, which is expected to be in 1996, it will be of particular relevance to franchisors who wish to exploit their trade marks throughout the Community.

10.10.2   Harmonisation

The European Commission is attempting to achieve a similar effect by requiring member states to harmonise their local intellectual property laws. While, as we shall see *below*, ownership and use of intellectual property rights are capable of distorting competition within the Community, and there are special rules as to that, it is also the case that where different intellectual property regimes apply in different states, so that the mutual rights and obligations of owners of intellectual property rights, licensees and third parties vary from state to state, that can also distort competition within the Community. The Commission has therefore issued a series of directives requiring member states to harmonise their intellectual property regimes in particular areas. The most significant of these, in relation to franchising, are those which affect trade marks and copyright and will be discussed in Chapters 11 and 13.

10.10.3   Competition law

The principles

It is fundamental to the idea of intellectual property rights that they entitle their owner, and those authorised by their owner, to do certain things and to restrict others from doing so. Under intellectual property law, viewed in isolation, the owner of an intellectual property right is entitled to grant licences on particular terms to licensees in certain territories and to other licensees in other territories on entirely different terms; he is entitled to refuse to give a licence at all.

It is a fundamental principle of the Treaty of Rome, however, by which the EU (or its original predecessor) was constituted, that so far as possible there should be an unrestricted market within the Community and that actions having a contrary effect should so far as possible be forbidden.

The conflict

There is therefore a clear conflict between the principles of intellectual property law and the principles underlying the Treaty of Rome. The Treaty itself acknowledges the issue without very satisfactorily resolving it. That has been left to the courts, and the position is still developing.

Articles 30 and 36

Article 30 of the Treaty of Rome prohibits restrictions on imports between member states and measures having equivalent effect. The enforcement of intellectual property rights in national courts may amount to 'measures having equivalent effect'. Article 30 is, however, qualified by art 36. This permits restrictions on imports where they can be justified on specific grounds, including the protection of intellectual property rights. However, the exemption does not apply where 'prohibitions or restrictions . . . constitute a means of arbitrary discrimination or a disguised restriction on trade between member states'. There are similar provisions in relation to the provision of services in arts 59 and 65.

Articles 85 and 86

Article 85 of the Treaty of Rome relates to agreements between undertakings, decisions of associations of undertakings and concerted practices which 'may affect trade between member states and the object and effect of which is to prevent, restrict or distort competition within the Common Market'. Article 85(1) prohibits such agreements, decisions and practices. However, under art 85(3), the Commission reserves the right to exempt from art 85(1) particular agreements or categories of agreement where they can be economically justified, if they contribute towards promoting technical or economic progress, while allowing consumers a fair share of the resulting benefit, provided also that they do not impose on the undertakings concerned restrictions which are not indispensable to the achievement of these objectives, nor afford them the possibility of eliminating competition in a substantial part of the products in question. The Commission may grant exemption in particular cases, or may grant an exemption in relation to a class of transactions having the same characteristics; the latter is called a 'block exemption'.

Article 86 restricts companies from exploiting monopoly positions within the EU in relation to particular types of goods or services, where the monopoly is abused and competition is restricted.

All franchises involve licences of copyright and trade marks; they all impose restrictions on the licensee as to its exercise of its rights under the licence, and questions always therefore arise in relation to art 85. There is no block exemption under art 85(3) relating specifically to licences of copyright or trade mark licences. There is, however, a block exemption in relation to franchising, and that provides which restrictions are and which are not to be regarded as consistent with art 85, both in relation to intellectual property rights and otherwise. This will be dealt with in detail in Chapter 16.

Article 86 raises the conflict between the Treaty of Rome and intellectual property law in stark form. All intellectual property rights put their proprietors in a 'monopoly position' in relation to those rights. Intellectual property encourages creative and inventive people to acquire those monopoly rights in order to make worthwhile the work required to develop the business which flows from those rights. Article 86, however, restricts severely how monopoly rights may be exercised.

A number of cases have dealt with this issue, most recently the *Magill* case (*RTE* v *Commission*, C-241/91P and *ITP* v *Commission*, C-242/91P) where the final judgment was delivered as this work went to press. A distinction is drawn between, on the one hand, the existence of monopoly rights arising under intellectual property law and, on the other, the way in which they were exercised. Exercise of a monopoly derived from an intellectual property right does not necessarily infringe art 86. There need to be particular economic circumstances and a restriction of competition by the owner of the right amounting to abuse.

A franchisor undoubtedly owns a monopoly in the bundle of intellectual property rights making up the franchise system. It is intrinsic to a franchise that those rights are made available to franchisees, but they may be offered on terms which are regarded by prospective franchisees as unpalatable, and sometimes a franchise may be refused outright however apparently well qualified a prospective franchisee may be. A fast food franchisor may not, for example, want more than one of his outlets, however excellent, in the same high street.

These are situations in which, translated into other commercial arenas, challenges have been mounted under art 86. It appears that no aspiring but disappointed franchisee has so far chanced his arm. If he did, it is by no means certain that the courts would regard the refusal to grant a franchise as an abuse sufficient to justify invoking the article; certainly not in all circumstances. If, in our example of the fast food franchise, the prospective franchisee was unable to secure the burger franchise of his choice, but could easily get a pizza one, the courts might feel that the burger franchisor did not have enough of a real monopoly to justify the complaint. Indeed, some would argue that it was hard to envisage any franchise which amounted to a monopoly to which art 86 would be relevant.

A company which owns intellectual property and as a result has a significant monopoly may be subject to challenge under art 86. A franchisor's relations with its franchisees can be regulated with relative certainty under the franchising block exemption. It may nevertheless be subject to challenge from competitors under art 86 and that, of course, affects both franchisors and franchisees.

10.11   Minor rights

Since the ingenuity of franchisors is unlimited, there is no limiting the types of intellectual property which might come into play in a franchise. This work concentrates on copyright, trade marks, registered and unregistered, and confidentiality.

10.12   Patents

The most significant area which is not covered in this work is the law relating to patents, since the present scope of franchising transactions does not merit a full discussion of patent law. It is however possible to envisage circumstances in which patent law might be relevant. If a franchisor were the proprietor of a patent in relation to an invention a franchisee would, in very simple terms, require a licence under the patent to make and sell the object, but it would not require a licence simply to buy the object from the franchisor and use it. Questions of patent law would therefore arise if a franchisor were to patent a particular recipe and authorise franchisees to prepare and sell food in accordance with that recipe. They would not, however, arise if a franchisor were to require franchisees to buy from it machinery, for example, which was covered by a patent, or even, which is possibly more likely, if the franchisor were to lease the machinery to the franchisees for the duration of their franchises.

Chapter 11

Trade Marks

Chapter 11

Trade Marks

11.1 Introduction

Trade marks usually form an essential part of the package of rights licensed under a franchise agreement. Trade marks enjoy a high degree of legal protection and, if used properly and renewed regularly, they can become assets which are capable of being used and licensed indefinitely.

English law offers two basic types of legal protection for trade marks:

(1) If a manufacturer or seller uses a trade mark in connection with goods or services for an appreciable length of time, or in circumstances where the mark is advertised and promoted extensively, that mark will become closely associated with those goods or services and the mark will be distinctive. The courts will then, in a passing-off action, allow the owner of the mark to prevent competitors from using the mark in connection with the same or similar goods or services. Passing-off actions are dealt with later in this chapter. Compared with registered trade mark protection, the passing-off action is inferior, but it is nonetheless valuable where a trade mark owner wishes to prevent unfair trade practices by competitors where the mark is either not registered or is for some reason incapable of registration.

(2) Extensive protection against the misuse of a trade mark by competitors can be obtained by registering it at the UK Trade Mark Registry. An application for registered trade mark protection has to be made in respect of specified goods or services. The owner of a registered trade mark has a range of rights and remedies conferred by trade mark law to prevent unauthorised uses of the mark by a competitor.

A limited and often overvalued degree of protection can be obtained by including a name or mark in respect of which exclusivity is sought in a corporate name registered at Companies House. The only protection conferred by this is that the Registrar of Companies will not allow another company with an identical or almost identical name to be registered with Companies House.

The preparation of this work has coincided with the first major overhaul of trade mark law in the UK for over 55 years. On 21 July 1994 the Trade Marks Act 1994 (TMA 1994) was enacted, repealing the Trade Marks Act 1938 and the Trade Marks (Amendment) Act 1984. It came into effect on 31 October 1994. References in this chapter to sections are to sections of the TMA 1994.

11.2   Conditions for registration

11.2.1   Definition of a trade mark

Before devising a mark or a series of marks, it is wise to consider what will be accepted for registration, and the categories of mark which will not be accepted. Section 1(1) of the TMA 1994 states that 'trade mark' means 'any sign capable of being represented graphically which is capable of distinguishing goods or services of one undertaking from those of other undertakings'; a trade mark may consist of, among other things, 'words (including personal names), designs, letters, numerals or the shape of goods or their packaging'.

11.2.2   Grounds for refusing registration

Registration may be refused on absolute (s 3) or relative (s 5) grounds.

Absolute grounds

Absolute grounds relate to the nature of a mark itself. A mark will not be registrable:

(a) where it is not a trade mark; in other words if it is not a sign which is capable of being represented graphically and is not capable of distinguishing goods or services;

(b) where it is devoid of any distinctive character, consists of signs or other *indicia* which refer to the nature, quality, geographical origin or other characteristics of the goods or services to which it is applied, or has become what is sometimes referred to as generic (s 3(1)), unless the mark has in fact acquired a distinctive character as a result of the use made of it;

(c) where the shape of a three dimensional mark arises from the goods themselves or is necessary to obtain a technical result or gives substantial value to the goods (s 3(2)).

The Act identifies other categories of mark which may not be registered for what can loosely be described as public policy reasons. A mark will not be registrable if it:

(a) offends accepted principles of morality;

(b) is of such a nature as to deceive the public or is prohibited by law (domestic or EU) (s 3(3));

(c) is applied for in bad faith (s 3(6)).

Relative grounds

These grounds concern the registrability of marks relative to potentially con-flicting earlier rights, now making the test of registrability the corollary of the test of infringement. Under the old Act, the fact that goods or services fell outside the specification of goods or services of an earlier mark did not mean that the new user of the mark could register for those goods or services, as these may have been regarded as goods of the same description rendering the mark unregistrable.

A trade mark will not now be registered if:

(a) it is identical with an earlier trade mark and is to be registered for iden-tical goods or services as an earlier mark (s 5(1));

(b) it is identical with an earlier trade mark and is to be registered for similar goods or services as an earlier mark, or it is similar to an earlier trade mark and to be registered for identical or similar goods or services, and as a result there exists a likelihood of public confusion, including a like-lihood of association (s 5(2));

(c) it is identical with or similar to an earlier trade mark and is to be regis-tered for goods or services which are not similar to those for which the earlier mark is registered if the earlier trade mark has a reputation in the UK and use, without due cause, would take unfair advantage of or be detrimental to the dinstinctive character or repute of the mark (s 5(3)). This is the first statutory recognition of the concept of dilution whereby use of a trade mark by a third party can devalue the original trade mark, even though it is used for different goods or services. How reputation is to be measured by the UK courts remains to be seen, but it is likely that evidence, similar to that currently used in passing-off actions, will be required to establish acquired distinctiveness;

(d) its use is liable to be prevented because of earlier rights, such as unreg-istered trade mark rights, copyright, design right or registered design right (s 5(4)).

These provisions make it even more important for exploiters of rights (for example, character merchandisers) to ensure that they obtain all necessary per-missions from rights owners so that protection can be obtained and infringe-ment avoided.

A trade mark may be registered, in spite of the existence of earlier rights, if the proprietor of an earlier trade mark or other earlier rights consents (s 5(5)).

If the applicant can show that there has been honest concurrent use by him of a mark which, on its face, conflicts with an earlier trade mark or earlier right, the application will not be rejected on that ground, although the owner of the earlier mark can oppose this. The Act refers to the honest concurrent use provisions of the old Act. The law which applied under the old Act will therefore continue to be relevant (s 7).

A possible change in practice is foreshadowed in s 8. After ten years from the introduction of the Community Trade Mark the Secretary of State may order the Registry to ignore the relative grounds of refusal unless the owner of earlier rights opposes registration. This would give rise to a system for trade mark filing, as currently exists in many other European countries, whereby the Trade Mark Registries will examine applications only for absolute grounds of registrability. This should speed up and simplify the process of obtaining a trade mark, but the validity of the trade mark will, consequently, be less certain, leading to increased costs of subsequent opposition and invalidity proceedings. These drawbacks have led to some resistance from the UK Trade Marks Registrar and trade mark agents.

11.3   Choosing a mark

The skill in choosing the right trade mark is to produce one which will both be attractive in the market place and enjoy strong legal protection. Generally, the following basic principles should be followed when selecting marks for goods and services which are intended for registration:

(1) *Descriptive words:* It is often assumed by businesses that a mark should be as descriptive of the goods or services as possible. In practice the opposite is the case, as a mark which is descriptive of the characteristics of the goods or services in question will not only be impossible or difficult to register, but will be difficult to enforce against a competitor, who can counterclaim that the mark is inherently non-distinctive and invalid.

(2) *Invented words:* From a legal point of view, probably the best mark is one comprising one or two words consisting of no more than three syllables which are easy to pronounce and to recognise. The classic example of a trade mark which satisfies this criterion is 'Kodak'. It is an invented word and did not, when coined, carry any obvious message about the nature of the products or services with which it was intended to be used. Now the name is associated with the products which the Kodak company provides.

(3) *Known words:* A known word, that is to say one generally found in a dictionary, is acceptable as a trade mark, but words which refer to any of the characteristics of the goods or services will be vulnerable. Examples of known words used as trade marks are 'Mars' and 'Jaguar'.

(4) *Devices, logos or other pictorial matter:* These are all acceptable as trade marks either in their own right or in combination with words or

182

names. Examples of famous device marks are the Rolls Royce 'Spirit of Ecstasy' and the 'Access' symbol.

When a prospective mark has been selected, searches can be made of the Trade Marks Register to establish not only whether the mark is likely to be registrable, but also if its use is likely to conflict with the rights of an existing mark owner.

It is also generally worthwhile searching the Companies Registry for competitor companies who may have developed protectable goodwill on the basis that they have traded under their corporate name.

It is also normally advisable to make searches in the trade to identify marks currently in use which are either identical or likely to be confused with the proposed new mark. Obvious sources of reference are local and national telephone directories and journals and directories associated with particular trades.

11.4   Classification of goods and services

An application for the registration of a trade mark must be made in respect of particular goods or services selected from the classification used by the UK Trade Marks Registry, which is the international classification compiled by the World Intellectual Property Organisation listing classes of goods, 1–34, and services, 35–42.

When a trade mark is registered, the exclusive right of the owner of that mark relates essentially to the goods or services comprised in the registration, known as the 'specification'. (It is not quite that simple, *see* 11.7 *below* for a more detailed discussion of the rules relating to infringement.) Applicants for trade marks must ensure that all the goods or services in respect of which they require exclusivity in the use of the mark are included in the specification submitted with the application. Specifications of non-UK trade marks should not be repeated verbatim in a UK trade mark application as the UK specifications are, by contrast with some countries like the US, fairly broad in scope. Further, when the mark is already in use, it should not be represented as having been registered before and unless that is so; and registration of the mark must not be claimed in relation to goods or services which are not covered by the specification of the registration, as each such representation or claim constitutes a criminal offence under the TMA 1994, s 95.

11.5   Registering a trade mark

11.5.1   Proprietorship

Section 32(3) of the TMA 1994 provides that when an application for a registered trade mark is made, the application shall state that the trade mark is being used by the applicant or with his consent in relation to those goods or services the subject of the registration, or that the applicant has a bona fide intention that it should be so used.

Questions may arise whether the applicant owns all rights to the mark *vis-à-vis* its originator. Where a mark is originated by an employee of the applicant there is normally no problem. However, if a mark is originated by somebody other than an employee of the applicant, such as a consultant or outside designer, rights may remain with the originator unless the applicant obtains confirmation of ownership by means of a written agreement with the originator. This is particularly important in the case of device marks, the drawings of which may enjoy copyright protection, and which may be assigned by means of a written agreement only.

11.5.2   The procedure

The formalities for making applications for registration and the prosecution of applications before the Trade Mark Registry are governed by the Trade Marks Rules 1994 (SI 1994 No 2583).

Applications have to be filed in accordance with the Registry's prescribed procedures and fees are payable in respect of each application for the registration of a mark in each class of goods or services. Applications may specify more than one class. Although it is open to an applicant to file an application himself, it is normally advisable to retain the services of a trade mark agent or solicitor to file and prosecute an application.

The prescribed fees payable at the time of the filing of the application are the only fees payable for first registration. Further fees become payable only at the time of the renewal of the registration of the trade mark.

Once an application for the registration of a trade mark has been filed with the Trade Mark Registry the application passes through a number of stages, leading to the grant of a registration for the mark. Typically, this procedure will take anything between 12 and 18 months. Difficult applications often take longer, particularly if hearings before the Registrar become necessary.

11.5.3   The Register

Before the passing of the TMA 1994, the UK Register of Trade Marks was divided into Parts A and B. Part A registration constituted a superior form of registration. The distinction between Part A and Part B of the Register was a rather intricate matter, but essentially a mark was capable of being registered in Part B of the Register if it did not comply with all of the requirements of s 9 of the Trade Marks Act 1938, but was nevertheless capable of distinguishing the goods in respect of which it was registered from other goods. One legal difference was that a Part A registration was incapable of being challenged after seven years, but a registration in Part B of the Register was capable of being challenged at any time.

The TMA 1994 abolished the distinction between Part A and Part B registrations, so that all future registrations are now in a single register. This is in keeping with the abolition of the previous requirements of a high degree of distinctiveness for registration of a trade mark in Class A.

11.5.4 Term of protection

Once registered, a trade mark will enjoy a potentially unlimited period of protection, provided registration is renewed. Since the passsing of the TMA 1994 the initial period of protection is ten years (formerly seven) from the date of the grant of the trade mark, with subsequent renewals due each ten years (formerly 14) thereafter.

11.5.5 Famous marks

The TMA 1994 provides that a mark which is treated as a 'well known' mark within the meaning of the Paris Convention is capable of blocking the registration of an identical or substantially similar new registration. In addition, for the first time in the UK, the proprietor of a well known mark has the right, by virtue of the TMA 1994, to restrain the use of the same or a similar mark on the same or similar goods if it is likely that such usage will cause confusion.

The protection of famous marks has been introduced into UK Trade Mark Registry law in (rather belated) compliance with art 6 of the Paris Convention of 20 March 1883 (as amended). Article 6 of the Paris Convention provides as follows:

> ... the countries of the Union undertake, ex officio if their legislation so permits, or at the request of an interested party, to refuse or to cancel the registration, and to prohibit the use, of a trade mark which constitutes a reproduction, an imitation, or a translation, liable to create confusion, of a mark considered by the competent authority in the country of registration or use to be well known in that country as being already the mark of a person entitled to the benefits of this Convention and used for identical or similar goods. These provisions shall also apply when the essential part of the mark constitutes a reproduction of any such well known mark or an imitation liable to create confusion therewith.

The enactment of art 6 in UK domestic law has considerable benefits for overseas franchisors, and indeed for all businesses with distinctive trading styles or strong brands. It means in practice that the UK Trade Mark Registry will reject applications for marks which are identical or likely to be confused with internationally well known trading styles or brands. It also gives the owners of these

185

names and brands the right to make representations to the Registry at the application stage or, in the case of a registered mark, to seek the removal of the trade mark from the Register. Owners of well known marks are therefore well advised to arrange for a watching brief in respect of new applications.

11.5.6   The Madrid Protocol

The Madrid Protocol is a proposal to establish a new international trade mark registration system which will exist in parallel with the existing Madrid Agreement for the International Registration of Trade Marks. The UK has refused to become a signatory to the Madrid Agreement, but has indicated a desire to accede to the Madrid Protocol and the Act contemplates the UK's participation.

If the UK does accede to the Madrid Protocol, it will then be possible for businesses based in the UK to obtain a portfolio of international trade mark registrations through a single application. This contrasts with the existing arrangements where separate applications have to be made in each country where protection is sought.

Likewise, it will be possible for businesses in other Madrid Protocol signatory states to obtain UK trade mark protection by filing applications overseas, designating the UK for trade mark protection.

11.6   Trade marks for services

11.6.1   Retail services

Marks for the provision of retail services, that is to say shop names, have been traditionally refused trade mark (formerly 'service mark') protection in the UK and the TMA 1994 retains that position. The attitude of the UK Trade Mark Registrar has been that the essence of retailing is the sale of goods rather than the provision of a service.

The protection of retail services by means of service mark protection was the subject of the test case *Re Dee Corporation plc* [1990] RPC 159. The case was decided under the old law but remains authoritative. In the case it was stated that services which were merely incidental to or an adjunct to the retail selling of goods, and which it was not the business or trade of the applicant to provide, would not support a service mark application since the constituents of the retail services relied on for registration were ancillary to and part and parcel of the function of trading in goods.

It is, however, open to retailers to seek trade mark protection in respect of branded goods sold in the store. It is not uncommon for retailers operating under franchises to seek extensive trade mark protection for their full range of products and to promote the marks extensively on in-store stationery, packaging and advertising.

11.6.2   The leasing of goods

The UK Trade Mark Registry has indicated an unwillingness to register trade marks in respect of the leasing of goods.

11.7   The licensing of trade marks

11.7.1   General

Licensing consists of the granting of permission to a third party to use a trade mark on agreed terms. The licensing of trade marks in the UK has been considerably simplified as a result of some of the changes introduced by the TMA 1994. In particular, the TMA 1994 made the following changes to the previous law and practice of licensing:

(a)   the creation of an express statutory right to grant sub-licences (s 28(4));
(b)   the abolition of the recording of licensees as 'registered users';
(c)   the removal on the prohibition on 'trafficking' in trade marks.

One consequence of the abolition of registered user agreements is the loss of the legal presumption that the use of a mark by a registered user is deemed to be use by the proprietor. Contractual controls on the use of the mark, and the means of ensuring that any goodwill generated by the use of a mark by a licensee accrue to the proprietor, are therefore now much more important.

Section 46(1) of the TMA 1994 provides that any use by a third party, whether formally appointed as a licensee or not, with the proprietor's consent, will be deemed to be use by the proprietor for the purposes of attacks on the mark of the sort described on p 189.

11.7.2   Statutory provisions

Under the Trade Marks Act 1938, licensees who were permitted by the owner to use a trade mark 'could be recorded as registered users'. This rather cumbersome practice was abolished by the TMA 1994, which now provides a much more straightforward basis for the grant of trade mark licences. The provisions are set out in ss 28(1)–(4) (inclusive). Each of the four subsections is considered separately *below*.

Section 28(1) of the TMA 1994 provides as follows:

(1)   A licence to use a registered trade mark may be general or limited.
      A limited licence may, in particular, apply—

(a) in relation to some but not all of the goods or services for which the trade mark is registered, or

(b) in relation to use of the trade mark in a particular manner or a particular locality.

Subsection 28(1)(*a*) makes it clear that a licence may be granted for part or all of the goods or services contained in the specification of the registration. Subsection 28(1)(*b*) gives statutory authority for the long-standing practice of franchisors, among others, of granting trade mark licences subject to certain restrictions, for example for use only in connection with the conduct of a business from particular premises or for its use within a particular geographical locality.

Section 28(2) provides as follows: 'A licence is not effective unless it is in writing signed by or on behalf of the grantor'. An oral licence to use a trade mark is not a valid licence at law, although the purported licensee may be a user of the mark for the purposes of s 46. It is essential to both franchisors and franchisees that a licence of a trade mark is recorded in a written agreement signed by the franchisor. From the franchisor's point of view, the absence of a written licence may have consequences which could jeopardise the validity of the mark. From the franchisee's perspective, the absence of a written agreement signed by a franchisor leaves the franchisee open to a claim for infringement.

Section 28(3) provides that: 'Unless the licence provides otherwise, it is binding on a successor in title to the grantor's interest'. It will be fairly uncommon for an agreement containing a trade mark licence to provide that the licence granted by the proprietor of the trade mark does not bind an assignee of the trade mark. This subsection also emphasises the importance to a franchisee of a written agreement.

Section 28(4) provides as follows: 'Where the licence so provides a sub-licence may be granted by the licensee; and references in this Act to a licence or licensee include a sub-licence or sub-licensee'. The TMA 1994 introduced into UK trade mark law the sub-licensing of trade marks. The absence of an express right to sub-license has in the past complicated agreements with master franchisors in the UK, particularly where the trade marks to be used by the ultimate sub-franchisees are registered in the name of the franchisor.

11.7.3   Registration of licences

Although the TMA 1994 dispenses with the previous system for recording registered user agreements, it is still possible to register a licence on the Register of Trade Marks by submitting particulars to the Trade Marks Registry.

Before the enactment of the TMA 1994, the principal reason why the owner of a trade mark would wish to register a licensee of a widely used trade mark as a registered user was to emphasise its ownership of the mark and the goodwill generated by it, both to the franchisee and to the public at large. The benefits to a trade mark owner of the registration of licences are less obvious under the new regime.

In contrast, there is a possible advantage to be gained by a franchisee from recording its licence at the Trade Mark Registry. This is particularly so where a licensee wishes to enjoy the right to institute infringement proceedings against third parties and to claim damages. Section 30 of the TMA 1994 gives licensees certain rights to bring proceedings for infringement by third parties. These rights may be excluded by contract and, in franchise arrangements, nearly always will be.

11.8 Revocation

A registered trade mark can be revoked or invalidated in certain circumstances. The grounds for revocation are (s 46):

(a) five years' non-use;
(b) suspended use for five years;
(c) the trade mark has become generic in consequence of acts or inactivity of the proprietor;
(d) the trade mark is liable to mislead the public as a result of use of it by the proprietor or with his consent. Use in a form which does not alter the distinctive character of the trade mark and use for export are regarded as use. However, use on similar goods (goods of the same description) will no longer constitute use. The relevant date for revocation will be the date of the application or such earlier date as the Registrar or court considers that grounds for revocation existed;
(e) bad faith on the applicant's part. Although it is not stated that, if an applicant has no bona fide intention to use the mark, it is a ground for invalidation, it is necessary to state in the application form that the mark is being used or that there is a bona fide intention to use the mark. If this statement were made but was not true, the trade mark could be declared invalid on the basis that the application was made in bad faith (s 32(3)). The Registrar can apply to the court for a declaration of invalidity (s 47(4));
(f) registration devoid of any distinctive character and not capable of distinguishing, ie not a trade mark. A trade mark can also be declared invalid if it was registered in breach of s 3(1)(*b*), (*c*) or (*d*) (*see* p 180 *et seq above*). If the mark is devoid of distinctive character, being descriptive of quality, quantity, etc or being a sign in the current language of or in the bona fide and established practices of trade, it will not be declared invalid if it has, after registration, acquired distinctiveness.

189

(g) an earlier mark exists. A trade mark can be declared invalid if the proprietor of an earlier right did not agree to the registration where there are the same or similar marks relating to the same or similar goods or services and there is a likelihood of confusion, unfair advantage or use detrimental to the repute of an earlier mark or other earlier intellectual property rights (s 47(2)).

If the proprietor has knowingly tolerated infringing use of a registered mark for five years he cannot apply for a declaration that a trade mark is invalid or object to the use unless the earlier mark was applied for in bad faith (s 48).

11.9   Infringement

The Department of Trade and Industry Press Release issued to introduce the TMA 1994 summarises the position on enforcement of trade marks as follows: 'The Act will provide wider infringement rights, making it easier for a business to protect valuable marks without having to resort to the complex and expensive common law action for passing-off'.

11.9.1   Elements of infringement

In each situation where registration can be refused, a trade mark owner can sue for infringement. The provisions are, however, broader, as infringement can be by a sign and is not restricted to signs which are registrable as marks. Infringement occurs if the following are used:

(a) an identical sign on identical goods (s 10(1));
(b) an identical sign on similar goods or a similar sign on identical or similar goods where, as a result, there is a likelihood of public confusion including the risk of association with the trade mark (s 10(2));
(c) identical or similar signs on non-similar goods if the mark has a reputation in the UK, and use, without due cause, would take unfair advantage of or be detrimental to the distinctive character or repute of the mark (s 10(3)).

11.9.2   What constitutes trade mark use

A trade mark is used, in particlar, by (s 10(4)):

(a) affixing it to goods or packaging;
(b) offering or exposing goods for sale, putting them on the market or stocking them under the mark or offering or supplying services under the mark;

(c) importing or exporting goods under the mark;

(d) using the mark on business papers or in advertising. This is important as this catches business names.

People who merely print labels or advertising material are also using the mark if they know or have reason to believe that this was not properly authorised (s 10(5)).

The definition of use is further extended to non-graphic use, so that speaking the mark aloud can amount to use. It is unclear whether this covers passive use, such as where a customer asks for a rum and Coke but is given Pepsi (s 103(2)).

11.9.3   Comparative advertising

Comparative advertising will now be permissible as s 10(6) of the TMA 1994 does not prevent the use of a registered trade mark by anyone to identify goods or services as those of the proprietor or licensee, provided that:

(a) it is in accordance with honest practices in industrial and commercial matters; and

(b) it does not, without due cause, take unfair advantage of, or is not detrimental to, the distinctive character or repute of the trade mark.

Clearly these provisions will be wide open to debate and the scope of comparative advertising may be limited, particularly if the comparative advertiser deliberately gives false information which would be actionable as a malicious falsehood.

11.9.4   Acts not amounting to infringement

Section 11(1) and (2) of the TMA 1994 provide that the following will not amount to infringement:

(a) the use of another registered trade mark in relation to goods or services for which that mark is registered;

(b) the use by a person of his own name or address;

(c) the use of indicia relating to the nature and quality or characteristics of goods or services;

(d) the use of a trade mark where it is necessary to indicate the intended purpose of a product or service (in particular, as accessories or spare parts)

if the use is in accordance with . . . honest practices in industrial or commercial matters.

Nor will a registered trade mark be infringed by the use, in the course of trade in a particular locality, of an earlier right which applies only in that locality. To take a hypothetical example, suppose a restaurant trading in Cornwall set up under the name McDonald before the McDonald's chain applied to register its own trade mark and had used that mark continuously ever since. In those circumstances no infringement would occur (s 11(3)), although an action in passing-off might be available to the Cornish restaurateur.

11.9.5 Minimising the risk of infringement

A range of practical steps can be taken to minimise the risk of infringing the trade mark owner's exclusive rights. The essential task is to establish, in the minds of customers, licensees and competitors, the proprietor's ownership, and exclusivity in and to the use of the mark.

(1) Registered trade marks should always be identified as such by the use of the ® symbol when the mark is registered or the ™ symbol when the mark is not registered, or the ™ symbol with a mark where registered protection has been applied for but has not yet been granted. In the case of particularly valuable marks or marks which are, for some reason, potentially vulnerable (for example because of the possibility that use may become generic) it may be advisable to be even more specific by, for example, including language such as '[name of mark] is a registered trade mark of [proprietor]'.

(2) As well as using the mark on the goods themselves there is merit in referring to the trade mark extensively in advertising. It is not uncommon to use advertising partly to promote the existence of the trade mark itself as distinct from the product carrying the mark. Evidence of advertising is also usually valuable evidence in trade mark infringement proceedings, particularly in answering defences of innocent infringement.

(3) When the mark is used in written text, it is not uncommon to print it in a way which emphasises its distinctiveness. The use of different-sized lettering, capitals, stylised lettering or even different colours for the mark itself, may be considered.

(4) It is important to develop a strategy for dealing with infringements as they arise. Equally, it is important to monitor applications for trade mark registration by competitors and, if appropriate, lodge oppositions. A number of companies provide trade mark owners with a watching service both within and outside the UK. The services offered are generally very flexible and range from the reporting of all applications made in a particular class to reporting only on applications made by a particular competitor. Given the quite modest charges made by watching firms, it is generally no bad thing to use their services, particularly in the case of franchisors with substantial trade mark holdings.

11.10   Unregistered marks: passing off

11.10.1   Importance of the remedy

The tort of 'passing off' is encapsulated in the time-honoured line, 'No man has a right to pass off his goods as though they were the goods of another'. This phrase identifies the heart of the tort of passing off: that there is a misrepresentation about the nature of the goods or services being provided by one trader to the extent that those goods or services are associated with another trader. Over time, the law of passing off has developed so that such misrepresentations are not limited to actual goods or services, but may extend to any false claim to a business connection by one trader with another which is calculated to cause damage to that other trader. An actionable passing off can readily arise in a franchising situation, particularly where an ex-franchisee is involved in making the misrepresentation, because passing off and franchising are closely linked in the sense that they are both concerned with the protection and exploitation of goodwill.

However, a misrepresentation alone will not be enough to amount to passing off and the other elements of the tort must be met. The plaintiff must establish a protectable goodwill within the jurisdiction, and that the defendant's actions amount to a deception causing damage to that goodwill or loss of sales.

From a franchising perspective, it is a prerequisite to determine who owns the goodwill which is generated by the franchisee's trading activities. Clearly, if the goodwill attaches solely to the business of the individual franchisee, the franchisor may find itself with no established goodwill on which to base an action for passing off, either against a third party competitor or a rogue ex-franchisee. The franchisor is ultimately responsible for the operating standards of the franchised system as a whole and the public's understanding of this fact. In these circumstances, the franchisor is the owner of the goodwill in the franchised system so far as the public is concerned. However, that is not to say that each individual franchise unit is incapable of generating its own goodwill. Over a period goodwill may be built by successful franchisees. Indeed, this goodwill is often the franchisee's principal asset. We will deal in greater detail with the nature and ownership of goodwill at p 195 *below*.

Having established goodwill, the franchisor must also show that there is, or is likely to be, damage to that goodwill as a result of the misrepresentation complained of. For example, damage may take the form of harm to the franchisor's reputation if the goods or services are inferior in quality, or it may result in the loss of the commercial opportunity to set up a franchise in the territory concerned.

In the context of franchising, the elements of passing off—goodwill, misrepresentation and damage—are usually reasonably clearly defined. It ought therefore to be possible to avoid some of the problems associated with passing off actions, such as the need to rely on survey evidence to establish reputation or a misrepresentation; the costs of survey evidence are often inversely proportional to the reliance placed on it by the courts.

11.10.2   Elements of passing off

The modern law of passing off is contained in the House of Lords decision in *Erven Warnink BV* v *J Townend & Sons (Hull) Ltd* [1979] AC 731 (the *Advocaat* case). This decision has, wrongly, assumed almost the status of an Act of Parliament in the blanket application of the judgments of Lord Diplock and, to a lesser extent, Lord Fraser. Lord Diplock looked at what a defendant had to do for his acts to amount to an actionable passing off, whereas Lord Fraser considered what a plaintiff had to establish in order to found a case in passing off.

Lord Diplock said:

> *Spalding* v *Gamage* and the later cases make it possible to identify five characteristics which must be present in order to create a valid cause of action for passing off: (1) a misrepresentation (2) made by a trader in the course of trade (3) to prospective customers of his or ultimate consumers of goods or services supplied by him, (4) which is calculated to injure the business or goodwill of another trader (in the sense that this is a reasonably foreseeable consequence) and (5) which causes actual damage to a business or goodwill of the trader by whom the action is brought or (in a *quia timet* action) will probably do so.

Lord Fraser said:

> [A plaintiff must show] (1) that his business consists of, or includes, selling in England a class of goods to which the particular trade name applies; (2) that the class of goods is clearly defined, and that in the minds of the public, or a section of the public, in England, the trade name distinguishes that class from other similar goods; (3) that because of the reputation of the goods, there is goodwill attached to the name; (4) that he, the plaintiff, as a member of the class of those who sell the goods, is the owner of goodwill in England which is of substantial value; (5) that he has suffered, or is really likely to suffer, substantial damage to his property in the goodwill by reason of the defendants selling goods which are falsely described by the trade name to which the goodwill is attached.

Two preliminary points should be made. First, neither of the passages quoted *above* should be taken as a definitive statement of passing off. Clearly, for example, passing off extends to matters other than the sale of goods as referred to by Lord Fraser. Second, while on a first reading the judgments appear to be complementary, they are not in fact, and are best regarded as a checklist of the

factors which are likely to be relevant in establishing whether or not an actionable passing off has occurred.

What is clear from the judgments of Lords Diplock and Fraser, and stated
with possibly greater succinctness in the *Jif Lemon* case, *Reckitt & Coleman
Products Ltd* v *Barden Inc* [1990] RPC 341, is the need for the three essential
elements before passing off can occur: goodwill, misrepresentation and
damage. Each element is examined separately in the sections that follow.

Goodwill

Goodwill is easier to imagine than define. Perhaps the most succinct definition
is that of Lord Macnaghten:

> What is goodwill? It is a thing very easy to describe, very difficult to
> define. It is the benefit and advantage of the good name, reputation, and
> connection of a business. It is the attractive force which brings in custom.
> It is the one thing which distinguishes an old-established business from
> a new business at its first start. The goodwill of a business must emanate
> from a particular centre or source. However widely extended or diffused
> its influence may be, goodwill is worth nothing unless it has power of
> attraction sufficient to bring customers home to the source from which it
> emanates.

Goodwill is a property right and can attach to a number of different facets of
the owner's business, the usual embodiments being a trade name, logo or 'get
up', and business premises. However, for the purposes of passing off it is not
necessary to dissect goodwill into its component parts. It is enough that the
plaintiff's goodwill as a whole or in part is damaged by the defendant's actions.

'Goodwill' and 'reputation' are not one and the same, although the terms are
often used as if they were interchangeable. This point can be illustrated by reference to the decision in *Anheuser-Buse Inc* v *Budejovicky Budvar NP* [1984]
FSR 413 (the *Budweiser* case). The plaintiffs, brewers of the well known
American beer *Budweiser*, attempted to restrain sales of beer in England
brewed by the defendants in Czechoslovakia (as it was then), even though this
was where the name had originated. At the time, the plaintiffs' beer, although
well known in England through exposure on television etc, was available for
sale only on American armed forces bases to which the general public did not
have access. The court held that although the plaintiffs' beer was well known
and so it had a reputation, because it was not available to the general public no
goodwill had accrued through a course of trade which was capable of being protected by passing off. While, therefore, it may be that a foreign franchisor has
a substantial reputation in its system or services, there is unlikely to be any protectable goodwill in this jurisdiction until it has established it through a course
of trading with the public. Nonetheless reputation is important in the sense that

the public, or a sufficient section of it, recognises the business of the plaintiff in which goodwill is claimed. With the introduction into UK trade mark law of the concept of the well known mark (*see* p 185), the attitude of the courts may develop in this area.

The level of trading which may be necessary to create protectable goodwill is a matter of degree depending on the nature and scale of the business activity concerned. For example, a prospective franchisor entering a territory for the first time will wish to know what protection he has in his 'get-up' or, as it is sometimes known, 'trade dress'. Equally, a competitor will wish to know whether he is safe in setting up a rival concern before the franchisor becomes established.

Mere advertising may be sufficient if a demand has been created by it and trade by the advertiser is imminent. However, preparing to trade (as opposed to advertising an intention to trade) is not enough to create goodwill. The position of the foreign franchisor is complicated by the fact that, as with other intellectual property rights, goodwill is territorial in nature. Goodwill created through many years of trading in, say, the USA cannot be transplanted into England and used as the basis for a passing-off action. Nevertheless, a franchisor need not be based in this jurisdiction; it is enough that its goods or services have been the subject of trade in the UK.

A useful illustration can be found in *Sheraton Corp of America* v *Sheraton Motels Ltd* [1964] RPC 202. The plaintiff had hotels in the USA and elsewhere but not in England. However, reservations for the hotels were regularly made through travel agents' offices in England and through the plaintiff's own office in London. The court held that this level of trading activity was sufficient to sustain a protectable goodwill. The greater the reputation of the plaintiff, the lower the level of trading which will be necessary to persuade the court that a protectable goodwill exists.

Goodwill can also exist regionally. If a trader's customers are all located in a clearly defined area the associated goodwill extends only to that area. While the courts will not readily confine goodwill in this way except in the clearest instances, a prospective franchisor should be aware of the potential dangers of setting up a localised franchise if the nature of the business is such that the franchise and its customers will be confined to a very specific area. As a precautionary measure in these circumstances some form of national advertising should take place.

Establishing ownership of goodwill, particularly in franchising, may not be straightforward.

It is helpful to think of there being, in the context of franchising, two kinds of goodwill.

The first is that arising from the trade marks, trade names, systems, get-up and so on common to the whole of a franchise system. This belongs to the franchisor. This is partly because it is intrinsic to the rights granted by the franchisor to the franchisee, rights by way of licence to use these disparate but commercially linked elements of the franchise business for a fee and for a period; it is what the franchisee shares in during the period of its franchise and loses when the franchise ends. It is also partly, and more simply, because the franchise agreement will normally provide that that goodwill belongs to the franchisor.

The other goodwill essentially reflects the going concern value of the franchisee's business. At its simplest it is no more than an accountancy convention, reflecting the fact that the business of a franchisee may be worth more to a purchaser than its net asset value. This goodwill is of little relevance for the purposes of a passing-off claim. (*See* the discussion of the *Devaney* case in 17.4.)

In the case of goods (but less so with the provision of services) there may be a number of legally separate entities dealing in those goods before they reach the consumer. The consumer may have no dealings with anyone other than the franchisee from whom the goods are purchased. But the goodwill in the goods belongs to whoever is, in reality, responsible for the quality and character of the goods, or whoever the public regards as being responsible. In franchising it is generally the case that the franchise system is operated under or by reference to a name, mark, logo, get-up or a combination of these, and it is in relation to these indicia, rather than particular goods or services, that the question of ownership of goodwill usually arises.

Nevertheless it may be desirable to join the franchisee as a co-plaintiff in any action, to avoid any doubt being cast by the defendant on the existence and ownership of goodwill. The ability to do this will be expressly provided for in a well drawn franchise agreement.

Misrepresentation

The misrepresentation must amount to more than a mere aside; that is, it must be believed by those to whom it is addressed and those persons must place reliance on it. In other words, there must be a deception on the relevant section of the public.

In franchising, the misrepresentation normally arises in one of two ways. First, there is the misrepresentation by a third party trader that it is a member of a franchise network, and second, there is the misrepresentation by an ex-franchisee that it is still a member of a franchise network. The misrepresentation is often made by the unlicensed use of the indicia of the franchised system (or indicia which are colourably similar), or by a false statement to consumers to the effect that the third party trader is associated with the franchised business.

As stated *above*, there must be a deception in the representations made. If the individual to whom the representation is addressed is not deceived by it, then there is no passing off.

Deceptive intent is not necessary in making the misrepresentation, although that will usually be the case. Indeed, neither negligence, recklessness or fraud are necessary, so that the situation is very different from, say, trade libel or malicious falsehood which require the presence of malice, and so intent or at least 'reckless indifference'.

The third party must make the misrepresentation in its capacity as a trader (used in its widest sense). It follows that an individual acting in a private capacity cannot commit an act of passing off. There is no requirement for those concerned to be engaged in a common field of activity, but in franchising this will almost certainly be the case. The existence of a common field of activity may be importance in establishing whether there has been a misrepresentation. It is not conclusive, however, and its existence will not overcome other factors such as a strong dissimilarity between the parties' respective marks or other media which may negate passing off.

To whom must a misrepresentation be addressed? The short answer is the 'public'. Lord Diplock in the *Advocaat* case identified the addressee as the 'customer or ultimate consumer' of goods or services. While in most cases it will be apparent whom the public consists of, an important distinction is to be made where the alleged misrepresentation is made to suppliers or others in the chain of distribution before the goods or services concerned reach the retail customers or ultimate consumer. Such individuals are likely to be more knowledgeable about the goods or services concerned and are likely to be less susceptible to being deceived as the result of a misrepresentation. It is therefore important to be able to identify the relevant class of individuals to whom the alleged misrepresentation is being made and to show that they are more (or less, if the defendant) likely to be deceived.

A misrepresentation can be made in a number of ways and in a variety of circumstances, from a direct misrepresentation to 'reverse' or 'inverse' passing off. In the latter case a defendant uses the plaintiff's actual goods to sell his own goods, rather than representing falsely that his goods are those of the plaintiff.

The franchise agreement generally gives the franchisee permission to use, *inter alia*, the franchisor's trade mark or get-up and know-how, and provides for the many other controls necessary to operate the system. Accordingly, a misrepresentation often made by an ex-franchisee is that it is licensed to operate the system by the franchisor (manifested by use of the franchisor's marks or get-up, or of those which are confusingly similar).

However, in fact, the ex-franchisee will be in the business of providing actual goods or services (pursuant to the system), whereas the franchisor is in the business of licensing its system (often supplying its franchisees with the means to operate it). Indeed, the franchisor does not usually compete with its franchisees or ex-franchisees, unless it could be said to do so by the operation of outlets which it owns. Therefore, in order to give the franchisor a sufficient nexus, the ownership of the goodwill must be said to vest in the person (the franchisor) with the overall responsibility for maintaining the operation of the system in the eyes of the public; the misrepresentation therefore arises where, say, an ex-franchisee holds itself out to the public as being the licensee of the franchisor in whom, in the eyes of the public, ultimate responsibility for the goods or services in question rests. This position is strengthened because of the public's perception of the close relationship between franchisor and franchisee.

Distinctiveness

The franchisor must be able to establish that its mark or get-up, or whatever way it says its goodwill is capable of being recognised and misrepresented, is distinctive of it. The mark or get-up of the franchisor will usually be the most recognisable (and therefore valued) aspect of the franchise system to the public. At first glance it ought to be relatively straightforward to show that the franchisor's mark or get-up is distinctive of it. Distinctiveness is usually established through use in the course of trade in the territory over time. As has already been seen in connection with the establishment of goodwill, the extent of use is also relevant in this regard. Further, in the case of descriptive (as opposed to distinctive) marks or get-up, the franchisor will need to establish that it has acquired a 'secondary meaning' which is distinctive and associated with it. These matters can be decided only on the circumstances and facts of each case.

A common problem associated with franchising in particular is the understandable desire of a franchisor to adopt a mark or get-up which is descriptive of its business or is in some other way generic. While anything is capable of being distinctive for the purposes of passing off, relatively small differences in marks or get-up of a descriptive nature will be sufficient to persuade the court that no passing off has occurred. Indeed, if the purported mark or get-up used is generic, then it is incapable of ever becoming distinctive whatever the scale and length of use. If the mark or get-up is a combination of the distinctive and generic, it is the distinctive part on which an action for passing off will be based.

In assessing distinctiveness it is not necessary to show that all members of the relevant 'public' regard the franchisor's mark as being distinctive of it but only that a significant proportion do so. The test of distinctiveness is a common sense test. It does not amount to a detailed comparison of the plaintiff's and defendant's marks or get-up side by side but takes account of the public's 'imperfect recollection' and of the overall impression left on the mind.

Distinctiveness may be lost by third parties using the mark or get-up of the franchisor or something which is colourably similar. Alternatively, a less than diligent but successful franchisor may forfeit distinctiveness by allowing the use of its mark or get-up to become generic in the minds of the public.

Damage

The need to prove damage to the plaintiff's goodwill is the last element required to complete the tort of passing off. This requirement is formulated in the decisions of both Lords Diplock and Fraser in the *Advocaat* case. Unless damage is

199

shown, a misrepresentation will not give the rights owner a cause of action. It is not necessary to prove actual damage so long as the likelihood of damage can be demonstrated. This must, however, be a likelihood of real or substantial damage.

Damage to a franchisor's business can arise in a number of ways. The first is the actual or potential loss of profit on sales, as the plaintiff and defendant in a franchising context will be in direct competition with each other. The second is damage caused as a result of the inferiority of the defendant's goods or services. The potential for harm is clear where the basis of the franchise network rests on the high regard in which the operation of the system by its franchisees is held by the public. The third is the loss of franchising opportunity, in other words the loss of an opportunity to enter into a franchise for the territory concerned with a third party because of the defendant's activities. Lastly, dilution of the franchisor's mark or get-up may also prove to be a significant head of damage.

In practical terms, franchisors should seek to rely on passing off only where they do not have registered trade marks to rely on or, where for some reason, both are appropriate. It can be difficult to obtain guidance from the decided cases, because many rely on particular facts. Establishing evidence of goodwill and misrepresentation can be difficult. Survey evidence is usually expensive to obtain and can prove unreliable. The scope of passing off is uncertain.

Chapter 12

Confidential Information and Trade Secrets

Chapter 12

Confidential Information and
Trade Secrets

12.1   Introduction

Confidential information, know-how and trade secrets—the terms are in practice interchangeable to some extent—are valuable assets. Like most other intellectual property rights, they are assets which have to be nurtured, or they fade
away.

12.1.1   Know-how

Franchisors lay out time, skill and effort, and invest money, in developing and
operating effective and profitable business systems. These systems may comprise methods of distributing, merchandising, packaging, promoting and marketing, which are used in connection with the sale of products or in the
provision of services. They may encompass a distinct design, decor or colour
scheme for premises, a layout for equipment or furniture, or procedures in
accounting, inventory control and management. All these specialised techniques may give the franchisor a competitive edge. Collectively, this amounts
to a body of non-patentable, probably non-copyright, information assembled by
the franchisor through its own trial and error. This is the franchisor's 'know-
how' (to use a modern word, which postdates many of the cases under which
it is protected).

It is inherent in franchising that the franchisee uses the franchisor's know-
how without having to undergo the franchisor's trial and error all over again.
This is not the least part of what the franchisee pays its fees for.

To preserve the franchisor's reputation, and as a means of maintaining uni-
formly high standards, franchisees are obliged to conduct their businesses in
strict accordance with the know-how made available.

The know-how will be made known not only to the franchisee; it will also
be acquired by others. Franchisees which are companies are often controlled by
one or two individuals. The individuals will acquire the know-how, but without

the personal right to use it. Conventionally, they will often be parties to the franchise agreement, as guarantors of the franchisee's obligations generally. The franchisee's employees, through their exposure to the franchisor's system, will also acquire the know-how. The franchisor will want to be protected against the unlawful use or disclosure of its know-how. This chapter examines the extent to which know-how can be protected under the law relating to confidential information and trade secrets.

12.1.2   Protection of know-how

We deal in Chapter 13 with the protection of know-how under copyright law. Patent protection is also available in principle, but in practice it is unlikely that a franchisor's know-how will be inventive enough to qualify. Even if it is, patent protection may not be cost-effective and protection would be limited to the inevitably narrow ambit of the patent claim. In practice, therefore, know-how has to be protected under the law of confidence, and that depends on the arrangements which the parties make between themselves. Unlike copyright, nothing very satisfactory arises automatically by way of intellectual property; contrary to popular belief, know-how is not protected as a matter of routine and the law of confidence has to be made to cover it if it is to be covered at all.

12.1.3   Confidentiality of know-how

Once information is classed as confidential, the recipient of that information must keep it confidential and must not use it to the detriment of the person who passed it on. In other words, the recipient of confidential information must not give that information to others and must not use it himself.

Confidential information can be protected in two ways. The first is by contract and the second is under general law. In franchising, the first is more important; practically all franchising arrangements are made by written contract, and most such contracts will incorporate obligations of confidentiality.

12.2   Protection by contract

Contractual provisions typically restrict the use and disclosure of certain information and contain wording restricting franchisees from running a competing business during and after the franchise term. The restricted information will comprise the franchisor's know-how—the business system and, specifically, the contents of the operations manual—and private information which the franchisee may acquire about the franchisor's own business and structure.

Any use of specified information may be effectively restricted by contract, subject only to general provisions of contract law. The most significant in this area relate to restraint of trade.

12.2.1   Restraint of trade

Express provisions in a franchise agreement protecting confidentiality are often combined with terms which restrict the ability of the franchisee to compete with the franchisor during or after the termination of the agreement. The franchisee is frequently forbidden to be involved in a business similar to or competing with the franchisor's within a certain radius of the business premises, for a specified period. Such clauses fall into the category of covenants in restraint of trade.

The courts view restrictions of this sort unfavourably and they will uphold them only if they are no wider than is reasonably necessary to protect the franchisor's interests, in terms of the activities covered, the geographical area to which the restriction extends and the length of time it lasts. As stated by Lord Macnaghten in *Nordenfelt* v *Maxim Nordenfelt Guns and Ammunition Co* [1894] AC 535, HL:

> The public have an interest in every person's carrying on this trade freely: so has the individual. All interference with individual liberty in trading, and all restraints of trade themselves, if there is nothing more, are contrary to public policy and therefore void. That is the general rule. But there are exceptions: restraint of trade and interference with individual liberty of action may be justified by the special circumstances of a particular case. It is sufficient justification, and indeed, it is the only justification if the restraint is reasonable—reasonable, that is, in reference to the interests of the parties concerned, and reasonable in reference to the interests of the public, so framed and so guarded as to afford adequate protection to the party in whose favour it is imposed, while at the same time it is in no way injurious to the public.

A distinction is made between restraints imposed on employees and restrictions on others. The distinction is based on public policy which, in the case of employees, favours their continuing ability to use their general skills and knowledge, so that they can set up in business or work for another employer. Covenants restricting employees are therefore construed strictly and are often unenforceable. This does not apply between franchisor and franchisee but may apply between either franchisor and franchisee, on the one hand, and their own employees, on the other.

A franchisor can use a restraint clause only in so far as it is necessary to protect its legitimate business interests. One example of such an interest is the goodwill attached to a business. Another legitimate commercial interest which can be protected by a covenant in restraint of trade is a trade secret. Until recently trade secrets were not distinguished from other confidential information. In *Faccenda Chicken Ltd* v *Fowler* [1985] FSR 105, [1986] FSR 291 CA, and the cases which followed it, however, a distinction is drawn between trade secrets and 'information which is merely confidential'. The definition of trade secrets has been most carefully delineated in cases involving employees, and is discussed in more detail later in this chapter. The enforceability of restrictive covenants is dealt with in more detail in Chapter 15.

12.3   Protection under the general law

To err is human, and enough franchise lawyers are human to make it necessary to examine what would happen if a franchisor's contractual documents were to prove inadequate, and it was necessary to rely on the general law of confidentiality for protection of know-how.

There is considerable doubt how the obligation of confidence arises when not by contract. The best view is that the legal principles are based on Equity. Certainly they are not derived from statute. For the necessarily limited purposes of this work, we will leave it at that, and confine ourselves to the consequences.

12.3.1   Preconditions

A number of criteria must be fulfilled as a precondition for establishing a franchisee's liability for breach of a franchisor's confidence:

(1) The information must have the necessary quality of confidence about it.
(2) The information must have been imparted in circumstances under which a duty of confidentiality arises.
(3) There must be an actual or expected unauthorised use or disclosure of that information.

12.3.2   Nature of confidential information

The first question is what constitutes confidential information.

English law, unlike that of many other jurisdictions, makes no distinction between the various categories of information which may be protected against breach of confidence. On one hand, trivial gossip will not be deemed as having the requisite level of confidentiality, and on the other hand, information of a personal, commercial or technical nature will be. Confidential information encompasses specific details such as sales figures, lists of customers and price lists, marketing and managerial procedures and information concerning the business system—the know-how discussed *above*—technological secrets and personal and other information, without any distinction as to subject matter.

Lord Greene MR, in the case of *Saltman Engineering* v *Campbell Co* (1948) 65 RPC 203, formulated a wide and easily satisfied test for confidentiality: confidential information is material which is neither public property nor within public knowledge. The standard of secrecy required is not absolute; relative secrecy suffices. The fact that the information in question may be known by rival businesses and their employees does not preclude a civil action for breach of confidence.

On the basis of Lord Greene's test, a franchisor's know-how will lose its confidential nature only if it becomes public property and forms part of the public's knowledge. The public for this purpose means those in the franchisor's trade. Lord Greene further stated that:

> it is perfectly possible to have a confidential document . . . which is the result of work done by the maker upon materials which may be available for the use of anybody; . . . what makes it confidential is the fact that the maker of the document has used his brain and thus produced a result which can only be produced by somebody who goes through the same process.

A slightly more stringent and subjective test of confidentiality was formulated in *Thomas Marshall* v *Guinle* [1978] 3 WLR 116 by Sir Robert Megarry VC, who identified the following four elements:

(1) The information must be information the release of which the owner believes would be injurious to him or of advantage to his rivals or others.
(2) The owner must believe the information is confidential or secret, that is, not already in the public domain.
(3) The owner's belief under the previous two heads must be reasonable.
(4) The information must be judged in the light of the usages and practices of the particular industry concerned.

12.3.3   Circumstances giving rise to confidentiality

The second question is when an obligation of confidence will arise. It is in fact easier to state the circumstances which will give rise to an obligation of confidence than those which do not. For example, doctor/patient, husband/wife and solicitor/client relationships all have obligations of confidence attached to them. Obligations of confidence also arise out of technical co-operation agreements and know-how licences, although it is likely that these agreements will deal with these obligations expressly.

Megarry J stated in *Coco* v *AN Clark* that where information of commercial or industrial value is given on a commercial basis, the recipient of the information has a heavy burden to discharge to refute the notion that he is bound by an obligation of confidence.

The tests

Two approaches are apparent from the cases. The objective test proposes that an obligation of confidence will arise whenever a reasonable man, standing in the shoes of the recipient of the information, would realise on reasonable grounds that the information was being given to him in confidence. Hence the importance of marking documents or other material 'confidential'.

A second test, known as the 'limited purpose test', can be used to identify the circumstances in which an obligation of confidence will arise. Under this test, an obligation arises whenever confidential information is disclosed for a limited purpose. The recipient of the information will then be under a duty to use the information for the limited purpose only and, if the recipient discloses or uses the information for any other purpose, he will be in breach of the obligation.

Employees

The obligation of confidence which arises under general law, as opposed to one imposed contractually, is different where employees are concerned. While the contract of employment subsists, the employee is bound by a duty of fidelity to the employer. The employee may not disclose confidential information acquired in the course of employment. This includes trade secrets and the confidential aspects of the employee's general knowledge and skill. Once a contract of employment is terminated, the position is different. The former employee is free to use general knowledge and skill, but is not free to exploit, without authorisation, the former employer's trade secrets. Trade secrets will continue to be protected by the employee's duty of fidelity. Other information, which would have been classified as merely confidential during employment, is no longer protected. A trade secret, at least in respect of employment cases, requires some higher degree of confidentiality to be categorised as such.

Neill LJ delivered the judgment of the Court of Appeal in *Faccenda Chicken v Fowler*. He stated that to determine if information can be protected by an implied obligation of confidence in a contract of employment, it was necessary to consider all the circumstances of the case, but the following matters were among those to which attention must be paid:

(1) The nature of the employment: employment in a capacity where confidential information is habitually handled may impose a high obligation of confidentiality, because employees could be expected to realise its sensitive nature to a greater extent than if they were employed in a capacity where material of that sort reached them only occasionally.

(2) The nature of the information: information would be protected only if it could properly be classed as the trade secret or, if not properly to be described as a trade secret, was in all the circumstances of such a highly confidential nature as to require the same protection as a trade secret. If information is restricted, and if it is specifically identified as comprising a trade secret, it will be easier for an employer to protect it as such.

As Butler-Sloss LJ said in the case of *Lansing Linde Ltd* v *Kerr* [1991] 1 All ER 418:

> We have moved into the age of multinational businesses and world-wide business interests. Information may be held by very senior executives which, in the hands of competitors, might cause significant harm to the companies employing them. 'Trade secrets' has, in my view, to be interpreted in a wider context of highly confidential information of a non-technical or nonscientific nature, which may become within the ambit of information the employer is entitled to have protected, albeit for a limited period.

Some information which an employee acquires, once learned, becomes part of the employee's own skill and knowledge, even if originally acquired in confidence. This category of information cannot be protected even by an express covenant. It is an essential principle that employees, after termination of their employment must be entitled to continue to use their general knowledge and skill. To restrain them from doing so would be contrary to public policy. In practice, of course, it is often difficult to draw the line between employees' general knowledge and skill and an employer's trade secret.

12.4 Third parties

Once a franchisor's confidential information is disclosed in breach of confidence, it may subsequently pass to third parties who may themselves use or disclose it. They may or may not receive the information knowing that it is confidential, or in circumstances where they ought to know.

A third party who receives information knowing it to be confidential might be liable under the general law of tort for inducing or procuring the breach of the franchisee's confidentiality obligations, or for unjustifiably interfering with the business relations between the franchisor and franchisee. If several recipients act collectively with the confidant to procure the disclosure this could constitute an actionable conspiracy.

Recipients of information who know or have reason to believe that it has been disclosed in breach of an obligation of confidence are bound to respect the confidentiality of the information in the same way as is the informant.

The legal position of an innocent third party is less clear. In the case of *Malone* v *Metropolitan Police Commissioner* [1979] Ch 344, Megarry VC said:

> If A makes a confidential communication to B, then A may not only restrain B from divulging or using the confidence, but also may restrain C from divulging or using it if C has acquired it from B even if he acquired it without notice of any impropriety . . . In such cases it seems

plain that, however innocent the acquisition of the knowledge, what will be restrained is the use or disclosure of it after notice of the impropriety.

There is, however, no conclusive authority in English law on the position of innocent third parties who are either bona fide purchasers for value of the information, or have in good faith changed their position in reliance on the information, for example, by installing equipment in the business premises in order to exploit a new business system.

Given this uncertainty it is advisable to include in franchise agreements wording requiring franchisees to obtain written confidentiality undertakings from third parties, preferably addressed directly to the franchisor.

12.5   Extinction of the duty of confidentiality

Generally, confidential information cannot be protected once it becomes public; it has to remain secret to be protectable. There is an exception to this general rule: where someone receives information in confidence and it loses that confidence as a result of the recipient's fault, he may be prevented from using that information, notwithstanding the publication. The justification for this is that it would be unfair to allow someone to have an advantage over others by allowing him to have a headstart in using that information.

12.6   Summary

(1) Obligations of confidentiality are much easier to enforce when contained in specific contractual wording than when inferred from general law.
(2) Even specific contractual restrictions may not be enforceable if unfairly in restraint of trade.
(3) The standards are different where employees are concerned. In particular, the courts differentiate between trade secrets and less confidential information.
(4) Whether between franchisors and franchisees, or between either and their employees, it is advisable to specify the restrictions required, and, what is more often overlooked, the information sought to be protected. General restrictions are more likely to be too vague, or too unfair, to enforce.

Chapter 13

Copyright

Chapter 13

Copyright

13.1 Introduction

English copyright law is principally to be found in the Copyright, Designs and Patents Act 1988 (CDPA). The bulk of its provisions came into force on 1 August 1989. Since then it has been supplemented by EC directives and statutory instruments giving effect to them in the UK. These are dealt with in 13.10 *below*. References in this chapter to sections are to sections of the CDPA.

The CDPA is a codifying act. It amends (sometimes substantially) and restates the existing law, but it does not have retrospective effect. In relation to works which came into being before 1 August 1989, the copyright position is governed by the Copyright Act 1956. That Act, too, had no retrospective effect, and works which came into existence before 1 June 1957, the effective date of the Copyright Act 1956, are governed by the Copyright Act 1911. And so on. This is of more than passing importance. Many of the signs and designs which make up popular culture, and many of the brands on which today's most successful franchises are based, are of some age and their first steps will have been governed by legislation quite different from the CDPA. For example, the cinema is one of the most potent sources of popular commercial images, but the treatment of films from the point of view of copyright is different under the CDPA from the position under the 1956 Act. Before the 1956 Act, films had no copyright status at all; there was merely a bundle of the rights in the various constituent parts.

13.2 The extent of copyright

Material is protected by copyright only if it falls into a category which the CDPA prescribes as eligible for copyright protection. These categories are: literary works; dramatic works; musical works; artistic works; sound recordings; films; broadcasts; cable programmes; the typographical arrangement of published editions.

The category of 'literary works', as we shall see, includes material which one would not immediately expect to find so named; specifically, it includes computer software.

The ingenuity of franchisors being what it is, it is possible to envisage franchise arrangements which encompass material in any of the categories named *above*. However, nearly all franchises feature copyright in literary and visual works, while few are concerned with the other categories. In practical terms, franchise arrangements are concerned mainly with operating manuals, software, and the artwork involved both in promotional and branding material and in designs such as for shop and restaurant layouts. To the extent that franchise arrangements do involve copyright material in other categories, it is likely to relate to the specific requirements of the franchised business (between franchisor and franchisee on the one hand and the outside world on the other), as opposed to the franchise relationship (between franchisor and franchisee). We will therefore concentrate on copyright as it relates to literary works and artistic works. It will be immediately apparent that, although the general principles of copyright are discussed, this chapter cannot be regarded as a the general statement (however brief) of copyright law, since matters not generally relevant to franchise arrangements are omitted.

13.3   Concept and expression

Copyright protects works, not ideas. Other species of intellectual property relate directly to ideas; copyright only indirectly. Patent law exists specifically to protect inventive ideas, and they may also be protected as know-how under the rules relating to confidentiality (*see* Chapter 12). For copyright to be of use in the protection of an idea, the idea needs to be reduced to a material form, and then it is the form not the underlying idea, which is protected. This is of crucial importance in relation to franchising, where the kernel of a business to be franchised often amounts to a concept which is not capable of protection as intellectual property.

Since copyright does not protect original ideas, there is nothing in copyright law to prevent one person from using original ideas developed by another, so long as there is no actual copying (or any of the other 'restricted acts' referred to in 13.9 *below*) of any copyright work incorporating the idea.

A recipe is a useful example. The combination of ingredients and the method of their preparation might be sufficiently original to qualify for patent protection. (A patent application would be unusual in practice, as few food products would justify the cost). The recipe might simply be kept secret, and disclosed only to a very small number of people, and then under an obligation of confidentiality. As a matter of copyright, there would be no protection for the concept of the recipe, but the recipe itself, if reduced to writing or other permanent form, and assuming all the other tests, for originality and so forth, were met, would be protected as a literary work. The owner of the copyright in the recipe would be entitled to prevent others from copying and publishing the recipe, even from adapting it. They would not, however, be entitled to prevent anyone from discerning from the recipe its underlying point, and reproducing it in entirely different language, let alone as food.

Copyright protects works, then, but only works of the type designated by the CDPA, and this chapter is confined to literary and artistic works.

13.3.1   Literary works

'Literary works' are defined in s 3 of the CDPA as:

> any work, other than a dramatic or musical work, which is written, spoken or sung, and accordingly includes—
>   (a) a table or compilation, and
>   (b) a computer program.

To constitute a work, it must be reduced to tangible form, in writing or otherwise (s 3(2)). 'Writing' is defined in s 178 as including 'any form of notation or code, whether by hand or otherwise and regardless of the method by which, or medium in or on which, it is recorded'. The intention is that any conceivable form of notation should count.

13.3.2   Artistic works

An 'artistic work' is defined in s 4 as:

>   (a) a graphic work, photograph, sculpture or collage, irrespective of artistic quality,
>   (b) a work of architecture being a building or a model for a building, or
>   (c) a work of artistic craftsmanship.

Architectural works and works of artistic craftsmanship require an element of 'artistic quality' to qualify, but graphic works, photographs, sculptures and collages do not. The requirement for 'artistic craftsmanship' has not proved straightforward.

It might appear that protection for 'works of artistic craftsmanship' would assist a franchisor whose business includes, for example, retail outlets such as fast food restaurants where the style of the furniture is consistent and distinctive. This is an area where franchisors' expectations of protection by intellectual property law are more often than not disappointed. Unfortunately, the courts have restricted the availability of protection under this head to the extent that it is not something on which any franchisor could place any great reliance.

215

The courts' attempts to put the judicial finger on what is and what is not artistic have been more revealing about the cultural pre-conceptions of those who make up the British judiciary than helpful to business people.

The case in which these matters were considered at greatest length was *Henscher* v *Restawile Upholstery* [1976] AC 64. The question there was whether a particular suite of furniture comprised a work of artistic craftsmanship. This was considered at first instance, by the Court of Appeal and finally by the House of Lords. There were seven judgments, one by the judge at first instance, one by the Court of Appeal and five in the House of Lords. The five Law Lords approached the matter in radically different ways. To summarise, a work would be of artistic craftsmanship if:

(a) people generally would think it was (Lord Reid);
(b) experts would think it was (Lord Morris);
(c) the judge would think it was (Lord Dilhorne);
(d) the craftsmanship (rather than the work) was artistic (Lord Simon of Glaisdale);
(e) the craftsman intended the work to be artistic (Lord Kilbrandon).

There was, however, unanimity that the suite of furniture in question was not a work of artistic craftsmanship.

The final approach was adopted in the subsequent case of *Merlet* v *Mothercare plc* [1984] FSR 358, which concerned a weatherproof cape for babies. The question was whether the cape was a work of artistic craftsmanship. Walton J held that it was a work of craftsmanship but not artistic craftsmanship. The test was the intention of the designer. Whether the designer intended to produce a work of art was relevant, rather than the degree and nature of the aesthetic *frisson* experienced by an individual on seeing the work. This was subsequently confirmed in the Court of Appeal. It is far from satisfactory, for more than one reason. The craftsman might, on any test, be misguided in his belief that there was art in his work, or his views might not be ascertainable. Underlying all the debate there is:

(a) no sense of the idea prevalent in the design world that, in craft, art and function are inextricably linked;
(b) the hint that, whatever the legal arguments, the taste of the judiciary will prevail; and
(c) considerable uncertainty.

13.3.3   Graphic works and photographs

Graphic works are defined in s 4(2) as including:

(a) any painting, drawing, diagram, map, chart or plan, and
(b) any engraving, etching, lithograph, woodcut or similar work.

216

Photographs are defined widely so as to include the results of technology developed from traditional photography, such as holograms. However, films (in the sense of motion pictures) are not included within the definition of photographs.

13.3.4 Names

By application of the rules outlined *above*, names are not in principle protected as a matter of copyright. This is so even if they are reduced to writing, even if they are the names of made-up characters (*see Tavener Rutledge Ltd* v *Trexapalm Ltd* [1977] RPC 275) or if they are made-up names (*see Exxon Corporation* v *Exxon Insurance Consultants International Ltd* [1982] RPC 81). If names are to be protected, they must be protected by trade marks or under the law relating to passing off (*see* Chapter 11).

13.3.5 Practical implications

All this is particularly relevant when a franchisor seeks to identify the intellectual property to be licensed to a franchisee. At the centre of many franchise operations is a way of doing business. Depending on the operation, that may include a small number of excellent ideas, or a highly detailed blueprint for a business operation. In either case, this will be reduced to writing and made available by franchisors to franchisees as an operations manual. The operations manual itself will (all things being equal) be protected by copyright. Competitors can be restrained from copying and adapting the manual, and indeed from doing any of the other 'restricted acts' described in 13.9 *below*. Copyright law will not, however, prevent a competitor from identifying the essential points of the operations manual and using them himself, or indeed reducing them to writing in his own words and making that available to his own employees or franchisees.

The most effective measure that a franchisor can take in these circumstances is to provide the operations manual in confidence to its franchisees. For all its difficulties, the law of confidence will occasionally protect a concept which cannot be protected by copyright. In *Fraser and Others* v *Thames Television Ltd and Others* [1983] 2 All ER, three actresses and their manager discussed with Thames TV the concept of a television series featuring a rock group comprising three women. An option agreement was prepared but was not proceeded with. Thames TV then independently produced the television series *Rock Follies*, which involved a rock group featuring three women. The court held that a person who had received an idea expressed in oral or written form was not entitled to disclose it or use it until it became general public knowledge, provided that the information was imparted in confidential circumstances and that the content of the idea was clearly identifiable, original, of potential commercial attractiveness and capable of reaching fruition. There was a breach of confidence, for which the plaintiffs were compensated. There was no possibility of a claim for breach of copyright.

It is undoubtedly easier for a legal system to police a system which protects works to the exclusion of concepts, since a work can be seen and identified, whereas the extent, content and even existence of a concept will always be open to argument. Nevertheless, one may doubt whether it is fair that some concepts are so valuable that people will pay large sums of money for the use of them (for example, the money paid by a television producer to reproduce a successful game show, or the money paid by a franchisee for access to a successful business system), but attract no copyright protection, whereas the most trivial sequence of words reduced to writing is imbued with the full majesty of the CDPA. Interestingly, in the film and television world, concepts, or formats, are bought and sold and licensed, and lawyers frequently connive to ignore the fact that concepts do not comprise any sort of intellectual property; 'format rights' are defined and provided for in legal documents just as if they really existed. There are proposals to amend the law to provide for a new format right, but it is unlikely that it will extend to a business format.

13.4   Skill and labour: originality

For literary and artistic works to be protected, they must be original (s 1). Since, as has been seen, copyright protects works and not the ideas underlying them, the originality must be in the form of expression rather than the underlying ideas. Lord Atkinson put this in the case of *MacMillan & Co* v *Cooper* [1923] 93 LJPC 113 in a way which, incidentally, illustrates the English approach to copyright as essentially a matter of facilitating commerce rather than fostering creativity:

> It is the product of the labour, skill and capital of one man which must not be appropriated by another, not the elements, the raw material, if we may use the expression, upon which the labour and skill and capital of the first had been expended. To secure copyright for the product it is necessary that labour, skill and capital should be expended sufficiently to impart to the product some quality or character which the raw material did not possess, and which differentiates the product from the raw material.

Notwithstanding these ringing words, the test of originality is not of great practical significance, since the standard is in practice low. Provided that a sequence of words (for example) has not been lifted directly from another source, it is in practice very unlikely that it would be possible to take the point that it was not original. For example, even a telephone directory could well be original and therefore subject to copyright protection, provided that the person who compiled it did so without copying existing material.

It is accepted law that copyright can subsist in a list, on the same principle that it subsists in an anthology of poems or the track listing for a compilation album assembling pop songs of, say, the early 1970s, provided that the compiler of the list has used skill in assembling it. There comes a point, of course, at which the skill used in assembling the list is minimal, and the question arises whether the list is still protected by copyright. The point usually arises in relation to databases, and the position is complicated there by new law (*see* 13.11.3 *below*).

13.5 Registration

Unlike some other jurisdictions, English law neither requires nor permits registration as a precondition of copyright protection.

13.6 The term

In copyright as in life, everything grows old and dies, except Peter Pan (as to whom, see s 301).

As with most other forms of intellectual property (the notable exception being trade marks), a degree of monopoly is allowed by the state in the hope that creative work and scientific research will be encouraged, and that the fruits of the work and research will come into common currency and, in due course, into the public domain.

The term of copyright is different for different types of work. The general rule for literary and artistic works is that copyright subsists until 70 years have elapsed from the end of the calendar year in which the author dies. There are exceptions for works of unknown or joint authorship and for computer-generated works. Until 1 July 1995, the period was life plus 50, rather than 70 years. The change is effected by a statutory instrument made pursuant to a European directive. At the time of writing the statutory instrument has not been published and the details, particularly the transitional provisions, are not yet known.

13.6.1 Unknown authors

In the case of works whose authors are unknown, including those published anonymously or pseudonymously, the period of copyright is 70 years from the end of the calendar year in which the work was first 'made available to the public'. If, before the end of this period, it becomes possible for a person having no previous knowledge of the facts to identify the author, the normal full period of copyright will apply. In the case of copyright material made available to franchisees, these rules are more likely to come into play because the identity of the author has been lost, rather than because of anonymous or pseudonymous publication.

13.6.2 Joint authors

Joint works are those produced by two or more authors, where their respective contributions cannot readily be distinguished. For the purposes of copyright, the period is calculated by reference to the death of the joint author who dies last.

13.6.3 Computer-generated works

Copyright subsists in computer-generated works (defined in s 178 of the CDPA) until the expiry of 70 years from the end of the calendar year in which they were made.

13.6.4 Employee authors

Where the term of copyright is calculated by reference to the death of the 'author', the death of the human author will be relevant even if he or she was at all times an employee. Under the CDPA, s 11(2), copyright is never vested in the author but in the author's employer.

13.6.5 Photographs

Although copyright in photographs follows the general rule for artistic works stated *above*, the copyright in photographs created before 1 August 1989 is radically different.

The Copyright Act 1911 came into force on 1 July 1912. Copyright in all photographs taken before that date has now expired. For all photographs taken between 1 July 1912 and 1 June 1957, the period of copyright was 50 years from the end of the calendar year during which the photograph was taken. The copyright in photographs taken after 1 June 1957 but before 1 August 1989 expires 70 years after the end of the calendar year when the photograph was first published. The copyright in photographs which remained unpublished on 1 August 1989 expires on 31 December 2039. The position may be affected by the forthcoming statutory instrument referred to in 13.6.

13.7 Qualifying for protection

The conditions to be satisfied if a work is to qualify for copyright protection are set out in ss 153–162. There are three tests, but one relates solely to broadcasts or cable programmes and is not considered here; the two remaining qualifications refer to the identity of the author and the country in which the work is first published.

13.7.1   The author

Section 154 deals with qualification by reference to the author. At the 'material time' the author must have been a 'qualifying person'.

For literary and artistic works which are unpublished, the material time is when the work was made, or, if the making of the work extended over a period, a substantial part of that period. For published literary and artistic works, the material time is the date of publication or, if the author died before the work was published, immediately before the author's death.

To be a 'qualifying person' the author must be one of the following:

— a British citizen;
— a British Dependent Territories citizen;
— a British national (overseas);
— a British Overseas citizen;
— a British subject or a British protected person within the meaning of the British Nationality Act 1981;
— an individual domiciled or resident in the UK or another country to which the relevant provisions of the Act has been extended or applied;
— a body incorporated under the law of a part of the UK or of another country to which the relevant provisions of the Act have been extended or applied.

As in relation to the term of copyright, qualification is determined by reference to the human author rather than the first owner. Where, for example, a work was created by a British citizen employed by a foreign company, the work would be protected by copyright in the UK by reason of the British citizenship of the author, and the nature of the employer, the first owner of the copyright, would not be relevant.

13.7.2   Country of publication

The CDPA protects works first published in the UK or created by a British person. The works of most authors in other countries are also protected because the UK grants reciprocal protection to countries which have acceded to the Berne and the Universal Copyright Conventions. There are many such countries, and the purpose of the treaties is to confer an agreed standard of protection, so that any work protected in a relevant country should effectively enjoy international protection through the jurisdictions of all other relevant countries. The USA, from which much of the copyright material relevant to franchisees emanates, is a party to both conventions, but complications may arise with works created by Americans before the dates of accession.

Literary and artistic works qualify for copyright protection irrespective of their authorship, if they are first published in the UK or another country to which the relevant part of the CDPA has been extended or applied.

There are rules to cater for simultaneous publication, and a work would be deemed to have been 'first published' in a country if it was published there within 30 days after actual first publication elsewhere.

'Publication' is defined in s 175(1) of the CDPA. It means the issue of copies to the public. The mere exhibition of artistic works to the public does not constitute publication.

Publication is of relatively minor importance in relation to franchising; the main types of work with which franchisors and franchisees are concerned—logos, operation manuals, operational software and so on—will never be published. However, it is possible to envisage franchise businesses in which copyright works are published. For example, a fast food chain would produce copyright material in the information packs which it produces for its customers and in the free gifts which it provides to children.

13.8   Ownership

Copyright protection depends, then, largely on the identity of the author. Ownership of copyright also starts with the author.

The first owner of copyright in a work will be the author, unless the work was created by the author in the course of his or her employment, in which case the copyright will automatically vest in the employer (s 11(2)).

13.8.1   Assignment

Copyright is freely transferable. Section 90(3) provides that for copyright to be transferred there must be an assignment in writing signed by or on behalf of the assignor. No further formality is required. (Despite this, copyright lawyers still tend to include in copyright assignments a certain amount of archaic language borrowed from their conveyancing colleagues.)

13.8.2   Commissioned works

There is no rule that someone who commissions a copyright work is entitled to the copyright in the work. Where the documentation is silent, the courts might infer a licence from the creator of the work to the commissioner to enable the commissioner to use it for the purposes envisaged. They cannot treat the commissioner as the legal owner of the copyright unless there is actually a written assignment, and only in special circumstances will they infer a beneficial interest on the part of the commissioner.

13.8.3   The implications for franchisors

Ownership of the copyright in material included in a franchise package is crucial to a franchisor. Since there is no system for registration of copyright in the UK, it is essential for franchisors to be able to deduce title to the relevant copyright works. In other words, they must possess a sequence of assignments and employment contracts starting with the author and ending with the franchisor, and all of them, even if originating elsewhere in the world, must have effect in the UK.

A licence, and particularly an implied licence, is of course less satisfactory to the recipient than an assignment, since the ability of a licensee to deal with the copyright is limited by the terms of the licence. If the work is successful and new applications become apparent, the commissioner will not want to have to seek the consent of the author to extend the use of the work, since the author will no doubt wish to charge for consenting.

13.9   Restricted acts

Restricted acts, in relation to a copyright work, comprise those things that the copyright owner can do, but, if anybody else does them, they are in breach of copyright unless they have a licence from the copyright owner.

To do a restricted act without a licence is a primary breach of copyright. There is also a category of acts of secondary infringement, where infringers are in breach only if they had an element of guilty knowledge and knew, or reasonably ought to have known, that they were in breach of copyright.

Where there is a breach of copyright, or a breach of copyright is threatened, a copyright owner may be entitled to damages or to seek an injunction preventing infringement. These remedies are dealt with in more detail in Chapter 17.

The primary restricted acts are:

— copying the work;
— issuing copies of the work to the public;
— performing, showing or playing the work in public;
— broadcasting the work or including it in a cable programme service; and
— adapting the work or doing any of the acts mentioned *above* in relation to an adaptation.

13.9.1   Copying

'Copying' is not a defined term, but s 17 elaborates on its meaning. 'Copying' in relation to a literary work means reproducing it in any material form. The section makes it clear that storing literary material in electronic form is included in the definition of copying.

A protected work is being infringed if a 'substantial part' is copied. A 'substantial part' can mean a large proportion of the work, a small proportion if that proportion has a commercial interest, or even a tiny proportion if it possesses key features by which the whole can be identified, for example the first four notes and the silent rest which precedes them in Beethoven's *Fifth Symphony* (if it were still in copyright, which of course it is not).

An artistic work will be copied if it is rendered in more or fewer dimensions than the work itself. Thus, a three-dimensional model based on a drawing will infringe copyright in the drawing, as will a two-dimensional drawing of a three-dimensional work.

13.9.2   Adaptation

There is also no definition in the CDPA of 'adapt' or 'adaptation'. It is, however, made clear that it includes translations, the dramatisation of a non-dramatic work, the rendering of a dramatic work into the form of a novel, abridgements, versions in graphic form or cartoon form, the arrangement or transcription of a musical work, and, in the case of computer programs, versions in different computer languages or codes.

An adaptation may itself, if sufficiently original, be protected by copyright in its own right, but that copyright cannot be exploited without the consent of the owner of the copyright work which was adapted.

Adaptation is not a restricted act in relation to artistic works. The style of an artistic work can therefore be reproduced, as long as the work itself is not copied. Copying of course includes the copying of a substantial part of an artistic work.

13.9.3   Parody

There is a widely held belief that a parody of a copyright work does not constitute an infringement of the copyright. That is not so. The rules are precisely the same as in any other case, and it is therefore a question whether there is copying of a substantial part of the work. It was held in *Schweppes Ltd and Others* v *Wellingtons Ltd* [1984] FSR 210 that the defendants' *Schlurppes* label infringed the plaintiffs' label *Schweppes*, and that it was no defence to say that the offending label was a parody. In *Williamson Music Ltd and Others* v *The Pearson Partnership Ltd and Another* [1987] FSR 97, it was held that the correct test in deciding whether a parody amounted to an infringement was whether it made use of a substantial part of the expression of the original work. It has never been a good defence to a claim in English law that the act complained of was intended as a joke.

13.9.4   Secondary infringement

The following acts constitute a secondary infringement of copyright:

(1) The importation of an article (other than for private or domestic use) into the UK without the licence of the copyright owner, if the importer knew or had reason to believe that the article was an infringing copy of a copyright work (s 22).

(2) — Possessing in the course of the business; or
    — selling or letting for hire or offering or exposing for sale or hire; or
    — in the course of the business exhibiting in public or distributing; or
    — distributing otherwise than in the course of a business to such an extent as to affect prejudicially the owner of the copyright:
    an article which is or which the person in question has reason to believe is an infringing copy of a copyright work without the licence of the copyright owner (s 23);

(3) — Making; or
    — importing into the UK: or
    — possessing in the course of a business, or
    — selling or letting for hire or exposing for sale or hire:
    an article specifically designed or adapted for making copies of a copyright work, where the person in question knows or has reason to believe that it is to be used for making infringing copies (s 24(1)).

(4) The transmission of a work by means of a telecommunications system (otherwise than by broadcasting or including in a cable programme service) knowing or having reason to believe that infringing copies of the work were made by means of the reception of the transmission in the UK or elsewhere (s 24(2)).

The last category is intended principally to catch transmission of copies by fax; the transmitter does not make the copies since they are printed by the recipient's machine, but the transmitter knows that they will be made.

There is a definition of 'infringing copy' in s 27 of the CDPA. An article is an infringing copy if its making constituted an infringement of the copyright in the work in question. The work is also an infringing copy if:

(a) it has been or is proposed to be imported into the UK; or
(b) its making in the UK would have constituted an infringement of the copyright in the work in question, or a breach of an exclusive licence agreement relating to that work.

13.10   European issues

The European Commission is currently taking a great interest in copyright and has issued directives with the aim of harmonising copyright law throughout the Union. The Commission has said that the following are its main aims:

(a) to encourage competition by the removal of national laws which distort competition between member states and create barriers to business;

(b) the creation of a single market in the field of copyright;

(c) the combating of piracy.

The following directives all greatly affect English copyright law and are relevant to franchising:

(1) Directive harmonising term of copyright and related rights: As from 1 July 1995, the term of copyright protection will be 70 years after the death of the author, and for neighbouring rights (with which we are not concerned here), 70 years after the work is put into circulation for the first time. The statutory instrument giving effect to the Directive has not yet been published.

(2) Directive on the legal protection of computer programs: This Directive was implemented into UK law by the Copyright (Computer Programs) Regulations 1992 (SI 1992 No 3233). This Directive had a limited effect in the UK as the CDPA anticipated most of its provisions.

(3) Directive on the legal protection of databases: This Directive offers a new form of intellectual property protection, separate from copyright, to electronic database producers. It gives the producers a ten-year protection period against the unfair copying of the contents of their databases. The Directive is restricted to information which is arranged, stored and accessed by electronic means and therefore is relevant to on-line databases.

13.11   Software

13.11.1   Protection as a literary work

Software is protected under copyright law as a literary work, irrespective of whether the components are ever written down. To the extent that graphics and sound are involved, artistic and musical copyright are also relevant. The rules already discussed, for example as to originality, apply to software in the same way as to an operations manual or any of the other copyright works with which franchisors and franchisees are concerned. So do the rules as to ownership.

As already discussed, the first owner of copyright is the author of the work, regardless of who commissions or pays for the work. This is subject to the exception that the copyright in a work created by an employee in the course of his or her employment belongs to the employer.

13.11.2   Commissioned software

Difficulties arise when a freelance programmer or a software house is commissioned to write a software program. A program may include contributions from the commissioner, the commissioner's employees and consultants, who may all provide varying degrees of originality. Even if it is agreed that the commissioner, who could be the franchisor, would own the software, there must be a written assignment of copyright to give effect to this. Ownership will not always be available, especially where the creator wishes to make the software available to others. It is then necessary to ensure that the appropriate rights are licensed. Not infrequently a franchisor makes available to franchisees software which is partly original to the franchisor but based on software licensed to the franchisor. The licence to the franchisor needs therefore to entitle the franchisor to:

(a) run the program itself;
(b) adapt it; and
(c) sub-license it in its adapted form.

These rights are unlikely to be available as a matter of routine and will need to be negotiated.

The franchisor will require similar rights from the individual adapter of the licensed software, unless the franchisor is in a position to require an outright assignment of the rights of the adapter.

It is vital that there is certainty as to which parties own which rights. A software package may include a number of different owners, or include separate modules or programs which may be separately owned. Problems will arise if one owner of the copyright refuses to co-operate with the rest, in which case, if possible, the objecting party's rights would have to be severed. To avoid disputes such as these, it is again wise to ensure that satisfactory agreements exist with all connected with the ownership and exploitation of rights.

13.11.3   Databases

The Directive on the legal protection of databases is mentioned in 13.10 *above*. This will have a dramatic effect once it is implemented into UK law, as producers will be given a ten-year protection period against the unfair copying of information contained in their databases. Protection will be given to information which might not be protected if it were not on a database. For example, a list might not be subject to copyright protection because there was not sufficient creativity involved in its production. However, if it were on a database, it would be subject to protection from copying once the Directive is implemented.

13.12 Moral rights

13.12.1 General

The CDPA gives certain new rights to authors of works. These rights are personal and are distinct from, although often parallel to, copyright. They are derived from civil law and have been current in other jurisdictions for many years but are new to the UK. The implications for franchising are not as great as in other areas, and they are therefore mentioned here only briefly.

These rights entitle an individual:

(a) to be identified as author of a work;
(b) to object to derogatory treatment of a work;
(c) to restrain false attribution of a work; and
(d) to preserve privacy of certain photographs and films.

13.12.2 The right to be identified as author

Section 77 gives the author of a copyright work the right to be identified as the author of that work. He or she has the right to be identified whenever the work is commercially published, and whenever it is adapted. The author of an artistic work has the right to be identified whenever the work is published commercially or exhibited.

The right to be identified must be asserted before there can be liability for infringement of the right. If an author wishes to enforce the right to be identified, he or she must first have asserted it both in the manner required by CDPA and in such a way as to bind any person said to be liable for infringement. There are two ways to assert this right:

(a) by an assignment of the copyright which includes a statement that the author asserts, in relation to that work, his or her right to be identified; or
(b) by an instrument in writing signed by the author asserting the right either generally or in relation to a specified act or description of acts.

The right to be identified does not apply in relation to a computer program, the design of a typeface, or any computer-generated work (CDPA, s 79(2)). Nor does it apply to anything done by or with the authority of the copyright owner where the copyright in a work originally vested in the author's employer by virtue of ss 11(2) and 9(2)(*a*) of the CDPA.

This right is not infringed by any act which would not infringe the copyright in the work. If there is a good defence to a claim for infringement of copyright, there is also a defence to any claim for infringement of this right.

13.12.3   The right to object to derogatory treatment of a work

The author of a copyright work has the right not to have the work subjected to derogatory treatment (CDPA, s 80). The right applies in relation to the whole or any part of a work. Unlike the right to be identified, there is no requirement for this right to be asserted before there can be infringement.

To establish infringement the author must prove that the work has been subject to 'treatment'; and that the treatment is 'derogatory'. 'Treatment' of a work can be defined as any addition to, deletion from, alteration to, or adaptation of a work. This does not include a simple translation.

The treatment of a work is 'derogatory' if it amounts to a 'distortion or mutilation' of the work or is otherwise 'prejudicial to the honour or reputation' of the author (s 81(2)(*b*)). So far, there is little guidance on how the courts will interpret these provisions.

The right is also infringed by any person who possesses or deals with infringing articles which are and which the person knows, or has reason to believe, to be infringing articles (s 83(1)). A person is liable who commits any of the following acts in relation to the infringing article:

(a) possesses it in the course of business;
(b) sells it or lets it for hire, or offers it for sale or hire; or
(c) in the course of a business exhibits it in public or distributes it; or
(d) distributes it otherwise than in the course of business so as to affect prejudicially the honour or reputation of the author or director.

As with the right to be identified, this right does not apply to a computer program or any computer-generated work. Furthermore, the right is not infringed by anything done for certain specified purposes, provided that, when the author is identified at the time of the relevant act or has previously been identified in or on published copies of the work, there is a 'sufficient disclaimer' (s 81(6)). Those purposes are:

(a) avoiding the commission of an offence;
(b) complying with a duty imposed by or under an enactment; or
(c) in the case of the British Broadcasting Corporation, avoiding the inclusion in a programme broadcast by them of anything which offends against good taste or decency or which is likely to encourage or incite or lead to disorder or to be offensive to public feeling.

A 'sufficient disclaimer' is defined in s 178 as a clear and reasonably prominent indication given at the time of the act and, if the author is then identified, appearing along with the identification, that the work has been subjected to treatment to which the author has not consented.

13.12.4   The right to restrain false attribution

A person has the right not to have a copyright work falsely attributed to him or her (s 84).

'Attribution' means a statement, express or implied, as to who is the author of the work. For example, the right is infringed by a person who, in the course of business, deals with a work which has been altered after the author has parted with possession of it, as being the unaltered work of the author, or deals with a copy of such a work as being a copy of the unaltered work of the author, knowing or having reason to believe that this is not the case (s 84(6)).

This right is infringed by any person who issues copies of a work on which there is a false attribution. This includes public exhibition of such a work and public performance. However, there will be an infringement only if that person knows or has reason to believe that the attribution is false. There can also be secondary infringement of any such works.

In addition to the statutory claim for false attribution, an author may also be entitled to make a claim for passing off, libel and breach of contract.

13.12.5   The right to privacy of certain photographs and films

A person who, for private and domestic purposes, commissions the taking of a photograph or the making of a film has, where copyright subsists in a resulting work, certain rights to privacy. Section 85(1) provides that a person has the right not to have:

   (a) copies of the work issued to the public;
   (b) the work exhibited or shown in public; or
   (c) the work broadcast.

These rights will be infringed by any person who does, or authorises the doing of any of those acts.

13.12.6   Duration of moral rights

The right to be identified as author, the right to object to derogatory treatment of a work and the right to privacy of certain photographs and films, continue to subsist so long as copyright in the works subsists (s 86(1)). However, the right of a person not to have works falsely attributed to him or her continues to subsist only until 20 years after the person's death. Moral rights are not assignable, although the CDPA provides for the transmission on death of the right to be identified as author, the right to object to derogatory treatment of the work and the right to privacy of photographs and films.

13.12.7   Consent and waiver of rights

There can be no infringement of a moral right if the person entitled to that right has consented. The author of a work can waive any of the rights by a signed instrument in writing. The waiver can relate to specific or general uses, and can be conditional or unconditional, and may be subject to revocation. This, from the point of view of franchisors and franchisees is the essential point. Moral rights are not intended to protect the writers of operations manuals, publicity material and so on, where the commissioner needs total freedom to make whatever use of, and whatever changes seem appropriate to, the work commissioned. It is therefore crucial that effective waivers of moral rights are included in all contracts under which writers and designers are engaged.

13.13   Design law

13.13.1   General

In this section the scope of legal protection conferred on industrial and aesthetic designs is outlined. Franchisors and franchisees rarely come into contact with design law, but they should bear in mind the scope of design protection, not least to ensure that the rights of others are not unintentionally infringed.

Copyright law no longer offers any realistic protection for designs in English law. Since 1 August 1989, designs of functional articles which satisfy certain criteria now enjoy design right protection, which is a new species of intellectual property introduced by the CDPA. Artistic designs are protected separately by means of registration under the Registered Designs Act 1949.

13.13.2   Design right

Design right is a form of legal protection which automatically covers original functional designs of part or the whole of an article. Protected designs enjoy protection against unauthorised copying for a period of ten years from the end of the calendar year in which articles featuring the design are first introduced into the marketplace.

Certain types of design are denied design right protection. Three of these are particularly important:

(1) Design right does not subsist in those parts of the design of an article which are used to fit or connect an article to another so that either article may perform its intended function. Design right protection is therefore

not available for those features of a spare part which enable it to fit on to the whole of a piece of equipment.

(2) Design right does not protect methods or principles of construction.

(3) Surface decoration is excluded from the scope of design right.

The first owner of a design protected by design right is the person who created the design. However, the employer of a designer is the first owner of any designs created in the course of a designer's employment. In addition, and contrary to the position under copyright law, when a design is created pursuant to a commission, the design right belongs to the commissioner rather than the designer.

13.13.3   Registered design protection

While design right is principally concerned with functional industrial designs, registered design protection is exclusively concerned with aesthetic designs: those which have strong eye appeal. For a design to be registrable it must be new, and must have features which appeal to the eye of a prospective purchaser when acquiring articles of that kind.

Registration in the UK is effected by filing an application with the Design Registry, which is a division of the UK Patent Registry. If the design is accepted for registration, it will confer an initial period of protection of five years and a maximum of 25 years' protection, subject to renewals being made at five-year intervals.

13.13.4   Designs and the business of franchising

UK design law is concerned mostly with the protection of designs which can be applied to finished articles. It will be rare that a franchisor will enjoy rights in designs which it will license to its franchisees. The more immediate area of concern is to avoid infringing third party rights by the importation into or sale in the UK of articles made to, or featuring, other people's registered designs or design right. The existence of designs in the UK similar to those either used or proposed to be used by a franchisor should become apparent during the course of the detailed market research which normally precedes the setting up of a franchise business. Prudent franchisors or those on notice of the existence of potentially protected designs will conduct a search of the Registry of Designs.

13.14   Data protection

There is no general law of privacy in England. The law protecting individuals, information about whom is kept on databases, arises under the Data Protection

Act 1984. It has nothing to do with copyright, but this is as good a place as any in this work to consider the matter.

The Act was passed as a result of obligations undertaken by the UK government. It is probably not unfair to say that it comprised the minimum which enabled the government to comply with its obligations, and that it was undertaken without any great political enthusiasm. There are currently proposals from the European Union for a new data protection regime. If it is enacted there will in due course be an upheaval in the law.

13.14.1 Relevance

The Data Protection Act 1984 is not of general application in franchising. It applies in some franchise businesses as between franchisees and their customers. An example is travel agencies where franchisees keep data about individual customers on computer. In the case of other franchise businesses the issue may not arise at all. It may or may not arise between franchisor and franchisee, but in any event it is only incidental to the relations between franchisor and franchisee, and is therefore dealt with in outline only.

13.14.2 The requirements of the Data Protection Act 1984

The Act relates to 'personal data', defined as 'data consisting of information which relates to a living individual who can be identified from that information (or from that and other information in the possession of the data user), excluding the expression of opinion about the individual but not any indication of the intentions of the data user in respect of that individual'. It therefore relates to living individuals, which excludes corporations and the dead.

The Act governs the affairs of 'data users': those who hold or deal with personal data on computer. Where such a person employs the services of a computer bureau (again, the term is defined in the Act), the Act regulates in different ways the computer bureau and its client.

A data user is required to register with the Data Protection Registrar. The process of registration requires a declaration of the source and intended use of the personal data to be handled by the data user. This is important in the context of franchising for reasons dealt with *below*.

Data users are subject to the jurisdiction of the Data Protection Registrar. In applying the Act, the Registrar is required to apply eight principles. They are as follows:

(1) The information to be contained in personal data shall be obtained, and personal data shall be processed, fairly and lawfully.
(2) Personal data shall be held only for one or more specified and lawful purpose.

(3) Data held for any purpose or purposes shall not be used or disclosed in any manner incompatible with that purpose or those purposes.

(4) Data held for any purpose or purposes shall be adequate, relevant and not excessive in relation to those purposes.

(5) Personal data shall be accurate and where necessary kept up to date.

(6) Data held for any purpose or purposes shall not be kept for longer than is necessary for that purpose or those purposes.

(7) An individual shall be entitled:

    (a) at reasonable intervals and without undue delay or expense (i) to be informed by any data user whether he holds personal data of which that individual is the subject; and (ii) to access to any such data held by a data user; and

    (b) where appropriate, to have such data corrected or erased.

(8) Appropriate security measures shall be taken against unauthorised access to or alteration, disclosure or destruction of personal data and against accidental loss or destruction of personal data.

Only the third and the seventh of these principles are commented on here. Franchise agreements regularly place an obligation on the franchisee to disclose information, particularly about customers, to the franchisor. Franchisees frequently keep that information on computer. They will have a conflict between their contractual obligations and their obligations under the Act (specifically by reference to the third principle) unless both their application for registration under the Act and their dealings with their customers provide for the disclosure of data to the franchisor.

The seventh principle gives individuals about whom data is kept the right of access to the data, and, in the case of inaccuracy, the right of correction. When the Act was passed, it was expected that individuals would avail themselves of this right to a much greater extent than is in fact the case. Nevertheless, the right is available. The cynical may conclude that if one wishes to hold data about individuals which they cannot read, it is better to keep the data on paper than on computer.

Chapter 14

Premises

Chapter 14

Premises

14.1 Control of the outlet

Most franchisors wish to maintain control of an outlet not only during the period of the franchise agreement but also on termination, whether by reason of expiration, breach of the franchise agreement or sale of the business by the franchisee. A good site can be difficult to replace. The franchisor can achieve this control by:

(a) taking an option to acquire the franchisee's interest in the outlet (be it leasehold or freehold) in certain circumstances; or

(b) itself acquiring an interest in the outlet.

14.2 Option to acquire

This method is more common where the location of the franchise outlet is not vital to the nature of the franchise operation. The franchise agreement will incorporate an option entitling the franchisor to acquire the franchisee's interest. To be binding on third parties the option must be registered as a notice against the franchisee's title at HM Land Registry or (in the case of unregistered land) as a Class C(iv) land charge at HM Land Charges Registry (Land Charges Act 1972, s 2(4) and Land Registration Act 1925, s 49).

There are two principal events which should trigger the right to exercise the option. These are:

(a) if a franchisee wishes to sell the business during the course of the franchise agreement; and

(b) at the expiration or earlier termination of the term of the franchise agreement.

In both instances, the existence of the option will significantly strengthen the franchisor's negotiating position.

14.2.1   Option price

The option to purchase may be at a pre-agreed value or at open market value at the relevant time. In the latter case, the treatment of improvements should be considered. It will often be agreed, for example, that no account will be taken of the value of any improvements for which the franchisor has paid, but that the franchisee's own improvements will be taken into account in the valuation. Goodwill is generally disregarded in assessing open market value since this will flow from the benefit of the franchise agreement.

14.2.2   Advantages

The advantages of protecting the franchisor's interest by taking an option are these. First, it is a relatively quick and straightforward procedure. Second, unless and until the franchisor chooses to exercise the option there is no need for the franchisor to become involved in the property chain. This is particularly significant in the light of the current state of the law concerning privity of contract discussed in 14.3.4 *below*.

14.2.3   Disadvantages

The option procedure has two possible drawbacks, however. First, if the franchisee's own interest is leasehold, it may be that, if the franchisor is terminating the franchise, the franchisee's landlord may also have grounds for forfeiting the lease. This would arise, for instance, if the franchisee were in arrears of rent or otherwise in breach of covenant or had gone into liquidation. In other words, problems with the franchise agreement may also signal that the franchisee is in breach of its obligations as tenant of the outlet.

The second drawback is one of timing and this applies whether the franchisee's property is freehold or leasehold. If the franchisee is unwilling to comply with the obligations to transfer the outlet to the franchisor, or if the franchisee is already in liquidation and the franchisor is negotiating with the liquidator, a transfer pursuant to the option might take some time to achieve. This could give rise to a break in the continuity of handover. Having said that, there will generally be a strong incentive on the part of any liquidator to deal rapidly with the franchisee's property interests.

14.3   Franchisor acquiring an interest

The franchisor may choose to increase the control it has over the franchise outlet by taking an immediate legal interest in the premises. As mentioned *above*, this method may be preferred if the location is particularly valuable.

Sometimes the franchisor will acquire outright the freehold interest in the site but, partly for reasons of cash flow and partly because of the nature of the property market, it is more common for the franchisor to take a leasehold interest. In either case, the franchisor will then grant to the franchisee a lease or sublease, as appropriate.

14.3.1   Security of tenure

Whether the franchisor has acquired the freehold or a leasehold interest in the outlet, it is vital to pay proper attention to the relevant provisions of Part II of the Landlord and Tenant Act 1954. As practitioners are aware, these provisions afford a measure of security of tenure to tenants who occupy premises for business or professional purposes and who are in actual occupation when the contractual term of their lease (or sublease) expires, unless the landlord can establish one or more specific grounds of opposition to renewal (Landlord and Tenant Act 1954, ss 24–28). To ensure that a franchisee cannot claim the right to a new tenancy under Part II of the 1954 Act on the expiration of the franchise agreement, the franchisor should obtain the franchisee's agreement that the security of tenure provisions will not apply. This agreement will be void unless it is authorised by the court on a joint application made by the parties under s 38(4) of the 1954 Act, before any tenancy commences. The franchisee should not be allowed into occupation of the premises before the grant of the court order. The procedure is generally quick and straightforward.

Part II of the 1954 Act can also give rise to problems for the franchisor on renewal, if its own interest in the premises is leasehold rather than freehold. These are discussed further in 14.6 *below*.

14.3.2   Lease or licence

The security of tenure afforded by Part II of the 1954 Act does not apply to licences. It has been argued that one solution for the franchisor is to grant to the franchisee a licence of the outlet rather than a lease. This method carries a significant risk. Whether a transaction is a licence or a tenancy does not depend on the label put on it by the parties. It depends on the nature of the transaction itself: *see Addiscombe Garden Estates Ltd* v *Crabbe* [1957] 3 All ER 563, [1958] 1 QB 513. The true substance of the transaction will be a tenancy if there is an agreement to grant exclusive possession of the outlet for a term and at a rent: *Street* v *Mountford* [1985] 1 AC 809. A franchisee will invariably be given exclusive possession of the outlet.

In some cases, the degree of control exercised by the franchisor, both in the documentation and as a matter of fact, will be sufficient to prevent a tenancy arising. In *Esso Petroleum Co Ltd* v *Fumegrange Ltd* [1994] EGCS 126 CA the Court of Appeal held that the degree of control retained by Esso under three linked agreements concerning a garage, a garage shop and a car wash was so significant as to be inconsistent with the exclusive right to possession remaining with the operator, Fumegrange. Among other things, Esso could make alterations to the premises, install a car wash and change the layout of the shop. It was clear that these very wide rights were genuinely required by Esso, and the Court of Appeal expressed itself satisfied that they were commercially justified. The outcome might have been otherwise if the operator could have shown that the apparently wide powers were merely a sham to avoid a tenancy arising.

If, as a matter of fact, the arrangement between the franchisor and the franchisee confers exclusive possession of the outlet, it seems highly likely that the arrangement will be construed as a tenancy, and will therefore enjoy the protection of Part II of the 1954 Act, whatever label the parties may choose to give it.

14.3.3   Advantages for the franchisor

The main advantage for a franchisor in taking a legal interest in the outlet and granting a lease or sublease to the franchisee is that it gives the franchisor additional control. The controls set out in the franchise agreement will of course also apply. Many of these controls can be mirrored in the franchise lease or sublease, together with cross-default provisions so that a default under one agreement also constitutes a default under the other. The advantage for the franchisor is that it will then have the benefit of the additional remedies which apply as between landlord and tenant. Thus a breach by the franchisee would entitle the franchisor, as landlord, to forfeit the lease or sublease and regain control of the outlet, subject to the tenant's right to apply for relief from forfeiture. This additional sanction can be very useful indeed for a franchisor.

14.3.4   Disadvantages for the franchisor

The principal disadvantages for the franchisor arise if the interest which it holds is leasehold, rather than freehold.

Liabilities to freeholder

The first problem is that the franchisor will take on an immediate and direct liability to the landlord to pay the rent and perform the obligations under the lease, even if the franchisee fails to do so. While the franchisor will generally ensure that it has the benefit of back-to-back obligations in the sublease, these will be of little comfort if, for instance, the franchisee goes into liquidation at a time when it is in breach of repairing obligations. As a matter of practice, this type of problem may not arise very frequently because the franchisor will be monitoring the franchisee's operations fairly carefully.

Privity of contract

The most significant drawback arises from the current law relating to privity of contract. Under this principle, the original parties to a lease remain liable on their covenants for the whole of the period of the lease, even after they have assigned their interests in the property. By way of example, a franchisor may take a new 25-year lease of an outlet and immediately grant a five-year sublease to a franchisee. At the expiration of the term of the sublease, the franchisee may choose not to renew its franchise agreement and, if the outlet has not proved particularly successful, the franchisor may dispose of its leasehold interest by way of assignment to a third party. Some ten or 12 years later, the assignee (or its successor) may experience financial difficulties, fail to pay the rent and permit the premises to fall into substantial disrepair. The landlord of the outlet could choose to seek recourse against the franchisor, as original tenant of the premises, for the breach of the assignee's covenants. Indeed, the landlord is highly likely to do so if the franchisor is of good financial standing. This principle applies even if the lease has been materially altered, for instance by substantial increases in rent on review. Furthermore, the franchisor's liability as original tenant will remain unaffected even where the lease is disclaimed by the assignee's trustee in bankruptcy or liquidator: *Warnford Investments Ltd* v *Duckworth* [1979] Ch 127.

A franchisor may acquire this direct and primary liability even if it was not the original tenant under the lease, but takes an assignment of an existing lease. This is because many landlords insist, as a condition of consenting to an assignment, that the assignee enters into a new direct covenant with the landlord to perform and observe the obligations contained in the lease, not just for as long as the lease is vested in the assignee, but throughout the term. Clearly, a franchisor will wish to resist this in negotiating a licence to assign.

In 1988, the Law Commission, recognising the need for reform of the law in relation to privity of contract, made a number of important recommendations, although these stopped short of a 'complete abrogation' of the principle (The Law Commission (Law Com No 174) Landlord and Tenant Law, Privity of Contract and Estate 29 November 1988). In the meantime, wherever possible, franchisors who are taking a new lease will no doubt seek to negotiate provisions limiting their liability to the period during which the lease is vested in them.

The problems which can arise on renewal under Part II of the 1954 Act if the franchisor's interest in the outlet is itself leasehold are discussed in 14.6 *below*.

14.4   The sublease to the franchisee

Where the franchisor intends to take a new lease of the outlet, or an assignment of an existing lease, it will, of course, be necessary for the franchise agreement to incorporate provisions relating to the proposed sublease of the outlet to the franchisee. These will include:

(a) an obligation on the part of the franchisee to make a joint application for a court order to ensure that the sublease is contracted out of the security of tenure provisions of Part II of the 1954 Act;

(b) a requirement on the part of the franchisee to supply all necessary information (and, if appropriate, guarantors) to assist the franchisor in obtaining the consent of the superior landlord to the grant of the sublease; and

(c) a provision entitling the franchisor to terminate the franchise agreement if either the court order or the superior landlord's consent has not been obtained after a stated period.

The sublease itself should, of course, contain provisions which mirror those in the franchisor's own lease. In other words, it should pass on to the franchisee responsibility for performing all the obligations owed to the superior landlord.

14.4.1   Restrictions on user

The sublease should also add further controls or tighten the existing controls in the lease. For instance, the lease might specify that the premises may be used for any retail purpose. Most franchisors will require the sublease to specify that the premises may be used only for the purposes specifically set out in the franchise agreement. Similarly, while the franchisor's lease may contain standard provisions concerning alienation, the sublease will generally impose an absolute prohibition on dealings except an assignment to a purchaser of the franchisee's business who has been approved by the franchisor under the terms of the franchise agreement and with whom the franchisor has entered into a new franchise agreement.

14.4.2   Rent

These more restrictive provisions may be unattractive to the superior landlord who will be concerned about their effect on rent reviews. Most superior landlords are keen to ensure that underlettings are at full market rent. Restrictions on user and dealings will invariably depress the rental value of the outlet. While the sublease will frequently require the sublease rent to be reviewed in line with that payable under the franchisor's lease, a superior landlord may wish to protect its position to cover the possibility that the franchisor's lease may cease to exist. This concern can generally be overcome by incorporating into the rent review provisions in the sublease for notional assumptions as to user and dealings which would apply in those circumstances.

The franchise sublease generally provides for payment of a rent to the franchisor which is at least equal to that which the franchisor pays to its landlord. As mentioned *above*, the sublease often also provides for increases in the sublease rent in line with increases in the rent payable under the franchisor's lease, following review. To protect the position of the franchisee on rent review, the franchisee's advisers may seek to include in the sublease an obligation on the part of the franchisor to use its best endeavours to achieve the lowest rent reasonably obtainable on review of the rent payable by the franchisor to the superior landlord, together with an agreement as to who should bear the cost of the rent review negotiations.

14.4.3   Other terms

The franchise sublease should be coterminous with the franchise agreement.

The franchisor's advisers will wish to incorporate in the sublease wide rights of entry for the franchisor to inspect and to ensure that the franchise agreement is being complied with.

The franchisor will also wish to qualify the covenant for quiet enjoyment so that it is expressly subject to the franchisee's observing the obligations contained in the franchise agreement.

The franchise sublease will generally incorporate a provision entitling the franchisor to determine the sublease on early termination of the franchise agreement by reason of breach or sale of the business by the franchisee. The extent to which such a provision is effective is discussed further in 14.5 *below*.

The treatment of any improvements carried out by the franchisee should be carefully considered. As a matter of general law, unless works carried out by a franchisee amount to 'tenant's fixtures', they must be left on the premises when the franchisee leaves at the end of its sublease. However, under Part I of the Landlord and Tenant Act 1927, a franchisee tenant will be entitled to compensation if he takes certain statutory steps before commencing certain works of improvement. No compensation is payable if the work is carried out as a result of a contractual obligation (Landlord and Tenant Act 1927, s 2). It is not possible to contract out of the compensation provisions contained in the 1927 Act. (Landlord and Tenant Act 1927, s 9).

14.5   Termination of the franchise agreement

14.5.1   Relief from forfeiture

As mentioned *above*, the franchisee's lease or sublease should incorporate cross-default provisions entitling the franchisor to forfeit the lease or sublease if the franchisee is in breach of the franchise agreement. If the breach is capable of remedy, however, the franchisee may be able to claim relief from forfeiture under s 146 of the Law of Property Act 1925. The franchisee's entitlement to relief will probably apply even if the cross-default provisions do not take the usual form of a landlord's right of re-entry but instead take the form of an option to determine. This is because a court will look at the events which give rise to the right to determine and can, in certain circumstances, treat the break clause as a right of re-entry. The relevant question will be whether the right to determine was exercisable irrespective of the breach, or only as a result of the breach.

It is also possible that the court's equitable power to grant relief could extend to certain provisions of the franchise agreement itself. This might arise if the court considers that, in fact, there are two documents setting out the terms on which the franchisee can occupy the premises, namely the franchise agreement and the franchise lease or sublease. If it was always contemplated that the franchisee would occupy the outlet for the purposes of carrying out the franchise agreement and, if the provisions of the franchise lease or sublease are sufficiently restrictive, a franchisee might argue that relief cannot be granted in relation to the lease or sublease alone without also granting relief in relation to the termination of the franchise agreement, because to do so would render ineffective the court's power to grant relief. As to the jurisdiction of the courts in cases other than leases *see Shiloh Spinners Ltd* v *Harding* [1973] AC 691, Lord Wilberforce at p 722. However, since such jurisdiction would be exercised only on terms requiring the breach to be remedied, this will not generally be a fundamental problem for the franchisor.

14.5.2   Option to take assignment

In addition to the provisions entitling the franchisor to determine the franchisee's lease or sublease in certain circumstances, franchise agreements frequently incorporate an option entitling the franchisor to take an assignment of the franchisee's lease or sublease on early termination of the franchise agreement whether by reason of breach or on a proposed sale of the business by the franchisee. As mentioned *above*, the option must be registered at HM Land Registry or HM Land Charges Registry if it is to be binding on third parties. In addition, if the franchisor is also the landlord of the franchisee, the option will be effective only if the franchisee's lease or sublease is contracted out of the security of tenure provisions of Part II of the Landlord and Tenant Act 1954. This is because the option entitling the franchisor to require an assignment will almost certainly be construed as having the effect of precluding the franchisee from making an application for a new tenancy under Part II of the 1954 Act and will thus be void under s 38(1) of that Act: *Joseph* v *Joseph and Another* [1967] Ch 78, [1966] 3 All ER 486. This difficulty can be avoided by ensuring that the lease or sublease is contracted out from the outset, but, it is not possible, procedurally, to obtain clearance for the option alone under s 38(4)(*b*) of the 1954

Act before the grant of a sublease which is not to be contracted out. This is because s 38(4)(*b*) only entitles the court to authorise an agreement on a joint application made by persons who are already the landlord and the tenant.

14.6   Renewal of the franchise headlease

It has been mentioned that, where the franchisor's own interest in the outlet is leasehold, difficulties can arise for the franchisor on renewal under Part II of the Landlord and Tenant Act 1954. To ensure that the franchisor can regain possession of the outlet from the franchisee, the franchisor will generally have ensured that the sublease is contracted out of the security of tenure provisions of the 1954 Act (s 38(4)). The franchisee will, therefore, have no statutory right to a new tenancy on the expiration of its sublease. However, since the franchisor will not be in occupation of the outlet at the expiration of its own lease (s 23(1)), the franchisor will likewise have no statutory rights of renewal against the franchisor's own landlord. There are a number of ways of dealing with this difficulty.

14.6.1   Franchisor's option to renew

The franchisor may be able to negotiate with its own landlord, at the time of taking the outlet, for the incorporation in the franchisor's lease of an option for renewal at the expiration of the term. The option could be exercisable on the same basis as if Part II of the 1954 Act had applied, so that the franchisor's landlord can resist the exercise of the option if it can establish any of the grounds for opposition set out in s 30(1) of the 1954 Act. Certain of those grounds are discretionary. The solution here might be to incorporate an arbitration clause. By this means, the franchisor may be able to secure control of the outlet for the duration of two consecutive long leases. The superior landlord will, of course, be concerned to ensure that the franchisor's lease is not perpetually renewable.

14.6.2   Renewal by the franchisee

It may be possible to set up a scheme whereby the franchisee secures a new lease under Part II of the 1954 Act, in effect, on behalf of the franchisor. Thus, if, for example, the franchisor has a 25-year lease and the franchisee is granted a series of consecutive subleases, each for a term of five years, the penultimate sublease might be granted for a term of only three years. The final sublease for the remaining two years of the term of the franchisor's lease would not be contracted out of the security of tenure provisions of the 1954 Act. At the expiration of the term of the franchisor's lease, therefore, the franchisee would generally be able to exercise rights of renewal against the superior landlord.

The scheme would ensure, by means of an option, that the franchisor, in effect, took the benefit of that new lease and granted a new, contracted-out, lease to the franchisee.

It must be said that the effectiveness of a scheme of this nature must be open to some doubt since, as a matter of substance, it would restrict the franchisee's full right to obtain a new lease on terms which would be no less favourable than those which would be settled by a court pursuant to the 1954 Act, that is to say, a new lease which is not contracted out of the security of tenure provisions of the 1954 Act: *Joseph* v *Joseph* [1967] Ch 78, [1966] 3 All ER 486; *Johnson* v *Moreton* [1980] AC 37; *Gisborne and Another* v *Burton* [1989] QB 390. That said, many such schemes have worked well in practice.

It may also be expected that superior landlords will be unwilling to consent (and may be acting reasonably in refusing consent) to the creation of a sublease which is not to be contracted out of the security of tenure provisions of the 1954 Act when a series of earlier subleases in favour of the franchisee have been contracted out.

It will be possible to obtain authorisation of the court under s 38(4)(*b*) of the 1954 Act to an agreement embodying this type of scheme only once the final sublease (which would not be contracted out of the 1954 Act) is in place (*see* 14.5.2 *above*). Clearly, at this stage, the necessary joint application to court will require the voluntary co-operation of the franchisee.

14.7   Reversionary lease

If the franchisor is of good financial standing, it may be able to negotiate with its landlord, at or near the expiration of the franchisor's lease, for the grant to it of a reversionary lease of the outlet. This may be more attractive to a superior landlord than the grant of a new lease pursuant to Part II of the 1954 Act direct to the franchisee, who is unlikely to offer such a good covenant. This method will be effective only if the franchisor has secured its negotiating position with its landlord by ensuring that the final sublease to the franchisee has not been contracted out of security of tenure provisions of Part II of the 1954 Act.

Chapter 15   ,

UK Competition Law

Chapter 15

UK Competition Law

15.1 Introduction

Franchise agreements may be subject to UK competition law. The more successful a franchise operation, the greater the likelihood that it will be subject to competition law issues, and the greater the potential for damage should the franchise agreements fall foul of the legislative requirements. It is therefore essential that competition law is considered both at the drafting stage and during the subsistence of the franchise agreement. The first legislative scheme to consider is under the Restrictive Trade Practices Acts 1976 and 1977, under which agreements which contain provisions restricting activities or for the provision of information in the field of commerce may have to be registered.

15.1.1 The Restrictive Trade Practices Acts 1976 and 1977

The Acts of 1976 and 1977 focus on the way in which agreements are drafted and are highly technical. It is only if these technicalities are understood that the many pitfalls of the Acts can be avoided.

The principal Act is the Restrictive Trade Practices Act 1976 (RTPA 1976, also 'the Act'). It divides agreements into four categories:

(a) restrictive agreements relating to goods (s 6);
(b) information agreements relating to goods (s 7);
(c) restrictive agreements relating to services (s 11); and
(d) information agreements relating to services (s 12).

Under the RTPA 1976, where an agreement is registrable, the parties must furnish particulars of the agreement to the Office of Fair Trading (OFT). If an agreement is then registered, the parties may be required to justify the agreement before the Restrictive Practices Court ('the Court'); otherwise the Court may declare the restrictions to be contrary to the public interest and void.

15.1.2 The Competition Act 1980

Where an agreement does not fall within the RTPA 1976, it may be subject to the Competition Act 1980 (CA 1980) under which agreements which involve or result from 'anti-competitive practices' can be examined by the Director General of Fair Trading ('the Director'), and thereafter be referred to the Monopolies and Mergers Commission (MMC) for further investigation. Unlike the RTPA 1976, which concentrates on the form of agreements, the CA 1980 is not invoked in specified instances, as the concept of 'anti-competitive practices' is fairly flexible and loosely defined; it is not limited to considering the terms of an agreement, but is more concerned with the course of conduct pursued by parties under an agreement, and the effects of such conduct.

15.1.3 The Fair Trading Act 1973

Under the Fair Trading Act 1973 (FTA 1973), an agreement can be referred to the MMC for investigation where it gives rise to a monopoly situation in relation to the supply of goods or services or the export of goods; or if the agreement gives rise to a merger situation, for example, where separate undertakings are brought under common ownership or control. Although the practices which may be investigated under the FTA 1973 and the CA 1980 are broadly similar, the procedure under the FTA 1973 is slower and more cumbersome as it involves an exhaustive and comprehensive enquiry into the market sector and is not confined to an investigation of specific practices.

15.1.4 The Deregulation and Contracting Out Act 1994

The extent to which this legislation impinges on franchise agreements will be examined in this chapter. The Deregulation and Contracting Out Act 1994 will also be considered. This introduces new powers for the Secretary of State for Trade and Industry to take agreements out of the registration procedure (i) if the parties' turnover and market share are below certain thresholds and (ii) if any agreement falls within a block exemption.

15.2 The Restrictive Trade Practices Act 1976

15.2.1 Introduction

The RTPA 1976 is frequently described as 'form-based' legislation because it is directed to the nature of the agreement and the restrictions contained in it, rather than on its effects on competition. Indeed the approach of the RTPA 1976 to agreements has often been likened to that of an English tax statute. The proposals for reform of the RTPA 1976, discussed later in this chapter, include the adoption of an 'effects-based' system modelled on the European Community law approach to restrictions on competition contained in art 85 of the EEC Treaty, which prohibits agreements that have as their object or effect the prevention, restriction or distortion of competition.

15.2.2   Application of the Act

The RTPA 1976 renders registrable any form of agreement for, *inter alia*, the supply of goods (s 6(1)) or the provision of services (s 11(1)) to which there are at least two parties who carry on business in the UK and under which 'relevant restrictions' are accepted by at least two parties to the agreement. Broadly speaking these are restrictions on the parties' commercial freedom of action. The general scheme of the legislation is that the Act requires particulars of these agreements to be furnished to the Director. The particulars are then entered into a Register of Restrictive Trading Agreements ('the Register'). Once they are registered, the Director is under a general obligation, subject to a number of exceptions considered later, to refer the agreement to the Restrictive Practices Court. On a referral by the Director, a presumption arises that the restrictions in the agreement are contrary to the public interest. Unless the parties are successful in rebutting this presumption, the Court declares the restrictions contrary to the public interest and therefore void. The Court may then make an order restraining the parties from giving effect to the offending restrictions or from making any other agreement to like effect.

The RTPA 1976 applies to agreements relating to goods or services, and to information agreements; those concerning information about goods or services (s 1(1)). The treatment of restrictions relating to goods on the one hand and to services on the other, is entirely separate.

15.2.3   Agreements

The Act extends beyond legally binding and enforceable agreements. No doubt intentionally, the Act does not define 'agreement'. Section 43(1) merely states that it 'includes any agreement or arrangement, whether or not it is intended to be enforceable (apart from the provisions of this Act) by legal proceedings'.

As clearly expressed by Lord Denning:

> People who combine together to keep up prices do not shout it from the housetops. They keep it quiet. They make their own arrangements in the cellar where no one can see. They will not put anything into writing, not even into words. A nod or a wink will do. Parliament was well aware of this. So it concluded not only an 'agreement' properly so-called, but any 'arrangement' however informal. . . .

Much of the case-law on this point concerns the circumstances which are sufficient to give rise to an 'arrangement' between the parties.

Where a franchisee is a company, its directors will normally be required by the franchisor to enter into non-competition covenants corresponding with those between the franchisor and franchisee in the franchise agreement. The significance of the words 'any agreement or arrangement' in s 43(1) is immediately apparent. The subsidiary agreement between the directors and the franchisor is entered into as a result of arrangements reached between the franchisor and franchisee. Under this arrangement at least two persons, namely, the franchisee and its directors, have accepted restrictions, thus bringing the arrangement as a whole within the RTPA 1976. It will make no difference that the restriction accepted by the franchisee and its directors are contained in two separate agreements, as the definition of 'agreement' is wide enough to embrace the overall arrangements.

Two or more persons

Only agreements made 'between two or more persons carrying on business within the United Kingdom' either in the manufacture, production or supply of goods (s 6) or in the supply of services (s 11) are registrable under the RTPA 1976. Section 43(2) provides that individuals in partnership with each other and 'interconnected bodies corporate' are to be treated as a single person. In turn, s 43(1) provides that 'interconnected bodies corporate' are bodies corporate of the same group (ie a body corporate and all other bodies corporate which are its subsidiaries within the meaning of the Companies Act 1985).

Accordingly, agreements exclusively between members of a single group of companies or of individuals in partnership with each other are not agreements between 'two or more persons' for the purposes of the RTPA 1976. A partnership must comprise individuals only for the partners to be treated as a single person.

Where the franchisor is not carrying on business in the UK, an agreement to which the franchisee and a director of the franchisee are separate parties would be an agreement between 'two persons'; the question would be whether the director was carrying on business in the UK in the supply of goods or services. Even if the answer is 'no', the point to watch for is the possibility of his starting up some activity at a later date. The RTPA 1976 makes no provision for this possibility and looks only at whether there is a duty to furnish particulars at the date an agreement is entered into. If an agreement later becomes registrable because one of the parties has accepted restrictions—has started up in business, strictly speaking—to comply with the time limits for furnishing particulars of agreements, the agreement would have to be sent in just *before* this happened— from a practical viewpoint this will rarely be possible. It is not unusual for the parties to find that an agreement which, at the time it was made, was not registrable because only one party was carrying on business in the UK in the supply of goods or services, becomes registrable later because one of the parties then starts a UK business.

In *Registrar of Restrictive Trading Agreements* v *Schweppes Ltd (No 2)* [1971] 1 WLR 1148; [1971] 2 All ER 1473, however the court made it clear that the provision relates only to the counting of parties to an agreement and is not intended to cause the interconnected bodies to be deemed to be the same person for any other reason.

Carrying on business within the UK

The RTPA 1976 applies to '. . . agreements (whenever made) between two or more persons carrying on business within the United Kingdom in the production or supply of goods, or in the application to goods of any process of manufacture . . .'.

It is a question of fact whether an undertaking is 'carrying on business within the United Kingdom', although some guidance is given by s 43(4), which provides that '. . . a person shall not be deemed to carry on a business within the United Kingdom by reason only of the fact that he is represented for the purposes of that business by an agent within the United Kingdom'.

The fact that some parties to an agreement do not carry on business in the UK does not necessarily prevent the Act from applying, provided that at least two of the parties do so. In addition, it would be irrelevant if only parties outside the UK were accepting restrictions, provided that there are two or more parties to the agreement who do carry on a relevant business in the UK. The 'two or more persons' carrying on business need not be engaged in the same kind of business.

This criterion will, in practice, generally be satisfied in the context of franchise agreements. Even where the franchisor is based overseas, this usually entails an arrangement whereby a sub-franchisor in the UK is appointed to enter into sub-franchise agreements and to manage the franchise network.

Relevant restrictions

What is a 'relevant restriction'? In relation to goods, s 6(1) of the RTPA 1976 applies to:

> . . . agreements under which restrictions are accepted by two or more parties in respect of any of the following matters—
>
> (a) the prices to be charged, quoted or paid for goods supplied, offered or acquired, or for the application of any process of manufacture to goods;
>
> (b) the prices to be recommended or suggested as the prices to be charged or quoted in respect of the resale of goods supplied;

(c) the terms or conditions on or subject to which goods are to be supplied or acquired or any such process is to be applied to goods;

(d) the quantities of descriptions of goods to be produced, supplied or acquired;

(e) the processes of manufacture to be applied to any goods, or the quantities or description of goods to which any such process is to be applied; or

(f) the persons or classes of persons to, for or from whom, or the areas or places in or from which, goods are to be supplied or acquired, or any such process applied.

Guidance as to the meaning of 'restriction' is given by s 43(1), which provides that 'restriction' includes a negative obligation, whether express or implied and whether absolute or not. The 'two or more persons' accepting restrictions need not be the same as the 'two or more persons' carrying on business; nor do the restrictions accepted by the parties have to be of the same kind or have the same effect.

In general, restrictions exist when the parties to an agreement accept some limitation on their freedom to make their own decisions on matters to do with the production of goods, the supply or acquisition of goods or services, or the application to goods of a manufacturing process. In practice, it can be difficult to identify relevant restrictions. Express restrictions are more readily identifiable, for example a restriction whereby the parties agree not to supply goods in a particular area. The identification of implied obligations, which s 43(1) envisages, is more problematic. For example, an express obligation between two parties to sell their goods at a particular price arguably gives rise to an implicit restriction not to sell at another price. It has even been suggested that the basic terms of a contract of sale constitute restrictions within the meaning of the Act (*see Registrar of Restrictive Trading Agreements* v *Schweppes* (No 2), *above*, and *Re Cadbury Schweppes Ltd's Agreement* [1975] 1 WLR 1018, 1031–1032 for dicta to this effect); and that the only reason these contracts fall outside s 6(1) is by virtue of s 9(3) of the RTPA 1976, considered *below*.

The favoured view, however, is that terms which merely define the positive obligations of the parties under the agreement are not restrictions within the meaning of the RTPA 1976. In general, the position would seem to be that an obligation constitutes a restriction where the obligation has the effect of restricting business freedom. For example in *Re British Basic Slag's Application* [1963] 1 WLR 727, the Basic company was obliged to purchase basic slag from eight steel manufacturing companies 'in an equitable and reasonable manner'. It was held that this was a 'relevant restriction' because it restricted the company in the way it purchased from each of the companies concerned.

Furthermore, a number of cases support the proposition that an obligation which does not restrict a pre-existing liberty does not constitute a restriction

254

within the meaning of the Act. The case of *Ravenseft Properties Ltd's Application* [1978] QB 52 supports the view that a party to an agreement does not accept a restriction within the meaning of the Act where he accepts a restriction which simply limits rights he would not have had unless he entered into the agreement. An example of this is a franchise agreement where the franchisee and its directors undertake not to use the franchisor's know-how. There was no entitlement to use the know-how without entering into the agreement, and so there is no restriction of a pre-existing liberty. However, it is uncertain how far the *Ravenseft* principle will be applied in general and, accordingly, it should be treated with caution. In particular it should be noted that Sched 3 to the Act provides for exemptions for various types of exclusive intellectual property licences, which, if the *Ravenseft* line of reasoning is correct, should be necessary, on the grounds that any restrictions on licensees on the use of the intellectual property would not be 'relevant restrictions' at all.

'Relevant restrictions' falling within the Act which are commonly found include obligations not to engage in another business, so that the franchisee is bound to devote his full personal attention to the franchise. The franchisor is interested in such a clause since it will ensure that the franchisee can run its business.

In addition, in order to prevent an ex-franchisee from exploiting the knowledge that he has acquired of the franchisor's business methods during the subsistence of the agreement, the franchise agreement will usually contain clauses which directly restrict the franchisee from competing with the franchised business both during the agreement and after its termination.

Other 'relevant restrictions' could include restrictions on the franchisee not to supply certain types of goods or services outside his territory, thereby protecting territory which is either occupied by another exclusive franchisee or is potentially franchisable, and stipulations of maximum prices at which goods or services are to be supplied. (Restrictions of this type would also raise important EC law issues.)

Conversely, the only 'relevant restriction' usually accepted by the franchisor is an exclusive territory clause under which the franchisor agrees not to operate or grant to any other person the right to operate a business in the territory of the franchisee. This clause acts as an incentive and makes the franchise arrangement more attractive to potential franchisees. Frequently, it is only the acceptance by the franchisor of this restriction that makes such franchise agreements registrable. The only exceptions are those agreements where there are two parties other than the franchisor who accept restrictions. This usually occurs when the franchisee is a limited company and the directors must also accept some restriction on their freedom of action as referred to *above*.

Some authors have argued that exclusive territoriality can be achieved without making the agreement subject to the need to furnish particulars. It has been suggested that this will be the case where the franchisor undertakes not to use or license the franchise trade name or mark within the franchisee's territory. The franchisor retains the option to trade on its own account in the territories which it is granting to the franchisee, by using a different name. Accordingly, the argument goes, the clause is not construed as a restriction on the franchisor. Since the franchisor is not accepting relevant restrictions as to goods or services, the only restrictions remaining in the agreement will be those imposed on the franchisee.

It is argued that when drafting a franchise agreement where the franchisee requires the grant of an exclusive territory, serious consideration should be given to defining the name of the business to include the franchisor's trade name, and preventing the franchisee from using that name outside the territory, and the franchisor from using it inside the territory, thus avoiding the provisions of RTPA 1976. If both the franchisor and the franchisee wish to avoid furnishing particulars, it is essential that the grant of an exclusive territory in the UK is limited to the business carried on under a particular name, thus reserving to the franchisor the ability to compete with the franchisee using other names and marks.

This argument fails to take account of two factors:

(a) the possibility that such a restriction may be treated as a 'relevant restriction' as to the 'form or manner' in which services are made available or supplied under s 11(1)(d) (see *Restrictive agreements as to services*, below);

(b) that where the substantive effect of the provision is a non-competition covenant, the provision will be a relevant restriction.

An agreement which adopts the approach of restricting competition through trade mark provision should, at the very least, be furnished on a 'fail safe' basis to the OFT. The duty, of course, is to furnish particulars of registrable agreements, not to have them placed on the register.

Even if RTPA 1976 is successfully excluded in the view of the OFT in relation to a particular agreement, it must nevertheless be borne in mind that where exclusive territories are granted other competition legislation and the EC provisions, in particular, may apply.

Disregarded provisions and excepted agreements

Once each of the elements in s 6(1) has been considered, the next step in establishing the applicability of RTPA 1976 to a franchise agreement is to take into account the fact that certain terms and restrictions in an agreement are disregarded. In addition, certain agreements are exempt from the operation of the Act. For example, s 28 excepts agreements described in Sched 3; ss 29–34 provide for the exemption of certain additional categories of agreement, by an order of the Secretary of State or other competent authority.

Where restrictions are disregarded they are 'blue pencilled' or struck out from the agreement and the remaining terms of the agreement are then considered to determine whether any relevant restrictions remain. If so, the agreement may still be taken outside the scope of the Act by virtue of the provisions of, *inter alia*, s 28 and Sched 3, other exemptions under ss 29–34, and other legislation.

Provisions to be disregarded   In respect of agreements relating to goods, s 9 of the Act provides for certain terms and restrictions to be disregarded. The most important provision, ss 9(3) and (6), provides for the disregard of any term 'which relates exclusively to the goods supplied, or to which the process is applied, in pursuance of the agreement'. Section 9(3) is limited to restrictions relating only to the same goods as are supplied under the contract. However, restrictions accepted as between more than one supplier, or more than one party to whom goods or services are supplied, are not disregarded.

Section 9(4) provides that where the restrictions in question have been made:

as between two or more persons by whom, or two or more persons to or from whom, goods are to be supplied, or the process applied, in pursuance of the agreement, sub-section 3 above shall not apply to those restrictions or to those information provisions unless accepted or made in pursuance of a previous agreement—

(a) in respect of which particulars have been registered under this Act; or

(b) which is exempt from registration by virtue of an order under Section 29 (agreements important to the national economy) or Section 30 (agreements holding down prices) below.

Section 9 (6) provides that:

no account shall be taken of any restriction or information provision which affects or otherwise relates to the workers to be employed or not employed by any person, or as to the remuneration, conditions of employment, hours of work or working conditions of such workers. In this sub-section 'worker' means a person who has entered into or works under a contract with an employer whether the contract be by way of manual labour, clerical work, or otherwise, be expressed or implied, oral or in writing, and whether it be a contract of service or of apprenticeship or a contract personally to execute any work or labour.

Therefore any restrictions contained in a franchise agreement requiring the franchisee to employ people with franchising experience, or to stipulate terms and conditions of employment would be disregarded.

In addition to the provisions of the RTPA 1976 outlined *above*, s 2(1) and

(2) of the RTPA 1977 provide for the disregard of certain restrictions in agreements containing 'financing terms', for example, loan and rental terms. Furthermore, s 2(3) of RTPA 1977 provides that:

> the Secretary of State may by statutory instrument make an Order specifying matters (in addition to those mentioned in Section 9 of the Act of 1976) which are to be disregarded for the purpose of determining whether an agreement is one to which that Act applies by virtue of Section 6 of that Act.

(*See*, for example, the Restrictive Trade Practices (Sale and Purchase and Share Subscription Agreements) (Goods) Order 1989 (SI 1989 No 1081).)

Exempt agreements   Once the restrictions that are to be disregarded have been struck out, if there are still restrictions accepted by two or more parties under the agreement the next stage in the analysis is to determine whether the agreement falls within one of the categories of exempt agreements provided by RTPA 1976. Section 28 of the Act provides that 'this Act does not apply to the agreements described in Schedule 3 to this Act'. Furthermore, s 9(7) provides that no account is to be taken of restrictions and terms which have been disregarded under s 9 when determining whether the agreement is one which falls within Sched 3 to the Act.

To qualify for exemption under s 28 and Sched 3, an agreement must be entirely encompassed by the provisions of one paragraph of Sched 3. Exemption cannot be obtained on an aggregate basis by showing that an agreement falls within the provisions of a number of paragraphs, although only partially within each paragraph. The main types of agreement exempted under Sched 3 which are relevant to franchise agreements are bipartite distribution agreements and agreements relating to intellectual property.

The conditions to be satisfied are strict.

Paragraph 2 relates to bipartite distribution agreements and provides that the Act:

> . . . does not apply to an agreement for the supply of goods between two persons, neither of whom is a trade association, being an agreement to which no other person is a party and under which no such restrictions as are described in Section 6(1) above are accepted or no such information provisions as are described in Section 7(1) above are made other than restrictions accepted or provision made for the furnishing of the information—
>
> (a) by the party supplying the goods, in respect of the supply of goods of the same description to other persons; or
>
> (b) by the party acquiring the goods, in respect of the sale, or acquisition for sale, of other goods of the same description.

The application of para 2 is limited to the extent that if another restriction, not qualifying for exemption under para 2, is accepted by either party, the Court will have jurisdiction even in relation to those restrictions falling within Sched 3, para 2. This is in contrast to the provisions of s 9(3) under which restrictions to be disregarded are 'blue pencilled' from the agreement, and if there are restrictions remaining, the jurisdiction of the Court is confined to these remaining terms.

Sched 3, para 3, 4, 5, 5A and 5B provide for the exemption of certain agreements whereby intellectual property (know-how, trade marks, patents and registered designs, copyrights and design right agreements, respectively) is licensed.

Information agreements as to goods and services

The Act also contains provisions for the registration of agreements concerning information about goods and services.

By virtue of the Restrictive Trade Practices (Information Agreements) Order 1969 (SI 1969 No 1842) (the 1969 Order) certain categories of information agreements were 'called up'. The information agreements brought under the control of the Act by the 1969 Order relate to:

(a) the prices charged or quoted or to be charged or quoted otherwise than to any of the parties to the relevant agreement for goods which have been or are to be supplied or offered, or for the application of any process of manufacture to goods;

(b) the terms and conditions on or subject to which goods have been or are to be supplied otherwise than to any such party or any such process has been or is to be applied to goods otherwise than for any such party.

The Schedule to the order describes the various agreements to which the order does not apply. In general these are agreements relating to exports, the divulging of information to government departments and other specified authorities listed in Part II of the Schedule and the gas and electricity industries.

When considering whether information agreements are registrable under the Act, various provisions in relation to goods agreements apply equally to information agreements about goods. The definition of an 'agreement' is the same and restrictions to be disregarded from goods agreements under s 9 are similarly disregarded in information agreements.

A franchise agreement which contains provisions for (1) the franchisor to inform the franchisee of prices charged for goods in other outlets owned or franchised by the franchisor and (2) the franchisee to inform the franchisor of his charges, would be an information agreement as to goods caught by the Act.

Although similar provisions exist for bringing information agreements relating to services under control as for information agreements as to goods, no such Order has yet been made under the RTPA 1976.

Restrictive agreements as to services

Section 11(1) of the RTPA 1976 provides that:

> the Secretary of State may by statutory instrument make an order in respect of a class of services described in the order (in this Act referred to, in relation to an order under this Section, as 'services brought under control by the order') and direct by the order that this Act shall apply to agreements (whenever made) which:
> (a) are agreements between two or more persons carrying on business within the United Kingdom in the supply of services brought under control by the order, or between two or more such persons together with one or more other parties; and
> (b) are agreements under which restrictions, in respect of matters specified in the order for the purposes of this paragraph, are accepted by two or more parties.

Section 11(2) provides the matters which may be specified in such an Order for the purposes of subs (1)(*b*) *above*. These matters correspond closely with those for goods under s 6(1) of the Act.

The Restrictive Trade Practices (Services) Order 1976, SI 1976 No 98, (the 1976 Order), which came into operation on 22 March 1976, 'brought under control' within the meaning of s 11(1) of RTPA 1976, all services without exception. The 1976 Order applies the provisions of RTPA 1976 to:

> ... agreements between two or more persons carrying on business within the United Kingdom in the supply of services brought under control by this Order, or between two or more such persons together with one or more other parties ...

In addition, the agreements must not be agreements described in Sched 1 to the RTPA 1976, which exempts certain services from being designated services. Section 13(3) of the RTPA 1976 precludes all the services described in Sched 1 to the Act from being described as designated services in any Order made under s 11. These are essentially professional services, such as those of lawyers, dentists, doctors and architects. Although restrictive agreements relating to professional services are 'brought under control' and fall within the RTPA 1976, restrictions that relate to those designated services will not be relevant restrictions for the purposes of the Act and so can be ignored.

Under the 1976 Order, restrictions must be accepted in respect of the matters specified in subparas (*a*) to (*e*) of art 3(2) of the 1976 Order, that is to say:

(*a*) the charges to be made, quoted or paid for designated services supplied, offered or obtained;

(*b*) the terms or conditions subject to which designated services are to be supplied or obtained;

(*c*) the extent (if any) to which designated services are to be made available, supplied or obtained;

(*d*) the form or manner in which designated services are to be made available, supplied or obtained;

(*e*) the persons or classes of persons for whom or from whom, or the areas or places in or from which, designated services are to be made available or supplied or are to be obtained.

In relation to disregarded restrictions and excepted agreements, the scheme of the Act in respect of services corresponds closely to that in respect of goods. Section 18 of the RTPA 1976, which is similar to s 9, provides for certain terms and restrictions to be struck out from the agreement for the purpose of determining whether any agreement is one to which the Act applies by virtue of an Order under s 11.

Thus, s 18(2) provides that no account shall be taken of any term which relates exclusively to a service supplied in pursuance of the agreement in question; s 18(3) provides that s 18(2) does not apply to any term of the agreement which imposes restrictions in respect of matters specified in the Order unless they are accepted in pursuance of a previous agreement in respect of which particulars have been registered under this Act; s 18(5) provides for provisions on standardisation to be disregarded; s 18(6) provides for the disregard of any restriction relating to employees.

Similarly, art 4 of the 1976 Order, which was added by the RTPA 1977, provides for the disregard of certain restrictions in agreements containing 'financing terms'.

Section 14(2) of the RTPA 1976, as amended by s 1(1) and (2) of the RTPA 1977, provides that an Order under s 11 of the 1976 Act may specify matters (in addition to those mentioned in s 18) which are to be disregarded for the purpose of determining whether an agreement is one to which the 1976 Act applies by virtue of the Order.

Sched 3, paras 4, 5 and 5A apply similar provisions to trade mark licences relating to services, patent licensing agreements and copyright agreements.

Sched 3, para 7 provides that the Act does not apply to an agreement where:

(a) there are only two parties, neither of whom is a service supply association, and

(b) one of the parties is a person who agrees to supply services and the other is the person to whom they are to be supplied, and

(c) no restrictions of the kind specified in the s 11 Order are accepted, except in respect of the supply of services of the same description to, or obtaining services of the same description from, other persons.

15.2.4   Registration

Where an agreement is registrable under the Act, its particulars must be supplied to the Director, who maintains the Register of Restrictive Trading Agreements. The Register, apart from sections containing sensitive or confidential information, is open to public inspection on the payment of a fee. Section 24 of Sched 2 to the RTPA 1976 sets out the particulars that must be furnished and the time limits for doing so. These particulars comprise the name and address of the parties and the whole of the terms of the agreement, whether or not relating to the relevant restrictions contained in it. Particulars must also be furnished of certain variations and of the determination of the agreement. Paragraph 1 of Sched 2 to the RTPA 1976 provides that 'the duty to furnish particulars in respect of an agreement which at any time is subject to registration shall not be affected by any subsequent variation or determination of the agreement'. Paragraph 2 goes on to provide that 'if at any time after an agreement has become subject to registration it is varied . . . or determined otherwise than by effluxion of time, particulars of the variation or determination shall be furnished to the Director'.

Any inaccuracy or incompleteness may expose the person furnishing the particulars to criminal sanctions. Under Sched 2 to the RTPA 1976, the particulars must be furnished before the date on which any restriction accepted under the agreement takes effect and, in any case, within three months from the date on which the agreement is made. In relation to variations which extend or add to the restrictions the time limit is similarly before the variation takes effect, and in any event within three months from the date of the agreement. In respect of other variations and the determination of an agreement, details must be provided within three months of the variation or determination.

Suspensory clauses

In practice, agreements frequently contain suspensory clauses under which the agreement is suspended from operation until the requisite particulars have been furnished. The purpose of these suspensory or safety clauses is to ensure that details of any agreement or variation are provided in time, by inserting a clause to provide that any registrable restrictions it contains do not come into effect until the day after it has been received by the Director. This is to avoid the serious consequences of a failure to furnish particulars within the time limits specified. However, the details of an agreement or variation incorporating such a clause must still be provided within three months of the day it was made.

Protective furnishing

Furthermore, a 'fail-safe' procedure can be utilised where there is genuine doubt about the registrability of an agreement. Under this procedure, parties to the agreement may furnish particulars while reserving their position on the question of registrability. The parties should set out in their notification the reasons for doubting whether the agreement is registrable. This is known as protective furnishing, giving complete protection from the serious sanctions for failing to comply with the RTPA 1976, contained in s 35 considered *below*. If the Director agrees not to place the particulars on the register, the obligation to furnish will nevertheless have been satisfied. Even if the director puts the agreement on the register, the parties need not necessarily be concerned; the Director has a discretion under s 21(2) to refrain from referring an agreement to the Court on the basis that the restrictions accepted are 'not of such significance as to call for investigation by the Court'. This discretion will usually be exercised by the Director unless he is convinced that the effect of the restrictions is seriously anti-competitive because, for example, they entail price restrictions. It is open to the parties to apply to the Court for a declaration as to whether the agreement is registrable and to apply for the removal of the agreement if they believe it has been wrongly placed on the Register, although this is rarely necessary.

15.2.5   Failure to furnish

When the parties fail to furnish the particulars to the Director within the time limits specified, then a number of serious consequences follow:

(1) The agreement cannot be defended before the Court.
(2) Section 35(1)(*a*) provides that 'the agreement is void in respect of all restrictions accepted or information provisions made thereunder . . .'. The question arises whether s 35(1)(*a*) renders void all restrictions including those which may be disregarded for the purposes of determining registrability. Counsel for the Director conceded in the case of *Re Agreements Relating to the Supply of Diazo Copying Materials, Machines and Ancillary Equipment* [1984] ICR 429 that a restriction in s 35 meant a restriction by virtue of which the agreement was subject to registration. This view is supported by the judgment of McKinnon J in the case of *Snushalls Team Ltd* v *Marcus* (1990) *unreported.*
(3) Section 35(1)(*b*) provides that:

> it is unlawful for any person party to the agreement who carries on business within the United Kingdom to give effect to, or enforce or purport to enforce, the agreement in respect of any such restrictions or information provisions.

Furthermore, s 35(2) provides that:

> No criminal proceedings lie against any person on account of a contravention of sub-section 1(*b*) above; but the obligation to comply with that paragraph is a duty owed to any person who may be affected by a contravention of it and any breach of that duty is

actionable accordingly subject to the defences and other incidents applying to actions for breach of statutory duty.

In practice, the most probable plaintiffs in an action for breach of statutory duty will be the franchisees themselves. However, knowingly or recklessly to furnish incomplete or inaccurate particulars under s 24 nevertheless constitutes a criminal offence.

(4) Under s 35(3):

... the Court may, upon the Director's application, make such Order as appears to the Court to be proper for restraining [any person party to the agreement who carries on business within the UK] from giving effect to, or enforcing or purporting to enforce:
    (a) the agreement in respect of any restrictions or information provision;
    (b) other agreements in contravention of sub-section (1) above. ...
Breach of any order under this sub-section may give rise to serious penalties for contempt of court.

Section 35 of the RTPA 1976 is a potential trap for unwary franchisors. If the requisite particulars are not furnished to the Director, then the restrictions are void and unenforceable. The franchisee may then set up a competing business in breach of the covenants in restraint of trade contained in the franchise agreement. If the franchisor then seeks to enforce these clauses, the franchisee will allege that the covenants are void by reason of s 35. This is a disastrous consequence for the franchisor. If there is any doubt about the application of the RTPA 1976, a suspensory clause should be included and particulars of the agreement should be furnished in time to the OFT.

15.2.6 Civil enforceability of agreements after particulars furnished

The terms of a registrable agreement particulars of which have been duly furnished will not be treated as void unless and until declared to be so by an interim or final order of the Court.

15.2.7 Consequences of registration

On the registration of an agreement, particulars of which have been furnished to the Director, there is a general obligation on the Director to refer the agreement to the Court. This duty is subject to s 21 of the RTPA 1976, which entitles the Director, under certain circumstances, to refrain from taking proceedings before the Court. This is where:

(1) (a) he thinks it appropriate because of any directly applicable Community provision or any exemption; or

(b) an agreement or the relevant restrictions have been determined; or

(2) under s 21(2) it appears to the Secretary of State, on the Director's representations, that the restrictions accepted under the agreement are of such significance as to call for investigation by the Court.

It should be noted, however, that under s 21(3), 'The Secretary of State may at any time upon the Director's representation withdraw any directions given by him under sub-section (2) *above* if satisfied that there has been a material change of circumstances since the directions were given'.

The OFT's view is that few franchise agreements cause problems in terms of effects on competition, but that they nevertheless make heavy calls on the OFT's resources. In general, the OFT views franchises as beneficial to both franchisors and franchisees. The franchisor is able to penetrate the market rapidly by gaining access to key sites and local and consumer know-how, while the franchisee is afforded access to the goodwill associated with the franchisor's brand name and to the managerial and marketing package provided under the agreement. Franchises enable independent traders with little or no expertise of their own to set up outlets and compete with larger undertakings. Effectively, franchise arrangements facilitate entry into the market and widen consumer choice by enhancing inter-brand competition. Clearly therefore, franchises can be pro-competitive, even if the agreement imposes restrictions on the franchisees' freedom of action. Conversely, the limited territorial protection granted to franchisees is a necessary restriction to protect the franchisor's investment in the franchise operation.

Accordingly, s 21(2) is frequently invoked by the Director in the context of franchise agreements in view of the advantageous characteristics of these agreements. It is possible that some agreements may nevertheless be restrictive of competition, for example, where there is limited inter-brand competition and the franchise dominates the particular market sector. There may also be cases where franchisees put to the OFT evidence of restrictive pricing arrangements. In such cases, the Director may refer the agreement to the Court to examine the nature of the restrictions.

Where an anti-competitive agreement falls outside the provisions of the RTPA 1976, it could be investigated by him under the CA 1980, but no such cases have yet arisen. The Director may also cause the existence of agreements that are restrictive of competition to be investigated by making a monopolies reference to the MMC under the FTA 1973, and the MMC may carry out such an investigation in the course of their inquiries.

15.2.8   Referral to the Court

If s 21 is inapplicable, the Director must refer the agreement to the Court. The parties may then decide to abandon the agreement or the restrictions contained in it, or seek to justify them before the Court. On referral, s 10(1) and 19(1), concerning goods and services respectively, provide that the restrictions are deemed to be contrary to the public interest unless the Court is satisfied of one or more of eight circumstances or 'gateways' and, further, that the restriction is not unreasonable having regard to the balance between those circumstances and any detriment to the public resulting or likely to result from the operation of the restrictions (the 'balancing provision').

In practice, when an agreement is referred to the Court, the parties frequently do not seek to justify it before the Court in view of the time and expense involved and the unlikelihood that they will succeed. Referral to the Court and arguing the agreement through the 'gateways' is expensive and is unlikely to be worthwhile in the franchising context. It is therefore more usual for the parties either to abandon the agreement or to seek exemption under EC law, thereby avoiding domestic law on the basis that the normal practice of the Director, pursuant to s 21(1)(*a*) of the RTPA 1976, is not to refer agreements to the Court if they are exempt under art 85(3) of the Treaty of Rome.

15.2.9   Agreements affected by EC law

At the moment the RTPA 1976 still applies to agreements even though they may be affected or expressly authorised by EC law unless, as previously mentioned, the agreement is exempt because it falls within the ECSC Treaty. However, the Director has a discretion, in such cases, to refrain from referring the agreement to the Court. Under The Registration of Restrictive Trading Agreements (EEC Documents) Regulations (SI 1973 No 950), the parties to a registrable agreement must inform the Director when seeking negative clearance, notifying an agreement to the European Commission, or when Community decisions are given or proceedings instituted. It should also be noted that the Deregulation and Contracting Out Act 1994 provides in s 10(2)(*b*) for an order to be made by the Secretary of State categorising those agreements which fall within block exemptions as 'non-profitable agreements', which are exempt from the duty to furnish particulars. To be a non-profitable agreement, the agreement must be:

(a) subject to registration;
(b) not already on the Register; and
(c) not a price-fixing agreement.

It seems likely that those agreements falling within the Franchising Block Exemption Regulation (*see* Chapter 16) will be made subject to an order categorising them as non-profitable agreements, subject to conditions (a) to (c).

15.2.10   *De minimis* agreements

There is currently no provision in the RTPA 1976 which excludes from the scope of the Act agreements which are 'insignificant' in terms of the size of the parties or their market shares. Section 10(1) of the Deregulation and Contracting Out Act 1994, however, inserts a new s 27A into the RTPA 1976, which defines a new category of 'non-notifiable agreement'. Agreements which fall under an EC Block Exemption Regulation may be designated as non-notifiable agreements (*see above*). An order may also be made by the Secretary of State designating agreements as non-notifiable by reference to the size of business of the parties in terms of turnover or market share, provided the conditions referred to in (a) to (c) in relation to agreements covered by a block exemption also apply. The present proposal (January 1995) is to lay down a turnover threshold of £5–10m and a market share threshold of 5–10 per cent (DTI Discussion Document (1995) 139 SJ 141). The thresholds would be alternatives, so that it would be enough to fall within one for an agreement to become non-notifiable. The turnover criterion would:

(a) take account of all the companies in the group of any of the parties; and
(b) relate only to UK turnover.

15.2.11   Restrictions contrary to the public interest

Irrespective of whether the parties have sought to justify restrictions before the Court, where the Court decides that the restriction is contrary to the public interest it will make a declaration accordingly.

15.2.12   Investigation by the Director

Under s 36, the Director may issue a notice requiring persons whom he has reasonable cause to believe are parties to a registrable but unregistered agreement to furnish him with information concerning the agreement. Failure to comply with any notice will constitute a criminal offence. Proposed reform of the RTPA 1976 would strengthen the Director's investigative powers and ability to uncover covert anti-competitive practices.

15.2.13   Final orders

The Court may (s 2(3)) make an order restraining:

(a) The persons party to an agreement who carry on business within the UK;
(b) a trade association or a services supply association of which any such person is a member; or
(c) any person acting on behalf of any such association.

They can be restrained:

(a) from giving effect to or enforcing or purporting to enforce the agreement in respect of those restrictions or those information provisions;

(b) from making any other agreement (whether with the same parties or with other parties) to the like effect; or

(c) where such an agreement as is mentioned in paragraph (b) has already been made, from giving effect to that agreement or enforcing or purporting to enforce it.

15.2.14   Civil enforceability after Court order

After the Court has considered restrictions, they may then be subject to civil proceedings. Where the restrictions have been approved by the Court as not contrary to the public interest, and if one of the parties has committed a breach of the restrictive term, the aggrieved party may then sue for damages and/or an injunction under normal common law principles, provided that the term is not otherwise unenforceable at common law by contravening the doctrine of restraint of trade and therefore being void as against public policy.

15.2.15   Conclusion

By virtue of the 'form-based' nature of the RTPA 1976, which is concerned mainly with the terms of an agreement as opposed to its effects on competition, it is possible to draft franchise agreements in such a way as to avoid the provisions of the RTPA 1976.

When drafting any agreement in such a way as to avoid furnishing particulars under the RTPA 1976, it must be borne in mind that such agreements may nevertheless be investigated under the CA 1980 if they produce anti-competitive effects and, more importantly, that the agreement may well be caught under art 85(1) of the EC Treaty. As will be discussed *below*, the CA 1980 focuses, in contrast, on the effect of an agreement on competition. Thus, it is possible for a franchisor to enter into an agreement with the franchisee which is inoffensive in terms of the RTPA 1976, and yet thereafter engage in highly anticompetitive practices pursuant to the franchise agreement, and vice versa.

In the context of franchises, there is less incentive to avoid the RTPA 1976, apart from the inconvenience of having to furnish particulars of the agreement. As previously mentioned, the OFT is favourably inclined towards franchises because of their pro-competitive characteristics, with the result that the Director will usually invoke s 21(2) to avoid referring such agreements to the Court.

Particulars of any registrable franchise agreement, and certain variations to it, should, though, always be furnished to the Director even in cases of doubt, to avoid the serious sanctions contained in s 35. In this respect, all franchise agreements should therefore contain a 'fail-safe' clause to ensure that these particulars are furnished within the strict time limits specified in the RTPA 1976.

15.3 The Competition Act 1980

15.3.1 Introduction

The Competition Act 1980 (CA 1980) brought about further control in the sphere of competition law by introducing new procedures in relation to 'anti-competitive practices', by focusing on particular firms. The procedure under ss 2–10 of the CA 1980 allows the Director to conduct a preliminary investigation into whether the practices of specific firms amount to 'anti-competitive practices' and, if necessary to refer the matter for investigation to the MMC. In many cases the Director has been able to negotiate suitable undertakings with the business concerned, thus avoiding a reference.

15.3.2 Anti-competitive practices

Under s 2(1) of the CA 1980, an anti-competitive practice is a course of conduct which of itself has or is intended to have or is likely to have the effect of restricting, distorting or preventing competition in connection with the production, supply or acquisition of goods or services in the UK.

15.3.3 Exemptions

The CA 1980 excludes certain courses of conduct from constituting anti-competitive practices. The RTPA 1976 and CA 1980 are mutually exclusive; if conduct is required or envisaged by a 'relevant restriction' in a registrable agreement the CA 1980 will not apply.

The Anti-Competitive Practices (Exclusions) (Amendment) Order 1994

The Anti-Competitive Practices (Exclusions) (Amendment) Order 1994 (SI 1994 No 1557) contains a *de minimis* exclusion. It provides that a course of conduct is excluded from constituting an anti-competitive practice if the person whose conduct is complained of either:

(a) has an annual turnover in the UK of less than £10 million and is not a member of a group which has a turnover of more than £10 million, or
(b) has (and whose group has) less than a 25 per cent market share.

The OFT has elaborated, in its guide to the Act, on the practices which it considers could be anti-competitive. These types of practice could conceivably occur in the franchising context, and fall within two main areas, pricing policy and distribution policy. In the former category are price discrimination; predatory pricing and vertical price squeezing. The latter category includes tie-in sales, full line forcing, rental-only contracts, exclusive supply, selective distribution and exclusive purchase.

This list is not exhaustive of the practices likely to be considered anti-competitive, and each case must be decided on its individual facts.

One further problem is the identification of the relevant market in determining whether a course of conduct amounts to an anti-competitive practice, and whether the market share threshold has been exceeded.

15.3.4   Conclusion

When considering any practice under the CA 1980, the first issue to address is whether the agreement is registrable under the RTPA 1976. If it is, then particulars must be furnished to the Director. However, in such cases, there is no longer a need to consider the anti-competitive effects of the 'relevant restrictions' in relation to the CA 1980 by virtue of their mutual exclusivity, although the other provisions of the agreement, which may have anti-competitive effects, and of course the competition provision of the EC Treaty must nevertheless be considered. If the CA 1980 is prima facie applicable, the next question is whether the business exceeds the thresholds of market share and turnover, bearing in mind the breadth of the definition of 'person'. If it falls within the *de minimis* exception then there is no further need to consider the CA 1980.

Chapter 16

EC Competition Law

Chapter 16

EC Competition Law

16.1 Introduction

16.1.1 Article 85

Article 85(1) of the EC Treaty prohibits all agreements between undertakings which may affect trade between member states and which have as their object or effect the prevention, restriction or distortion of competition within the Common Market. The article provides a non-exhaustive list of examples of matters which restrict competition, such as fixing selling prices or trading conditions; limiting or controlling production of markets; or sharing markets or sources of supply.

Article 85(2) provides that any agreements prohibited by art 85(1) shall be void. Article 85(1) applies using the 'blue pencil' rule, so that only those provisions of an agreement which infringe art 85(1) will be void, and not the agreement as a whole, unless it proves impossible to sever the offending terms.

Article 85(3) allows for exemption from art 85(1) of agreements or categories of agreements which '[contribute] to improving the production or distribution of goods or to promoting technical or economic progress while allowing consumers a fair share of the resulting benefit'. It is a condition of exemption that any restrictions are 'indispensable to the attainment of these objectives' (art 85(3)). In addition, the agreement must not enable the parties to eliminate competition in respect of a substantial part of the products in question.

16.1.2 Exemption and negative clearance

A system of 'notification' of agreements with a view to obtaining either an exemption under art 85(1) or a 'negative clearance' (statement that art 85(1) does not apply) was set up under Regulation 17/62 and is administered by the EC Commission. The advantage of notification is protection from fines pending a decision from the EC Commission. Regulation 19 also provides for the adoption of regulations by the Commission exempting certain categories of agreement.

The Commission Block Exemption Regulation 4087/88 ('the Regulation') for categories of franchise agreements was adopted in November 1988.

16.1.3   Agreements having no significant effect on competition

If, however, an agreement has no significant effect on competition it will fall outside art 85(1) altogether and it will not be necessary to consider the Regulation. The Commission notice of 23 December 1994 on agreements of minor importance lays down certain turnover and market share criteria, and an agreement falling within its scope may be treated by the EC Commission (but not necessarily by the national courts or the European Court of Justice) as *de minimis* or insignificant, and outside the scope of art 85(1).

The *de minimis* provisions catch agreements:

(a)   which cover goods or services which do not represent more than 5 per cent of the total market for such goods and services in the area of the Common Market affected by the agreement. The relevant market in goods and services must be established by looking at other goods which 'are considered by users to be equivalent in view of their characteristics, price and intended use'; and

(b)   where the aggregate annual turnover (which includes the corporate groups to which participants belong) does not exceed 300m ECUs.

Many franchisors may well consider that their system falls within the notice on agreements of minor importance. There will always be reservations, however; growth rates cannot be predicted accurately and the thresholds may be exceeded in the future; it can often be difficult to be sure how narrowly the Commission will define the market.

16.1.4   Effect on trade

Whether or not distribution franchise contracts affect trade between member states seems to have been conclusively determined by the European Court of Justice in *Pronuptia de Paris GmbH* v *Schillgalis* [1986] 1 CMLR 414. In the judgment it states:

> Clauses which result in a sharing of markets between franchisor and franchisees or between franchisees constitute restrictions of competition within the meaning of art 85(1) . . . Distribution franchise contracts which contain clauses leading to market sharing between franchisees are liable to affect trade between states.

It seems clear that exclusive rights granted by a franchisor to franchisees, and location clauses which oblige the franchisee to carry on the business only from an identified address, constitute restrictions on competition, as does a provision restricting the area in which a franchisee may actively exploit his franchise. Since most franchise agreements use one of these approaches, it is likely, following the court's statement of the law, that in those cases trade between member states will be affected.

Although the court refers to distribution franchise contracts, it seems from the *ServiceMaster* decision (OJ No 6 332, p 38) that the Commission takes the view that, for all practical purposes, there is no distinction to be drawn between such contracts and service franchise contracts.

Whether one is drafting a new agreement or reviewing an existing agreement, the same considerations will apply. There are two initial questions:

(1) Is the agreement restrictive of competition under art 85(1) of the EC Treaty or will it be?
(2) If the answer is yes, will the agreement be able to benefit from the Block Exemption Regulation?

16.2 Restriction on competition

Whether a franchise agreement restricts competition is answered by the judgment of the European Court of Justice in the *Pronuptia* case, when it identified market sharing, the tying of products and price fixing as restrictive of competition under art 85(1). It also pointed out that restrictions on the disclosure or use of know-how and confidential information, restrictions for the protection of the franchisor's branding, and the imposition of the use of systems are not restrictive of competition to the extent that they are essential for the protection of franchisers from competition or preservation as the case may be.

The Commission has identified in the Regulation those provisions regarded as restrictive of competition under art 85(1).

Exemption is granted pursuant to art 1.1 to franchise agreements entered into between two undertakings which include one or more of the following restrictions:

(a) the grant of exclusive territorial rights, which can include the franchisor's agreeing not to supply its goods to third parties in the territory;
(b) the imposition of a location clause restricting the franchisee to operating from premises specified in the contract;
(c) a prohibition against a master franchisee concluding agreements with third parties outside the contract territory;
(d) a prohibition against the franchisee seeking customers outside the contract territory; this prohibition is likely to affect mobile franchisees more than those which are tied to premises;
(e) an obligation on the franchisee not to manufacture, sell or use, in the course of the provisions of services, goods competing with the

franchise; where the subject of the franchise is to sell or use in the course of the provision of services both certain types of goods and spare parts or accessories, this obligation may not be imposed for the spare parts or accessories.

This list includes the provisions most frequently seen in franchise agreements which can be regarded as restrictive of competition.

16.3   The Block Exemption Regulation

In answering the second question, whether the agreement can benefit from the Block Exemption Regulation, it is necessary to review the definitions in the Regulation.

16.3.1   Definitions

(a) 'franchise' means a package of industrial or intellectual property rights relating to trade marks, trade names, shop signs, utility models, designs, copyrights, know-how or patents, to be exploited for the resale of goods or the provision of services to end users;

(b) 'franchise agreement' means an agreement whereby one undertaking, the franchisor, grants the other, the franchisee, in exchange for direct or indirect financial consideration, the right to exploit a franchise for the purposes of marketing specified types of goods and/or services; it includes at least obligations relating to:

— the use of a common name or shop sign and a uniform presentation of contract premises and/or means of transport;
— the communication by the franchisor to the franchisee of know-how;
— the continuing provision by the franchisor to the franchisee of commercial or technical assistance during the life of the agreement;

(c) 'master franchise agreement' means an agreement whereby one undertaking, the franchisor, grants the other, the master franchisee, in exchange for direct or indirect financial consideration, the right to exploit a franchise for the purposes of concluding franchising agreements with third parties, the franchisees;

(d) 'franchisor's goods' means goods produced by the franchisor or according to its instructions, and/or bearing the franchisor's name or trade mark;

(e) 'contract premises' means the premises used for the exploitation of the franchise or, when the franchise is exploited outside those premises, the base from which the franchisee operates the means of transport used for the exploitation of the franchise ('contract means of transport');

(f) 'know-how' means a package of non-patented practical information, resulting from experience and testing by the franchisor, which is secret, substantial and identified;

(g) 'secret' means that the know-how, as a body or in the precise configuration and assembly of its components, is not generally known or easily accessible; it is not limited in the narrow sense that each individual component of the know-how should be totally unknown or unobtainable outside the franchisor's business;

(h) 'substantial' means that the know-how includes information which is of importance for the sale of goods or the provision of services to end users, and in particular for the presentation of goods for sale, the processing of goods in connection with the provision of services, methods of dealing with customers, and administration and financial management; the know-how must be useful for the franchisee by being capable, at the date of conclusion of the agreement, of improving the competitive position of the franchise, in particular by improving the franchisee's performance or helping it to enter a new market;

(i) 'identified' means that the know-how must be described in a sufficiently comprehensive manner so as to make it possible to verify that it fulfils the criteria of secrecy and substantiality; the description of the know-how can either be set out in the franchise agreement or in a separate document or recorded in any other appropriate form.

16.3.2 Checklist

These definitions provide their own checklist:

(1) Is there a franchise agreement to which two undertakings are parties? If the franchisee is a small proprietorial company the franchisor will normally require that the principal shareholders and directors join in the franchise agreement to guarantee its performance by the franchisee and to protect the franchisor's know-how. The shareholders and directors may well not be undertakings (as that expression is interpreted), in which case they can be parties to the contract without difficulty. If the shareholders and directors are undertakings, then for the purposes of EC competition law, they would be regarded as forming part of the same economic unit as the franchisee.

(2) Does the franchisor possess intellectual property rights relating to trade marks, trade names, shop signs, utility models, designs, copyrights, know-how or patents, which are to be exploited for the resale of goods or the provision of services to end users?

(3) Are goods sold or services provided to end users?

If the franchisee is a manufacturer or wholesaler not dealing with end users the Regulation cannot apply. Manufacturing agreements are described by the Commission in its Regulation as industrial agreements which are manufacturing licences based on patents and/or technical know-how combined with trade mark licences. The Commission did not include franchising at wholesale level since it lacked experience in that field. The terms of the definition clearly do not include such categories of franchise.

(4) Does the agreement contain the following elements:

   (a) the grant by one undertaking to another of the right to exploit a franchise for marketing specified goods and/or services?

   (b) a direct or indirect financial consideration?

   This wording in the definition recognises that apart from the initial fees and continuing franchise fees (management service fees) a franchisor may receive indirect financial rewards, such as a mark-up on product sales.

   (c) obligations relating to at least (i) the use of a common name or shop sign, and (ii) the uniform presentation of layout design and decor of premises; and/or (iii) in those cases where the franchise is mobile (where the franchisee travels to customers rather than the reverse) a uniform design and appearance of the vehicles used; and (iv) the communication by the franchisor to the franchisee of know-how; and (v) the provision of continuing back-up services by the franchisor?

   (d) a package of non-patented practical information comprising the franchisor's know-how resulting from its experience and testing?

   (e) that the franchisor's know-how as a body or in the precise configuration and assembly of its components is not generally known or easily accessible?

   (f) that know-how is important for the sale of goods or the provision of services to end users?

   (g) that know-how at the date of the agreement is useful to the franchisee by being capable of improving his performance or by helping him to enter a new market?

   (h) a description of the know-how in detail; is there, for example, an operations manual?

If all these elements are present they constitute a franchise and the franchise agreement will satisfy the definition in the Regulation.

Technical compliance is not sufficient; there must be compliance in reality. Franchising is a method of marketing goods and services and is a member of a family of related transactions involving the manufacture and distribution of goods and the provision of services. Many of the features of these transactions are to be found in franchising arrangements and there are similarities between the provisions of the agreements which are used by the whole family. One should not expect to be able to blur the differences to benefit from the franchising exemption when the transaction is not truly a franchise. This Regulation will not benefit those who pay only lip service to its provisions while disguising the true nature of their transaction.

16.4   Effect of the Regulation on franchise agreements

The effects of the Regulation on the terms of the franchise agreement are considered next.

16.4.1   Territorial restrictions

The grant by the franchisor of exclusive territorial rights, coupled with undertakings by the franchisor not to appoint another franchisee or itself to carry on business within the territory, is permitted (art 2(a)). The franchisor may also undertake not to supply goods manufactured by it, to its specification or bearing its trade mark, to third parties within the territory allocated to the franchisee (art 2(a)).

The franchise may be restricted by a location clause to trading only from the premises identified in the contract (art 2(c)). The franchisee should be permitted to move to alternative premises with the franchisor's consent. The franchisor cannot withhold its consent to such a move if the alternative premises match the franchisor's normal criteria for trading premises (art 3.2(i) and 8(e)).

The franchisee can be prohibited from soliciting or touting for custom from those whose residence or business premises are outside any allocated territory, but he cannot be required to refuse to do business with a non-solicited customer from outside the territory (arts 2(d) and 8(c)).

A master franchisee can be prohibited from selling franchises outside his territory (art 2(b)).

While the issue of exclusivity, so far as art 85(1) is concerned, has been dealt with in the Regulation, the commercial considerations, which have given rise to many difficulties in practice, remain. There also remains, for the time being, the fact that the grant by a franchisor of exclusive rights will, where there are two or more parties to the franchise agreement who carry on business in the UK, inevitably lead to the application of the Restrictive Trade Practices Act 1976 to the agreement (*see* Chapter 15).

The commercial considerations revolve round the difficulties, particularly in the early stages of the development of a franchise business, of fairly defining a territory. The tendency is to allocate an area which is too large. Many franchisors who have tried to establish exclusive territories have created problems for themselves by having unexploited areas and by being unable to force the franchisee to expand his business to fill the demand which has been created for the goods or services offered by the franchised network. Such a situation affects franchisees as well as franchisors since there is an open invitation in the unexploited area to others to provide the facilities which the network is not supplying.

The obvious solution—of establishing performance targets, allowing for the effects of inflation and true growth—is not so easy to achieve either. It is not a separate issue since the performance capability of any territory allocated must be based on an accurate assessment of its potential, giving the franchisee the necessary scope for establishing and developing his business without inhibiting the growth of the franchised network. If the franchisor cannot fairly define the territory it is unlikely to be able to establish fair and realistic performance criteria to apply throughout the term of the contract. The ability to grant exclusive territorial rights without adverse competition law consequences will not affect the commercial considerations, and while location clauses will continue to be used widely, there may not be an increase in the grant of exclusive territorial rights.

16.4.2   Franchise goods

The franchisee can be prohibited from manufacturing, selling or using in the course of the provision of services, goods competing with the franchisor's goods (defined as goods produced by the franchisor or according to its instructions and/or bearing the franchisor's name or trade mark) (art 2(e)). The obvious course for franchisors to adopt would be to ensure that all goods sold or used in the franchised business should be manufactured by the franchisor or to its instructions and/or bearing the franchisor's branding. In some cases this is done, but in many cases it is not possible. A strongly branded product may just not be available for 'own brand' labelling, or the range and volume of products may make it impracticable to arrange.

Without prejudice to this, the franchisor must not refuse to designate as authorised manufacturers third parties proposed by the franchisee for reasons other than that of protecting the franchisor's intellectual property rights, or maintaining the common identity and reputation of the franchised network.

The franchisee can be required, so far as is necessary to protect the franchisor's intellectual property rights or to maintain the common identity and reputation of the franchise network:

(a) to sell, or use in the course of the provision of services, exclusively goods which match minimum objective quality specifications laid down by the franchisor (art 3.1(a));

(b) to sell, or use in the course of the provision of services, goods manufactured only by the franchisor (art 3.1(b));

(c) to sell, or use in the course of the provision of services, goods manufactured by nominated third parties where it is impracticable owing to the nature of the goods which are the subject matter of the franchise to apply objective quality specifications (art 3.1(b));

(d) to sell the goods only to end users, other franchisees and others within the manufacturer's distribution network (arts 3.1(e) and 4(a));

(e) to use his best endeavours to sell the goods (art 3.1(f));

(f) to offer for sale a minimum range of goods (art 3.1(f));

(g) to achieve minimum sales targets and plan orders in advance (art 3.1(f));

(h) to keep minimum stocks (art 3.1(f));

(i) to provide customer and warranty services (art 3.1(f));

(j) to honour guarantees whether the goods have been obtained from the franchisor, nominated suppliers, other franchisees or other distributors of the goods which carry similar guarantees in the Common Market (art 4(b)).

The franchisee cannot be prevented from:

(a) buying the goods from other franchisees or other distributors of them (art 4(a));

(b) fixing his own prices, although the franchisor may recommend prices (art 5(e)). It should be noted that the Commission can withdraw the benefit of the exemption given by the Regulation if 'franchisees engage in concerted practices relating to the sale prices of the goods or services which are the subject-matter of the franchise' (art 8(d)). In view of this provision franchisors should prohibit such concerted practices in the franchise agreement, so that if it does arise, action may be taken to require the practice to be discontinued or to terminate the agreement;

(c) obtaining spare parts or accessories for the franchisor's goods other than from the franchisor (art 2(e)); or

(d) supplying goods or services to non-solicited end users because of their place of residence (arts 5(g) and 8(c)).

The provisions relating to products taken as a whole indicate that the position on tied supplies of goods may be summarised as follows:

(1) The franchisee can be required to sell or use in the provision of services only franchisor's goods (as defined) and no others. This requirement cannot be imposed in respect of accessories or spare parts for these goods.

(2) The franchisee must be permitted to obtain franchisor's goods from other franchisees or other distributors of such goods.

(3) In so far as it is necessary to protect the franchisor's intellectual property

rights or to maintain the common identity and reputation of the franchised network:

(a) the franchisor can require the franchisee only to sell goods obtained from it or from nominated suppliers where it is impracticable, owing to the nature of the goods, to formulate objective quality specifications;

(b) to sell exclusively goods which match minimum objective quality specifications laid down by the franchisor.

(4) The franchisee cannot be prevented from obtaining supplies of goods of a quality equivalent to those offered by the franchisor, but without prejudice to 1 and 3(a) *above*.

The combined effect of (3) and (4) is that the franchisee may be obliged to deal in goods supplied by a nominated supplier where it is impracticable to formulate objective quality criteria. In the *Pronuptia* case the court gave two examples to illustrate this. The first was the nature of the products, such as fashion goods (not a surprise since the case involved a fashion goods franchise), and the second was where the cost of monitoring compliance with the specification would be too high, as could be the case if there were a large number of franchises.

To take advantage of either or both examples it is probably sensible to use the opposition procedure under the Regulation (art 6), given that the agreement otherwise complies with its requirements. To resolve these issues (apart from any others which may be relevant) the following questions will have to be addressed:

(1) Is what is proposed necessary to protect the franchisor's intellectual property rights or to maintain the common identity and reputation of the franchised network?

(2) Is it impracticable to formulate objective quality criteria by reason of the nature of the goods or the cost of monitoring compliance in the light of the numbers of suppliers involved?

There has been much comment, particularly in the USA, over the 'nature of the goods' provision, which is said to prevent a fast food operation from nominating the brand of beverage to be served by franchisees. A case can be made that a franchisor should be able to nominate brands of product to maintain the common identity of the network. It is also suggested that a case can be made, as it was for fashion goods, that it can be impracticable to formulate objective quality criteria for food where subtle variations of flavour and consumer taste are involved.

16.4.3   Competition

The franchisor can require the franchisee:

(a) not to manufacture, sell or use in the course of the provision of services goods which compete with the franchisor's goods; this requirement cannot be extended to spare parts and accessories for such goods (art 2(e));

(b) in so far as it is necessary to protect the franchisor's intellectual property rights or to maintain the common identity and reputation of the franchised network, not to engage directly or indirectly in any similar business in a territory where the franchisee would compete with a member of the franchised network, or the franchisor, during the agreement and for a reasonable period, not exceeding one year, after the agreement ends in the territory where the franchisee has exploited the franchise (art 3.1(c)). This prohibition can extend to non-solicited customers who reside or have their place of business outside the franchisee's allocated territory;

(c) in so far as it is necessary to protect the franchisor's intellectual property rights or to maintain the common identity and reputation of the franchised network, not to acquire financial interests in the capital of competitors which would give the franchisee power to influence the economic conduct of the competition (art 3.1(d)). It is understood that the Commission takes the view that 'power to influence' means power to compel by agreement or weight of voting. There is unlikely to be a problem in practice if the business in which the investment is made is a listed company. However, if it is a small proprietorial company there is great temptation for the investing franchisee to influence the economic conduct of the business by reference to knowledge derived from the franchisor's know-how, if the business encounters difficulties. The franchisee may be prohibited from being personally involved in the conduct of a competing business in which he has invested.

16.4.4 Know-how

The franchisor is entitled to protect its know-how and can impose obligations on franchisees:

(a) not to use the know-how other than for the purpose of exploiting the franchise, during or after the end of the agreement, but only until the know-how becomes generally known or easily accessible other than by breach of an obligation by the franchisee (arts 3.2(d) and 5(d));

(b) not to disclose the know-how to third parties during or after the termination of the agreement (art 3.2(a)); and

(c) to require staff of the franchisee to keep confidential the know-how imparted to them to enable them to discharge their duties as employees of the franchisee.

16.4.5   Generally

The franchisor must oblige the franchisee to indicate his status as an independent undertaking (art 4(c)). This is, in any event, quite a frequent requirement in franchise agreements. The Business Names Act 1985 contains provisions which support this approach.

In so far as is necessary to protect the franchisor's intellectual property rights or to maintain the common identity and reputation of the franchised network, the franchisee can be required to make advertising contributions and not to advertise unless the nature of such advertising has been approved by the franchisor.

The franchisor must not prohibit the franchisee from challenging the validity of the intellectual property rights which form part of the franchise. However, the franchisor can provide for the termination of the agreement if a franchisee does mount such a challenge (art 5(f)).

The Regulation contains a list in art 3.2, which is not intended to be exhaustive, of typical franchise contract clauses which are not considered to be restrictive of competition and are thus permissible without any qualifications. They do not call for any special comment.

As EC competition law stands, the conduct of the parties can be investigated to see whether, in practice, they are behaving in a manner which contravenes the requirements of the Regulation. This is recognised in art 8(e) which provides that the franchisor must not use its rights to inspect the location (or vehicle), to veto a move to new premises, or to withhold consent to an assignment of the franchisee's agreement (in other words a sale of the business) for reasons other than protecting the franchisor's intellectual property rights, maintaining the common identity and reputation of the franchise network or verifying that the franchisee is performing his obligations under the agreement.

The franchisor can require franchisees to introduce modifications of the franchisor's commercial methods (art 3.2(f)).

The exempting provision in art 1.1 refers to 'franchise agreements to which two undertakings are party'. This does not exclude directors/shareholders who are not undertakings (as that expression is construed) from being parties to the franchise agreement; this is frequently the case with small company franchisees. However, if a shareholder or director is an undertaking it would be wise to have a separate agreement containing the usual guarantees and undertakings as to confidentiality.

16.5   Difficulties of interpretation

A number of issues which arise out of the Regulation can be categorised as drafting uncertainties. There are also what are clearly mistakes, and treatment of issues in a manner which indicates that the Commission should have given more consideration to the underlying practices. In the EU there are different legal systems (common law and civil code) which approach the interpretation of legislative provisions very differently. This difference clearly has to be respected, but the problem for practitioners is that judges in member states may resolve the anomalies differently. This inconsistency of approach will create problems for international franchise operations who can find that what is accepted as complying with the Regulation in one member state will not be so accepted in another.

The first issue is the way in which the Regulation treats goods. The multiplicity of expressions dealing with goods and the ways in which the provisions are expressed invite confusion. Thus:

(1) Paragraph (9) of the preamble contains the first reference and states 'where the franchisees sell or use in the process of providing services, goods manufactured by the franchisor or according to its instructions and/or bearing its trade mark, an obligation on the franchisees not to sell, or use in the process of the provision of services, competing goods, makes it possible to establish a coherent network which is identified with the franchised goods'.

(2) The paragraph continues, 'However, this obligation should only be accepted with respect to the goods which form the essential subject-matter of the franchise'.

(3) Paragraph (12) of the preamble states, 'To guarantee that competition is not eliminated for a substantial part of the goods which are the subject of the franchise, it is necessary that parallel imports remain possible'.

(4) Article 1.3(d): '"Franchisor's goods" means goods produced by the franchisor or according to its instructions, and/or bearing the franchisor's name or trade mark'.

(5) Article 2(a): '. . . itself exploit the franchise, or itself market the goods or services which are the subject-matter of the franchise under a similar formula'.

(6) Article 2(a): '. . . itself supply the franchisor's goods to third parties'.

(7) Article 2(d): '. . . seeking customers for the goods or the services which are the subject-matter of the franchise'.

(8) Article 2(e): '. . . goods competing with the franchisor's goods which are the subject-matter of the franchise'.

(9) Article 3.1(a): '. . . goods matching minimum objective quality specifications laid down by the franchisor'.

(10) Article 3.1(b): '. . . to sell, or use in the course of the provision of services, goods which are manufactured only by the franchisor or by third parties designated by it, where it is impracticable, owing to the nature

of the goods which are the subject-matter of the franchise, to apply objective quality specifications'.

(11) Article 3.2(h): '. . . to allow the franchisor to carry out checks of the contract premises . . . including the goods sold and the services provided . . .'.

(12) Article 4(b): '. . . where the franchisor obliges the franchisee to honour guarantees for the franchisor's goods . . .'.

(13) Article 5(b): '. . . supplies of goods of a quality equivalent to those offered by the franchisor'.

(14) Article 8(b): '. . . the goods or services which are the subject-matter of the franchise . . .'.

(15) One or other or a combination of the expressions 'the goods which are the subject-matter of the franchise' and 'the services which are the subject-matter of the franchise' appears in arts 3.1(b), 3.1(f), 4(a), 5(e) and 5(g).

All these different descriptions give rise to a number of questions.

16.5.1   The essential subject-matter

The preamble refers to 'goods which form the essential subject-matter of the franchise'. The word 'essential' does not appear in any of the operative articles in the Regulation. There is no guidance on which goods are the subject-matter of the franchise. Although the preamble does not deal with the issue, the articles of the Regulation refer to 'services which are the subject-matter of the franchise'.

Does the reference to goods mean all the goods which the franchisor stipulates must be sold in the franchise business, or does it mean some; if the latter, which are the subject-matter of the franchise and which are not? As far as services are concerned does it mean, in the case of a fast food franchise, the entire menu range offered by the franchise system or part only; if part only, which items are the subject-matter of the franchise and which are not?

The preamble refers to 'goods manufactured by the franchisor', while the definition of franchisor's goods in art 1.3(d) uses the word 'produced'. Is a subtle difference intended or are both terms identical in meaning? In which case why use different words?

It should be possible to assume that where it is intended to refer to 'franchisor's goods', that that term would be used, but there are references in arts 3.1(b) and 5(c) to goods 'manufactured' by the franchisor. Would that make them franchisor's goods even though the definition of 'franchisor's goods' uses the word 'produced' and not 'manufactured'? Has the definition not been used because it is intended in those two provisions to exclude goods produced according to the franchisor's instructions and/or bearing the franchisor's name or trade marks? If that was the intention, why? The reasoning is difficult to follow because there does not seem to be any risk to what the regulation is seeking to achieve if the defined term had been used, unless 'manufacture' is intended to mean something different from 'produce'. To add to the confusion art 5(b) refers to 'goods of a quantity equivalent to those offered by the franchisor', and since that expression is qualified as being without prejudice to arts 2(e) and 3.1(b), the purpose of art 5(f) is in doubt.

These different uses of terms, and the issue of what is the subject-matter of the franchise, whether one is dealing with goods or services, cause problems. Poor wording introduces uncertainty to an area where the intentions are fairly clear. At least one hopes they are.

16.5.2   Master franchise agreement

The definition of 'master franchise agreement' appears to be limited to those cases where the objective is to enter into sub-franchise arrangements. There are cases where the master franchisee undertakes an obligation to open a significant number of units in its own ownership, often as a precondition to sub-franchising. In those circumstances the agreement would not be a master franchise agreement within the definition.

16.5.3   The opposition procedure

The opposition procedure under art 6 appears to be available only where there are franchise agreements and not where there is a master franchise agreement; the article specifically refers to 'franchise agreements', which is a defined term. As 'master franchise agreement' is a separate defined term, and is not mentioned in the article, it does not seem that the procedure can be available in these circumstances.

16.5.4   Business selling same types of goods/services

Article 5 (a) provides that where businesses selling the same types of goods or providing the same types of services enter into franchise agreements they are not within art 1. This means that totally independent competing groups which are in the same product or service line, who decide to enter into franchise agreements, disqualify each other from benefiting from the Regulation. It should be noted that the exclusive purchasing and exclusive distribution regulations have the word 'reciprocal' in a similar provision, which clearly makes more sense. It would be open to a national court to take the view that where the circumstances envisaged in art 5(a) exist, the Regulation does not assist. In any event one is bound to question whether this sort of provision should have been included in the Regulation at all. It seems to have been borrowed from the other regulations which deal with totally different economic and competitive considerations and business practices.

16.5.5   Market sharing

The Regulation envisages two types of market sharing: where there is a defined territory, and where there is a location clause. Although the fact that not all franchises are territorial is recognised, the Regulation assumes in some provisions that they are.

The provision for post-termination restraints is one such case. Where there is a territory the Regulation is clear. Where there is no territory, while the permitted post-termination restraint allows the franchisor to restrain the franchisee from competing in the territory where he formerly exploited the franchise, one is left with the difficulty that there is no defined territory.

In practice this problem might be overcome by defining a radius which equates to a reasonable catchment area which the franchisee's location serves. That seems to be within the Regulation, but it would be better if the two different approaches had been treated as separate cases.

The provisions of art 3.1(c) and 3.1(d) appear to give rise to an anomaly. Franchisees can be prevented during the term of the agreement from competing with a member of the franchise network, including the franchisor. Franchisees cannot be prevented from taking an interest in a competing business so long as that interest does not give them power to influence the economic conduct of that business. Post-termination franchisees can be prevented, for a reasonable period not exceeding one year, from being directly or indirectly engaged in a competing business in the territory in which they have exploited the franchise.

Two questions arise. First, is the franchisee a member of the franchise network for the purposes of art 3.1(c)? Second, given that the franchisee has taken up a permissible interest in a business which competes within the franchisee's area of exploitation, can the franchisor, post-termination, require the franchisee to give up that interest on the basis that, under the permitted provision in art 3.1(c), there can be imposed a post-termination restraint against the franchisee's being engaged directly or indirectly in a competing business in the area where it has exploited the franchise?

As a separate matter, it is unfortunate that the Regulation does not remove uncertainty and permit a one year post-term restraint. This would avoid disputes about whether the period was reasonable or not. A period of one year is likely to be appropriate in a significant majority of cases. In many, it may not be long enough.

16.5.6   Development agreements

The Regulation makes no provision for development agreements. These are in essence option arrangements, under which the developer secures the right to open an agreed number of franchised outlets over an agreed period of time within an exclusive area. They pose the risk of running counter to the EC rules on competition to the extent that they relate to an exclusive territory within which the developer will have rights. It is common in such agreements to provide that a franchise agreement, as defined in the Regulation, will be entered into once the premises have been found and approved, or a territory specific to an identified location has been agreed. In paras 17, 28 and 36 and art I of the Commission's *Computerland* decision [1987] 2 J Int Fran & Dist L 89, OJ (1987) L 222, the issue of development area agreements was discussed and exemption given. Unfortunately the decision does not explain fully the structure which Computerland used for its agreements, although it may be inferred from paras 28 and 36. Unless the Regulation is amended to take account of development agreements and the various approaches adopted, they will need to be individually notified.

16.5.7   Interest of franchisee in competing business

The Regulation requires a franchisor to permit franchisees to have an interest in a competing undertaking, provided such an interest does not give the franchisee the power to influence the economic conduct of that business. This provision ignores the great temptation for the franchisee to 'leak' the franchisor's know-how to the competing business to enhance his investment. The likely effect of a prohibition on such investments will be so insubstantial and would have such an insignificant effect on trade between member states that franchisors should be able to prohibit franchisees from taking investments in other businesses unless such investments are in publicly traded shares.

16.5.8   Value of know-how

In the definition of 'substantial' it is provided that 'the know-how must be useful for the franchisee by being capable, at the date of conclusion of the agreement, of improving the competitive position of the franchisee, in particular by improving the franchisee's performance or helping it to enter a new market'.

While this test will clearly be met on the occasion of the first contract between the parties, most contracts provide for renewals or extensions after the initial term, and it may be difficult to satisfy a test which ignores the reality when the renewed or extended contract is concluded. The definition should be adjusted to take account of this factor, although there is a compelling argument that the franchisee would not wish to enter into a second (or third) contract unless he perceived a benefit in doing so.

Chapter 17

Remedies

Chapter 17

Remedies

17.1   Introduction

The working relationship between a franchisor and franchisee should be close and requires 'co-operation and good faith as between the parties to the agreement if it [is] to work effectively'. So said Sir Peter Pain in the unreported judgment in *Body Shop International plc* v *Rawle and Others* given in the Queen's Bench Division of the High Court on 9 July 1992. Ideally, the relationship between the franchisor and franchisee should be established and maintained with the long term in mind. Few franchisors will find it profitable to be at odds with their franchisees, and vice versa. Sometimes, however, the relationship breaks down and both parties may need to consider the remedies available.

17.2   Before the relationship breaks down

17.2.1   Direct negotiations

One of the reasons for the breakdown of the relationship may be that there is little or no effective communication between the parties. If problems arise, it is in both parties' interests to address the issues at an early stage to try to rescue the relationship and reconcile what may be conflicting aims. Continuing contact with franchisees should be part of normal procedures in all franchise systems.

17.2.2   Confidentiality of concessions

Although all the franchisees in a network will be bound by the same or similar terms, a franchisor must be prepared to take account of each franchisee's individual circumstances when assessing his overall performance. In exceptional circumstances, to preserve a relationship which the franchisor believes has a future, a franchisor may decide to make concessions even though it would be justified in terminating the agreement. If this is the case, the franchisor should be aware of the effect on other franchisees in the network who, if they learn that concessions have been made, may consider that they have been unfairly treated. To guard against this, the franchisor should ask the franchisee to sign an agreement that he will not disclose to other franchisees the terms of any discussions or settlement reached.

17.2.3   Threat of termination by the franchisor

If a dispute arising from alleged breach by a franchisee cannot be resolved by discussion, the next step for the franchisor is often to send a warning letter to the franchisee. Such a letter would point out that the franchisor considers the franchisee to be in breach of the agreement. It should specify the acts or omissions complained of and the particular clauses of which the franchisee is said to be in breach; it should stipulate the contractual or other period within which the breach must be remedied (if capable of being remedied). It should make clear that if the franchisee does not remedy the breaches within this time limit, the franchisor may assert its right to terminate the agreement by serving formal notice and may also claim damages. It is important from both parties' points of view that (in the case of the franchisor) the complaints and (in the case of the franchisee) any mitigating circumstances are well documented in preparation for any litigation which may follow. The franchisor should leave the franchisee in no doubt that it will take all steps necessary to protect its interests, even though the franchisor's objective at this stage may well be to persuade the franchisee that the situation is serious but not beyond recall.

17.2.4   Complaint by the franchisee

If the franchisor is alleged to be in breach of the contract, the franchisee should similarly send a detailed written complaint. The franchisee may also threaten to terminate the agreement, claim damages and costs and refuse to comply with any post termination restraints.

17.2.5   Alternative Dispute Resolution (ADR)

ADR embraces a variety of dispute resolution techniques, the principal method being mediation. These techniques are increasingly used in commercial disputes, but their appropriateness in franchising cases is not clear as the relationship already has communication as part of its structure. Many issues which franchisees may wish to raise (for instance system standards and issues of control) are matters which franchisors view as non-negotiable. Franchisors have to consider the whole network, not only the views of an individual franchisee. Whether and, if so, the extent to which, mediation may have a role in franchising is yet to be determined. Mediation is more structured than direct negotiations between the parties, as a third party mediator is effectively in control. It is less formal than litigation or arbitration and relies on the co-operation of the parties. It can precede arbitration or litigation.

Mediation begins with a meeting of the parties convened by the mediator, who is neutral and unbiased. Generally, this is a joint session at which each party makes a short presentation of its case.

The mediator then holds a series of private meetings with each party in turn, at which they have the opportunity to discuss the dispute with the mediator frankly and in confidence. By speaking to both parties, exploring possibilities with them, putting forward new ideas and communicating information between the two, the mediator helps them towards a solution. If a settlement is reached, it will be drawn up in a formal document and become binding. If the process fails, the mediator can be asked to express a non-binding view on the merits of the arguments.

Mediation differs from litigation and arbitration as follows:

(1) The mediator has no authority to make a binding ruling. The mediator's role is to assist the parties to arrive at their own solution, which will be largely shaped by commercial considerations and will be final. Litigation and arbitration impose a decision on the parties, based on the facts proved and legal principles rather than commercial considerations.

(2) The court can adjudicate only on issues which have been specifically pleaded by the parties to the action, whereas in mediation the parties are free to discuss whatever they wish and may even re-negotiate the terms of their original agreement. The remedies in litigation and arbitration are limited by law, and alternative solutions, outside the scope of the law, cannot be contemplated. For example, mediation might result in a franchisee's agreeing to give up one territory which is not successful in order to concentrate on another. This could not be ordered by the court or an arbitrator.

(3) The mediation process is voluntary and confidential.

(4) Mediation can be set up at short notice and can be successful in a single day. The method encourages the parties to focus on the key issues only. For these reasons it can be an extremely efficient and cost-effective method of dispute resolution.

(5) Mediation also can be used at any stage of a dispute, although generally the earlier the better. It can be used concurrently with any of the other methods such as direct negotiation, litigation or arbitration.

17.2.6 Arbitration

The agreement may provide expressly that disputes between the franchisor and franchisee arising out of the agreement shall be referred to arbitration. Such an agreement may also specify the rules which will govern the arbitration, for example the Arbitration Scheme of The British Franchise Association, which is administered by the Chartered Institute of Arbitrators (*see* Appendix 3).

From the franchisor's point of view, a duty to arbitrate in a case of breach of any clause of the agreement may not always suit its purpose. It is often preferable, at the outset, to provide for arbitration in respect of selected relevant provisions only. In particular the franchisor should reserve the right to apply to the court where the franchisee is acting in breach of his post-termination obligations, so that the franchisor may seek an injunction and other orders restraining the franchisee from continuing to act in breach.

As general rule, where the agreement provides that the parties are under a duty to arbitrate, if one party issues court proceedings in breach of this duty, the other can apply to court for a stay of proceedings pending arbitration.

The advantages and disadvantages of arbitration are as follows:

(1) An arbitration is heard in private rather than in open court and the proceedings are therefore confidential.
(2) Arbitration may be less costly than litigation because it is less formal and may involve fewer representatives. However, as the arbitrator has to be paid, it may be more expensive than using the court system where the costs of the judge's time and court premises are not charged to the parties. The British Franchise Association (BFA) Scheme has cost provisions favourable to a franchisee.
(3) The procedure is flexible and may therefore be quicker than court proceedings. However, especially where there is a number of arbitrators, delays can be inordinate and the non-availability of an arbitrator may be used as a tactic to delay matters. Under the BFA Scheme a single arbitrator is appointed.
(4) The arbitrator appointed generally has particular expertise in franchise disputes.
(5) The arbitrator appointed will personally control the preparation for the hearing.
(6) Arbitrators have less power than judges.
(7) The arbitration award is final and binding on both parties; appeal to the High Court is available on a point of law only, whereas a court decision can be appealed on questions of law or fact.
(8) Although in most cases awards are implemented without recourse to the court, if the losing party does not comply with the final award, an application must be made to court to enforce it.

17.3 Following breakdown of the relationship

17.3.1 Litigation

Litigation may be the inevitable result where co-operation and good faith have broken down. Although most well drafted agreements will provide that failure by the franchisor to enforce its rights under the agreement promptly will not constitute a waiver of these rights, nonetheless failure to do so will give the franchisee in question and other franchisees in the network the wrong impression.

Litigation is usually considered an extreme step, as it is seen as lengthy and costly. If the franchisee's disposable income and assets are below a certain level he may apply for legal aid to fund either wholly or in part an action which he is bringing or defending. If it is granted, the franchisor, even if successful, is unlikely to be able to enforce any order for costs or damages made in its favour.

In many cases the issue and service of a writ will result in early settlement of a dispute; indeed most court actions are settled at some stage after the commencement of proceedings but before trial. Where the franchisee clearly has no arguable defence, the franchisor may be able to apply to the court for summary judgment. This application can be made even before the franchisee has served a defence.

In some cases, even though the franchise agreement may set out very clearly the steps which the parties are required to take to fulfill their obligations, the only way of enforcing those obligations is to issue proceedings. The court has wide powers and can make orders preventing the party in default of its obligations from infringing the other party's rights, or requiring the party in default to comply with its obligations.

Finally, where it is evident that litigation cannot be avoided, it is usually in the interest of both parties to act sooner rather than later. For example, where one of the parties is seeking an injunction, delay may be fatal. Likewise, where the franchisee is in arrears with payments of franchise fees, the franchisor may well need to force the issue before the arrears mount up; if the franchisee is in financial difficulty, it is unlikely that he will be in a position to pay a substantial sum by way of a single payment, and the franchisor may have difficulty enforcing payment of agreed monthly instalments. If the franchisor is bringing a claim, it is important that it is seen by the other franchisees in the network to act swiftly and decisively. Equally, if the franchisee has a good claim and is committed to bringing proceedings, he should try to pre-empt the franchisor by bringing his claim first so that he can control the litigation.

17.3.2   Termination of the agreement

If one of the parties fails to perform one of the fundamental terms of the agreement they are effectively repudiating it, that is, acting in a way which clearly evidences an intention not to perform or be bound by the contract. The case of *Alfred C Toepfer International GmbH* v *Itex Italgrani Export SA* [1993] 1 Lloyd's Rep 137 confirms that a contract has not been repudiated unless either a clear statement of unwillingness or inability to perform has been made, or it is shown on a balance or probabilities that the party will be unable to perform its obligations. A fundamental term is one the breach of which will deprive the innocent party of effectively the whole or a substantial part of the benefit of the agreement. Non-payment of sums due under the agreement is not necessarily a fundamental breach since it is capable of remedy. Breach of a fundamental term does not mean that the agreement is automatically terminated. To end the agreement, the innocent party must show that he has accepted the repudiation, and to do this should give formal notice to the party in breach that the agreement is at an end.

Furthermore, if the innocent party delays in accepting the other party's repudiation, this may be construed as indicating an intention that the agreement should continue notwithstanding the breach. The general principle is that the innocent party must be reasonably diligent in seeking relief and that the position of the party in breach should not be prejudiced as a result of any delay.

In other cases, where the breach is remediable or not sufficiently serious to constitute repudiation of the agreement, the innocent party should give notice of termination. It is rare for the agreement to include express provision for the franchisee to terminate. In most cases the franchisee will have to rely on its rights under contract law. The termination clause in the agreement should set out clearly the procedure for termination, including the time within which breaches (if remediable) must be remedied. It is important that the party wishing to terminate complies with the prescribed procedure for notices set out in the agreement, and that termination is effective. For example, notice must generally be given in writing and sent by recorded delivery to the other party's registered office or last known trading address.

In the case of *Body Shop International plc* v *Rawle and Others* (*above*) the defendants sought to rely on the fact that a writ had been issued before the notice period had expired and before the agreement had effectively terminated. The defendants argued that the action was premature, but were not successful on that point because the writ was issued only shortly before the notice period expired.

A procedural error of this kind would obviously not be an absolute bar to proceedings, but it may lead to an order requiring the costs wasted by commencing proceedings prematurely to be paid by the offending party.

Once notice has been given, the innocent party should not take any steps which could be deemed to constitute waiver of its right to terminate. For example, any subsequent discussions should be expressly stated (preferably in writing) to be without prejudice to the innocent party's right to terminate.

17.4   Post-termination obligations

Obligations to be fulfilled after termination of a franchise agreement are relevant where the agreement is terminated by either party for breach; where the franchisee sells his interest in the franchised business; or where he is not entitled to exercise his right of renewal on expiry of the agreement, or decides not to do so.

Usually the post-termination obligations are relatively onerous for the franchisee because they are aimed at protecting the franchisor's trade names, trade marks, reputation and goodwill.

17.4.1 Precautions on termination

The franchisor should ensure that the franchisee complies with his post-termination obligations promptly. There are two main reasons for this. The first is to effect a 'clean break'. In other words, the franchisor can start to recruit a new franchisee and fill the gap in the market, and the former franchisee can divest himself of the encumbrances associated with the franchise. Second, if the franchisee will not co-operate, delay of more than a few weeks (where this cannot reasonably be explained) may well prevent the franchisor from applying for interlocutory relief. It is a useful precaution for the franchisor to send a letter in standard form to each outgoing franchisee reminding him of his obligations. This applies particularly to the non-compete covenants. This should be followed by an early inspection of the premises to ensure that it no longer bears the name or identity of the franchisor. Arrangements should be made to collect equipment, manuals and any other materials bearing the franchisor's name or trade mark or in which the franchisor has copyright or other rights.

17.4.2 Telephone lines

The franchisor should also ensure that the franchisee executes any documents necessary to ensure that the telephone and facsimile lines are transferred to the franchisor or its nominee. The franchise agreement will generally include a clause to this effect. If it does not, or if there is any reason why the franchisor is not entitled to rely on that clause, the franchisor will have to argue that the telephone number is part of the goodwill of the business and that the franchisee is not entitled to take this goodwill. In the unreported Court of Appeal decision in *Western Staff Services (UK) Ltd* v *Storm and Others* on 13 May 1980 it was held on appeal that 'the goodwill of the plaintiffs necessarily embraces the most valuable manner by which the business is exercised, namely the telephone'. The franchisor should also continue to monitor closely the franchisee's activities in the territory in which he formerly operated.

17.4.3 Non-compete clauses

The non-compete clause is fundamental to the protection of the franchisor and its franchisees from unfair competition. Once the agreement has terminated or expired, 'what [franchisors] want to be able to do is to continue to enjoy the benefit of the goodwill attaching to the name . . . and the businesses associated with it by granting a further franchise to some other person for the area in question' (*Prontaprint plc* v *Landon Litho Ltd* [1987] FSR 315). If the non-compete clause is unenforceable, the franchisor is unable to stop the franchisee competing against any new franchisee in the territory. More importantly, if a covenant of this kind is unenforceable, 'as soon as they have managed to get going on the expertise, advice and assistance given to them by the [franchisor], other franchisees are going either to withdraw or not renew their agreements and franchising will, effectively, become inoperable' (*Prontaprint plc* v *Landon Litho Ltd*).

The position at law is that a restrictive covenant is prima facie invalid unless the party seeking to rely on it can show that it is, in terms of area and period, reasonable to protect its legitimate business interests. The franchisor will argue that it has a legitimate interest in running a franchising business and that, without a restraint of this kind, that will be, effectively, impossible. Conversely, the franchisee will argue that the restriction is wholly unreasonable and goes further than is necessary to protect the franchisor's legitimate interests.

A number of authorities deal specifically with the enforceability of such clauses. For the most part, these fall into two categories: vendor/purchaser and employer/employee covenants.

Herbert Morris Ltd v *Saxelby* [1916] 1 AC 688 falls into the former category. In this case, Lord Shaw observed that 'the law . . . declines to permit the vendor to derogate from his own grant'. Put at its simplest, without a covenant not to compete by the vendor, a purchaser would not get what he is contracting to buy. However, different considerations apply to an employer who is taking a covenant from an employee. In that situation, while the employer is not entitled to protect itself against the use by an employee of the ordinary skills acquired through his particular employment, the employee is prevented from taking unfair advantage of information which he acquires while in the employer's service (*see* Chapter 12).

One of the difficulties for both parties' advisors is that the law is constantly changing, as can be seen from the recent cases.

Geographical limitation

In the case of *Prontaprint plc* v *Landon Litho Ltd* (*above*), it was held on an interlocutory application that the following covenant was 'not one which would be likely at full trial to be held to be unenforceable':

> The licensee agrees that he shall not at any time within three years from the determination of this agreement engage in or be concerned or interested directly or indirectly in the provision of the Service or anything

similar thereto within a radius of half a mile of the Premises or within a
radius of three miles from any premises in the United Kingdom at which
the Service or anything similar thereto is carried on by any other licensee
of the licensor or by the licensor or itself.

This clause is widely drawn in respect of the geographical area, but a clause
which is limited to a specified radius around the territory formerly operated by
the franchisee is more likely to be upheld than a restriction which extends to
the territories of other franchisees. The court does of course have the power to
'blue pencil', that is, delete any part of a clause which it holds to be unreasonable, and enforce the rest. In the recent case of *Kall Kwik Printing (UK) Ltd* v
Bell and Another [1994] FSR 674, a geographical restriction of a 700 metre
radius from the printing centre formerly operated by the defendants was held
to be reasonable.

The period of limitation

Again, there is no hard and fast rule governing what period of limitation is reasonable. A useful guideline is the Block Exemption Regulation of the European
Commission relating to categories of franchise agreements which are exempted
from the competition laws of the European Community contained in art 85 of
the EC Treaty. This Regulation provides that the period of non-competition
should not exceed one year after the agreement ends (*see* Chapter 16).

In the case of *Prontaprint plc* v *Landon Litho Ltd* (*above*) the restriction was
for a period of three years after termination. This was followed by the unreported decision in *Prontaprint plc* v *Devaney (Patrick James Noel)* in July
1992 where judgment was given by Mr Timothy Lloyd QC (sitting as a deputy
High Court judge) on an interlocutory application. In the latter case, the
covenant was not to compete for a period of one year. On an interlocutory application for an interim injunction pending trial, the judge held that, while the
franchisor's case was seriously arguable, it was not overwhelmingly likely to
succeed in enforcing the post-termination restriction and that the defendant
might establish at trial that the clause was unfairly in restraint of trade. The
main distinction between this case and the earlier *Landon Litho* case is that the
defendants in the earlier case had set up the business from scratch, rather than
buying an existing business; they had been supported in setting up a business
about which they knew little or nothing until the franchisor provided expertise.

In contrast, in the case of *Devaney*, the franchisee argued successfully, for
the purposes of interlocutory relief, that in the case of a takeover of an existing business with the purchase of its goodwill, the benefits are less than they
would be where the franchisee starts a business from scratch. 'In those circumstances the goodwill in the franchised business does not arise solely from
the franchisor's activities and, the franchisee will say, the franchisor should

reasonably and legitimately claim protection for only a limited part of that goodwill'. That argument, if it had prevailed at the trial, would have been in direct contrast with the *Landon Litho* case, where it was confirmed that the goodwill belonged to the franchisor. Unfortunately, we shall never know what the trial judge would have found, as the case was settled. However, it is the author's view that the franchisee's arguments could not have prevailed. The franchisee's argument in *Devaney* cannot be correct since it would have the effect of allowing the franchisee to benefit from the goodwill and reputation established and already owned by Prontaprint. The judge appears to have been influenced by the fact that the defendant had paid his predecessor franchisee for the business, and contrasted that with the position of an original franchisee. In principle there is no difference, since the original franchisee pays the cost of entry to the network and provides the capital to establish the business. The franchisee who buys it from him pays the value of that business as a going concern, which may or may not be more than the accumulated cost of the business to the outgoing franchisee, depending on how well the business has performed. That sale does not include the ownership of the goodwill in the name and system. Fragmented ownership of such goodwill as contended for by the franchisee in *Devaney*, would be destructive of franchising. After a few franchise sales, if the franchisee were correct, no one would know who owned what goodwill in the name and system and whether such ownership was general or limited in area. The effect would be that the franchisor could not grant franchises in any area where a sale had taken place. The purpose of a franchise is to give a franchisee a limited licence to use the franchisor's name and system and the goodwill associated with them for a limited period, but the argument in *Devaney*, if followed at a full trial, would make the franchise agreement effectively operate as an absolute unencumbered grant of those rights. If that reasoning is correct there is not only a disincentive to franchise, but a positive reason not to do so. It would be surprising if the *Devaney* argument were upheld at trial since the overwhelming view of the courts has been to accept that the goodwill in the name and system belong to the franchisor (*see* Chapter 11).

Office Overload Ltd v *Gunn* [1977] FSR 39 was another interlocutory decision. In this case the restrictive covenant was for a period of one year after termination of the agreement within the area (six miles from the centre of Croydon) formerly exploited by the franchisee. Lawton LJ on appeal found that in considering the reasonableness of a restrictive covenant it was material that the party giving the covenant gained virtually no benefit from the contract. In the case of *Kall Kwik (UK) Ltd* v *Bell and Another* (*above*), a period of 18 months after termination of the agreement was upheld. Harman J said:

> I have no hesitation in concluding that 18 months is, prima facie, a reasonable period to apply . . . But a period of 18 months for a business

where there is goodwill, which goodwill is the property of the plaintiff and which is being required by the plaintiff for the continuing conduct of business at the premises or within the 700 metres of these premises, seems to me a period of time which is highly likely to be that during which goodwill annexed to the defendants would persist . . . .

The usual wording includes the phrase 'that the franchisee will not be engaged, concerned, interested or employed in the operation of a similar business'. In the case of *Batts Combe Quarry Ltd* v *Ford and Others* [1943] Ch 51 the construction of the wording 'engaged, concerned, interested or employed' was considered. In this case, a vendor of a business provided financial assistance and other support, including advising and assisting in negotiations, for his sons who were establishing a new business in competition with a business which their father had sold. It was held by the court that providing finance and assisting in the negotiations for the establishment of the new business constituted being 'concerned or interested in' the business and therefore amounted to a breach of covenant not to compete.

17.4.4 Non-solicitation of former customers

As with the non-compete clause, a prohibition on soliciting former customers must be limited in time to a specified and reasonable period (for instance, the year) after termination; and to customers with whom the franchisee (not other franchisees) dealt during a limited period (for instance, two years) before termination.

17.4.5 Option to purchase

If it seems likely that the agreement will be terminated because of breach by the franchisee, and the agreement is about to expire, the franchisor should be vigilant, endeavouring to anticipate the franchisee's future activities. He may be planning covertly to operate a competing business or to sell the franchised business to an allegedly 'unrelated' third party immediately before expiry with a view to competing with that third party following expiry. Of course, it may be difficult to anticipate the franchisee's plans and the agreement should therefore safeguard against all eventualities.

Some franchise agreements provide the franchisor with an option to purchase the business within a period before termination if the franchisee does not exercise his right to renew the agreement. This would safeguard against the situation where a successful franchisee elects not to renew the agreement on expiry because he intends to participate in indirect or disguised connections with a competing business thereby circumventing the non-compete clause.

17.5   Causes of action

The remedies available to the parties will depend on the act or omission of which the innocent party complains.

17.5.1   Misrepresentation

Allegations of misrepresentation are often raised by franchisees, either in the statement of claim if the franchisee has issued proceedings, or in his defence and counterclaim if the franchisor has commenced proceedings to recover outstanding franchisee fees or damages for breach of contract. In many cases, before the franchise agreement is signed, the franchisor will have supplied the franchisee with projected turnover figures or profit forecasts. The BFA Code of Conduct (para 3.2) provides that where there are 'direct or indirect references to future possible results, figures or earnings to be expected by individual franchisees it shall be objective and shall not be misleading'. The Code of Conduct does not form part of the contract unless expressly stated to do so. The BFA Best Practice Guide states that:

> any statement indicating that a franchisee can expect to make profits or achieve any level of return without any qualifying explanation would not be within the Code. The franchisor would have to state the basis upon which such a statement is made so that there is no possibility of a reasonable person being misled.

The franchisee, when entering the agreement, may have relied on figures provided by the franchisor as an accurate statement of the turnover or profit that he would be able to achieve. The Best Practice Guide states that:

> the information MUST CLEARLY STATE the basis of presentation of the financial projections . . . Franchisees must therefore be WARNED that they should understand that no franchisor can warrant with accuracy any financial performance in any particular case. A franchisee should take his own proper accountancy advice in considering his franchise proposition.

A well drafted agreement will include a clause excluding liability in respect of all financial information provided by the franchisor to the franchisee before the agreement is signed. It is arguable whether such a clause is enforceable and this is discussed in further detail in Chapter 8. The BFA guidance should be followed in preparing pre-contractual documents and in the contract wording.

In the case of *Esso Petroleum Co Ltd* v *Mardon* [1976] QB 801 a statement was made by Esso concerning the potential throughput of a petrol station, on the basis of which the defendant entered into a lease for the station. It was held on appeal that this statement constituted a contractual warranty because it was a factual statement on a crucial matter made by a party who had, or professed to have, special knowledge and skill, with the intention of inducing the other party to enter into the contract. It was also held that the statement was a negligent representation made by a party holding himself out as having special expertise in circumstances which gave rise to the duty to take reasonable care to see that the representation was correct. This duty of care existed during the pre-contractual negotiations and survived the making of the written contract. In a franchise situation, the court will look at all correspondence between the parties before the agreement was signed, minutes of meetings and any information provided to the franchisor by the franchisee showing his monthly or annual income and outgoings. In some cases the franchisee may have relied on market research carried out on his behalf to assess the viability of a franchised business in a new area. The franchisee should ensure that any report is addressed to him, so that he has a cause of action against the author of the report. The franchisor should ensure that any clause in the agreement excluding liability for such information is sufficiently wide to cover such reports.

17.5.2 Breach of contract

From an evidential point of view, it is preferable to rely on an express term of the agreement rather than an implied term. It is therefore essential that the agreement is carefully drafted, unambiguous, and signed by all the parties, including any guarantor.

By the franchisee

Where the franchisee is in breach of contract the franchisor should ascertain the reason. The franchisee may be dissatisfied with the franchisor. The most common breach is failure by the franchisee to submit weekly or monthly reports and to pay franchise fees. Often the franchisor must look at the underlying problem behind this failure. The franchisee may be failing to perform in other areas. He may be deviating from the franchise system, for example by selling products other than those authorised by the franchisor, or using administrative or operational procedures other than those set out in the operations manual. This may contribute to the franchisee's failing to achieve sufficiently high standards in respect of the goods it produces or the services it provides. Often customers may complain direct to the franchisor.

The franchisor may carry out quality control checks which will highlight a franchisee's deficiencies. The franchisee may fail to achieve an expected target which may or may not be set out in the franchise agreement. If it is not, the franchisor may have to rely on the franchisee's obligation to devote his full time and attention to the business and to promote goodwill. A more flagrant breach is where the franchisee operates another business on the back of the franchised business and fails to account for the profits from it in his franchise fee returns. There will generally be a prohibition in the franchise agreement on the franchisee's being involved in the operation of another business during the term of the agreement. It may be difficult to assess the loss to the franchisor, so the franchise agreement should confer a right of entry for the franchisor's authorised agent for the purpose of carrying out an on-site audit. The agreement should also include the right to take copies of and remove books and records if necessary.

The type of evidence which will be relevant in the event of such breaches will include:

(a) the field reports following site or centre visits by the franchisor and any follow-up correspondence recording the franchisee's performance;
(b) notes of meetings and telephone conversations, and correspondence between the parties during the currency of the agreement;
(c) the operations manual and any updates;
(d) auditor's evidence of turnover and whether this corresponds to till receipts and entries in the franchisee's books of account;
(e) evidence of orders or purchases where it is believed that the franchisee is operating a competing business.

By the franchisor

The franchisee is most likely to complain about the franchisor's lack of training and support. He may complain that the franchisor has failed to supply equipment in breach of the agreement. If his complaint is that the franchisor has failed to comply with its initial obligations, this should be clearly and promptly stated in writing. Without such supporting evidence, it is difficult for the franchisee to convince a court that the criticisms are genuine, particularly if the franchisee does nothing for several years, and then raises the issues in his defence and counterclaim only when the franchisor has commenced proceedings. If these issues are raised by the franchisee, the franchisor will need to produce the franchisee's training record and any assessments provided by either party following training courses.

Procurement of breach

The question of procurement of breach of contract may be relevant where the franchisor suspects but is unable to prove fraud on the part of a former franchisee who, it believes, is assisting in the running of a competing business following termination or expiry of the agreement while remaining ostensibly unconnected with the competing business. For example, in the case of *British Motor Trade Association* v *Salvadori and Others* [1949] Ch 556, [1949] 1 All ER 208, the defendant was attempting to circumvent a restrictive covenant by acting through an 'unrelated agent'. It was held that if that agent facilitated a breach of the restrictive covenant in circumstances where the agent knew of the covenant, he would be guilty of procuring a breach of contract.

17.5.3 Other causes of action

Other causes of action include trade mark infringement, passing off, copyright infringement and misuse of confidential information, which are considered in earlier chapters.

17.6 Remedies

The remedies most commonly sought by franchisors and franchisees are damages and injunctions.

17.6.1 Damages

Damages can of course be liquidated or unliquidated. Liquidated damages include claims by the franchisor for non-payment of franchise fees or invoices for goods provided to the franchisee pursuant to the franchise agreement. If the franchisor has a lease of premises occupied by the franchisee it may have a claim for non-payment of rent. Conversely, it would be unusual for the franchisee to have a claim for liquidated damages against the franchisor.

Unliquidated damages may be claimed by either the franchisor or the franchisee for breach of the franchise agreement, for example where the franchisee is operating a competing business during or following termination of the franchise agreement, or where the franchisor has not complied with its duties to support the franchisee. When assessing the measure of damages payable by the party in breach, the court may take into account the following:

(a) the turnover that the franchisee would have achieved if he had used his best endeavours to promote and extend the business or, in the case of breach by the franchisor, if the franchisor had supported him in accordance with its obligations under the agreement. The court may consider evidence such as the average turnover of the other franchisees in the network;

(b) the costs incurred by the innocent party in dealing with the breach or termination of the agreement, including legal fees and lost management time. Obviously, lost management time may be difficult to quantify;

(c) where a franchisee is in breach of the agreement by failing to promote the business or exploit the territory to its full potential, the profits that the franchisor would have made in the period required by a replacement franchisee to promote the business or exploit the territory. This will include damages for the period during which the franchisor is recruiting a replacement franchisee.

The party claiming damages will have to show that the losses were incurred as the natural and probable consequence of the other party's breach and that it was foreseeable that these losses would have occurred in the event of breach of the agreement. It is rare that either party will claim an account of the profits that have been made by the party in breach of the agreement. Generally speaking, the sum payable on an account of profits is likely to be less than the sum the innocent party would have made but for the other's breach.

Interest

Franchise agreements usually provide for the payment of interest on outstanding franchise fees and other sums due under the agreement. Interest on damages should always be claimed either at the rate of interest specified in the agreement, or, if higher, at the prevailing court rate, currently 8 per cent.

Duty to mitigate

The party claiming damages has a duty to mitigate its loss by taking all steps reasonably necessary to protect its interests. This is more likely to be relevant to a franchisor claiming damages in respect of lost profit following termination of the franchise agreement during the period it takes to recruit a new franchisee. The franchisor must show that it has taken all practical steps to appoint a replacement franchisee, and if it has not taken over the franchised business itself during the interim period, why it has not done so.

17.6.2   Injunctions

The other common remedy is an injunction. A claim for an injunction rests on an allegation that the other party is threatening, or intends to continue, the acts complained of unless he is restrained, and that there is no other adequate remedy such as damages. At its simplest, an injunction is an order of the court preventing a party from committing a breach of contract, although in practice it may go further and restrain any action which would infringe the other party's rights. An injunction is an equitable remedy and its grant is in the court's discretion. Furthermore, the party bringing the action must come to court 'with clean hands', which means, essentially, that he must have been blameless in his dealings with the other party.

An injunction is commonly claimed by a franchisor where the franchisee is in breach of the post-termination restrictive covenants. A franchisee may claim an injunction where a franchisor has wrongfully terminated the franchise agreement and he requires the franchisor to treat him in the same way as other franchisees in the network.

A distinction should be drawn between an injunction and the remedy of specific performance which may not be available in the context of franchise agreements. As a general rule, an order for specific performance of a contract will not be made where the court's constant supervision would be required to ensure compliance. Such supervision may be required in, for example, contracts for personal services.

In the case of *Shiloh Spinners Ltd* v *Harding* [1973] AC 691 the House of Lords confirmed that 'the impossibility for the courts to supervise the doing of work' may be rejected as a reason for denying a plaintiff specific performance. In the case of *North American Financial Group Ltd* v *SMR Enterprises Inc* (1984) it was held by the US District Court, Northern District of Illinois, Eastern Division, that specific performance could not be ordered for a contract which was partially for personal services.

However, in *Posner and Others* v *Scott-Lewis and Others* [1987] Ch 25, an order was made for specific performance of a personal services contract. It was held that the performance required was merely the execution of an agreement for the provision of the relevant services, which needed little continuing supervision by the court. The need for supervision was not enough in itself to justify refusing an order for specific performance. Emphasis would also be placed on questions such as whether the order sufficiently defined what performance was necessary, and whether damages would constitute a sufficient alternative remedy.

Types of injunction

An injunction may be granted to restrain the guilty party from acting in breach of his obligations under the agreement. This is known as a prohibitive injunction. An example is where the franchisee is in breach of his post-termination obligations by carrying on a business which is similar to or competes with the franchised business within or near his former territory.

A mandatory injunction is an order that a breach be undone and that the guilty party take some positive action to comply with its obligations under the agreement. An example is where the franchisee is ordered to deliver up literature, signage, etc in accordance with the franchise agreement. The franchisee might apply for a mandatory injunction if the franchisor has terminated the agreement and the franchisee claims that termination was wrongful and that the agreement remains in place.

Interlocutory injunctions

In any interlocutory application, the applicant seeks to persuade the court that it needs the relief sought urgently, and that an injustice will result if it has to wait until the action comes to trial. As mentioned *above*, the most common situation in which injunctive relief would be appropriate is where a franchisor wishes to restrain a former franchisee from carrying on a business similar to the franchised business within or around the territory following termination or

309

expiry of the agreement. It would be pointless for the franchisor to wait until the action came to trial, which is likely to be at least one year after termination or expiry of the agreement; the covenant restraining the former franchisee from carrying on such a business may well be limited to one year. The general principles which will apply to most applications of this type were expounded in the case of *American Cyanamid Co* v *Ethicon Ltd* [1975] AC 396. These are, briefly, as follows:

(1) Is there a serious issue to be tried?
(2) Does the balance of convenience lie in favour of the plaintiff or the defendant?

Serious issue to be tried   This does not mean that the plaintiff must show that its case will succeed at trial on its merits, simply that it has an arguable case, although the courts are now prepared to consider the merits (*see below*). The defendant will try to show that there is no arguable case to be tried or, in other words, that there is no breach.

The balance of convenience   If the court has decided that the plaintiff has an arguable case, it will consider the balance of convenience. It will weigh the effect on the plaintiff if an injunction is wrongly refused, against the effect on the defendant if an injunction is wrongly granted. In making this assessment, the court will consider whether an award of damages at trial could adequately compensate the franchisor or the franchisee for their losses.

If the franchisor is making the application, it may argue that if an injunction is not granted, and it later wins at trial and damages are assessed, will the court be able to quantify the measure of damages? Where the former franchisee is continuing to use the franchisor's trade name and trade mark, thereby indicating that his business is still connected with the franchisor's business, the franchisor can argue that its damages will be the loss of goodwill during the period between termination or expiry of the agreement and the date of the full trial. During that time the franchisor may not have a business in the territory, and will be exposed to the gradual loss of goodwill which arises from the former franchisee's presence in or around that territory.

The franchisor's ability to re-franchise the territory or trading area will depend on its ability to satisfy prospective franchisees that it can deliver the goodwill associated with its name and system, etc to the new franchisee. The continued presence of a franchisee in dispute will be a serious deterrent and will seriously impair the value of the goodwill in that territory or trading area.

The franchisor may also argue that the goods or services provided by the former franchisee are inferior to those provided by the franchisor and other franchisees, and that its goodwill is being further damaged by association with poor quality goods or services.

The franchisor will inevitably argue that such loss of goodwill is impossible to quantify or assess and may not, ultimately, be recoverable if the franchisee does not have the financial resources.

However, the franchisee may argue that if an injunction is granted, he will effectively be prevented from carrying on business and will be forced to close down. If he succeeds at trial and is awarded damages, these will be based on his loss of business for the period from the grant of the injunction to the full trial. He will argue that this damage will be unquantifiable, since it will be impossible for him to tell what his sales would have been. The counterpart to this argument is, of course, that in an enquiry as to damages the court would consider other network experience from which considerable comparative guidance could be obtained.

The franchisee may also argue that the grant of an injunction against him will be decisive in that, if he has to change his trading name or style or seek alternative employment, it is highly unlikely that he will be in a position to return to his present business a year or two later. But this argument is flawed in that, once the parties have embarked on proceedings, there is little or no possibility of resuming a close working relationship.

Could the parties pay damages?   The plaintiff must give a 'cross-undertaking in damages'—an undertaking to compensate the defendant for his losses if the injunction is later found to have been wrongly granted.

Unless there is evidence to the contrary, the court will assume that the defendant is in a position to pay damages, and may make this assumption even where the defendant is legally aided as in the case of *Prontaprint* v *Devaney, above*. On the evidence, the defendant was the owner of a house of reasonable value which was subject to a modest mortgage. It was held that he was not without means and not unable to meet a liability for damages.

The defendant may bring evidence to show that he could meet an award of damages, and, if he can also show that damages would adequately compensate the defendant, an injunction should be refused.

If the defendant is a limited company the plaintiff may be able to refer, for example, to the last accounts filed at Companies House, which will show the company's financial position, whether the accounts are up to date, whether the company has made a loss or has a charge over its assets, and its net assets.

Preserving the status quo: If the balance of convenience has failed to come down decisively one way or another, the court will be reluctant to grant an injunction which alters the status quo, for example, a business in which there has been a considerable investment and which has been firmly established in the market place. It will, however grant an injunction to stop a defendant starting such a business.

In the case of *Office Overload Ltd* v *Gunn* (*above*), the franchisee had already started a competing business. In fact, he began to compete with the franchisor's business even before the franchisor's notice to terminate the contract had expired. The franchisee submitted that damages would be an adequate remedy and that, since there was no question that the franchisor would not be able to meet an award of damages against him, the injunction should not be granted. This submission was rejected on the basis that the court will in principle grant an injunction if covenants in restraint of trade are prima facie valid and there is prima facie an infringement. Lord Denning MR pointed out that actions for breach of restraint of trade clauses are rarely fought to the end but usually decided at the interlocutory stage. Bridge LJ distinguished *American Cyanamid Company (above)*, since here there was no dispute on the affidavit evidence before the court, and no question of law to be decided.

In *Kall Kwik Printing (UK) Ltd v Bell and Another (above)*, Harman J referred to two points:

> Firstly that it is, in my view, always true that preventative justice is better than remedial justice. It is better to prevent a wrong than to allow it to happen and then make payments to compensate for it. Secondly, that the status quo before the repudiation made by the defendants and accepted by the plaintiff in September was undoubtedly that the plaintiff had a right to have the business carried on at the centre and to have profits from it. That status quo has been completely disrupted and it is right, in my view, that one should go back to that status quo if it be possible.

In that case, the franchisees had repudiated the agreement by moving to premises 700 metres down the road from the printing centre formerly operated by them, and were running a print and copy business from those premises.

Delay or acquiescence   It is essential that whoever makes the interlocutory application, whether franchisor or franchisee, avoids delay because it is of the essence of the application that the relief is urgently required. Delay will also be relevant to the balance of convenience argument, since delay will enable a franchisee to establish itself in the market place. Furthermore, the argument that the franchisor will suffer irreparable harm if the franchisee is allowed to continue in business is not convincing if it has taken no steps to try to stop the franchisee's activities. Any apparent delay must therefore be explained in the evidence as far as possible. For example, the plaintiff will generally need time to obtain evidence that the defendant is acting in breach of the agreement. It may sometimes be reasonable initially to negotiate with the other party, in which case it should be agreed with the other party that the consequent delay would not be relied on in court to oppose the plaintiff's application.

The strengths of the parties' cases   In general, the court will be reluctant to assess the likely outcome of the action because the evidence is incomplete, and is only in writing with no cross-examination of witnesses. An exception is where the grant or refusal of an interlocutory injunction will effectively determine the action. In the case of *Lansing Linde Ltd* v *Kerr* [1991] 1 WLR 251 it was held that where the decision is likely, in practice, to dispose of the proceedings, the court should consider the effect of the plaintiff's succeeding. This will apply to most situations where the franchisor is seeking to enforce restrictive covenants which are of limited duration and may therefore expire before the case comes to trial. In such cases, the judge must consider whether the covenant appears to be valid and enforceable and, if it is, should grant the injunction to enforce it.

The decision in *Kall Kwik Printing (UK) Ltd* v *Bell and Another* (*above*) appears to have reversed the trend, which was previously in favour of the franchisee. Contrast the decision of Harman J who granted an interlocutory injunction in favour of the franchisor, with *Prontaprint* v *Devaney* (*above*) in which the court held that Mr Devaney was likely to suffer irreparable loss and would have to close down his business if prevented from trading in his former territory or the surrounding area. This would effectively put an end to the proceedings, but the judge noted, if an injunction were not granted and a speedy trial ordered, the franchisor was likely to continue to trial because of the importance of the question to its business generally. Mr Devaney, of course, had the right to conduct his business by virtue of the franchise agreement only. His knowledge of how to do so had come from the training and confidential know-how provided by the franchisor. By continuing to trade in the same business, the court was sanctioning the post-termination exercise of rights which had been brought to an end.

17.6.3   Anton Piller orders

An Anton Piller order will rarely be appropriate in a franchise situation. The purpose of the order is to preserve evidence pending trial of an action. It may be relevant where the franchisor suspects dishonesty on the part of the franchisee and believes that he is likely to destroy material evidence if forewarned of the franchisor's intention. Most well drafted franchise agreements, though, include a right of entry for the franchisor to inspect the franchisee's books and records and take copies, and the franchisor will usually make use of this right if it suspects the franchisee of dishonesty.

17.6.4   Mareva injunctions

The Mareva injunction is often referred to as an order 'freezing' the defendant's assets. It is most commonly used where a party in breach of an agreement has funds deposited with a bank which could easily be transferred out of the jurisdiction of the court to put those funds out of the innocent party's reach. This type of injunction has never yet been sought in the context of a franchise dispute. The Mareva injunction may conceivably be relevant where the franchisee is not a UK citizen and has substantial savings in a bank account.

17.7 Other orders

17.7.1 Delivery up

There is a distinction between the statutory remedies for breach of specific intellectual property rights such as trade marks and copyright which are considered in Chapters 11 and 13, and the right to delivery up which arises out of the agreement itself.

In most situations the franchisor will not have the right to force the franchisee to hand over his own property to the franchisor. The franchisor's only entitlement is to stop this property being used in such a way as to infringe its rights, usually by use of its trade mark. This may of course be achieved by destruction or alteration of the goods (by obliteration of offending trade marks), or by delivery up of the goods to the court.

Generally the agreement will provide that on termination or expiry, the franchisee must return certain items to the franchisor. These will include:

(a) items of equipment supplied by the franchisor and bearing the franchisor's trade mark;
(b) operational manuals;
(c) documentation bearing the franchisor's trade mark such as headed notepaper, invoices, statements, compliment slips and promotional literature;
(d) menu cards, posters and price lists.

17.7.2 Possession orders

A possession order may be appropriate where the franchisor has granted a lease of its property to the franchisee. *See* Chapter 14.

17.7.3 Declarations

Although either party can apply to the court for a declaration that a particular clause of the agreement is valid or, conversely, unenforceable, or that the other party has infringed its rights, this will rarely be of any practical use. However, the threat of an action claiming this relief may be used effectively as a negotiating tool by the franchisee, particularly where the franchisor has serious concerns about the validity of certain clauses, such as the franchisee's covenant not to compete.

17.7.4 Bankruptcy and winding-up proceedings

Where a franchisor has a liquidated claim which it does not believe is disputed by the franchisee, it might consider serving a statutory demand. The demand will require payment of the amount outstanding, setting out details of how the claim has arisen. If there is a genuine dispute, however, it is likely the franchisor will have to abandon the demand and start ordinary court proceedings against the franchisee.

If the demand is not dealt with satisfactorily or is formally disputed, and the debt is in excess of £750, the franchisor can apply for a bankruptcy order against an individual or apply to wind up a company. In the case of a company franchisee, the franchisor may also consider applying immediately for a winding-up order without first serving a statutory demand. The franchisor will have to show that it has sought payment from the franchisee but that no payment has been made and that there is a substantial reason for non payment. This was illustrated in the case of *Taylor's Industrial Flooring* v *M & H Plant Hire (Manchester)* [1990] BCC 44.

The threat of bankruptcy or winding-up proceedings by service of a statutory demand may well be sufficient to persuade a franchisee to come to the negotiating table.

17.8 Enforcement

This chapter concentrates on the remedies appropriate to both parties in a franchise dispute. There are no enforcement issues specifically relevant in this context.

Chapter 18

The Franchise Contract

Chapter 18

The Franchise Contract

There are many misconceptions about the role of the franchise contract in a franchise arrangement. There are those (including some lawyers) who believe that the contract is the driving force and that if that is correctly drafted, all will be well. There are also periodic calls for standard form contracts, as if to suggest that all franchise contracts are so similar one only need change the names and all will be well.

18.1   Introduction

These views are, of course, fallacious. The commercial arrangements are the driving force and the contract needs to be tailor-made to reflect them. There will be occasions when a commercial objective cannot be achieved in the agreement because there is a legal obstacle, but the contract can never drive the deal. Standard contracts are not only not possible, despite similarity of boilerplate provisions, but positively dangerous. As will be appreciated from reading this work, the legal nature of franchising arrangements is hybrid and makes such an approach a minefield for the inexperienced. One of the important functions of the discussion and debate leading to the preparation of the contract is the legal audit which is thereto conducted to ensure that the basis on which the contract is prepared is sound. In addition, the franchisor's business system, accounting and reporting systems, and initial and ongoing support functions are examined for their practicability and effectiveness.

As explained in Chapter 6, there are various forms of agreement which may be required to accommodate the commercial arrangements. The contractual document which is fundamental, whatever else may be necessary, is the franchise agreement for the operation of an individual franchise unit. Before we discuss its provisions, there are some background aspects to be considered.

The fundamental objectives which both franchisors and franchisees seek to achieve are the development and exploitation of a single brand identity, supported by a common business system to operate profitably. While the concept is simple, a wealth of consequences follows, and needs to be addressed in the contractual documentation when one chooses to franchise.

The agreement has an effect beyond the two parties who enter into it. Clearly, they have a responsibility to each other, but there are others who have an interest in their performance of their obligations: other franchisees and consumers. Other franchisees are concerned since the success of the network depends on the success of each of their fellow franchisees; each franchisee whose standards fall below par is a threat to the reputation of the brand and the network.

The consumer patronises the business whose branding he or she recognises and in which the consumer has confidence. Consistent standards of product and service are essential to retain customer loyalty. The consumer has an interest in being provided with what he or she expects. The franchisor needs to be in a position to ensure that the consumer is not let down and that no franchisee lets down the rest of the network.

18.2   Preliminary considerations

The British Franchising Association (BFA) Code of Ethics (*see* Appendix 2) has been adopted by the BFA and, essentially, by other members of the European Franchise Federation (EFF). Each member of the EFF has been permitted to make some adjustments to accommodate differences in practices between member states. The BFA adjustments appear in an addendum called *Extension and Interpretation*, which makes it plain that the Code does not form part of a franchise agreement unless it is expressly so provided. The remedy for alleged non-compliance is to complain to the BFA, whose members undertake to comply with the Code. The BFA Articles of Association provide a disciplinary mechanism in connection with such complaints.

If a franchisor wishes to advertise for franchisees in the national press the contract (*inter alia*) will have to satisfy the NPA requirements.

One cannot ignore the Block Exemption Regulation (BER) (*see* Chapter 6) when preparing the franchise contract. The importance of the Regulation is emphasised by the provisions in the Deregulation and Contracting Out Act 1994, which will lead to a relaxation of the requirement to furnish particulars under the Restrictive Trade Practices Act 1976, if the BER applies.

18.3   Control by the franchisor

There is a conflict between the legal need to write contracts with precision, and the need for the franchisor to have flexibility to require the franchisee to introduce changes into the business system, the products and services range and the business's appearance so that it retains its competitiveness in the marketplace. The usual technique for achieving this is to insert substantive obligations in the franchise agreement and to provide for the business systems and methods to be conducted in accordance with an operations manual which can be varied and updated as need be. This approach has been endorsed by the European Commission in the BER, where the need to have a document identifying franchising know-how is acknowledged in the definition of know-how. Also, in art 3.2(f) of the BER it is acknowledged that a franchise agreement would contain an obligation on the franchisee 'to apply the commercial methods devised by the franchisor including any subsequent amendment thereof . . .'.

Franchise agreements are often said to be unfair and loaded in favour of the franchisor. By its nature, however, the arrangement must allow the franchisor to make determinations and give directions which an individual franchisee may consider to be unfair to him. A franchisee will often be concerned with the effect which a franchisor's directions have on him personally. The franchisor has wider interests to consider. Essentially, the franchisee is being granted a licence to use the franchisor's branding and know-how. The franchisee will be required to sell the range of products and provide the services laid down by the franchisor, consistent with the branding, and in the interests of uniformity at all network outlets. Most franchisors provide continuing support services, including field visits, market research, research and development, monitoring of performance and a range of advisory services to assist and encourage a franchisee in achieving the best results of which he is capable. The franchisor cannot do it all for the franchisee; the franchisee has a lot to do for himself, but franchising essentially requires a franchisee to operate in a controlled and limited environment. Undisciplined challenges to that environment may not only be bad for that franchisee, but can have an adverse effect on the whole network. The franchisor therefore needs to have an extensive array of controls and the ability to intervene to enable standards, quality and uniformity to be maintained.

18.4   Payment of fees

A discontented franchisee may withhold payment of franchise fees and/or advertising contributions. Given that frequently the franchisor's only source of income is franchise fees, withholding of fees by any franchisee is serious, and if a number do so it can destroy the franchisor's business and with it the network. Indeed, there have been cases where that has happened. There are other side effects. If a franchisee fails to pay as an expression of discontent, effectively he is still demanding the restoration of what he regards as his entitlement but for which he is not prepared to pay. Effectively, the franchisor and other franchisees are subsidising him. Furthermore, if he uses the franchisor's name and system he will be receiving continuing benefits while continuing to

321

refuse to pay. If the refusal to pay extends to advertising contributions, there is no doubt whatever that the franchisees who do pay will be subsidising the non-paying franchisee. That will mean that the relationship will almost certainly come to an end even though both may suffer far more than is necessary.

18.4.1   Counterclaims

Typically, franchisees who do not pay and are sued allege that the franchisor has failed in some respects to perform its obligations (even in some cases the sudden realisation three or more years after the event, that the franchisor's initial obligations were not performed) and the allegations are used to support a counterclaim. There may be a valid counterclaim; there may not. In franchising there is no such thing as black and white. The function of a franchisor is to create opportunities and a climate from which franchisees may benefit. The extent to which they benefit will invariably owe a lot to their own abilities, skills and commitment. The various performance levels in any franchise network clearly demonstrate that some do better than others even though all are working to the same formula. There are no guarantees and both the franchisor and franchisees are human and there will be errors of judgment by both. This is the same in all walks of life. In franchising each tends to expect more of the other, so the disappointment tends to be greater when difficulties arise.

18.4.2   Unfair contract terms

Unfortunately, the Court of Appeal, following *Stewart Gill Ltd* v *Horatio Myer & Co Ltd* [1992] 1 QB 600, applied the Unfair Contract Terms Act 1977 to a franchise agreement in the case of *Fastframe Franchises Ltd* v *Roman Lohinski* (Court of Appeal 3 March 1993, *unreported*). The decision is of some importance, although the franchisor's case does not appear to have been fully presented to the Court of Appeal or, if it was, the court did not deal with the issues in its decision.

The facts were that Fastframe Franchises Ltd entered into a franchise agreement with Mr Lohinski, who withheld payment of royalty and marketing services fees because he claimed:

(a) that the franchise agreement gave him a monopoly/exclusivity within his marketing area;
(b) that the marketing services fund was misapplied; he complained that no advertising was placed in his area and that the advertising was on a national basis which was not much use to him and that it supported the parallel service (*see below*);
(c) that the franchisor had established a parallel service to commercial customers which infringed his monopoly.

The matter came before the Court of Appeal having been the subject of Ord 14 proceedings before Master Munrow, and on appeal from him to Harman J.

The court considered that there were arguable issues which suggested unfairness since, although the defendant's right to raise these issues was not affected, he would be obliged to pay the plaintiff what he owed without being able to set off what he claimed. If ever there was an open invitation to defendant franchisees in such cases to raise spurious issues it would be hard to find it better put. What is troubling about the decision is that the court appears to have taken the defendant's case for granted, as if there was no question that there was substance to it. Perhaps the plaintiff did not argue the point, since the court does not appear to have addressed whether there were questions as to the sustainability of the counterclaims.

The court repeats the defendant's assertion that he had 'exclusive' rights. What the contract provided was that the defendant (franchisee) had 'prime responsibility' for an area. The word 'prime' is incompatible with 'exclusivity', and the word 'responsibility' is incompatible with the terms which would express a right or, as is perhaps more appropriate, the granting of a licence. In addition, if there was a grant of exclusive rights the Restrictive Trade Practices Act 1976 would have applied; particulars of the agreement should have been provided to the Director General of Fair Trading; they were not; any exclusivity would thus be void.

The second issue related to advertising. The defendant's complaint was that advertising contributions were not spent on his business and in his area. Quite apart from the fact that this was not correct, the relevant provision in the contract required the plaintiff (franchisor) to spend advertising contributions on 'promoting the system'. How this obligation could be construed to lend credibility to the defendant's claim is difficult to fathom. Was the court's acceptance of the claim based on the fact that the plaintiffs did not raise this issue? We do not know because the issue is not dealt with in the judgment; it may be that it was not, and the point was assumed by the court to have been conceded.

The last issue related to the establishment by the franchisor of a parallel initiative which franchisees were invited to join. For the defendant to have a valid claim under that head he would have to establish that it infringed his 'exclusive rights', a point dealt with *above*, and that the marketing funds were wrongly applied. As to the latter, the words 'promote the system' would be significant, but what was also significant, and again apparently ignored, was that the plaintiff had made considerable advances to the promotional and advertising spend and had subsidised its activities.

As a separate issue, it is also to be regretted that the decision does not examine the nature of and extent to which the exemption contained in Sched 1 to the Unfair Contract Terms Act 1977 may apply to franchise agreements.

It is to be hoped that this Court of Appeal decision will not encourage franchisees to risk jeopardising franchise networks by raising spurious claims to which the court will lend credibility by denying franchisors enforceable judgments for sums owed. If that is the case the prospects are bleak. It is to be regretted that the Court of Appeal's decision was not based on a full analysis of franchising, which would have shown that the overriding balance was indeed correct and that the reasonableness test had been satisfied.

For all these reasons, not least the inevitability of counterclaims whether or not justified, most franchisors provide in their contracts that all payments to be made by the franchisee to the franchisor should be made without deduction or right of set-off. If there are payments for products or other non-fee payments one would expect standard conditions of sale to apply, dealing with issues of non-supply, under-supply or faulty or defective supplies. These issues should be kept separate from fee payments, even if the franchisor receives his income from product mark-up and has no other fee income.

The various forms of legal documentation have been described in Chapter 6. With domestic franchises there will be the following forms which are used depending upon the nature of the arrangements.

18.5   Area development agreements

Area development agreements are not as common in the UK as in some other countries, notably the USA. Few domestic franchise companies employ this technique although companies from the USA have brought to the UK development agreements which mirror their arrangements in the USA. There can be legal problems unless these arrangements are carefully structured to avoid the provisions of the Fair Trading Act 1973 (*see* Chapter 6). The terminology in use is confusing, but an area development agreement is widely understood to be an arrangement between franchisor and franchisee which does not involve sub-franchising. Where sub-franchising is contemplated, the arrangement is called 'master franchising'. The terminology is most widely used and understood in these senses. Sub-franchising issues are dealt with in Chapter 20 where master franchising agreements are considered.

18.5.1   Commercial objectives

Before drafting the necessary documentation, one must understand the commercial objectives.

For the franchisor, the advantage of an area development agreement is that the franchisor deals with a single franchisee rather than a number; the franchisee will be a different type of business person than a single franchisee; the franchisor is able to plan growth in an agreed framework and ensure that the franchisee's 'umbrella' organisation is properly structured.

For the franchisee there is an opportunity to develop a much larger organisation and accordingly to structure his business and its finances to accommodate the expected growth. In some cases, the prospects are particularly attractive to institutional venture funds since the expected size of the resulting business justifies the investment. The most likely area of debate in such a case will be about exit routes. The franchisee has the comfort of knowing that he will have the opportunity to grow to a certain size provided he performs his contractual obligations.

The development agreement provides the framework for the area developer to become the owner and operator of a number of franchised outlets. The developer will require protection in the form of territories and rights which may or may not be exclusive. He will have the right to establish a predetermined number of franchise outlets within an agreed period. The developer's interest will be focused on numbers of outlets in a manageable geographic area.

18.5.2 Terms

The area development agreement is essentially a form of option ('development right') frequently having the characteristics of a put and call option. Each time the development right is exercised, the franchisor and the area developer enter into a unit agreement.

The agreement will contain detailed provisions in relation to the development programme and the procedure for selecting, approving and developing locations, as well as the detailed business infrastructure to be established by the area developer. The area developer will have to undertake certain central obligations concerning business organisation and functions. His senior staff will have to undergo specific training. The franchisor is likely to require that the person to be appointed managing director or general manager is approved by the franchisor, and passes the franchisor's training course. In addition it is not uncommon to find a requirement that the managing director or general manager should have a minimum equity stake in the business.

There are a number of problems to be considered in structuring the arrangements:

(1) What is to be the number and density of the outlets?
(2) Are exclusive or non-exclusive rights to be granted?
(3) Will the area developer be limited to opening the number of outlets agreed on in the contract, or will he be permitted to open more? If so, on what basis?
(4) What degree of transferability will there be? Will the area developer be permitted to dispose of his right to develop the area? That would be

unusual, as most franchisors expect an area developer to complete the development schedule before seeking to sell the business.

(5) To what extent will the area developer be permitted to dispose of individual units without affecting the development right, and on what conditions? The issue is not whether the area developer can sell individual units, but whether he can do so before he has fully developed the territory (as required by the contract), or if he does so thereafter, must he replace the outlet sold with another, and if so, on what terms?

(6) What provisions are to be made for termination of the arrangements? There are three component parts to consider: the development right; the total development agreement; and individual unit agreements. These are considered in turn *below*.

The development right

The development right would normally be capable of termination in the event of failure to meet the development schedule. If the area developer has exclusive rights, should he merely lose his exclusivity? Whether or not he has exclusive rights, should he lose the right to continue to pursue the development schedule? If so, are there ways in which he may be able to protect himself against a rate of progress slower than planned? The franchisor will attach great importance to the maintenance of the development schedule and may feel that the failure to do so would operate too much to the detriment of the development of the network. Whichever way the franchisor decides to approach the problem there is no clear answer. At worst, the franchisor would have parallel systems being operated in the same area by the original area developer and one subsequently appointed. The practical problems which can arise in such circumstances may lead the franchisor to require that the defaulting developer's agreement should be capable of termination for failure to sustain the development schedule.

The total development agreement

Under a total development agreement, a developer is required to observe and perform the 'non-development right' provisions in the development agreement and implement the detailed infrastructure provisions referred to earlier. Failure to do so would not normally lead to termination unless the developer had been given an opportunity to put matters right. But if, after warnings, the default is not remedied and the franchisor terminates the agreement, one would expect termination to bring the development agreement, including the development right, to an end. This would have to be the case, since if the general provisions relating to the area developer's business structure are ignored, it would be futile to permit him to continue to develop by opening further units. Such a breach would also be expected to lead to a position where the individual unit agreement would likewise be capable of being terminated, since the business structure, designed to provide the basis for the supervision and control of those units, would not be in place.

Individual unit agreements

There could be problems with an individual unit which could lead to termination of the agreement relating to the unit. Whether the termination should affect the main agreement must depend on:

(a) why the agreement is terminated;
(b) how many such agreements are terminated within a particular period; and
(c) whether the breach of the individual unit agreement is sufficiently serious to amount to a breach of the main agreement.

Consequences of termination

The consequences of terminating each of these three elements must next be considered and provided for. The following questions will be relevant:

(1) Does the loss of the development right affect the continued operation of the individual outlets, and if not can the developer still apply to open new outlets, but independently of the development arrangement? What would be the consequences if he did?
(2) If the whole of the development agreement is terminated, should the individual unit agreements also be in jeopardy?
(3) One would also expect that all the normal consequences of termination of a franchise agreement would be equally applicable. Where the franchisor is to have an option to purchase on termination, the scale of the business to be purchased could cause problems for it because the amount of money involved could be considerable.

18.6 The franchisor's strategic plan

The franchisor, in structuring its franchise package, makes a number of strategic decisions concerning its *modus operandi* which will impact the franchise documentation. The issues dealt with by the documentation will have to address three distinct stages:

(1) From recruitment to the establishment of the franchisee in business.
(2) The continuing business relationship.
(3) Termination of the relationship for whatever reason.

The decisions which the franchisor will make will concern the following:

(1) Do I want to be involved in the property chain (*see* Chapter 14)?

(2) If the franchisee is property-based, how will I cope with the finding and conversion of the premises?

(3) If the franchisee is mobile, what will be the appropriate means of transport, and how will it be identified, obtained and equipped?

(4) How will I train the franchisee and what level of training will his staff require (and if so how many of them do I train)?

(5) How will I provide for the franchisees' accounting and reporting systems?

(6) Will I introduce networked computer systems with modem access?

(7) How will I control the use of trade secrets and confidential information?

(8) What will be the appropriate method for dealing with and controlling trade marks and trade names?

(9) What arrangements will there be for supplies of products and services to the franchise network?

(10) What level of support and monitoring will I provide and how will this be delivered?

(11) How will I market and promote the sale of franchises?

(12) What level of research and development and market research into new products and services do I intend to introduce? How will I update the franchises? What will be my response to suggested innovations of franchisees?

(13) What different approaches are needed to franchises which are companies, individuals or partnerships?

(14) What level of income do I need to be profitable and how it will be achieved?
   — Can I mark up products?
   — Can I tie the franchisee to buy these products?
   — If I charge a percentage of the franchisee's gross revenues what should that percentage be?
   — How should I structure the initial (up-front) payments and at what level should they be fixed?

(15) What advertising and promotional support will I provide?
   — Is national or local advertising best?
   — Should there be a mix and if so what is the right mix?

(16) What level of contribution to advertising and promotion will be required from franchisees?

(17) What will be the length of the agreement? Will it be subject to extensions or renewals and, if so, on what basis?

(18) On what terms will the franchisee be permitted to sell the business?

(19) Do I want an option to purchase the business and if so on what terms:
— If the franchisee wishes to sell?
— In the event of termination?

18.7 Drafting the agreement

The resolution of these issues will enable the draftsman to prepare the franchise agreement. There is, however, more to some of the issues than may be apparent on the surface. Sometimes two contracts are prepared, one dealing with the pre-opening issues, and the other with the continuing relationship. There is no need in principle for two contracts, and there is a risk of conflicts and overlaps between the two if care is not taken. However many contracts are prepared, the issues to be dealt with will remain the same.

18.7.1 Pre-contract issues

There are invariably discussions between the franchisor and the prospective franchisee which culminate in the execution of the contract. In the course of those discussions the franchisor provides information to the prospective franchisee to help him decide whether or not to take up the franchise. With the increasing use of computers and the demands of banks for business plans, franchisors often prepare very detailed financial projections or work with franchisees to enable them to prepare their own business plans. This creates scope for claims that a franchisee was misled, and franchisors should ensure that the contractual documentation places the pre-contract discussions and disclosure in the correct perspective.

18.7.2 Unfair contract terms

Franchisors' liabilities are discussed in Chapter 8, and earlier in this chapter the Unfair Contract Terms Act 1977 was mentioned. The EC Commission has issued a Directive (93/13/EEC) to approximate the laws and practices of member states relating to unfair contract terms in consumer contracts, which has been introduced in the UK by regulation. In some EU jurisdictions (Germany, for example), laws already in existence relating to standard term consumer contracts have been applied to franchise agreements. The definition of 'consumer' in the Directive and in the Unfair Terms in Consumer Contracts Regulations 1994 (SI 1994 No 3159) which implements the Directive, is 'a natural person who in making a contract to which these Regulations apply is acting for purposes which are outside his business'. Since the only purpose for which a franchisee will enter into a franchise contract is for the purposes of his business, the Regulations will not apply to franchise agreements.

18.7.3   Premises

The franchise package may deal with premises in a number of different ways:

(a) the provision by the franchisor of standard plans and specifications for the franchised outlets which will be adapted either by the franchisor or the franchisee's own surveyor or architect subject to approval by the franchisor;

(b) the provision by the franchisor of a manual with property specifications, from which the franchisee's surveyor, architect or shopfitter will prepare detailed plans and specifications for the franchised outlet to be approved by the franchisor;

(c) a complete service by the franchisor consisting of the preparation of plans and specifications followed by the necessary works to convert the premises into the franchised outlet (a turnkey operation);

(d) the hiring by the franchisee of a shopfitter, either from a list approved by the franchisor or freely chosen by the franchisee, who will be employed to convert the premises into the franchised outlet in accordance with the franchisor's plans and specifications and subject to the franchisor's approval.

Where the franchisor is not itself doing the work, the quality and standards will be monitored by the franchisor for compliance with its standards, while the franchisee will have responsibility for ensuring the correct quality of day-to-day supervision.

18.7.4   Vehicles

Where a vehicle is to be acquired as part of the package, the manner of fitting out and equipping it will have to be detailed. The franchisor may arrange for the works to be carried out, or provide sufficiently detailed plans and specifications to enable the franchisee to organise it for himself. The specifications will invariably include the colour scheme and livery for the vehicle.

18.7.5   Price, financing and deposit

The price of the initial package will be specified, as will the manner of payment. This may be in cash in full on signature, although this is rare. More often a deposit is required on signature, with payment of the balance to follow on delivery of the equipment or at other identified stages, such as commencement of training.

There may be an allowance for the fact that finance has to be arranged, in which case the contract may be conditional on satisfactory finance being obtained. What is to be regarded as satisfactory finance should be defined carefully. If hire-purchase finance is to be obtained for vehicles and fixture and fittings, the contract must accommodate the fact that the finance house will acquire title.

Whether or not delivery charges, installation charges, shopfitting works and VAT are included in the price the initial package should be clear.

It should also be clear whether, and in what circumstances, any deposit paid, or a part of it, is returnable to the franchisee. At this early stage the franchisor will wish to retain the right to withdraw from the transaction. It may be that training will show the franchisee to be unsuitable for the particular type of franchise. If the franchisor withdraws from the transaction, the deposit should be returnable to the franchisee in full, unless the franchisee fails the training course, in which case the franchisor should be entitled to recover his costs to date.

The position is different if the franchisee wishes to withdraw. The franchisor may be prepared to take a risk on its own withdrawal, but if the franchisee can withdraw without cost after training, the deposit will not amount to much evidence of good faith. It is therefore usual to provide for the franchisor to be able to retain the whole or part of the deposit to reimburse it for the expenses in which it has been involved. The franchisor will also wish to avoid providing a training school to prospective competitors.

18.7.6 Rights of the franchisee

The franchisee will be given such of the following rights as may be relevant:

(a) to use the trade marks and trade names of the franchisor and to benefit from the goodwill associated with them;

(b) to use the brand image and the design and decor of the premises (including layouts, fixtures, fittings and equipment) developed by the franchisor in projecting that image;

(c) to use the franchisor's trade secrets, know-how, system and methods;

(d) to use the franchisor's copyright material;

(e) in appropriate cases to use the recipes, formulae, specifications, processes and methods of manufacture developed by the franchisor;

(f) to conduct the franchised business on or from premises approved by the franchisor (usually premises are specified in the agreement) identified under the franchisor's name and brand etc, and in accordance with the franchisor's system and methods. Many franchise schemes carry with them the promise of exclusive rights, but this is not an essential feature and in many cases exclusivity is not given. Exclusive rights, if granted, vary according to whether the franchised business is physically immobile (such as a retail shop) or mobile. In the case of a retail shop, exclusivity would be based on a radius from the premises, within which the franchisor will not franchise another similar unit. In the case of a mobile franchise an area within which the franchisee may carry on his business may be exclusive or non-exclusive and the franchisee may be forbidden to solicit or tout for business outside the area. The grant of exclusive rights involves issues of competition law which are dealt with in Chapters 15 and 16. It is difficult to lay down any set radius, for what is reasonable will vary considerably from case to case, but the franchisor cannot hope for successful growth in its own business if its units are so close together that none can operate profitably;

(g) the right (as well as the obligation) to obtain supplies of products from the franchisor and/or nominated suppliers at special prices. The franchisor can often obtain quite good reductions for franchisees using the bulk-purchasing power of the chain. The issue of product supply has been dealt with in Chapters 15 and 16.

18.7.7   Term and renewals

The term of the agreement has to be considered. A franchise relationship should be capable of subsisting in the long term. The BFA Code provides that the 'duration of the agreement . . . should be long enough to allow the individual franchisee to amortise his initial franchise investment'. This ethical principle, which is vague and anomalous in many respects, is expanded on by the BFA in the *Extension and Interpretation* attached to and incorporated in the Code which states:

> It is recognised:
>
> — that franchise contracts are ordinarily offered for a uniform term within a network;
> — that for a minority of the largest franchise opportunities amortising the initial investment may not be a primary objective for the franchisee. In such cases the objective should be to adopt a contract period which reasonably balances the interests of the parties to the contract;
> — that this section could be subject to national laws concerning the restraint of trade and may need to be met through renewal clauses.

There may be reasons (for example where there is a product tie, and one follows the cases concerning petrol station solus agreements commencing with *Esso Petroleum Co Ltd* v *Harpers Garage (Stourport) Ltd* [1968] AC 269, [1967] 1 All ER 699) why the initial term should not exceed, say, five years. In these cases the franchisee should ideally be given an option to renew the agreement.

It is a requirement of the Code that the agreement should contain 'the basis for any renewal of the agreement'.

Some franchisors do not like to grant too long a term in the belief that there may be developments in the law to which they would like to have the opportunity to respond sooner rather than later. In any event, it is invariable practice to grant a franchisee an option to renew provided he has performed his obligations under the agreement, updates, refurbishes and re-equips the franchised unit, and enters into a new agreement in the franchisor's then current form.

There is, however, a detectable trend for some franchisors to use renewal to impose wider conditions. These may include 'revamp' and relocation clauses.

Revamp clauses

A 'revamp' clause may require the franchisee to strip the shop back to the shell, and completely refit it to accommodate a new presentation, with costs perhaps equal to or greater than those incurred when he originally set up. The franchisee can of course decide not to renew on those terms, perhaps because the franchisor cannot demonstrate an acceptable return on capital investment for the franchisee. The franchisee may not be able to raise the money from the banks, who are equally uncertain about financial viability. The franchisor, who will benefit from any increase in product mark-up or franchise fees based on gross sales, regardless of the effect on the franchisee's net return, has a conflicting interest at this point. However, a revamp clause may be necessary to keep the business competitive and up to date.

Such a clause is not in itself unfair, but the way in which it is enforced can be. A franchisor who has such a provision in mind should observe the following requirements, which follow the BFA membership criterion that pilot-testing must be carried out: A revamp is analogous to opening a new operation in many significant respects.

(1) The 'revamp' should be previously tested by the franchisor, in practice, who should be able to demonstrate its effect on the financial performance of the units where it has been tested.
(2) The testing should be in a sufficient number of representative operational units to ensure that there are sufficient comparables to enable an informed decision to be made by franchisees. The franchisor should make the decision as to the sufficiency of the number of units at which testing should take place.
(3) The franchisor should be prepared to assist his franchisees in making arrangements with their banks for financing or refinancing the revamping.
(4) Revamps should not be required so often that a franchisee cannot reap the financial rewards of the expenditure, both in terms of recovering of investment and increased profitability over a reasonable period.

Relocation clauses

Under a 'relocation' clause, the franchisor makes it a condition of renewal that the franchisee closes down his present premises and moves to fresh premises which the franchisor may decide offer a better trading opportunity, or larger accommodation to suit the franchisor's new ideas. This, in essence, requires the franchisee to set up an entirely new business with all the inherent risks and considerable expenses, as well as the cost of disposal of the existing premises and of maintaining them until disposal, which may be at a loss.

Problems which can arise when a franchisor decides that a completely fresh approach is necessary, even though it may be completely right and change may be essential. There are ways in which such issues can be handled properly. The following considerations arise:

(1) Is it really necessary for the franchisee to be required to move? Is it possible for the old and the new to live alongside each other? A franchisee may not be able to afford to relocate and the franchisor does have a responsibility to him. The franchisee may well have a successful operation earning good profits for him and a good flow of franchise fees for the franchisor. The franchisor must exercise the utmost good faith consistent with his responsibilities, and should be prepared to demonstrate that change is necessary for future competitiveness and to update the system.

(2) The franchisor must be able to demonstrate, by his own adequate pilot-testing, that the relocation is likely to be cost-effective for the franchisee.

(3) The franchisor should be prepared to assist the franchisee in making his financing arrangements with his bankers.

(4) In no circumstances should a franchisor use revamping or relocation as an excuse for unfairly ridding himself of any franchisee. His motive should be to enhance and promote the franchise system and its profitability equitably for both franchisor and franchisee.

18.7.8   Future developments

Quite apart from the position on renewal of the agreement, the franchise network must, over the years, maintain and renew its freshness of image, appeal to the consumer and competitiveness in the marketplace. It may be prudent to require the franchisee in his contract to set aside amounts for the future modernisation and upgrading of the premises and equipment.

In these days of rapid technological progress, many franchisors have to consider the possibility that some new technology will have to be introduced in the future. Computerised cash registers (electronic point of sale or EPOS) are a recent example of a major technological development in retailing. The system fulfils many functions, such as stock control and recording gross income and categories of income. There may be a link with the franchisor's computer, which can provide franchisees with monthly profit and loss account and stock order lists. This is the sort of service a franchisor should provide and would be welcomed by franchisees if it is consistent with the original package.

If a franchisor wishes to have the right to introduce such a system or other new development in the future, he will also need to reserve the right to require the franchisee to spend whatever is necessary to install and run the system, regardless of the benefits. This is clearly untenable since the franchisee would be exposed to an obligation, unilaterally imposed, to spend without limit, and so the franchisor will have to be precise in its plan and proposals. One method of overcoming the problem is for the franchisor to delineate the scope of the planned requirements and to indicate limits of capital and running costs so that the franchisee can make an informed decision before undertaking a commitment.

18.7.9 Franchise and management fees

The franchisor's gross revenue will largely, and in some cases wholly, depend on the payment of franchise fees and/or management services fees by the franchisees. A franchisor will be concerned to ensure that franchisees fully disclose all income on which the management service fees are calculated, and will seek to secure its position. Obviously, there will always be those franchisees who see the payment of fees calculated by reference to gross income as a challenge but in franchising there is an overall structure which puts the cheat at a disadvantage.

The structure contains a number of features which will inevitably be reflected in the contract and in the system which has been developed by the franchisor and is operated by the franchisees. Thus:

(1) The franchisor, in establishing the system based on its experience in the marketplace, will have laid down guidelines for financial achievement. It will illustrate to franchisees, when training them, what their gross and net margins should be at given levels of turnover, and the percentage which each group of expense items should bear to turnover. A concealment of gross income would inevitably distort those margins. The margins could, of course, also be distorted by incompetence or by 'leakage' attributable to staff or customer theft, but if that is the case the franchisor should quickly be able to assist the franchisee in identifying the cause, and advise on or initiate appropriate remedial action.

(2) The franchisor will establish standard-form accounting systems and reporting procedures in order that it can be informed about the performance of each franchisee's business.

(3) The franchisor will require the right to spot audit the franchisee's financial records without prior warning.

(4) The accounting system and reporting procedures will enable the franchisor to monitor the franchisee's performance and to detect warning signs if all is not well.

(5) The franchisor's field support staff, who provide back-up to franchisees by regular visits, will have the opportunity of discussing performance with franchisees, and making spot checks on stocks, books and other records to verify the accuracy of the information which the franchisee is reporting to the franchisor. These checks are part of the support which a franchisor provides, since inaccurate information, whether intentional or unintentional, hampers the franchisor's ability to provide assistance and guidance.

(6) The franchisor, in collecting and collating the information from each franchisee, builds up a record of each franchisee's performance and is able to establish an average for the whole network. Any franchisee whose achievements are markedly below average will be a candidate for special attention so that the cause may be identified and remedial action taken.

(7) The franchisee should be required to make a return of gross revenue for Value Added Tax purposes. Copies of these returns and any assessments to VAT made by Customs and Excise should be obtained by the franchisor and compared with the figures submitted to it.

(8) The franchisor will have access to the franchisee's supply sources. If it knows what the franchisee is buying it will have a very good idea of what his gross sales figures should be if the business is operated properly. Visits by field support staff should reveal if the franchisee is purchasing products from non-approved sources which are not put through the system could provide the opportunity to falsify figures as well as distort the performance of the outlet.

(9) In some cases the franchisor may be able to obtain information from large customers of the network with whom arrangements have been made for the supply of goods and/or services by the network.

18.7.10   Obligations of the franchisor

The contract should detail the obligations undertaken by the franchisor on a continuing basis. Their nature and extent will have been defined by the franchisor when answering the questions detailed *above*. It is not a wise practice to omit from the contract obligations which the franchisor intends to undertake, and the opportunity should be taken clearly to define their nature and scope so that there is no room for future misunderstanding.

18.7.11   Obligations of the franchisee

The franchisee may have the following obligations imposed on him:

(a) to carry on only the business franchised, on approved premises and strictly in accordance with the franchisor's methods and standards;

(b) to observe certain minimum opening hours. These will usually be the hours which enable the business to be operated most profitably within the scope of the franchisor's system without incurring disproportionate overheads;

(c) to pay franchise and other fees. The financial aspects are dealt with in Chapter 7;

(d) to follow the accounting and reporting systems laid down by the franchisor. The purpose is twofold. First, the franchisor has a means of checking and calculating any fees to which it may be entitled. Second, these systems should provide management information and show whether or not the projected gross and net profit margins are being achieved;

(e) not to advertise without prior approval of the advertisements by the franchisor. The franchisor will invariably handle all national advertising but this would not usually prohibit the franchisee from conducting local or other advertising. The franchisor will wish to have control of the contents of advertisements which make use of its trade mark or trade name to ensure that the standards associated with them are maintained;

(f) to use and display such point-of-sale or advertising material as the franchisor stipulates. Also to use bags, boxes, wrappers and other consumables which may bear the franchisor's trade mark. Point-of-sale and advertising material may be supplied free of charge, as part of the advertising arrangements, but other items would have to be paid for;

(g) to maintain the premises in a good, clean, sanitary condition and to redecorate when required to do so by the franchisor. Provisions of this kind often cause difficulty in practice. The franchisor will always be striving to ensure that the premises have the best possible appearance, while the franchisee will be reluctant to spend his money;

(h) to maintain business insurance cover. The purpose of this provision is to protect the franchisee from the consequences of fire, public liability, employees' liability, liability to third parties, product liability and other claims. It protects the franchisee's business and his livelihood. In some cases franchisors are able to arrange insurance schemes for the benefit of the network. Indeed, some insurance brokers have offered specialist services to franchisors. Some franchisors require the franchisee to take out keyman life assurance where this is economically feasible;

(i) to permit the franchisor's staff to enter the premises to inspect and see whether the franchisor's standards are being maintained and the terms of the agreement are being observed;

(j) to train his staff in the franchisor's methods and to ensure that they maintain the standards of service associated with the franchisor's branding and system;

(k) not to assign the franchise contract or the business without the franchisor's consent. The assignability of the contract or the business is an essential feature. If there is no right to do so there is less incentive to the franchisee to invest in and build the business. The franchisor, however, will need to approve the purchaser. There is rarely difficulty in practice in arranging a transfer of the contract or business provided the purchaser of the franchisee's business meets the franchisor's selection standards and successfully passes through any necessary training. There is a tendency on the part of some advisers to approach these provisions in a franchise agreement as if they are analogous to a lease. This results in an insistence on the words 'such consent not to be unreasonably withheld' being inserted in the agreement. This is a false analogy. Most franchisors deal with many prospective franchisees before both parties are happy to enter into a contract. When a franchisee is selling his business, he is in effect recruiting a new franchisee for the franchisor. Since a franchisor may find that only 5 to 10 per cent of prospective franchisees it interviews are suitable, there is no reason to suppose that the franchisee will necessarily be more successful. If the franchisor concludes that the prospective franchisee put forward is not suitable, no third party can enforce the creation of the close relationship which is necessary. Many contracts provide for a fixed or percentage fee based on the sale price to be paid to the franchisor to cover its costs of processing the transaction and of training and establishing the new franchisee. Some franchisors are able to introduce purchasers from their waiting list of prospective franchisees, and charge for the introduction, as would a business transfer agent. Some franchise agreements grant an option for the franchisor to purchase the franchisee's business when the franchisee wishes to sell. Any such option should secure at least as good a deal for the franchisee if he were to make a bona fide arm's length sale in the open market. Any provision which requires the franchisee to sell to the franchisor at a value (such as net asset value) which does not reflect the going concern market value should be unacceptable.

Restrictions imposed on the franchisee are affected by the BER. The most common restrictions fall under four headings the last of which is not dealt with in the Regulation:

(a) product sourcing, supply and control of range of products to be dealt with by the franchisee;
(b) restrictions on other competing activities both during the term of the agreement and after its termination;
(c) protection of the franchisor's know-how during the term of the agreement and after its termination;

(d) a restriction on the franchisee to prevent him taking staff away from other franchisees.

It will be recalled that the franchisor's control of products can be considerable if they are 'franchisor's goods' as defined in the Regulation. Controls on other goods are more difficult to impose except on quality criteria, or where it is impracticable owing to the nature of the goods to establish quality criteria.

The franchisor can require the franchisee to devote the whole of his efforts to the franchised business and can prevent franchisees from soliciting or touting outside their allocated territory.

18.7.12   Death of the franchisee

The death of the franchisee or of the principal shareholder of a franchisee company should be dealt with in the contract. The franchisee or principal share-holder may want to ensure that in the event of death:

(a) his personal representative(s) and/or dependant(s) will be able to keep the business going until one of them can qualify as franchisee and take an assignment of the franchise agreement or undertake the obligations formerly assumed under its contract by the deceased principal share-holder; and/or

(b) that, if they cannot or do not wish to qualify, arrangements can be made to keep the business going until a suitable assignee can be found at a proper price. The franchisor may agree to offer to provide management (for a fee) during the critical few weeks following death. All reputable and ethical franchisors will be sympathetic and helpful, whatever the contract provides, but it is best if the contract clearly specified what will happen.

18.7.13   Arbitration clause

There is an increasing tendency to introduce into franchise agreements a pro-vision for the arbitration of disputes. The BFA introduced an arbitration scheme administered by the Chartered Institute of Arbitrators (*see* Appendix 3). Arbitration is a useful procedure and is particularly apt for franchise transac-tions although it is not considered desirable by all franchisors and their advis-ers as a method of resolving disputes. There is a role for arbitration as a method of resolving disputes or differences which arise in a franchise transaction. A franchise agreement is the basis for a long-term arrangement which should be able to survive genuine differences of opinion. The alternative is confrontation, termination and litigation. Arbitration is not a form of confrontation but it gives the opportunity to deal with a difference speedily, in confidence, and largely at the convenience of the parties. It is usually less expensive, and arbitrators can be selected from a specialist panel who will realistically understand and cope with the problems.

Some aspects of franchise agreements are particularly appropriate for the arbitration procedure. Examples are whether a franchisee has performed his contract sufficiently well to justify any renewal rights which the franchisee may have; and differences in respect of royalty or franchise fee calculations.

However, most franchisees would not wish to arbitrate about whether or not standards had been observed. Again, a franchisor may need to enforce his rights quickly, for example on termination, by applying to a court for immediate action.

There is a trend towards mediation and conciliation procedures as methods of dispute resolution (*see further* Chapter 17).

18.7.14   Termination

The agreement may provide that it can be determined after the expiration of the fixed period, or there may be express provision for determination on the service of notice. Inevitably, the agreement will provide for termination by the franchisor in the event of any default by the franchisee under his obligations in the franchise agreement. Most agreements provide for the franchisee to be given an opportunity to remedy any defaults which can be remedied within a specific period before the franchisor can exercise the right of termination, subject to safeguards against the habitual offender. Indeed, the BFA Code requires such a provision to be inserted in agreements.

Many franchisors treat breaches with varying degrees of seriousness, but most take a strong view of breaches which raise questions of the integrity of the franchisee. Some regard dishonesty in the disclosure of gross income, and thus the amount of the fee to be paid, as fundamental, and will wish to be able to terminate in such a case without giving the franchisee an opportunity to put matters right. Where the franchisee has provided misleading or false information in his franchise application, a franchisor may wish to be able to terminate the agreement. A franchisor is also bound to take a serious view of a franchisee who is found to be making confidential information available to competitors or potential competitors.

The termination of an agreement of a defaulting franchisee is always a sad time for the franchisor, but a bad franchisee will invariably cause disquiet among other franchisees, who could be adversely affected by his poor performance. Fairness and firmness should characterise the franchisor's dealing with all its franchisees but particularly with those with whom it experiences difficulties.

Whatever the circumstances in which the franchise agreement is terminated, the franchisee should be left with the assets of the business for which he has paid. He will be stripped of his right to carry on business under the trade name and to use the franchisor's trade mark, system and know-how, and he will lose all the other advantages available to a franchisee. He may also have to move trading premises or substantially change his business in view of post-termination restrictive covenants in the agreement.

Where the franchisor owns the freehold or lease of the premises, and granted a lease or an underlease to the franchisee, the franchisee will find that on termination of the franchise agreement he has lost his lease also. A franchisee should, when signing the initial contract, see that there are safeguards for the cash investment he is making. On termination in these circumstances, the franchisee should be no worse off than he would have been if the landlord were a third party. In fact, he may be slightly better placed, since if there were a third party landlord and the franchisee could not trade from the premises, he would have commitments under the lease until disposal. He would have no such commitments if the franchisor is his landlord and retakes possession.

The objective when framing termination provisions is to ensure that the franchisor recovers total control of his industrial and intellectual property rights, his system and his goodwill. Thus, the contract should provide that on termination:

(a) the use of the brand name and goodwill associated with it must be discontinued;

(b) the use of the system and know-how must be discontinued;

(c) all outward signs and the appearance of premises and vans must be changed to avoid confusion and to prevent the franchisee from trading on the franchisor's goodwill;

(d) customer contact must stop; their custom is part of the franchisor's goodwill;

(e) the franchisee must be prevented from competing with the franchisor and the network from the premises on which he conducted the franchise business.

18.8 Ancillary agreements

There may be ancillary provisions or agreements. If the franchisor is a product supplier the franchise agreement may include standard terms and conditions of sale or there may be a separate supply agreement. Increasingly there is a need for software licences where the franchisor's system includes use of software.

There may be a trade mark licence (*see* Chapter 11). There may be a lease between franchisor and franchisee of the premises (*see* Chapter 14). There may be equipment or vehicle leases. There may also be supplementary obligations undertaken by shareholders or directors of the franchise.

If there are ancillary agreements they must not conflict with or detract from the franchise agreement and they should be co-terminous.

341

Chapter 19

International Franchising: the Legal Issues

Chapter 19

International Franchising: the Legal Issues

19.1 Introduction

The 1990s are proving in terms of international franchising to be what the 1950s were to US domestic franchising. International franchise systems are growing rapidly and are likely to continue to do so. Franchise systems possess many of the elements required to take a business from one territory to another. The existence of a system which is usually well documented in operational manuals coupled with the training programmes which franchisors establish, enable a franchisor to contemplate crossing national borders with some degree of confidence. While the differences between countries cannot be ignored, franchising systems are designed to be extended.

A franchisor wishing to move to another country will have many business decisions to make but having done so it will need to know what areas of law should be considered in order to see what legal adjustments need to be made.

Many of the legal issues a franchisor would need to investigate before expanding overseas would have to be investigated even if it did not intend to franchise. The fact that there are strange or ostensibly restrictive laws need not deter a franchisor. What is important is to move into another territory with knowledge of the position in order to make an enlightened decision. There are a number of areas of law to consider. The taxation issues are dealt with separately in Chapter 21.

19.2 Government attitudes

Many governments have a positive attitude to franchising, but even so there may be laws which affect the viability of a franchise in a particular country. For example, in some countries there are restrictions on ownership of certain types of business or on the use and protection of confidential information. The government may provide incentives for certain types of business and in certain areas where it wishes to stimulate and encourage growth of business. Some governments may wish to encourage indigenous businesses rather than have foreign ideas imported. There may also be an emphasis on assisting certain segments of the population.

19.3   Legal status and relationship of the parties

Franchising is invariably based on contractual relationships but the nature of the relationship is not interpreted in the same way in all jurisdictions. There may be restrictions on the capacity in which parties may contract. The application of local rules may, in the absence of proper drafting of the contract, create an agency or employment relationship which was not intended. This can have uncomfortable consequences on third party liability and the incidence of taxation and social security costs. Any action to challenge the franchisor's or franchisee's status is most likely to be taken by aggrieved third parties or the tax authorities, although there have been actions by franchisees.

19.4   Competition laws

Although competition laws are not directed at franchise agreements, their general application means they have an effect on some of the provisions commonly found in franchise agreements. This is not surprising since franchisors are striving for uniformity, while competition laws seek to create a competitive environment free from restrictions. The European Commission and the European Court of Justice have recognised the competitive nature of franchising arrangements. The Office of Fair Trading has also repeatedly recognised that franchise arrangements rarely have an adverse effect on competition and the consumer. The Secretariat of the Organisation for Economic Co-operation and Development (OECD) (not supported by its government members) has produced a positive analysis of franchising in the context of competition laws (*Competition Policy and Vertical Restraints; Franchising Agreements* OECD, Paris, 1994).

The nature and extent of competition laws differ from country to country, as will the enforcement of particular provisions. A number of issues which have competition law implications commonly arise:

(a) the tying of products;
(b) the sourcing of products;
(c) the control of the quality of products;
(d) the control of the range of products and services to be offered by the franchisee;

(e) territorial and market sharing arrangements:
- exclusivity;
- non-exclusivity but the franchisee is prohibited from activity outside the territory;
- location clause;
- customer restrictions;

(f) the control of prices;

(g) non-competition provisions:
- during the term of the contract;
- after termination;

(h) restrictions on the use of know-how, trade secrets and confidential information.

To the extent that any of these practices forms part of the franchisor's contract, advice will be needed. It is also wise to obtain advice as to whether any other provisions would be considered anti-competitive under local law.

19.4.1   Unfair competition

No franchisor will wish to train franchisees so that they can trade competitively with the franchisor. To protect itself against competition from a franchisee, the franchisor has to ascertain what weapons the local legal system provides. The franchisor will wish to restrain the franchisee from engaging in a competitive business during the term of the franchise agreement and for a period following termination, within a certain area. The competition law of the local legal system may influence these provisions. In some countries there are constitutional provisions which can affect the viability of such restraints.

In addition, the franchisor will wish to ensure that the franchisee cannot make unauthorised use of its know-how or pass it on to third parties. The nature or extent of the laws which deal with this issue will require investigation.

19.5   Intellectual property laws

The franchisor's intellectual property forms the backbone of the franchisor's business. It may include:

- trade marks;
- trade names;
- goodwill;
- know-how, methods, trade secrets;
- copyright material including designs;
- patents.

347

The method of registering and protecting these rights in each territory must be investigated. Although the law in many countries follows a similar pattern, there can be significant differences. It is not unknown for franchisors to seek to set up business in a country only to find that someone else is already using their name and has established rights to it in priority to the franchisor. There are some countries which afford protection to well known international brands, even though they are not registered.

In franchise transactions, the use of the franchisor's rights is permitted by licence in some form or other, and it is essential to use the correct method of licensing each different right to avoid adverse claims and to enable the franchisor to maintain control over its property rights. It may be necessary to license the intellectual property separately from the franchise agreement.

19.6   Corporate law

In deciding whether to set up a branch or operational subsidiary overseas, apart from the taxation implications, local corporate laws have to be considered to ascertain whether some form of incorporation is necessary or desirable, and whether, as is often the case, foreign companies which establish a place of business in the country in question are required to register. Some territories have prohibitions against foreign nationals owning the majority of shares in companies, but there is a trend away from this sort of restriction. Another reason for studying corporate laws is that a franchisee may choose to incorporate the business which is to be licensed.

The franchisor will have to develop some method for ensuring that the shareholders and directors and their families cannot acquire the know-how and trade secrets, and subsequently use them in competition with the franchisor or other franchisees. There must be a clear understanding of the corporate laws, and the roles, duties and responsibilities of shareholders and directors. Appropriate steps must be taken to ensure compliance with the terms of contracts.

19.7   Special franchise laws

There are very few countries which have franchise-specific laws, but where they exist they present a potentially formidable obstacle to entry to the marketplace.

19.7.1   The USA

The USA leads the way in legislative regulation of franchising. To complicate matters more there are two systems, federal and state. Each has its own laws and there are 50 states which by no means always legislate alike. The laws are directed not only at pre-contractual issues, but also, in some cases, at aspects of the relationship.

At the federal level there is a pre-contract disclosure requirement contained in a rule promulgated by the Federal Trade Commission (FTC), which also polices compliance. This law does not, at present, give rise to any private right of action, but the FTC can and does apply to the courts for remedies including injunctions to prevent continuing trading.

At state level, there are states which have not only pre-contract disclosure laws, but also a requirement that the franchisor register with a state regulatory authority, which is usually associated with the office which deals with the regulation of securities. These laws require either registration before the sale of a franchise can take place, or the delivery to the franchisee of a disclosure document at an early stage in discussions, and in any event not later than usually ten days before a contract is signed. Most states have neither registration nor the pre-contract disclosure, but the FTC rule applies.

Fortunately there is some degree of co-operation between the state regulators, which has resulted in the adoption of a Uniform Franchise Offering Circular.

Some states have laws which affect the right of a franchisor to terminate or to refuse renewal of the franchise agreement.

More recently, commencing in Iowa and currently being considered in other states and at the federal level, there have been moves to legislate far more widely to restrict franchisors' activities. The Iowa law has in part been successfully challenged as unconstitutional, and some franchisors have announced that they will not extend their activities in Iowa while the current law is in force. Recent changes to the Iowa law soften but do not entirely remove the problems.

19.7.2   Canada

The Province of Alberta in Canada requires pre-contract disclosure. At the time of writing the law is about to be changed. A new Act is expected to:

(a) require franchisors to disclose information about the franchise, the franchisor and the franchise system, so that prospective franchisees may make an informed investment decision;

(b) provide effective civil remedies to deal with breaches of the Act;

(c) provide for fair dealing between franchisors and franchisees; and

(d) provide a mechanism to allow for industry self-management.

Regulations will set out the ground rules in more detail.

19.7.3   Brazil and Mexico

Both Brazil and Mexico have recently introduced legislation which requires pre-contract disclosure.

19.7.4   France

In France the *Loi Doubin* was adopted at the end of 1989 and regulations have been introduced under it. The law does not specifically relate to franchising but to trade marks, trade name and logo licences made subject to an undertaking from the licensee of an exclusive or quasi-exclusive nature. Since all franchise arrangements involve such a licence, this law, which requires pre-contract disclosure, has a direct application to franchise agreements.

19.7.5   Australia

In Australia there were unsuccessful attempts in the latter half of the 1980s to introduce a Franchise Agreements Bill, prompted by a court decision that a franchise was a security. Since then there has been political pressure from one or two states to introduce laws. In response, the federal government established a task force which was charged with establishing a voluntary code. This code is now in position and progress is currently the subject of review. The government has indicated that if it is not satisfied with the way in which the code operates it may introduce legislation. One is inclined to believe that legislation will be introduced in Australia; the only issue is when. The code requires registration with the Franchising Code Administration Council Limited. It is enforced by peer pressure and by unwillingness on the part of financial and other institutions to deal with those who do not register. The Code requires pre-contract disclosure. The disclosure document must be updated at least annually, and be provided to the franchisee at least seven days before signing the franchise agreement. The Code also includes a dispute resolution procedure.

19.7.6   Elsewhere

There are currently no other franchise-specific laws elsewhere in the world, although there have been discussions in some countries which have not resulted in any action. Many franchise associations enforce voluntary codes of ethics. The Italian association introduced a detailed code with effect from 1 January 1995. In South Africa a code has been promulgated by the Business Practices Committee which administers the Harmful Business Practices Act (Act No 71 of 1988). 'If the information on the Disclosure Document is incorrect or incomplete or the cooling-off period is not applied the Franchisee may have a claim for damages or for the annulment of the franchise agreement', according to Louise A Tager, chairman of the Business Practices Committee.

One development may have some influence on international franchising. UNIDROIT, which is a governmental organisation for the unification of private law, recently appointed a study group which has recommended that a guide be prepared on the lines of the UNCITRAL *Legal Guide in Drawing up*

International Contracts for the Construction of Industrial Works. Work on such a guide has begun; it may in the future influence the shape of master franchise contracts.

In 1994 the World Intellectual Property Organisation published a franchising guide. It included the following statement:

> From a legal standpoint, franchising relies on contract law and therefore, does not necessarily require any special regulatory or legislative structure in order to function and develop. It is, therefore, appropriate to stress at the outset that no specific regulation of franchising has or would be necessary for franchises to thrive in any economy. However some governments have nevertheless chosen to adopt legislation to regulate franchising. Over-regulation could, however, have the effect of discouraging investment in this area.

19.8   Special industry laws

The franchisor should investigate whether the target territory has any laws which concern or affect the type of operation in which he is engaged. For example, fast food or restaurant businesses are affected by legislation which regulates standards of cleanliness in the interests of public heath. These requirements must be carefully checked so that the franchisor can adapt its methods to the target territory's requirements. There may be special labelling and packing requirements for products, and products may be subject to local regulatory requirements and specifications.

19.9   Vicarious liability

One of the fundamental features of franchising is that the franchisee is an independent business person responsible for running his own business, albeit in accordance with the franchisor's format and using the franchisor's branding. The franchisee has total control of the day-to-day conduct of the business operation, owns the assets and hires and fires staff. The franchisor would not expect to be considered liable to those with whom the franchisee deals for any acts or defaults by the franchisee. The possibility that third parties dealing as customers or suppliers with the franchisee will not recognise that the franchisee is independent of the franchisor can be dealt with by various methods. In the UK, a trader using a name other than his own is subject to the Business Names Act 1985, which requires notice to be given in a particular way. The European Commission has made it a condition of the application of the block exemption regulation for categories of franchise agreements that the independent status of the franchisee is made clear. The issue must be investigated and appropriate action taken.

19.10   Real estate laws

Laws affecting real estate and leasehold property vary from territory to territory and what may be permissible in one country may not be in another. There may or may not be protection for business tenants. In some countries a franchisor who becomes involved in the property chain may find it is unable to obtain possession and terminate the sublease if the franchise agreement is terminated. Property laws must be evaluated to ascertain whether the manner in which the franchisor's scheme is structured in its home territory is capable of being repeated in the target territory. If it is not, adjustments or fundamental rethinking may be necessary, particularly where franchisors wish to retain the ownership or control of premises.

19.11   Exchange controls and limits on royalties

Some countries have restrictions on the import and export of currency. It is necessary to ascertain whether such restrictions exist and, if so, what they are. There may be a requirement that consent be obtained for inward investment, and that it is given only subject to certain conditions. These conditions may affect the right of the investor to remit profits in whole or in part. Careful evaluation will have to be made to see how these laws will affect the franchisor's investment.

There is little point in selling know-how and granting rights to others to exercise the right to carry on business under a franchise agreement if it is a profitless exercise for the franchisor, in the sense that it is unable to turn its entitlement to income into cash in hand except in the target territory where it may have little use for it.

In some territories, usually coupled with exchange controls, there are limitations on the rate at which royalties may be paid, if at all. Certain countries take the view that low-level know-how and trade secrets should not entitle the owner to any royalty income. Others take the view that royalty income should be limited for a period of time, after which no further charge can be made.

19.12   Contract laws

The law of contract differs from country to country. There are different legal systems, the common law system and the civil law system, and even in dealings between countries where the same systems apply, different legislative approaches lead to differences in the legal requirements which have to be considered and taken into account. In particular, methods of interpreting documents differ significantly between the two systems. The common law concept of a clause being void for uncertainty may not impress a civil law judge, who will decide what the parties meant to achieve and enforce that intention. It is clearly unsafe to assume that contracts can be entered into on the same basis from one country to another. Care is needed to ensure that the correct form and procedures are followed.

19.13   Planning laws

Careful investigation has to be made into the extent to which there are any restrictions on the use to which premises can be put. Local building requirements or building regulations may affect the proposed franchised outlets, having a marked effect on operation, the layout of facilities, the availability of suitable premises in the right location, and thus the rate at which the franchise network can grow.

It often transpires that when the calculations of growth rate are taken into account, coupled with the difficulty in obtaining suitable locations for particular types of business, a completely different financial projection emerges from that which the franchisor originally envisaged. The local regulations in relation to building may require a higher standard of construction than is normally provided for in capital requirement projections, and unless a thorough investigation is made of these factors, the franchisor is not in a position to give the right guidance to franchisees or, indeed, to know the extent to which its operation is viable.

19.14   Employment laws

There are wide variations in employment laws, some of which, notably social security laws, result in additional costs to the employer. Local legislation may inhibit the ability of the franchisor or the employer to dismiss staff without compensation. These laws must be assessed so that realistic decisions about how to cope with the differences, while keeping the business viable, can be made.

19.15   Excise and duties

The cost (including shipping costs) of importing any materials, equipment and plant and machinery which cannot be obtained locally must be taken into account, as should any excise or other customs duties (including VAT) which may be levied on them in the target territory. This, coupled with the need to make technical changes in equipment from time to time, may require the franchisor to use locally manufactured products, or products manufactured in a country whose imports to the target territory bear excise taxes and custom duties at an acceptable rate. It is clearly important to include the cost of import and excise taxes and duties, which can be significant, in the cost calculations and profit projections.

19.16   Import/export controls

In some territories there may be restrictions on what may be imported or exported, and certain standards may have to be achieved before imports are allowed. There may be quotas limiting how much can be imported from certain countries. The franchisor must be sure that it is possible to import into a target territory whatever it requires. Its product requirements in this respect must be capable of meeting the criteria established by the target territory in order to qualify for import, or alternative arrangements must be made.

Chapter 20

International Franchise Documentation

Chapter 20

International Franchise Documentation

20.1   The options

The franchisor, in considering its method of entering international franchising, will be influenced by the resources available to it and by what it regards as the most effective method for the achievement of its objectives.

The options available to an international franchisor include:

(1) For the franchisor to establish its own outlets. This is at the upper end of the scale of expense and the franchisor will need sufficient manpower and financial resources to establish and sustain such an operation. But having established its own outlets, its options then are:
    (a) to continue to expand its own outlets;
    (b) to franchise directly to others;
    (c) to contract with a sub-franchisor under a master franchise agreement;
    (d) to enter into a joint venture agreement with a local partner.
    In short, the franchisor has the full spectrum of arrangements available because it has done the most important exercise itself: established its name and branding, and proved that the business can be operated successfully in the target territory.

(2) To contract with each franchisee and undertake the franchisor's responsibilities directly. This technique is limited in that the further away the franchisor is from the target territory the more difficult it is to service the franchisees. But where it is used, it is often combined with the establishment of a subsidiary or a branch if the franchisor's resources enable it to do so and if there are no tax disadvantages (*see* Chapter 21).

(3) To enter into a master franchise agreement; *see below*.

(4) To enter into area development agreements (*see* Chapter 18) which enable the franchisor to cover a territory with fewer franchisees.

(5) To enter into an arrangement with a joint venture partner (or partners), coupled with a master franchise agreement or an area development agreement; or a series of joint ventures under area development agreements.

Whichever option is chosen, the franchisor will face the same challenges:

(a) selecting the right local entity or entities with whom to do business;
(b) controlling quality standards;
(c) achieving the rate of growth he is seeking;
(d) overcoming lack of familiarity with the country and his local 'partner' or staff.

20.2   Joint ventures

It is not the purpose of this work to deal with joint ventures in themselves, but there are some franchising aspects of joint ventures. In addition to the normal joint venture contract, there will be a franchise contract, probably a master franchise, an area development and/or a unit agreement, between the franchisor and the joint venture vehicle. This means that in addition to the normal joint venture dealings each will have with the other, the franchisor will have a considerable influence over the joint venture through the franchise documentation. This introduces an additional possibility for friction in the relationship, in that one party may be disappointed by the 'franchise' performance of the other. This potential for friction must be taken into account when establishing the relationship and drafting the joint venture documentation.

20.3   Master franchise agreements

The master franchise agreement reflects the commercial bargain which has been struck between the franchisor and the sub-franchisor to:

(a) evaluate the viability of the system in the target territory;
(b) equip the sub-franchisor to become the franchisor in the target territory;
(c) introduce the franchisor's system to the target territory;
(d) develop the growth of the system in the target territory; and
(e) result in the sub-franchisor's providing the full range of the franchisor's services to sub-franchisees in the target territory.

In these transactions the aspirations of the parties and balance of negotiating power will vary from case to case, as will the skill, financial resources, knowledge and experience of the prospective sub-franchisor. Negotiations for master franchise agreements often run into difficulty over certain issues, for example:

(1) The franchisor demands too much by way of initial fee.
(2) The franchisor requires too high a proportion of the continuing franchise fees, which may make it difficult if not impossible for the sub-franchisor to trade profitably.

(3) The prospective sub-franchisor finds it difficult to come to terms with the conceptual issues and the controls to which it will be subjected. This is more likely where the sub-franchisor is a large company.

(4) The prospective sub-franchisor underestimates the capital cost and time frame involved before the operation becomes profitable.

(5) The franchisor will not accept that his name does not carry a premium value in the target territory; or that there may be business, legal, market and cultural differences between the country of origin and the target territory which call for changes to the system and the operational manuals.

The master franchise agreement will have to accommodate the issues identified during the commercial discussions. In many of these issues, there is no such thing as the right answer since these agreements, unlike unit agreements, are all negotiated. The principal issues in negotiating and preparing a master franchise agreement are as follows:

(a) the rights to be granted;
(b) the term;
(c) territory;
(d) exclusivity;
(e) performance schedule;
(f) franchise fees;
(g) withholding taxes;
(h) training;
(i) trade marks and other intellectual property rights;
(j) sale of the business;
(k) default and termination;
(l) choice of law and venue.

20.3.1   The rights to be granted

The rights to be granted will include the use of the franchisor's trade marks, trade names, goodwill, know-how, confidential information, copyright material and all the usual elements found in franchise transactions.

20.3.2   The term

The term of the agreement does not usually present problems, although there have been draft agreements proposing what is clearly an unrealistic five-year term. Since the purpose of the transaction involves establishing the sub-franchisor in the target territory with a corresponding investment, the longer the term, the greater the opportunity to develop the territory properly. A sub-franchisor with only a five-year term would in any event be subject to a shorter term than the sub-franchisees would expect. This is clearly unworkable.

The contract should provide for the grant by the sub-franchisor to sub-franchisees of a longer term, or what turns out to be a longer term, than the sub-franchisor has left under his agreement. Otherwise, a sub-franchisee may find that his agreement is terminated by operation of law because the sub-franchisor's agreement has come to an end. The problem would arise where, for example, the master franchise agreement is for 25 years and ten-year sub-franchise agreements are entered into 15 or more years after the master franchise agreement. Realistic terms for master franchise agreements are 25 to 50 years, with rights of renewal.

Assuming it is agreed that the sub-franchisor should have a right of renewal there will be the normal issues to consider. In what circumstances should the right of renewal be denied? On what terms should it be granted? Will there be scope for the franchisor to introduce changes, particularly bearing in mind the time since the original document was entered into? If so, on what basis can that be done? Will any charge be made for granting extended rights, and if so how will the charge be calculated? Leaving negotiation to the time the right is exercised could effectively leave the sub-franchisor with no rights at all since if the charge cannot be agreed there can be no contract. What will be the continuing development schedule? How will changes in the method of exploiting the franchised business be dealt with? For example, larger regional franchise units with satellite operations may be preferred to smaller stand-alone units. This would have an effect on the number of regional outlets to be opened and kept in operation even though turnover may be enhanced.

20.3.3   Territory

Most sub-franchisors, like the operators of individual units who seek the comfort of exclusive territory, seek the widest possible territorial rights. In fixing the extent of the territory to be exploited by the sub-franchisor, the franchisor's overall international marketing strategy and how the individual sub-franchisors fit into that strategy must be taken into account.

Ideally, the territory should be one in which the sub-franchisor has the knowledge, experience and capacity to cope. One of the reasons for a master franchise agreement is to have the sub-franchisor stand in the shoes of the franchisor. It would defeat this object if territories were of such a nature and/or extent that the sub-franchisor is not capable of proper exploitation.

20.3.4   Exclusivity

Most sub-franchisors wish to have exclusive rights to the territory allocated to them. This enables them to invest with the comfort of knowing that they are the sole exploiters of the opportunity in the territory. Exclusivity is normally tied to performance and can be lost if performance criteria are not met. This can lead to practical problems if one has a network which is being developed by a sub-franchisor who fails after a period of time to meet the performance schedules.

In practical terms, the loss of exclusivity without the loss of the continuing right to grant further sub-franchises raises issues similar to those discussed in Chapter 18 in relation to area development agreements.

20.3.5   Performance schedule

A performance schedule which sets out the projected annual and cumulative rates of growth of the network in the target territory is a common feature of master franchise agreements. Without it, the franchisor would not have the confidence that a commitment exists which should result in the proper exploitation of the territory. Unless a sub-franchisor is prepared to accept a realistic performance schedule for the establishment of operational units, the master franchise route can lose some of its attractions. The performance schedule is obviously of great importance where exclusive rights are granted because it protects the franchisor against under-exploitation.

These are practical difficulties in establishing performance schedules. At the time the contract is being negotiated the parties may not have sufficient knowledge to enable them to judge what rate of expansion could be achieved. What is certain is that the franchisor's expectations are likely to be on the optimistic side, while those of the sub-franchisor will be on the pessimistic side. Most sub-franchisors prepare business plans as part of the process of deciding whether or not to take the opportunity on board and these will include some assessment of the growth rate which the business is capable of achieving. Otherwise, the sub-franchisor would not be able to make a balanced business judgment about whether or not to go into the proposition, and the level of resources which would need to be committed to it.

Some advocate trial period agreements to deal with the problem of an unknown name and an untried system, where the parties do not feel confident that they can agree a performance schedule which is fair to both. Undoubtedly there is a need for flexibility. When fixing a performance schedule, there is much to be learned from reviewing the performance of competitors. Many franchisors are prepared to accept a realistic minimum. If the business is successful, it is unlikely that the sub-franchisor would not wish to expand it to the full. It is important that the sub-franchisor is obliged to expand sufficiently to ensure that it achieves a critical mass quickly enough to achieve the springboard for effective growth.

20.3.6   Franchise fees

Initial fees

One of the most difficult questions in the negotiation of a master franchise agreement is how much the franchisor should receive for the grant of the rights, the transfer of know-how and setting up the sub-franchisor in the territory.

Some franchisors' expectations are so high that would-be sub-franchisors are frightened off. There are instances in which unrealistic figures have been agreed only to be resented by the sub-franchisor when it realises that it cannot make money either at all or sufficiently quickly to justify the high initial cost.

There are a number of factors which could be taken into account when trying to calculate what would be a proper level of front-end charge by a franchisor. The degree of importance to be attached to each will differ from country to country, depending upon the practices to be found in each. The factors are:

(a) the actual cost to the franchisor of dealing with the sub-franchisor, setting it up and proving the concept works within the target territory;
(b) the cost and time it would take the sub-franchisor to acquire the requisite know-how and skills to operate a similar business in his territory;
(c) the value of the territory as estimated by the franchisor;
(d) the estimated aggregate amount of initial franchise fees which could be charged by the sub-franchisor to his sub-franchisees.

Franchisors based in countries where high initial fees are charged to franchisees tend to have much higher expectations under (c) and (d) *above*, and therefore demand more than may be considered realistic in the target territory. As the medium to long-term interests of the franchisor are probably best served by having well motivated and successful sub-franchisors, the franchisor may be wise to adapt its expectations.

Continuing fees

Continuing fees are normally calculated on the aggregate amount of the gross network sales to the ultimate consumer. The level at which they are fixed has to provide the franchisor with an acceptable return; at the same time, these payments are deductions from the gross income of the sub-franchisor and have a direct effect on his profit. If the fees are too high, the sub-franchisor will not be able to run its business profitably; the network will not be properly supported and risks failure.

These are normally calculated on the aggregate amount of the gross network sales to the ultimate consumer. While the level at which they are fixed obviously has to provide the franchisor with a good economic reason to be involved, these payments represent a straight deduction from the gross income of the sub-franchisor. This directly affects the bottom line, and if they are too high the sub-franchisor will not be able to run his business profitably. In these circumstances, the network will not get proper support and the franchisor will be presented with conflict rather than income.

Franchisors who operate their domestic operations on, say, a 5 or 6 per cent fee to their own unit operators sometimes propose a 3 or 4 per cent fee from the sub-franchisor. That sub-franchisor may not be able to charge more than 5 or 6 per cent to its sub-franchisees, which might be extremely attractive in the absence of an obligation to share the income with the franchisor. But if the subfranchisor has to pay to the franchisor 2 or 3 per cent of its sub-franchisees' revenues, which is equal to 60 per cent of its own revenue, the proposition is doomed to failure. Clearly, the effect on the network of initial fees and the viability of the sub-franchisor's business, have to be carefully thought through.

Payments

The method of making payments should relate to the way in which the sub-franchisor will deal with sub-franchisees. For example, if sub-franchisees pay their fees monthly by the tenth day of the month, an obligation on the sub-franchisor to make payments at the same time might be difficult to meet. Yet one frequently encounters provisions of this nature in contracts. The payment periods and accounting periods at both levels complement each other.

Another question is whether the sub-franchisor is to be obliged to pay franchise fees to the franchisor even if he has not been paid by his sub-franchisees. This will be a subject for negotiation, but the franchisor may be reluctant to share the sub-franchisor's credit risks. There should always be a provision requiring the sub-franchisor to ensure that sub-franchisees observe and perform the terms of sub-franchise agreements, which would mean that failure by the sub-franchisor to collect fees and financial reports would be a breach of contract. A defaulting and non-paying sub-franchisee will not only not be paying fees, but will probably not be submitting returns of sales, which in turn will make it impossible to know what should be remitted. A formula can be written into the contract to cover such a situation.

Allowance needs to be made for delays in the banking system since payments sometimes still take an inordinate time to travel from bank A in country X to bank B in country Y.

The franchisor will invariably stipulate the currency in which payment is to be made. Franchisors usually prefer payment in their own currency. This requires the establishment in the agreement of a conversion date, and it is also sensible to identify which bank's quoted rate will be used for conversion on that date. Provision is usually made for the costs of remittance and conversion to be borne by the sub-franchisor. If by reason of exchange controls, currency conversion cannot take place, provision should be made in the agreement to establish the alternative action to be taken.

In view of the long-term nature of master franchise contracts, provisions are often inserted to allow for the possibility that exchange controls may be introduced in the future.

20.3.7   Withholding taxes

The contract should deal with the way in which payments will be treated and characterised for tax purposes in both the franchisor's country and the target territory. Any double taxation agreement should be examined to ensure that the franchisor may if it so wishes receive payments free of withholding tax. The contract should enable the franchisor to obtain the benefit of any double taxation agreement by the provision of evidence of payment in the target country in such form as may be necessary to enable the relief to be claimed.

Some franchisors insert 'grossing-up' provisions in their contracts. These provide that if tax is deductible, effectively it has to be borne by the sub-franchisor who must increase his payment to the franchisor, so that the franchisor receives net the amount it would have received had there been no deduction. The effect of such a provision is to increase the level of fees payable by the sub-franchisor as he is effectively paying the franchisor's tax liability on the payments which are remitted to it. This cost would not be recoverable from the franchise network, and if a sub-franchisor is forced into accepting such a provision, the sub-franchisor should check his projections and cash-flow forecasts to ensure that the additional burden does not make the proposition unacceptable.

20.3.8   Training

The degree of training support will, of course, vary from case to case. Many franchisors find it sensible, particularly in the early stages, to ensure that both the sub-franchisor's staff, and the sub-franchisees and their staff, are trained at the franchisor's domestic training facility. The reason is usually that the quality of training at the domestic base cannot be reproduced and, even though there will be changes to accommodate local requirements, training to the level affected at the domestic facility is essential.

One would expect the contract to say how, and how many of, the sub-franchisor's team will be trained, and to identify them by their job title. In appropriate cases, a franchisor may provide an opening crew for the first few units which are established in the target territory. The crew will provide on-site training for the sub-franchisor's staff. Normally, the training is provided free of charge, but the sub-franchisor and its sub-franchisees would be expected to pay all their expenses relating to getting to and from the training site and their subsistence and other expenses during the course of the training. The intensity of training and support during the pilot stage in the target territory can be quite high, and will be reflected in the initial franchise fee.

The agreement may also provide for the sub-franchisor to establish its own training facilities in the course of time, and for the franchisor to provide the necessary back-up and training aids to enable this to be done.

20.3.9   Trade marks and other intellectual property rights

The franchisor will need to protect, by whatever method is appropriate in the target territory, its trade marks and other intellectual property rights. The contractual arrangements will deal with licensing the use of the rights and the protection of the franchisor's position. The master franchise contract should be clear whether the sub-franchisor may sub-license these rights. If the sub-franchisor is to be permitted to sub-license, the parties will need to establish whether that is permitted under local law.

20.3.10   Sale of the business

The master franchise agreement should contain provisions as to how the agreement may be assigned and the sub-franchisor's business sold. The principles are the same as those which apply to the sale of a franchised business by a sub-franchisee, but there are some differences in detail because the level of investment is much greater, and the skills which the purchaser will require will not be the same as those required for the operation of a franchised unit.

A purchaser of a sub-franchisor's business will not only have to demonstrate his financial capacity, but also his ability to understand the franchise system and to manage the business of a sub-franchisor. The criteria to be applied should be specified, as should any conditions which are considered appropriate. The possibility that an interested purchaser could be a competitor should not be overlooked. Alternatively, the purchaser might be a large company wishing to expand and diversify its business, calling for provisions to confine the franchisor's know-how and confidential information to those employed in the franchised business, and to avoid its being available elsewhere in the purchaser's organisation or group of companies.

It may be necessary to impose training and approval requirements on any purchaser, and on any managing director or general manager for which provision should be made in the agreement.

In framing these provisions, which address the issue of who controls the sub-franchisor, it may be necessary to allow for the introduction of institutional or venture fund finance, and for the possibility that the sub-franchisor may wish to obtain a listing for its shares on a public market.

20.3.11   Default and termination

Of prime concern to the franchisor will be the degree to which the sub-franchisor monitors and controls the quality and standards of his sub-franchisees. The sub-franchisees are, after all, trading using the franchisor's know-how and systems, and are benefiting from the goodwill associated with its name and trade marks. The franchisor is at risk if things happen which are adverse to its interests. The sub-franchisor is the custodian of those interests in his territory. The agreement should provide for monitoring standards, but if all else fails, the franchisor must have remedies. These are based on the default provisions in the contract.

Expressions in a contract such as 'material or substantial defaults'are often difficult to interpret. What a franchisor regards as 'material or substantial' a sub-franchisor may regard as not so 'material or substantial', and how a court would determine the dispute could be open to question. If an expression such as 'material default' is to be used, it should be defined, as, for example, any default under the agreement of which the franchisor has given notice to the sub-franchisor requiring it to be remedied and which remains unremedied after a fixed period of time, which may be as much as 30 or 60 days. Money defaults may be treated more seriously, with a shorter period of notice. Quality control defaults may need a longer period for the default to be put right because it will invariably involve enforcing rights against sub-franchisees.

Failure by a sub-franchisor to ensure that its sub-franchisees comply with the terms of their contracts is a serious issue, and may require reasonable time and careful handling to secure compliance. The problem is not necessarily best solved by requiring the sub-franchisee to undertake legal proceedings. The solution of operational problems which have led to a lowering of standards can often be dealt with by direct discussion and persuasion, rather than resorting to law. The parties must acknowledge that there are a wide range of methods available to cope with these problems. Ultimately, of course, the franchisor must be able to bring matters to a head to protect its interests and the integrity of its intellectual property rights.

A master franchise agreement, like most commercial agreements, will provide for termination in the event of insolvency, bankruptcy or liquidation.

The consequences of termination are usually drastic. The sub-franchisor will generally lose the right to continue, will have to de-identify his business premises, and be bound by effective post-term restraints on competition and the use of the franchisor's know-how.

One of the dangers for franchisors and sub-franchisees is that on termination of the master franchise agreement the agreements with sub-franchisees will automatically terminate: *Austin Baldwin & Co Ltd* v *Greenwood and Baltey Ltd*; *Same* v *Magnetic Car Company Ltd* [1925] 42 RPC 454. Franchisors frequently provide themselves with the option to require the defaulting sub-franchisor on termination to assign all sub-franchisor agreements to the franchisor. But if the sub-franchise agreements have automatically terminated there would be nothing to assign. The master franchise agreement should therefore make express provision to ensure that the sub-franchise agreements are to survive the termination long enough for the franchisor to exercise the option.

Other questions about the future of the sub-franchises which arise on termination of the master franchise include:

(1) Will the franchisor be obliged to take them over?

(2) Will the sub-franchisor be able to make a virtue out of termination and
· claim payment of a sum of money by way of compensation for the
'takeover' of his business?

(3) Will the franchisor, having terminated the sub-franchisor for good
cause, want to take over what could be a badly run network of disgruntled sub-franchisees, who are intent on making difficulties, and be faced
with the expense of putting the business right? Should the sub-franchisor, rather than expect compensation, expect on the contrary to be liable
to the franchisor for the costs of coping with the problems left behind?

(4) What is to happen to any property (including leases), which the sub-franchisor has acquired for leasing or sub-leasing to the sub-franchisees,
and which may have a capital value which the franchisor cannot afford
to pay? This can create difficulties which arise from the integrated structure of the sub-franchise arrangements.

Another issue is whether the master franchise agreement should terminate as a
whole if the development schedule is not maintained. This issue is discussed in
relation to area development agreements in Chapter 18.

Should the sub-franchisor be entitled to terminate the franchise agreement
if the franchisor is in material default of his obligations, or becomes bankrupt
or is put into liquidation? If so, what should be the consequences for the sub-franchisor and his network? Should the sub-franchisor be entitled to continue
as before, using to the full the franchisor's intellectual property rights, including the name and know-how, and, if so, on what basis? Is it right that the sub-franchisor may have to run the risk of losing his business when the franchisor
is at fault, whether the fault arises voluntarily or involuntarily?

The issues are many and varied, and the list which is given is far from complete but will serve to indicate their complexity and the problems which arise
in negotiations.

20.3.12   Choice of law and venue

All contracts should specify the law which applies and the venue for the resolution of disputes. Parties should consider whether or not they wish to have disputes referred, or capable of being referred, to arbitration or mediation.

As far as choice of law is concerned, some jurisdictions may be less attractive than others, but the ultimate sanctions against a sub-franchisee would have
to be sought in the country in which the business was being conducted.
Although there are contrary views, on the whole, the law of the country where
the sub-franchisor will be conducting his business is usually the most appropriate.

There are other considerations. Most courts will not enforce 'public issue' provisions in accordance with foreign laws. Restrictive covenants, competition law and exchange controls are the types of provision which fall into this category. The treatment of the intellectual property rights which the sub-franchisee is licensed to use will fall to be dealt with under the law of the country in which the business operates. The laws of state A relating to trade marks would not affect the treatment of trade marks in state B where the sub-franchisor is carrying on business. Another factor is that the sub-franchise agreements would undoubtedly be subject to the law of the country in which the sub-franchisor is operating. It seems illogical for the master franchise agreement (out of which all rights are granted to the sub-franchisees) to be governed by a different legal system from that which governs the contracts for the operational units.

This chapter has not dealt exhaustively with the provisions to be found in an international master franchise agreement. Obviously, the terms will vary from case to case, and will reflect the outcome of the give and take of the commercial negotiations. International franchising is growing fast and the techniques are in a state of constant development.

Chapter 21

International Tax Issues

Chapter 21

International Tax Issues

21.1 Introduction

Chapter 9 deals with tax issues which arise when the franchisor and the franchisee are both resident in the UK for tax purposes. This chapter deals with specific tax issues which arise when either the franchisor or the franchisee is based in a country other than the UK.

The general principles which have to be understood when considering an international business operation or structure are first outlined. This is followed by a section on Value Added Tax. The chapter moves on to relate some of these general principles to international franchising structures before concluding with some brief observations on some international tax planning opportunities.

21.2 General principles

21.2.1 Residence and domicile

Exposure to UK tax will depend, in the cases of both companies and individuals, on residence and, in the case of individuals only, on domicile. The basic principle is that a UK-resident person will be liable for UK tax on worldwide income and capital gains, whereas a non-resident person will be liable for UK tax only on income from UK sources and capital gains attributable to UK assets held for the purposes of a UK trading activity. A summary of the rules relating to residence is therefore necessary.

Residence of companies

The following rules apply to determine the residence status of a company in the UK:

(1) Subject to (3) *below*, a company, wherever incorporated, will be UK resident if it is managed and controlled in the UK. This test was laid down by Lord Loreburn in *De Beers Consolidated Mines Ltd* v *Howe* [1905] 2 KB 612: 'a company resides . . . where its real business is carried on . . . and the real business is carried on where central management and control actually resides'. The test is aimed at the highest level of control of the business (eg where important policy decisions are taken) rather than necessarily where the business operations take place. This is a question of fact to be determined by reference to the circumstances of the case. Usually this control is exercised by the board of directors of the company in board meetings, in which case the place where the board meetings are held will determine the residence status of the company (under this test). If, however, management and control is exercised in some other way (eg a parent company exercising the powers which might otherwise be exercised by the board of a subsidiary or a controlling individual shareholder taking all decisions outside the forum of board meetings), the test should be applied having regard to the particular factual circumstances, and the location of the board meetings may not be conclusive. The Inland Revenue has issued a Statement of Practice (SP1/90) which summarises the Revenue's approach in applying this test.

(2) With effect from 15 March 1988 all companies which are incorporated in the UK are automatically UK resident (wherever they are managed and controlled) unless the company ceased to be UK resident (under the management and control test) before 15 March 1988 in pursuance of a Treasury consent obtained under Income and Corporation Taxes Act (ICTA) 1988, ss 765–767 (Finance Act 1988, Sched 7, paras 1 and 2), or (3) *below* applies to the company.

(3) With effect from 30 November 1993, any company which is UK resident under either of the above UK rules but which is also:
    (a) resident in another country under the laws of that other country; and
    (b) treated under the terms of any applicable double tax treaty between the UK and that other country as being resident in the other country (under the treaty 'tie breaker' rule);

will also be regarded as being non-UK resident for all UK tax purposes (Finance Act 1994, s 249). This means that the residence of companies which would otherwise have been resident in two countries (dual-resident companies) will be determined by reference to the 'tie breaker' test in the applicable treaty (assuming a treaty exists and that it includes the appropriate form of 'tie-breaker' provision). The usual 'tie-breaker' test is based on the place where 'effective management' is exercised. This is not necessarily the same as 'management and control'; 'effective management' may be related to the place where day to day business decisions and action are taken.

Residence and domicile of individuals

With individuals, three concepts have to be considered: residence, ordinary residence and domicile.

An individual will be treated as resident in the UK in any tax year (commencing on 6 April) if he is present in the UK for at least 183 days in aggregate in the tax year in question (ICTA 1988, s 336). He may also be treated as resident in the UK if, although not resident in the UK for at least 183 days in the particular tax year, he makes regular visits to the UK which average three months or more a year over a period of four years: *IRC* v *Lysaght* (1928) 13 TC 511.

There is no statutory definition of 'ordinarily resident', but case law indicates that a person will be treated as ordinarily resident in the UK if he is habitually so resident, and three years' actual or intended continued residence is the standard test for habitual residence: *IRC* v *Lysaght* (1928) 13 TC 511 and *R* v *Barnet London Borough Council ex p Nilish Shah* [1983] 2 AC 309.

The above represents the briefest possible summary of the relevant rules. A fuller explanation can be obtained from the Inland Revenue's own guide, IR 20, Residents and Non-Residents.

The concept of domicile (as developed by conflict of laws principles) is also relevant to the tax treatment of individuals. The rules summarised *below* apply in connection with income tax and capital gains tax liabilities. For inheritance tax purposes there is an additional statutory test (related to the number of years of residence spent in the UK) but this is not dealt with in this summary (*see* Inheritance Tax Act 1984, s 267).

Broadly, a person is domiciled for income tax and capital gains purposes where he has or is deemed by law to have his permanent home. A person acquires a 'domicile of origin' at birth. This will be his father's domicile at the date of the child's birth in the case of a legitimate child born during the father's lifetime; and his mother's domicile at the date of the child's birth in the case of an illegitimate child or a child born after his father's death. A child's domicile will then generally follow the domicile of the parent from whom he took his domicile of origin (although special rules can apply if the parents live apart or if the father dies). An adult (someone aged 16 years or over) will change his domicile to a domicile of choice if he is, in fact, resident in a particular country and intends to reside in that country permanently or indefinitely: *Re Clore (deceased)* [1984] STC 609. If a person ceases to reside in a country which has become his domicile of choice without adopting a new domicile of choice, his domicile of origin will revive. Women married before 1 January 1974 automatically took the domicile of their husbands on marriage and during the subsistence of the marriage. Since that date, a married woman is able to acquire her own domicile of choice just as any other person can.

There has been a number of proposals for changes in the law of domicile.

The latest proposals were announced in 1991. They would have made it easier for some people to change their domicile and could have resulted in some long-term UK-resident persons acquiring a UK domicile. Following representations, the government announced in May 1993 that it had no plans to introduce new legislation.

Residence of partnerships

The residence of a partnership is determined by reference to the country in which the trade or business of the partnership is controlled or managed (ICTA 1988, s 112). Residence is not determined by the country in which the individual partners are resident or by whether or not some of the partnership's business is conducted in the UK, although these factors may help to indicate where control and management is likely to be located.

21.2.2   Scope of liability

The relevant principles of UK domestic law are outlined *below*, but in many cases the extent of a business's liability to UK tax will be affected by the provisions of a double tax treaty (*see* pp 379–380 *below*).

Companies

A UK-resident company will be charged to corporation tax (at rates of between 25 and 33 per cent) on its worldwide income and gains whether or not remitted to the UK (ICTA 1988, s 8(1)).

UK law prescribes that a non-resident company will be liable for UK tax in respect of the profits of any trade conducted in the UK and any income from UK investments. If the company is carrying on a trade in the UK through a branch or agency then it will be assessed to corporation tax on:

(a) any trading income arising directly or indirectly through or from the branch or agency; and

(b) any income from property or rights used by, or held by or for, the branch or agency (eg bank deposit interest received by the branch).

(ICTA 1988, s 11(2) and *see also* ss 78 and 82 of the Taxes Management Act 1970 for certain exclusions relating to independent agents and brokers.)

It will, therefore, be necessary to determine whether a non-resident company is carrying on a trade in the UK (as to which, *see below*) and whether a branch or agency (defined rather unhelpfully in s 834(1) of ICTA 1988 as 'any factorship, agency, receivership, branch or management') exists. A branch will, for example, exist whenever an office presence is established.

If no branch or agency exists, a non-resident company will be liable to income tax (at 25 per cent) rather than corporation tax on its UK trading profits. If, however, there is no UK branch or agency then the UK Inland Revenue may in practice have difficulties in enforcing a tax liability. Furthermore, the provisions of a relevant double tax treaty may also exclude this liability since treaties invariably provide that there will be no UK tax liability unless profits are generated through a UK 'permanent establishment' (*see below*).

A non-resident company will also be subject to UK income tax at 25 per cent on any other income from UK investments (under Schedule D Case III or VI; ICTA 1988, s 18). Under the terms of Inland Revenue Extra Statutory Concession ESC B13, bank deposit interest will not, however, normally be assessed to tax unless the interest is earned by or through a UK branch or agency.

A non-resident company is not subject to UK tax on its capital gains unless it is carrying on a trade in the UK through a branch or agency, in which case it will be subject to corporation tax on any capital gains arising in respect of:

(a) assets situated in the UK and used for the purposes of the trade at or before the time when the capital gain accrued; and

(b) assets situated in the UK and used or held for the purposes of the branch or agency at or before that time, or assets acquired for use by or for the purposes of the branch or agency (Taxation of Chargeable Gains Act (TCGA) 1992, s 10(3)).

There will be no liability to tax on such capital gains if the company is no longer carrying on a trade through the branch or agency at the time of the disposal of the asset TCGA 1992, s 10(2)). However, tax cannot be avoided simply by exporting the asset or ceasing to carry on the trade through a branch or agency before disposal of the asset; a disposal of the asset is deemed to take place for capital gains purposes on the export of the asset or on the company's ceasing to trade through a branch or agency (TCGA 1992, s 25).

Individuals

An individual resident and ordinarily resident in the UK will be liable to UK income tax on his worldwide income (the maximum rate of income tax being 40 per cent). If the individual is resident but not ordinarily resident or not domiciled in the UK for tax purposes, any income from a foreign source, including profits of a trade or profession exercised exclusively abroad (ie income taxable under Schedule D Cases IV and V), will be taxed only if remitted to the UK (ICTA 1988, ss 13 and 65). Such individuals can also benefit from special rules relating to employment income (taxable under Schedule E) if the employment is exercised wholly or partly abroad. These rules go beyond the scope of this work.

An individual resident or ordinarily resident in the UK will be subject to capital gains tax on the disposal of capital assets, at his marginal rate of income tax. However, if the individual is not domiciled in the UK, tax will be payable only in respect of the disposal of non-UK assets if the gain in question is remitted to the UK (TCGA 1992, ss 2 and 12).

A non-resident individual will be subject to income tax on the profits of any trade carried on in the UK (Schedule D Case I: ICTA 1988, s 18), and in respect of income from UK investments (Schedule D Cases III or VI: ICTA 1988, s 18). In the case of interest, Inland Revenue Extrastatutory Concession B13 may apply (*see above*).

A non-resident individual is not subject to capital gains tax unless he is carrying on a trade in the UK through a branch or agency, in which case he will be liable to tax on the same basis as a non-resident company (TCGA 1992, s 10(1); *see above*).

Partnerships

Very basically, partners in trading partnerships are assessed as follows:

(a) UK trade: resident and non-resident partners are liable to UK tax in respect of UK trading profits.

(b) Non-UK trade: resident partners are liable to UK tax on their profit share. Non-resident partners are not liable to UK tax.

Normally the profits of a UK-resident trading partnership are treated as profits of a UK trade even if certain partnership business activities take place abroad. However, in practice it is understood that the share of profits attributable to the non-UK activities to which a non-resident partner is entitled is not assessed to tax by the Inland Revenue.

Each partner is treated as owning a fractional share in the partnership assets for capital gains tax purposes and a partner's liability to capital gains tax on the disposal of a partnership asset will depend on each individual partner's residence status rather than the residence of the partnership (TCGA 1992, s 59 and *see also* Inland Revenue Statement of Practice D12).

Place of trade and source of investment income

It will be clear from the above principles that it is often necessary to determine whether trading income is derived from a UK trade or whether investment income is derived from a UK source (UK investments) before the scope of any potential liability to UK tax can be established. Some brief comments on these issues follow.

Place of trade   If a person is carrying on a trade, it will be necessary to determine whether that person is trading 'with' the UK or 'within' the UK. If the trade is being undertaken within the UK, a UK trade is being carried on.

In the case of a trade involving the supply of goods no single fact is conclusive, but case law indicates that considerable weight will be placed on where contracts with UK customers are actually made. If contracts are concluded in the UK, this will tend to indicate that the trader is trading within the UK: *Grainger & Son* v *Gough* (1896) 3 TC 462 and *Pommery & Greno* v *Apthorpe* (1886) 2 TC 182. Technical contract law rules are applied to determine where the contract has been concluded. However, the place of contracting is not the sole determinant and if, looking at the situation as a whole, the profits are generated in the UK the trader may well be considered to be trading in the UK. This will particularly be the case if the trader manufactures or processes the goods in the UK. In *Greenwood* v *F L Smith & Co* (1922) 8 TC 193 Atkins LJ said:

> The contracts in this case were made abroad. But I am not prepared to hold that this test is decisive.
>
> I can imagine cases where the contract of resale is made abroad, and yet the manufacture of the goods, some negotiation of the terms, and complete execution of the contract takes place here under such circumstances that the trade was in truth exercised here. I think that the question is, where do the operations take place from which the profits in substance arise.

This case was cited with approval by the House of Lords in *Firestone Tyre & Rubber Co Ltd* v *Lewellin* (1957) 37 TC 111. The final sentence of the extract quoted above perhaps goes to the heart of the matter and is more likely to be applied by the courts than a test based solely on the place of formation of the contracts.

Most of the cases have involved the sale of goods. In the case of a trade involving the provision of services it seems likely that the courts would again seek to establish where the profits are being generated. The trade is therefore likely to be treated as carried on 'within' the UK if services are being performed in the UK. If services are performed outside the UK, even though the customers may be based in the UK, the trade is likely to be a trade undertaken 'with' the UK. In view of the diverse nature of the service activities, these comments must be treated as broad generalisations.

Source of investment income   It will generally be reasonably clear whether the income in question is derived from a UK investment and therefore has a UK source. Thus, for example, interest received from a UK resident debtor will generally be derived from a UK source.

In the context of franchise operations, circumstances may arise in which royalties derived from intellectual property rights are regarded as 'pure income profit' rather than as a gross receipt in a trading computation (*see* Chapter 9, pp 145–146). The source of royalties received from intellectual property rights will depend on the location of the property from which the royalty is derived.

It will have a UK source if the intellectual property is located in the UK (eg patents granted under the laws of the UK and royalties in respect of UK copyright under the Copyright Designs and Patents Act 1988). Royalties received from overseas intellectual property (eg foreign patents and copyright protected under foreign law) will be derived from a foreign source.

Double tax relief

As explained *above*, a UK-resident person will be liable for UK tax on worldwide income and capital gains and a non-UK-resident person may be liable for UK tax in respect of income derived from the UK. A UK-resident person may also be liable for overseas tax on overseas income and capital gains and a non-UK resident person may be liable for tax in the relevant overseas country on income and capital gains which have been taxed in the UK. Both UK domestic law and double tax treaties to which the UK is a party contain provisions designed to eliminate double liabilities.

UK domestic law—unilateral relief   UK tax legislation provides for unilateral relief from double taxation by allowing a UK resident taxpayer to set foreign tax suffered as a credit against any UK tax liability on the foreign income. Section 790(4) of ICTA 1988 provides for this credit where there has been '. . . tax paid under the law of the territory outside the UK and computed by reference to income arising or any chargeable gain accruing in that territory . . .'. The maximum relief that a taxpayer can obtain will be the lower of the foreign tax suffered and the UK tax on the foreign income; the taxpayer effectively ends up paying tax once, but at the higher of the effective rates payable in each country. There will generally be no unilateral relief if the taxpayer makes a loss on its overall income (ie including any income from its UK activities), as there will be no UK tax payable on the foreign income. This was the position in *George Wimpey International Ltd* v *Rolfe* [1989] STC 609. A taxpayer in this situation will not be able to use foreign tax credits against other sources of income which give rise to a UK tax liability.

Unilateral relief will not be available where the income or gains are regarded as having a UK source. However, the Inland Revenue has extended the availability of unilateral relief by a concession which provides:

> Payments made by a person resident in an overseas country to a person carrying on a trade in the UK as consideration for the use of, or for the privilege of using, in the overseas country any copyright, patent, design, secret process or formula, trade mark or other like property may in law be payments the source of which is in the UK, but are nevertheless treated for the purpose of credit (whether under double taxation agreements or by way of unilateral relief) as income arising outside the UK except to

the extent that they represent consideration for services (other than merely incidental services) rendered in this country by the recipient to the payer (ESC B8).

Accordingly, unilateral relief may still be available even if the source is technically in the UK provided the income is not derived from services being performed in the UK.

Unilateral relief is likely to be relevant where there is no applicable treaty with the country of source, or where there is but it does not deal with the tax liability in question.

Double tax treaties   The UK has entered into treaties with most countries (other than tax haven or low tax jurisdictions, for obvious reasons). These treaties operate to give relief from double taxation in two main ways. One is to give one country the exclusive right to tax specific categories of income or gains (as a result of which the taxpayer can claim exemption from tax in the other country). The other is to require one country to give credit when assessing tax for any tax paid on the income or gains in question in the other country.

Most of the UK's treaties are modelled on the OECD Model Convention. Some of the more important provisions (relating to the income and profits of an international business) of the Model Convention are commented on *below*.

The business profits article (art 7 in the Model Convention) provides that one country cannot impose tax on the business profits of a trader resident in the other country unless the trader is carrying on its trade in the first national country (ie trading within that country) through a 'permanent establishment' situated in that country.

The Model Convention (art 5) defines 'permanent establishment' to include a fixed place of business through which the business of an enterprise is wholly or partly carried on, including a place of management, a branch, an office, a workshop. Agents (other than agents who have no power to contract on behalf of the principal or independent 'general commission agents') can also constitute a permanent establishment.

If a trader resident in one treaty country does have a permanent establishment in the other country, the treaty will provide that the other country can tax only the profits which the permanent establishment might have been expected to produce if it were a distinct and separate enterprise engaged in the same or similar activities under the same or similar conditions dealing with the non-resident trader on an independent basis. This will mean that the country in which the permanent establishment is based should only tax the non-resident trader on the profits which would have been earned by an independent third party performing the activities actually performed by the permanent establishment. Any tax paid in respect of the activities of the permanent establishment in the country in which it exists would then be available as a credit to set against any tax payable in the country of the treaty partner (where the taxpayer is resident).

Most franchise fees which are not royalties should fall within the scope of the business profits article.

The OECD Model Convention provides (in art 12) that royalty income received by a person in one treaty country can be taxed in the other treaty country only if the person:

> carries on business in the other country through a permanent establishment situated therein, or performs independent personal services in the other country from a fixed base situated therein and the right or property in respect of which the royalties are paid is effectively connected with such permanent establishment or fixed base.

Thus, if a UK-resident franchisor were to receive a royalty from a USA franchisee, and if the franchisor had no relevant permanent establishment in the USA, no US tax should be payable on the royalty; it will be taxable solely in the UK. In practice some treaties provide for an exemption (as is the case with the UK/USA treaty), and others provide for a reduced tax rate.

So far as interest is concerned, art 11(1) of the Model Convention provides that the country of residence of the recipient of the interest may tax the interest. In addition, art 11(2) provides that the other country can tax the interest, but limited to 10 per cent of the gross amount of the interest. This effectively limits the amount of 'withholding tax' that can be imposed by the country of the payer to 10 per cent. The 10 per cent liability will be available as a credit against the recipient's tax liability in its own country. If the recipient of the interest carries on business in the UK through a permanent establishment, or performs independent personal services in the UK from a fixed base in the other country, and the debt claim in respect of which interest is paid was effectively connected with that permanent establishment or fixed base, arts 11(1) and (2) will not apply (art 11(4)); both countries will have taxing rights (but with credit rules applying).

The interest article in any particular double tax treaty may well be substantially different from the Model Convention, and it will be necessary to consider the detailed provisions of the relevant treaty.

If a person in one treaty country makes a capital gain on the disposal of an asset in the other country, the general rule in the Model Convention is that the gain will be taxable only in the country where the person is resident (art 13). However, the Convention permits both countries to levy tax if the gain relates to land situated in the other country or to the business property of a permanent establishment in the other country (art 13(1) and (3)).

Where tax is payable in both countries, most treaties provide for credit to be given for foreign tax paid against the liability in the taxpayer's home jurisdiction (the 'elimination of double taxation' article).

21.2.3 Computation of profit and transfer pricing

Where property is sold between associated persons, the Inland Revenue can substitute market value for the sale price where there is a sale at an under-value, and substitute market value for the purchase price where there is a purchase at an overvalue: ICTA 1988, s 770. Two persons are associated for this purpose where one controls the other or where both persons are under common control ('control' being defined by ICTA 1988, s 340 in accordance with ICTA 1988, s 773(2) and (3)). This legislation is designed to ensure that UK profits cannot be artificially manipulated to minimise UK tax liability. It does not apply if the company benefiting from the overcharging is a UK resident trading company.

The legislation catches more than transfers of goods, and specifically includes '. . . lettings and hirings of property, grants and transfers of rights, interests or licences and the giving of business facilities of whatever kind . . .' (ICTA 1988, s 773(4)). The section therefore covers the pricing of services and fees or royalties paid in respect of intellectual property rights.

The UK transfer pricing legislation deals with the UK position only. If a UK franchisor sells goods to its foreign subsidiary at an undervalue and the UK Inland Revenue substitutes market value for the sale price, the subsidiary will not necessarily be able to deduct the whole of the revised price in its own country as an expense. The subsidiary will have to seek to persuade its own tax authority to revise its allowable expenses. Mutual agreement procedures under double tax treaties are intended to address the problem of competing claims for profits between authorities in the two treaty countries, but may in practice fail to provide a satisfactory solution. In the European Union the Arbitration Convention is designed to establish more workable procedures to address this problem.

21.2.4 Collection

Withholding tax

In each of the following cases UK law requires the payer to deduct tax at the rate of 25 per cent from the payment of:

(a) capital sums paid on the sale of patent rights by non-resident vendors (ICTA 1988, s 524);

(b) copyright royalties (other than royalties relating to films) payable to someone whose usual place of abode is abroad (ICTA 1988, s 536);

(c) design right royalties payable to someone whose usual place of abode is abroad (ICTA 1988, s 537B);

(d) rent payable under a lease of property from a non-resident landlord unless a UK collecting agent has been appointed (in which case the agent can be assessed in respect of the landlord's liability) (ICTA 1988, s 43). For payments made on or after 6 April 1996 new rules will apply (Finance Act 1995, s 40).

(e) yearly interest payable from a UK source to someone whose usual place of abode is abroad (ICTA 1988, s 349(2)(*c*)).

The above rules apply specifically to payments to overseas persons. In addition the rules relating to 'annual payments' discussed in Chapter 9 should be considered since they apply equally to national and international payments.

In many cases (but not including rent payable to an overseas landlord) a double tax treaty entered into between the UK and the recipient's own country will provide for a reduction in or elimination of the tax deduction required by UK law (whether the obligation to deduct arises under the specific provisions referred to *above* or under the principles discussed in Chapter 9 concerning 'annual payments'). However, it will be possible to rely on a double tax treaty only where the authority of the Inland Revenue to pay at the reduced or nil rate has been obtained in advance. If payments are made under deduction of tax, eg before this authority has been obtained, the recipient will be entitled to apply to the UK Inland Revenue for repayment of the tax over-deducted. Where payments are made gross in accordance with authority given by the Inland Revenue, the payer will be able to obtain a tax deduction for the payments; a deduction will not be available if payments are made gross in reliance on a treaty but without receiving authority to pay gross. (The Double Taxation Relief (Taxes on Income) (General) Regulations 1970 (SI 1970 No 488) reg 3.)

Branches and agents of non-residents

Part VIII of the Taxes Management Act 1970 contains provisions under which UK tax liabilities can be assessed on UK branches or agents of non-resident persons. Certain exemption exists for independent investment managers and general commission agents and brokers (*see* ss 78 and 82). These provisions are being replaced by provisions introduced by the Finance Act 1995; the broad effect of the new provisions is that a non-resident's tax liability in respect of income from transactions carried out by independent investment managers or brokers acting in the normal course of their business should generally be limited to tax, if any, deducted at source (*see* the Finance Act 1995, ss 128, 129 and Sched 23).

21.3   Value Added Tax (VAT)

21.3.1   Introduction

The general principles of VAT and the VAT treatment of supplies made within the UK are dealt with in Chapter 9. This section outlines the VAT position where a UK trader receives a supply from a supplier based in another member state of the European Union or from a non-EU trader, and where a UK supplier makes a supply to a recipient based either in another EU member state or to a non-EU trader. For simplicity, references are made to goods or services being supplied by a franchisor to a franchisee but the same principles would apply in the event, for example, of a supply by a franchisee to one of its customers or suppliers by third parties to either a franchisor or a franchisee.

The member states of the EU are Austria, Belgium, Denmark, Finland, France, Germany, Greece, Ireland, Italy, Luxembourg, Netherlands, Portugal, Spain, Sweden and the UK (which for VAT purposes includes the Isle of Man but not the Channel Islands). Some of the overseas territories of these countries are included for VAT purposes.

Where goods are imported into the UK from outside the EU, VAT and customs duties will normally be payable. VAT is charged and payable as if it were a duty of customs, and Customs and Excise legislation is applied to VAT in the same way as it applies to customs and excise duties (Value Added Tax Act (VATA) 1974, ss 1(4) and 16(1)). The subject of customs and excise duties and procedures is not dealt with in this work.

21.3.2   Non-EU supplier

Supplies of goods

If an EU person (eg a UK franchisee) imports goods into an EU member state from a person who is not registered or required to be registered for VAT in any member state (eg a US franchisor), the EU importer will be required to account for VAT on the importation of the goods (Sixth VAT Directive, art 21(2) and VATA 1994, ss 1 and 2). The supplier/franchisor will not generally be obliged to register for UK VAT although registration may be necessary if it takes a supply of the goods in the UK, eg the supplier imports the goods into the UK and subsequently sells those goods to a UK franchisee.

If a non-EU franchisor acquires goods inside the EU, and sells them to a franchisee in the EU, the franchisor will normally be making a taxable supply for VAT purposes and if the value of all relevant supplies exceeds the relevant registration threshold (currently £46,000 per annum in the UK), it will be required to register for VAT.

Although the franchisee will be liable to account for VAT on its imports, this will not normally be more than a cash flow cost since the franchisee should be able to recover this tax as input tax (*see* Chapter 9 at 9.4.5).

The general rules explained *above* may be varied if the UK recipient of the goods 'intends to remove the goods to another member state' and the goods are, in fact, removed to another member state within one month of the date of importation. In such a case, no VAT will be due on their import into the UK, subject to compliance with procedural requirements (VAT (General) Regulations 1985 (SI 1985 No 886) as amended, reg 42). No import VAT will be due in the member state where the goods are received but the UK trader will make an intra-community supply to the trader in the other member state (*see* 21.3.4 *below*). This is likely to mean that a VAT charge equivalent to import VAT will arise in the member state where the goods are received. It may be possible to take advantage of this relief where the goods are being imported by a master franchisee located in a member state and such imports are only made to facilitate onward supplies to franchisees in other member states.

Supplies of services

If a non-EU franchisor is supplying services, it will be necessary to determine whether the services are supplied outside or within the EU. Services are generally supplied where the supplier belongs. Section 9(2) of VATA 1994 provides that a supplier belongs in the UK if:

(a)   it has a business establishment or some other fixed establishment in the UK and no such establishment elsewhere; or

(b)   it has no such establishment in the UK or elsewhere but its usual place of residence is in the UK; or

(c)   it has such establishments both in the UK and elsewhere and its establishment which is most directly concerned with the supply is in the UK.

A person will have a business establishment in the UK if it carries on business through a branch or agency in the UK (VATA 1994, s 9(5)). A non-EU franchisor will have a business establishment in its own country. Accordingly, it can make a supply in the UK only if it falls within (c) *above*; supplies will take place in the UK where the supply is more directly concerned with the UK branch than with the business carried on in the franchisor's own country. If a franchisor is involved in direct franchising, without establishing any branch in the UK, the supply will take place outside the EU and no VAT liabilities will arise for the franchisor.

If the franchisor has established a branch in the UK and the services are provided by this branch, a supply will be made in the UK. The franchisor will be liable to register for VAT in respect of this branch and will be treated as an EU trader for the purposes of VAT.

The Sixth VAT Directive provides that certain services (commonly referred to as 'reverse charge services') shall be treated as supplied in the country of the recipient of the supplies (eg in the country of the franchisee), and that the recipient (the franchisee) must account for VAT in its own country. The position regarding reverse charge services is dealt with in detail *below* at pp 386–389.

21.3.3   UK supplier to non-EU recipient

Supplies of goods

If a UK franchisor exports goods to a place outside the EU, the supply will be zero-rated (no VAT need be charged) subject to compliance with procedural requirements (Sixth VAT Directive, art 15, applied by VATA 1994, s 30(6)).

Supplies of services

If the recipient of a supply of services is located outside the EU, VAT will be payable unless the services are 'reverse charge services' or other special types of services detailed in the VAT (Place of Supply of Services) Order 1992 (SI 1992 No 3122) which specifies rules for determining the place of supply of these special types of services. In the main these services relate to land, transport services of intermediaries and services which involve immediate physical performance (eg sporting activities). If the services are reverse charge services and the recipient belongs in a country outside the EU, the supply will be outside the scope of VAT (The Value Added Tax (Place of Supply of Services) Order 1992, art 16). Input tax recovery will not be adversely affected by the existence of such services.

21.3.4   Intra-EU supplies

Introduction

There will be intra-EU supplies of goods and services where a franchisor makes supplies from a base in one member state and the franchisee is based in another member state. There may also be intra-EU supplies where a non-EU franchisor establishes a master franchise company in a member state to supervise its EU franchise network. This master franchise company will provide the various goods and services under the franchise agreement and may be liable to register for VAT in its country of operation.

Following introduction of the single market on 1 January 1993, the VAT position for intra-EU supplies should, in theory, be the same whichever two EU countries are involved in the transactions. However, despite the long term aim of harmonising VAT across the EU, there are still substantial differences between the national laws of the member states and these may result in different VAT consequences depending on the countries in which the supplier is operating.

A review of the differences between the domestic laws of the different member states goes beyond the scope of this chapter, which deals solely with the position where the franchisor has established its business in the UK and is registered for VAT in the UK.

Supplies of goods

If a UK-registered person acquires goods to be brought into the UK from another member state, it will generally be liable to account to Customs and Excise for VAT on the value of those goods (VATA 1994, s 10). Provided that person does not make exempt supplies it should be able to recover the whole of this VAT as input tax (*see* Chapter 9 at 9.4.8 and 9.4.9).

If a UK franchisor disposed of goods to a franchisee in another member state before 1 January 1993, the supply was zero rated in the UK. The franchisee would have to account for VAT in its own country on the importation of the goods.

From 1 January 1993, the supply of goods to a franchisee in another member state will be zero-rated only if the franchisee is VAT registered in another member state (VAT (General) Regulations 1985, reg 57A). The franchisor must obtain the franchisee's VAT registration number and must include this on any VAT invoice raised (VAT (General) Regulations 1985, reg 13). If the franchisee is not registered, VAT will have to be charged.

The position is less straightforward if the supplier makes 'distance sales' to a member state over a specified threshold. A 'distance sale' is the supply of goods to a person not registered for VAT in the other member state. Where the franchisor's sales to non-registered persons in a specific member state exceed that country's threshold (which may be either 35,000 ECU or 100,000 ECU (approximately £26,400 or £75,400 respectively) the place of supply for those goods will become the member state where the goods are acquired. As the franchisor will be making supplies in another member state, it may become liable to register for VAT in that country and to charge VAT in that country on the distance sales. If the franchisor does not have a place of business in that country it may have to appoint a fiscal agent in that country to be responsible for its VAT obligations there.

Supplies of services

A franchisor will often perform services for its franchisees in return for fees in accordance with the franchise agreement. It will not, generally, receive separate fees for the distinct services that it provides although, in some cases, it may receive a separate fee in respect of advertising.

The VAT legislation provides that the following services are treated as being supplied where they are received ('the reverse charge services' (VATA 1994, Sched 5)):

(1) transfers and assignments of copyright, patents, licences, trade marks and similar rights;
(2) advertising services;
(3) services of consultants, engineers, consultancy bureaux, lawyers,

accountants and other similar services; data processing and provision of information (but excluding from this head any services relating to land);

(4) acceptance of any obligation to refrain from pursuing or exercising, in whole or part, any business activity or any such rights as are referred to in paragraph 1 *above*;

(5) banking, financial and insurance services (including re-insurance, but not including the provision of safe deposit facilities);

(6) the supply of staff;

(7) the letting or hire of goods other than means of transport;

(8) the services rendered by one person to another in procuring for the other any of the services mentioned in paragraphs 1 to 7 *above*.

Many of the services commonly provided by the franchisor (eg advertising, consultancy, certain services relating to data processing, the supply of information and the supply of staff) fall within the list of reverse charge supplies, although this will not necessarily always be the case; items which do not fall within the list of reverse charge supplies include, for example, training and maintenance and repair of equipment.

Before 1 January 1993, if reverse charge services were supplied by a UK franchisor to a franchisee in another member state, the services were treated as being supplied in the UK (ie where the franchisor had established its business). This was a zero-rated supply provided the franchisee received the services in the course of its business. The franchisee would then have had to account for VAT in the member state where it was registered. If the franchisor made a supply of non-reverse charge services, the supply took place in the UK and the franchisor was required to charge UK VAT.

From 1 January 1993, supplies of non-reverse charge services are unaffected. So far as reverse charge services are concerned, a supply will take place in the country where the recipient of the supply is located if the recipient receives the supply in the course of its business. This means that no UK VAT is chargeable by the supplier. UK law additionally provides that this rule will apply only if the recipient is registered for VAT in another member state (VAT (Place of Supply of Services) Order 1992, art 16), and Customs and Excise initially stated that the UK supplier must obtain its recipient's VAT registration number to avoid charging VAT in the UK. However, European law provides that the recipient must be a 'taxable person' but does not require it to be registered for VAT (Sixth Directive, arts 4(1) and 9(2)(e)). This has led to suggestions that the new legislation is in breach of European law and, in March 1993, Customs and Excise announced that a supplier is not required to charge VAT on its reverse charge supplies (even if it had not obtained confirmation that its customer was so registered) provided that the supplier could satisfy itself that the supplies were made for the purposes of the recipient's business. It should be relatively straightforward for a franchisor to satisfy itself that its franchisees are receiving the supplies for the purposes of their businesses. It may nevertheless be prudent for the franchisor to obtain its franchisee's VAT registration number to avoid any possible disputes with Customs and Excise as to whether the supply was received in the course of the franchisee's business. A franchisor may wish to consider including in franchise agreements an obligation for franchisees located in other member states to provide their VAT registration numbers.

As a VAT-registered franchisee will be the person liable to account for VAT on reverse charge services in its own country, the franchisor will not be required to register for VAT in other member states in respect of such supplies. However, European law permits a member state to introduce in its domestic law a provision making the supplier jointly and severally liable for the franchisee's VAT liability arising from the reverse charge. (Sixth Directive, art 21 (1)(b)). When negotiating the terms of a franchise agreement, the franchisor may wish to consider whether an indemnity is required from the franchisee to cover this contingent liability.

An understanding of reverse charge supplies is important not only in the context of the supplier making such supplies to its franchisees, but also because a franchisor may receive such supplies. The franchisor will, for example, sometimes provide advertising services to its franchisees and, in this context, may deal as principal rather than agent when obtaining those services. If the advertisements are provided to the franchisor by a supplier registered for VAT in another member state, the franchisor will be liable to account for UK VAT under the reverse charge provisions (VATA 1994, s 8). When the supplier invoices its franchisees in respect of these advertising services, the franchisees may also be liable to account for VAT in their own country under the reverse charge provisions.

As the various services provided under the franchise agreement will, generally, be provided in return for one fee, it is necessary to determine the nature of the supply. The franchise fee may be viewed as being paid in return for a single composite supply (one combined supply, of all the services provided by the franchisor) or as being paid in return for a multiple supply (several distinct supplies for a number of separately identifiable services). If the supply is correctly viewed as a single composite supply (ie the goods and/or services supplied make up a single indivisible supply, or there is one dominant supply with other incidental supplies as an adjunct), the VAT treatment will depend on the nature of the service (as a whole) or the dominant supply which is being provided by the franchisor. If the correct analysis is that there are a number of separate supplies, it will be necessary to consider separately the nature of each specific supply provided by the franchisor and apportion the fee to each distinct service. Whether the supply is correctly viewed as a single composite supply or as a multiple supply is essentially a question of fact which the courts have in particular cases found difficult to resolve, as can be witnessed by the decisions in *Card Protection Plan Ltd* v *Customs and Excise Commissioners* [1994] STC

199 and *Bophuthatswana NCC* v *Customs and Excise Commissioners* [1992] STC 741. In practice, the distinction will become relevant only if the supply (or supplies) includes a mixture of non-reverse charge and reverse charge services.

21.4   Overseas franchisor with UK franchisees

21.4.1   Direct franchising

It is sometimes possible for a non-resident franchisor to establish a UK franchise network without the need for any form of establishment of its own in the UK; the non-resident franchisor may be able to provide all the franchise services from the franchisor's own country with occasional visits to the UK franchisees by the franchisor's staff. In this situation, it may be that the non-resident franchisor is not trading in the UK or that it has no UK permanent establishment for the purposes of an applicable double tax treaty (*see* pp 376 and 379 *above*). In either case there will be no exposure to direct taxation in the UK.

A franchisee paying franchise fees to a franchisor will have to consider the capital revenue distinction in respect of fees and whether any withholding tax obligation arises (particularly for continuing fees). The same principles as those applicable in a wholly domestic context will apply; the franchisee will for example, have to consider whether the fees amount to 'annual payments' (*see* Chapter 9, pp 143–146). In addition the franchisee should consider whether any withholding tax provision specific to the case of payments to a non-resident person or a person whose usual place of abode is abroad will apply (*see* 21.2.4 *above*). In many cases it will be arguable that no withholding tax obligation arises, although references in the franchise documentation to 'royalties' may be suggestive of 'annual payment' treatment. In cases of doubt the solution may lie in the terms of an applicable double tax treaty since treaties sometimes provide for an exemption from UK tax on royalties. As indicated at p 382 *above*, a UK franchisee can rely on the provisions of the double tax treaty to pay at a 'nil' or reduced rate only if the prior clearance of the Inland Revenue has been obtained. The franchisee should complete the relevant form (obtainable from the Revenue's Financial and Intermediaries Claims Office (International)) which is then forwarded to the franchisor. The franchisor completes relevant sections of the form and sends it to its own tax authority. If everything is in order that authority will return the form to the Inland Revenue who will then grant authority for payments to be made gross.

21.4.2   Operating through a branch or subsidiary

A franchising relationship requires the performance of services by the franchisor for its franchisees and supervision of the franchisees, rather than the passive receipt of income. In many cases, an overseas franchisor will need to establish some form of presence in the UK to perform the services required under the franchise agreement. If the overseas franchisor establishes a real presence (eg opens an office/training centre and employs staff to support the franchise network) it may well also be trading within the UK through a UK permanent establishment and will therefore incur a liability to UK tax on the profits of the UK presence (*see* 21.2.2 *above*).

In this situation the franchisor will wish to consider whether to operate through a UK branch of the overseas company or a UK subsidiary. This will involve consideration of the tax position in both countries and commercial and regulatory factors which extend beyond the confines of this chapter.

UK branch or subsidiary

If a non-resident company trades through a UK branch, it is likely to be exposed to UK corporation tax in respect of the branch profits (*see* pp 120–121 *above*). The profits will also form part of the non-resident company's profits and may be assessed to tax in its own country, usually with credit being given for the UK tax paid against the overseas tax liability.

An important potential tax advantage of operating through a branch is to achieve double relief for any trading losses incurred by the branch. This can be particularly advantageous in the initial years of establishing a UK operation when it may be that losses will arise. Depending on the tax laws applying in the non-resident's own country, the franchisor may be able to set losses arising from the part of the trade carried on in the UK against its worldwide income. In addition, the branch will be able to carry these losses forward against future trading income of that branch (ICTA 1988, s 293(1)).

If the activities in the UK can be limited to activities which do not amount to the carrying on of a UK trade, then use of a branch structure can avoid any UK tax liability arising. If the branch's activities consist of the supply of certain non-trading services exclusively to the branch's head office (eg possibly simply collecting information for the head office or acting in some other non-trading representative function) it may be that a non-trading 'representative office' status can be obtained and no UK tax liability would arise. If, however, the same activities were to be undertaken by a subsidiary established by the franchisor, the subsidiary would be treated as carrying on a service trade and the Inland Revenue would expect it to be remunerated on an arm's length basis (perhaps costs plus an agreed percentage, typically between 10 and 15 per cent). In the context of franchising operations, where the UK presence is likely to be required to enable support services to be supplied to the franchise network, a trading activity is likely to exist. The franchise fees relate at least partly to the provision of these services. In many cases the 'representative office' status is not therefore likely to be available.

If a non-resident company operates through a separate UK resident subsidiary in the UK, the subsidiary will be taxed in the same way as any other UK-resident company. It will be particularly advantageous to use a separate UK-resident subsidiary company where the UK activity is generating taxable profits which are to be retained in the UK for expansion of the business and the applicable tax rate in the UK is lower than in the non-resident's own country.

Some other tax issues to be considered are as follows:

(1) The applicable tax rate: Under UK domestic law a branch of an overseas company will be taxed at the full corporation tax rate of 33 per cent, whereas a subsidiary is capable of benefiting from the small companies rate of 25 per cent (*see* Chapter 9 pp 120–121). However, many double tax treaties include a 'non-discrimination article' which will ensure that a branch can also take advantage of the small companies rate.

(2) Repatriation of profits: If a branch is used, there will be no further tax to pay on repatriation of profits. If a subsidiary is used different methods for repatriation can be considered, to include fees for services supplied and interest and royalty payments (which may reduce the UK taxable profit, subject to the normal rules concerning deductibility, transfer pricing principles and withholding tax issues) and payment of dividends (non-deductible, generating an advance corporation tax liability and a possible tax liability in the overseas country on the receipt, subject to available credits for UK tax liabilities).

If losses are likely to arise in the initial years it may be appropriate to operate initially through a branch (to utilise the losses as described *above*) and to transfer the overseas business to a subsidiary when the branch has become profitable. It will, however, be necessary to consider the tax consequences of this reorganisation, taking into account the implications in both the UK and in the non-resident's own country.

So far as UK tax liabilities are concerned, there should be no immediate charge to UK tax on any capital gain where the non-resident company transfers assets to a UK-resident company as part of a scheme to transfer the whole or part of a trade carried on in the UK through a branch or agency to a UK-resident company at a time when the companies are in the same 'group' (TCGA 1992, s 172). A 'group' has the same meaning as is generally used for transfers between UK-resident groups of companies (contained in the TCGA 1992, s 170—basically 75 per cent ownership) except that the definitions are amended to include non-resident companies (TCGA 1992, s 172(5)). Where these conditions are satisfied, the capital assets of the branch will be deemed to be transferred at such a value as will give rise to neither a gain nor a loss (TCGA 1992, s 172(2)). This means that the UK subsidiary will take over the assets at the non-resident company's base cost (together with any indexation allowance).

If the transfer includes capital assets which have attracted capital allowances, s 343 of ICTA 1988 should be available to ensure that the new subsidiary takes over the non-resident's written down values for capital allowance purposes (as a result of which no balancing charges or allowances should arise). This section can also permit any unutilised trading losses to be transferred to the subsidiary. A transfer of any stock or work in progress held by the branch at book value should avoid any trading profit arising in the UK, subject to the making of an appropriate election in cases where the market value of the stock exceeds book value (Finance Act 1995, s 140).

The detailed requirements of the relevant legislation should be examined before proceeding with the incorporation of a branch. The review should also cover other potential tax issues, such as VAT and stamp duty.

Master franchisee

When structuring an international franchise operation it will be relevant to consider the precise scope of the activities to be performed in the UK. If the UK presence is to take on the role of a master franchisee, participating in the identification of franchisees and the granting of franchises in the local territory, this may involve a larger slice of profit being allocated to the UK than if the role is solely that of providing certain support services to the network. This comment will apply whether there is a branch presence or a subsidiary. If, however, there is a subsidiary providing the master franchisee role, franchise fees are likely to be paid by the subsidiary to the non-resident franchisor and withholding tax issues will have to be considered (the same issues as referred to in 21.4.1 *above*). In this context, the fact that a subsidiary may be granting franchises and supplying support services may in some cases result in the fees payable by the subsidiary to the non-resident franchisor having more of the character of a pure royalty, and increase the risk of 'annual payment' treatment; the role being performed by the franchisor in return for the fees it receives will have to be considered carefully, as will the terms of any applicable double tax treaty. These potential withholding tax issues will not arise if a branch operation is established, although this will not necessarily be a reason in itself for selecting a branch rather than a subsidiary.

Hybrid structure

If it is desirable to minimise UK tax (eg because UK tax rates are higher than the rates applicable in the non-resident franchisor's home country) a hybrid structure (rather than a structure involving a master franchisee) could be considered. The idea would be for the UK base to be given responsibility solely for support services; decisions relating to the granting of franchises and the process of granting franchises would be dealt with from the non-resident base, justifying a greater proportion of the global profit being retained there. This should be achievable whether a UK branch or subsidiary is established, although in practice a clearer separation between the roles of the franchisor and its UK establishment might be achieved through use of a subsidiary; the role of a subsidiary could be set out in an agreement which defines in a legally binding way the limited role to be performed by the subsidiary.

21.4.3   Appointment of an independent master franchisee

The main tax issues associated with the appointment of an independent master franchisee by a non-resident franchisor are likely to be the same as apply in connection with a domestic franchise arrangement: the tax treatment of initial fees (capital or income?) and possible withholding tax issues. These issues are covered in Chapter 9 and at 21.2.4 *above*.

21.5   UK franchisor operating overseas

21.5.1   Direct franchising

If a UK franchisor is undertaking franchise operations in other countries, it will be necessary to consider whether it is exposed to tax in that country. This will clearly depend on the domestic tax law of that country. However, if the UK has concluded a double tax treaty with that country there should be no exposure to overseas tax on franchise income if there is no permanent establishment in that country, subject to consideration of withholding tax issues (relating, for example, to royalties).

Trading income or annual payments

It will be necessary to determine whether the franchise fees received by the UK franchisor constitute trading income or 'annual payments'. The distinction between carrying on a trading activity and receiving annual payments is explained in Chapter 9 at 9.3.2. In essence, a franchisor receiving trading income will, subject to the comments in the following paragraph, be entitled to deduct all its trading expenses against that income and have the benefit of a more favourable regime relating to utilisation of losses. If the franchisor is receiving annual payments it will not be able to offset its expenses against this income.

If the income is properly regarded as trading income, it will then be necessary to decide whether this is in respect of a trade carried on in the UK (Schedule D Case I) or wholly carried on outside the UK (Schedule D Case V): *Spiers* v *Mackinnon* (1929) 14 TC 386. To determine which is the appropriate treatment, it will be necessary to decide whether the franchisor is carrying on a separate distinct trade of franchising overseas, or whether the activity forms part of its general trading activities as will be more likely if a franchisor simply expands its existing trading operations into the overseas market through direct franchising. It will generally be beneficial for the UK-resident franchisor to argue that the overseas activities form part of its existing UK trade. This will enable any losses derived from the overseas activities to be set against trading income in the UK. If the overseas activities are held to constitute a separate trade (taxable under Schedule D Case V), any losses will generally be available for offset only against profits of the trade or income from other trades taxable under Schedule D Case V. They cannot be set against profits of the UK trade (ICTA 1988, s 391).

Where the UK franchisor is receiving income in respect of overseas intellectual property rights (eg copyright royalties), this will be taxable under Schedule D Case V as it will be foreign source income (ICTA 1988, s 18(3)). If the income is also subject to tax in the franchisee's country, the UK Inland Revenue should grant unilateral relief against double taxation under the ICTA 1988, s 790 (*see* p 378 *above*).

Unilateral relief

When structuring its international franchise arrangements, a UK-resident franchisor should ensure that it does not prejudice any claim for unilateral relief (basically, a credit against UK tax for tax incurred abroad) in respect of profits that have already been taxed in a franchisee's own country, particularly if the franchisor is not able to obtain the benefit of a double tax treaty. Unilateral relief is available for tax paid in another country only if that tax is 'computed by reference to income arising or any chargeable gain accruing in that territory' (ICTA 1988, s 790(4)). The legislation does not afford any relief where overseas tax is charged in a particular overseas country in respect of income or chargeable gains arising or accruing in a different overseas country. Although a country will not generally tax a non-resident person on profits made in other countries, the availability of unilateral relief could be prejudiced if a person in, say, France is appointed to collect franchise fees from both French and German franchisees on behalf of a UK-resident franchisor. If, in this situation, the franchise fees were taxed in France (eg by way of withholding tax), no unilateral relief would be available on so much of the income as arises in Germany. However, the provisions of relevant double tax treaties should be considered, as it may well be that they operate to prevent any overseas tax from being imposed or provide for credits.

21.5.2 Overseas branch or subsidiary

If a UK franchisor requires its own presence to be established in another country in order to service its franchise network in that country, a decision between a branch presence and use of a subsidiary will have to be taken. Similar issues to those discussed in 21.4.2 (for an overseas company trading in the UK) will arise. For example, if a master franchise structure is being considered for the overseas country in question and if tax rates in that country are higher than in the UK, a hybrid structure (as explained in 21.4.2) might be worth considering.

Utilising losses

If the overseas activity is incurring losses and is part of a single trade undertaken by the UK franchisor in both the UK and the overseas country, use of a branch will enable the losses to be utilised in the UK against any taxable profits of the trade arising elsewhere. If the loss is derived from a separate trade undertaken abroad (perhaps in rare circumstances where it is not a natural extension of the UK franchising activity), the loss will arise under Schedule D Case V and will not be available for offset against UK trading income. A non-resident subsidiary, on the other hand, is a distinct legal entity and its UK parent will not be entitled to set the subsidiary's losses against the parent's own profits.

Avoiding UK taxation

If the UK and the overseas activities are both profitable, a non-resident subsidiary can be used to avoid UK taxation (subject to the controlled foreign company 'CFC' legislation) (*see* 21.6.1 *below*). This may be advantageous where UK tax rates exceed the relevant tax rates in the subsidiary's own jurisdiction (not currently a common situation) as UK tax will be paid only when profits are distributed to the UK parent. If most of the subsidiary's profits will be repatriated to the UK (other than by repayment of the principal of loans) this will negate any potential tax saving arising from using the subsidiary.

As with a non-resident trading company operating in the UK, a UK trader operating overseas may initially operate through a branch and subsequently decide to incorporate that branch. Overseas tax issues will have to be considered. Some of the main UK tax issues are touched on *below*.

Capital gains

Perhaps the most significant potential UK tax charge on the transfer of the branch to a subsidiary will be corporation tax on any capital gains arising in respect of the assets (including goodwill) transferred to the subsidiary. In these circumstances, the assets will be deemed to have been disposed of at market value. However, this chargeable gain can be deferred where a UK company carrying on a trade outside the UK through a branch or agency incorporates that branch or agency provided that the trade carried on through that branch or agency, or part of it, together with the whole assets of the company used for the purposes of the trade or part (or together with the whole of those assets other than cash) is transferred to a company not resident in the UK in exchange for securities consisting of shares, or of shares and loan stock, issued by the non-UK resident company to the UK resident company (TCGA 1992, s 140). The relief will be available only where the UK-resident company will have not less than one-quarter of the ordinary share capital of the non-UK resident company after the incorporation of the branch (TCGA 1992, s 140(1)(c)).

A similar relief is available under the TCGA 1992, s 171 where the branch is transferred to another UK-resident company in the same group (as defined in the TCGA 1992, s 170).

All the gains will be deferred where the consideration is wholly shares or shares and loan stock. If part of the consideration is cash, a proportion of the net gains arising will be immediately chargeable. The deferred gain will become chargeable when the transferor disposes of any of the shares or the loan stock (TCGA 1992, s 140(4) or when the non-resident company (within six years of the transfer) disposes of any of the assets on which a gain was deferred at the time of the transfer (TCGA 1992, s 140(5)).

The capital gains issues outlined *above* could arise in respect of both tangible assets used in the branch and in respect of intellectual property rights associated with the branch. Similarly, on the establishment of an overseas subsidiary to commence activities in that country (ie without the prior establishment of a branch), there could be a disposal or part disposal of some of the franchisor's intellectual property rights (eg if rights are granted to the subsidiary), particularly if the rights have an international dimension. If the franchisor has not previously operated in a particular territory, values of any assets and rights relating to that territory may be low so that the capital gains issue is of no great significance. If the franchisor is already operating there (through a successful branch), values may be significant, but it should be possible to defer any potential gain by means of the relief described *above*. The starting point when considering the tax implications of the relevant proposals must be to understand what intellectual property rights are involved and what rights are to be transferred or granted to the new subsidiary.

Other issues

Other UK tax issues will include the following:

(1) If the transfer to the subsidiary includes assets on which capital allowances have been claimed, the parent will have to consider whether there is any exposure to balancing charges on those assets (*see* Chapter 9, pp 133–134).

(2) The transfer of assets to a subsidiary can also give rise to transfer pricing issues in respect of, for example, the transfer of trading stock (ICTA 1988, s 770; *see* 21.2.3 *above*).

The commentary *above* focuses on UK tax issues. The decision between a branch and a subsidiary presence may well depend principally on the tax, regulatory and commercial issues in the overseas country, to which appropriate consideration will have to be given.

21.6 International tax planning

Some tax planning opportunities have been identified in the preceding sections of this chapter. There follow some brief comments on the use of tax havens and typical international corporate structures. These comments are designed to give the reader an indication of some pitfalls to be avoided, some opportunities which may be available and some of the more sophisticated international planning techniques. It is hoped that these will alert the reader to take specialist advice in this complicated area.

21.6.1 Tax havens and low tax jurisdictions

General

In structuring an international franchise network, a franchisor may seek to mitigate its worldwide tax exposure by establishing a group company in a tax haven or low tax jurisdiction. This company could, for example, be used to hold intellectual property rights and to receive income from the licensing of such rights. If the profits of this company were tax-free or were taxed at a low effective rate, this could facilitate the build-up of a fund free of significant taxes which could eventually be repatriated to the parent company (causing the parent company to receive taxable income, but having benefited from a deferral of the tax liability). In the meantime the funds may be utilised to assist expansion of the franchise network, for example by loans to other group companies (possibly at no tax cost).

However, tax authorities have been increasingly aware of the use of tax havens and have introduced various provisions to prevent tax liabilities in their own jurisdictions from being avoided by diverting profits to a tax haven. Some of the provisions of UK law are discussed *below*, as are some of the potential pitfalls associated with tax havens.

Residence

If a UK franchisor is establishing a company in a tax haven jurisdiction, the first issue to consider is whether it will be possible in practice to ensure that the subsidiary does not become UK resident for tax purposes. If so, the company would pay UK tax on its profits.

The management and control tests referred to in 21.2.1 *above* will be relevant in this context. It will be necessary to ensure that management and control is not exercised in the UK. It will normally be necessary to ensure that at least a majority of the board of directors of the tax haven company are not UK resident individuals and that, in any event, all board meetings take place outside the UK. In addition, management decisions must in reality be taken at the overseas board meetings and such meetings should not take place solely for the purpose of rubber stamping decisions already taken in the UK (at, for example, meetings of the board of the UK franchisor).

Place of trade

The principles briefly referred to in 21.2.2 *above* will need to be considered. If, for example, the role of the tax haven company is to provide support services to overseas franchisees and if, in reality, those services are provided from a base in the UK, using UK-based personnel of the franchisor, it may be that the Inland Revenue could successfully argue that the tax haven company is trading in the UK through a UK branch or agent. This would result in a UK tax liability on the profits of the tax haven company. In practice, it is often difficult to run a business efficiently without encountering problems of this nature. This may in turn lead to consideration of use of a tax haven company for a more passive activity (not involving active provision of services), so that operating the business of the tax haven company from outside the UK can more easily be accommodated.

Receipts and withholding tax

If royalties are paid to a tax haven company, withholding tax deductions may well be required. One possibility may be to route royalties into a tax haven company via a Netherlands company, since the Netherlands do not impose a withholding tax on royalties (*see further* 21.6.2 *below*). Alternatively, consideration could be given to the possibility of fees being paid to the tax haven company for a range of services to be provided under the franchise agreement, with the tax haven company then sub-contracting the provision of the services to the UK franchisor or a company in its group. An appropriate part of the fee would be paid to the UK sub-contractor, but it may be that a specific role or specific rights can be assigned to, or vested in, the tax haven company to justify retention of part of the fee offshore.

Transfer of assets abroad

If the UK-resident franchisor is an individual (sole trader or partner), he may be exposed to UK income tax on any income of a tax haven company established by him, under the anti-avoidance provisions of either ss 739 or 740 of the ICTA 1988. The establishment of any form of offshore structure by a UK ordinarily-resident individual will invariably require consideration of these sections. Most international franchising operations are likely to operate through a corporate structure, using existing corporate funds or facilities to expand abroad, possibly involving a tax haven vehicle. In this context, ss 739 and 740 should not normally be relevant. It is not therefore considered appropriate to deal further with these provisions and reference should be made to specialist tax books for a commentary on this legislation.

Controlled foreign companies (CFC) legislation

The CFC legislation (ss 747 to 756 and Scheds 24 and 25 to ICTA 1988) can apply where a non-resident company is controlled by UK-resident persons (whether or not companies). Where applicable, a proportion of the profits can be apportioned for tax purposes to corporate shareholders having an interest of at least 10 per cent. The legislation can therefore be relevant whenever a UK company establishes a subsidiary in a low tax jurisdiction. A list of countries is published by the Inland Revenue in two parts. If a company is resident and carrying on business (90 per cent of its income) in a country in Part I it will be regarded as falling outside the scope of the CFC legislation. The same is true for countries in Part II unless the company benefits from one of the reliefs referred to in Part II.

The CFC legislation also contains a number of exclusions; an apportionment will not be made in the following cases:

(1) If the chargeable profits of the foreign company do not exceed £20,000 (ICTA 1988, s 748(1)(*d*)).

(2) No apportionment is made unless the foreign company is resident in a country in which there is 'lower level of taxation'. The rate of taxation will not be treated as 'lower' where the amount of tax payable is less than 75 per cent of the amount that would have been payable in the UK on certain assumptions set out in the legislation, including an assumption that the company is resident in the UK. Formerly the percentage was 50 per cent, but this was raised following the lowering of UK corporate tax rates. (ICTA 1988, s 750 and Sched 24).

(3) No apportionment is made if the foreign company adopts an acceptable distribution policy (ie distributing at least 50 per cent of its profits to its shareholders in the case of a trading company, or 90 per cent of its profits in other cases) (ICTA 1988, s 748(1)(*a*) and Sched 25, Part I).

   (4) If the public quotation exemption applies (broadly where 35 per cent of the shares of the CFC are held by the public and are quoted on a recognised stock exchange) (ICTA 1988, s 748(1)(*c*) and Sched 25, Part III).

   (5) If the exempt activities exemption applies. This requires a real presence in the jurisdiction in which the foreign company is based and the exemption will not apply if the main activity is (*inter alia*) the receipt of income (such as royalties). (ICTA 1988, s 748(1)(*b*) and Sched 25, Part II).

   (6) If the 'motive test' applies; no tax charge arises if the transactions generating the profits were carried out for reasons other than reducing UK tax (ICTA 1988, s 748(3)).

It will often be impossible to avoid the application of the CFC legislation save by using the acceptable distribution exemption. If trading status can be established for the CFC, the 50 per cent distribution requirement can mean that a significant part of the profits can benefit from an indefinite deferral of tax. Even if the 90 per cent distribution policy must be adopted, the distribution must take place within 18 months of the relevant year end and this can effectively mean that a two years' deferral of tax can be achieved for 90 per cent of the income and indefinite deferral on the remaining 10 per cent. A valuable role can therefore be provided by a tax haven company where substantial international operations are taking place and the other main pitfalls (relating, for example, to residence status and withholding tax) can be overcome.

Capital gains

The CFC legislation applies to attribute a CFC's income to UK corporate shareholders; it does not apply to capital gains made by an offshore company. Section 13 of the TCGA 1992 provides that a UK-resident or ordinarily resident person (including a company) who has at least a 5 per cent holding in a non-resident 'close' company shall have attributed to it an appropriate proportion (by reference to entitlement on liquidation) of the non-resident company's gains unless the gains are remitted to the shareholders within two years. This legislation applies, however, only where the non-resident company would be a close company if it were UK-resident, and will not therefore apply if the UK parent is a non-close company (*see* the definition at p 129 of Chapter 9).

Transfer pricing

The UK transfer pricing legislation discussed in 21.2.3 *above*, and similar legislation in other countries, will have to be borne in mind. Where such legislation applies, all dealings between the tax haven company and other associated companies will have to be conducted on arm's length terms. Transfer pricing legislation will normally operate to negate the benefit of any attempt to pass profits into a low tax country on an artificial basis.

21.6.2 International group structures

The appropriate structure for a particular international operation will be developed having regard to the circumstances of the case. Some of the factors to be considered have been mentioned in this chapter. One example of a group structure for a multinational group with its headquarters in the UK is set out *below*, followed by a commentary which explains how the structure may be arrived at and the role to be performed by each company in the group. The aim of the commentary is to give an indication of some planning opportunities and to illustrate how an international structure may be developed.

Example

Factual assumptions   A UK franchisor will be undertaking franchising operations in a number of European countries. It will need a local presence in each country and proposes to establish subsidiaries to perform a master franchisee role (finding and vetting prospective franchisees, granting franchises, providing support services, etc). It has considered the alternatives of branches or subsidiaries and has concluded, having regard to both tax and commercial issues, to establish subsidiaries.

The franchisor has already registered its trade marks in the relevant countries (for protection purposes), but little value should attach to ownership of these rights since the franchise business has not been tried out in the local markets.

The structure proposed for this group is as follows:

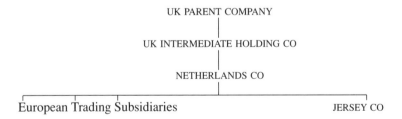

The Jersey company   When planning the international structure, the franchisor may wish to know whether it can secure tax savings by establishing a tax haven company. The structure *above* includes a Jersey company by way of example. Initially the franchisor might wish to consider the possibility of the Jersey company being a European master franchisee (ie participating in the process of granting franchises to European franchisees). The difficulty with this in the example may well be that the master franchisee role will require personnel operating from a fixed base in each of the European countries. It may therefore be difficult to avoid a taxable presence in each of the countries, thereby negating the potential advantages of use of a tax haven company. This leads to the conclusion that the Jersey company has to perform a more passive role. In this example, the UK franchisor decides to assign to the Jersey company the trade marks it has registered in the relevant European countries and other relevant intellectual property rights. The assignment will be treated as a disposal for capital gains purposes taking place at market value (since it is a disposal between connected parties), but the values are low and no significant tax charge therefore arises.

The Netherlands company   Subsidiaries are established in each of the relevant European countries and these subsidiaries will perform the master franchisee role for each country. Each of the subsidiaries will receive a licence from the Jersey company to use the relevant trade marks in return for licence fees/royalties. The main difficulty here is that most European countries will require a deduction of withholding tax on payment of the royalties to the Jersey company. A Netherlands company is therefore introduced into the structure. One of the roles of this Netherlands company will be to act as an intermediate licensor. The Jersey company will grant a licence to the Netherlands company and the Netherlands company will in turn grant licences to the European master franchisees. The idea here is that royalties can be paid to the Netherlands company free of withholding taxes, or at reduced withholding tax rates under treaties between the relevant European countries and the Netherlands. The possible application of provisions in treaties designed to stop treaty abuse will have to be considered. So far as payments on by the Netherlands company to the Jersey company are concerned, Netherlands law does not require a deduction of tax from royalties and royalties can therefore be paid to the Jersey company free of withholding taxes. An advance ruling is obtained from the Netherlands authorities to agree the measure of taxable profit the Netherlands authorities will require to be made in the Netherlands. The Netherlands company will also be involved in the process of maintaining trade mark registrations, dealing with European trade mark agents, prosecuting infringements, etc so that it performs more than a purely passive licensing role and has a commercial role in the structure.

A controlled foreign company   The Jersey company will be a controlled foreign company. Since it is performing a purely passive licensing role it will not be carrying on a trade and will therefore have to distribute 90 per cent of its profits (as calculated for CFC purposes) to avoid the application of the CFC legislation. Tax savings will nevertheless be obtained as a result of use of the Jersey company. Ten per cent of the profits will not have to be distributed to the UK company and might be utilised to assist continuing overseas expansion. So far as the 90 per cent is concerned, this has to be distributed as a dividend to the UK company within 18 months of the company's year end. This effectively achieves a deferral of tax for two years in respect of this 90 per cent. Furthermore, as will be seen *below*, the role of the Netherlands company as a 'mixer company' may effectively reduce further the tax on the Jersey company's profits.

Taxation of dividends   Consideration is then given to the tax treatment of dividends flowing up from the European master franchisees and from the Jersey company to the UK parent company. It is first assumed that the shares of the master franchisee company and the Jersey company will be held directly by the UK parent company, in other words there are no intermediate holding companies in this structure. Dividends paid up to the UK company will be taxable in the UK. However, the treaties between the UK and the relevant European countries in which the master franchisees are based provide that, in calculating the UK tax, credit is given for the underlying tax paid by the master franchisee companies on the profits out of which the dividends are paid. Thus the basic principle is that for profits which are taxed at a higher rate than the applicable UK rate, no further tax will be payable on the dividend received. For dividends received from companies which pay tax at a lower rate than in the UK, further tax will be payable.

The following very basic example (*see* overleaf) illustrates how this works. The example assumes that each company has £100,000 of pre-tax profits available to distribute. A reserve is first made by each company for the tax which will be paid on these profits, and the net after-tax amount is then distributed to the UK company. It is assumed that the applicable UK rate of tax is 33 per cent. It will be seen that the effective tax rate on the £400,000 of profit, following the distribution up to the UK company, is 40.25 per cent. The fact that tax credits for the foreign tax are given on a country-by-country basis means that for those countries where the tax rate is higher than the UK, tax credits are effectively wasted (tax credits cannot be set against the tax payable on the dividends received by the UK company from subsidiaries which pay tax at a lower rate than the UK rate).

The 'mixer company'

It is therefore decided to interpose a Netherlands 'mixer company' as the holding company of the master franchisee companies. The Netherlands company enjoys the Netherlands 'participation exemption' which means that the company does not pay Dutch tax on the dividend income received. The dividends received from the master franchisees and from the Jersey company are effectively 'mixed' and paid on as one dividend to the UK company. This enables the tax credits to be added together, resulting in excess unutilised

	Master Franchisee 1	*Master Franchisee 2*	*Master Franchisee 3*	*Jersey Co*
Pre tax profit for distribution	£100,000	£100,000	£100,000	£100,000
Local tax rate	25%	40%	55%	0%
Post tax profit to be distributed	£75,000	£60,000	£45,000	£100,000
UK tax at 33% to pay on dividend received after foreign tax credit	£8,000*	0	0	£33,000
Net after-tax profit	£67,000	£60,000	£45,000	£67,000
Total net profit:	£239,000			
Effective tax rate on £400,000 of profit:	40.25%			

*The actual dividend of £75,000 is grossed up at the local rate of 25% to produce UK taxable income of £100,000. The foreign tax credit of £25,000 is then set against the UK tax of £33,000 to produce a net amount payable of £8,000.

credits which arose in the above example being set against profits which have borne tax at a lower rate than the UK rate. Thus, in the above example, the UK company would receive a dividend of £280,000 (the post-tax profits distributed up through the Netherlands company). This dividend will be subject to tax at the UK rate of 33 per cent giving rise to a tax liability (before foreign tax credits) of £92,400. Against this liability can be set the foreign tax credits which average out at a rate lower than 33 per cent, so that the effective tax rate on the pre-tax profit of £400,000 originally identified as being available for distribution is the UK rate of 33 per cent; a 7.25 per cent reduction in the effective tax rate. This mixing process also has the effect of enhancing the value to the UK parent company of the use of the Jersey company; the foreign tax credits relating to the higher European tax jurisdictions are effectively used in part against the UK tax otherwise payable on the Jersey profits. The possible application of the controlled foreign company rules to the mixer company would need to be considered.

The UK intermediate holding company   The commentary *above* ignores the position of the UK intermediate holding company. This may be required to perform the role of a 'dividend trap company'. Such a company does nothing other than receive dividends. It may be required where the parent company has charges on income arising, for example, as a result of interest payments on borrowings. The foreign tax credits on the dividends may mean that no relief can be obtained for the charges in the parent company. Furthermore, it will not be possible for the excess charges to be surrendered to another company in the group; the charges must exceed the 'profits' of the company before a surrender can be made (*see* the ICTA 1988, s 403(7)). The dividend trap company is designed to avoid these problems; the borrowings will be in a separate company.

As noted *above*, the Netherlands company may have the benefit of the participation exemption. This also provides an exemption from tax on capital gains realised by the Netherlands company (eg in the event of a sale of shares of one of the European master franchisee companies).

This illustrates how an international group structure might evolve and suggests some planning opportunities. Each element of the structure has to be examined in detail, applying some of the general principles which are referred to earlier in this chapter, and considering more detailed technical issues which go beyond the scope of this work.

Appendices

Appendix 1

Commission Regulation (EEC)No 4087/88
(THE BLOCK EXEMPTION REGULATION)

OF 30 NOVEMBER 1988
ON THE APPLICATION OF ARTICLE 85(3) OF THE TREATY TO
CATEGORIES OF FRANCHISE AGREEMENTS

THE COMMISSION OF THE EUROPEAN COMMUNITIES,

Having regard to the Treaty establishing the European Economic Community,

Having regard to Council Regulations No 19/65/EEC of 2 March 1965 on the application of Article 85(3) of the Treaty to certain categories of agreements and concerted practices, as last amended by the Act of Accession of Spain and Portugal, and in particular Article 1 thereof,

Having published a draft of this Regulation,

Having consulted the Advisory Committee on Restrictive Practices and Dominant Positions,

Whereas:

(1)   Regulation No 16/65/EEC empowers the Commission to apply Article 85(3) of the Treaty by Regulation to certain categories of bilateral exclusive agreements falling within the scope of Article 85(1) which either have as their object the exclusive distribution or exclusive purchase of goods, or include restrictions imposed in relation to the assignment or use of industrial property rights.

(2)   Franchise agreements consist essentially of licences of industrial or intellectual property rights relating to trade marks or signs and know-how, which can be combined with restrictions relating to supply or purchase of goods.

(3)   Several types of franchise can be distinguished according to their object: industrial franchise concerns the manufacturing of goods, distribution

franchise concerns the sale of goods, and service franchise concerns the supply of services.

(4)   It is possible on the basis of the experience of the Commission to define categories of franchise agreements which fall under Article 85(1) but can normally be regarded as satisfying the conditions laid down in Article 85(3). This is the case for franchise agreements whereby one of the parties supplies goods or provides services to end users. On the other hand, industrial franchise agreements should not be covered by this Regulation. Such agreements, which usually govern relationships between producers, present different characteristics than the other types of franchise. They consist of manufacturing licences based on patents and/or technical know-how, combined with trade mark licences. Some of them may benefit from other block exemptions if they fulfil the necessary conditions.

(5)   This Regulation covers franchise agreements between two undertakings, the franchisor and the franchisee, for the retailing of goods or the provision of services to end users, or a combination of these activities, such as the processing or adaptation of goods to fit specific needs of their customers. It also covers cases where the relationship between franchisor and franchisees is made through a third undertaking, the master franchisee. It does not cover wholesale franchise agreements because of the lack of experience of the Commission in that field.

(6)   Franchise agreements as defined in this Regulation can fall under Article 85(1). They may in particular affect intra-Community trade where they are concluded between undertakings from different Member States or where they form the basis of a network which extends beyond the boundaries of a single Member State.

(7)   Franchise agreements as defined in this Regulation normally improve the distribution of goods and/or the provision of services as they give franchisors the possibility of establishing a uniform network with limited investments, which may assist the entry of new competitors on the market, particularly in the case of small and medium-sized undertakings, thus increasing interbrand competition. They also allow independent traders to set up outlets more rapidly and with higher chance of success than if they had to do so without the franchisor's experience and assistance. They have therefore the possibility of competing more efficiently with large distribution undertakings.

(8)   As a rule, franchise agreements also allow consumers and other end users a fair share of the resulting benefit, as they combine the advantage of a uniform network with the existence of traders personally interested in the efficient operation of their business. The homogeneity of the network and the constant co-operation between the franchisor and the franchisees ensures a

constant quality of the products and services. The favourable effect of franchising on interbrand competition and the fact that consumers are free to deal with any franchisee in the network guarantees that a reasonable part of the resulting benefits will be passed on to the consumers.

(9) This Regulation must define the obligations restrictive of competition which may be included in franchise agreements. This is the case in particular for the granting of an exclusive territory to the franchisees combined with the prohibition on actively seeking customers outside that territory, which allows them to concentrate their efforts on their alloted territory. The same applies to the granting of an exclusive territory to a master franchisee combined with the obligation not to conclude franchise agreements with third parties outside that territory. Where the franchisees sell or use in the process of providing services, goods manufactured by the franchisor or according to its instructions and/or bearing its trade mark, an obligation on the franchisees not to sell, or use in the process of the provision of services, competing goods, makes it possible to establish a coherent network which is identified with the franchised goods. However, this obligation should only be accepted with respect to the goods which form the essential subject-matter of the franchise. It should notably not relate to accessories or spare parts for these goods.

(10) The obligations referred to above thus do not impose restrictions which are not necessary for the attainment of the abovementioned objectives. In particular, the limited territorial protection granted to the franchisees is indispensable to protect their investment.

(11) It is desirable to list in the Regulation a number of obligations that are commonly found in franchise agreements and are normally not restrictive of competition and to provide that if, because of the particular economic or legal circumstances, they fall under Article 85(1), they are also covered by the exemption. This list, which is not exhaustive, includes in particular clauses which are essential either to preserve the common identity and reputation of the network or to prevent the know-how made available and the assistance given by the franchisor from benefitting competitors.

(12) The Regulation must specify the conditions which must be satisfied for the exemption to apply. To guarantee that competition is not eliminated for a substantial part of the goods which are the subject of the franchise, it is necessary that parallel imports remain possible. Therefore, cross deliveries between franchisees should always be possible. Furthermore, where a franchise network is combined with another distribution system, franchisees should be free to obtain supplies from authorised distributors. To better inform consumers, thereby helping to ensure that they receive a fair share of the resulting benefits, it must be provided that the franchisee shall be obliged to indicate its status as an independent undertaking, by any appropriate means which does not

jeopardise the common identity of the franchised network. Furthermore, where the franchisees have to honour guarantees for the franchisor's goods, this obligation should also apply to goods supplied by the franchisor, other franchisees or other agreed dealers.

(13)   The Regulation must also specify restrictions which may not be included in franchise agreements if these are to benefit from the exemption granted by the Regulation, by virtue of the fact that such provisions are restrictions falling under Article 85(1) for which there is no general presumption that they will lead to the positive effects required by Article 85(3). This applies in particular to market sharing between competing manufacturers, to clauses unduly limiting the franchisee's choice of suppliers or customers, and to cases where the franchisee is restricted in determining its prices. However, the franchisor should be free to recommend prices to the franchisees, where it is not prohibited by national laws and to the extent that it does not lead to concerted practices for the effective application of these prices.

(14)   Agreements which are not automatically covered by the exemption because they contain provisions that are not expressly exempted by the Regulation and not expressly excluded from exemption may nonetheless generally be presumed to be eligible for application of Article 85(3). It will be possible for the Commission rapidly to establish whether this is the case for a particular agreement. Such agreements should therefore be deemed to be covered by the exemption provided for in this Regulation where they are notified to the Commission and the Commission does not oppose the application of the exemption within a specified period of time.

(15)   If individual agreements exempted by this Regulation nevertheless have effects which are incompatible with Article 85(3), in particular as interpreted by the administrative practice of the Commission and the case law of the Court of Justice, the Commission may withdraw the benefit of the block exemption. This applies in particular where competition is significantly restricted because of the nature of the relevant market.

(16)   Agreements which are automatically exempted pursuant to this Regulation need not be notified. Undertakings may nevertheless in a particular case request a decision pursuant to Council Regulation No 17 as last amended by the Act of Accession of Spain and Portugal.

(17)   Agreements may benefit from the provision either of this Regulation or of another Regulation, according to their particular nature and provided that they fulfil the necessary conditions of application. They may not benefit from a combination of the provision of this Regulation with those of another block exemption Regulation,

HAS ADOPTED THIS REGULATION:

Article 1

1   Pursuant to Article 85(3) of the Treaty and subject to the provisions of this Regulation, it is hereby declared that Article 85(1) of the Treaty shall not apply to franchise agreements to which two undertakings are party, which include one or more of the restrictions listed in Article 2.

2   The exemption provided for in paragraph 1 shall also apply to master franchise agreements to which two undertakings are party. Where applicable, the provisions of this Regulation concerning the relationship between franchisor and franchisee shall apply *mutatis mutandis* to the relationship between franchisor and master franchisee and between master franchisee and franchisee.

3   For the purposes of this Regulation:

(*a*) 'franchise' means a package of industrial or intellectual property rights relating to trade marks, trade names, shop signs, utility models, designs, copyrights, know-how or patents, to be exploited for the resale of goods or the provision of services to end users;

(*b*) 'franchise agreement' means an agreement whereby one undertaking, the franchisor, grants the other, the franchisee, in exchange for direct or indirect financial consideration, the right to exploit a franchise for the purposes of marketing specified types of goods and/or services; it includes at least obligations relating to:

— the use of a common name or shop sign and a uniform presentation of contract premises and/or means of transport,

— the communication by the franchisor to the franchisee of know-how,

— the continuing provision by the franchisor to the franchisee of commercial or technical assistance during the life of the agreement;

(*c*) 'master franchise agreement' means an agreement whereby one undertaking, the franchisor, grants the other, the master franchisee, in exchange of direct or indirect financial consideration, the right to exploit a franchise for the purposes of concluding franchise agreements with third parties, the franchisees;

(*d*) 'franchisor's goods' means goods produced by the franchisor or according to its instructions, and/or bearing the franchisor's name or trade mark;

(*e*) 'contract premises' means the premises used for the exploitation of the franchise or, when the franchise is exploited outside those premises, the base from which the franchisee operates the means of transport used for the exploitation of the franchise (contract means of transport);

(*f*) 'know-how' means a package of non-patented practical information, resulting from experience and testing by the franchisor, which is secret, substantial and identified;

(*g*) 'secret' means that the know-how, as a body or in the precise configuration and assembly of its components, is not generally known or easily accessible, it is not limited in the narrow sense that each individual component of the know-how should be totally unknown or unobtainable outside the franchisor's business;

(*h*) 'substantial' means that the know-how includes information which is of importance for the sale of goods or the provision of services to end users, and in particular for the presentation of goods for sale, the processing of goods in connection with the provision of services, methods of dealing with customers, and administration and financial management; the know-how must be useful for the franchisee by being capable, at the date of conclusion of the agreement, of improving the competitive position of the franchisee, in particular by improving the franchisee's performance or helping it to enter a new market;

(*i*) 'identified' means that the know-how must be described in a sufficiently comprehensive manner so as to make it possible to verify that it fulfils the criteria of secrecy and substantiality; the description of the know-how can either be set out in the franchise agreement or in a separate document or recored in any other appropriate form.

Article 2

The exemption provided for in Article 1 shall apply to the following restrictions of competition:

(*a*) an obligation on the franchisor, in a defined area of the common market, the contract territory, not to:
  — grant the right to exploit all or part of the franchise to third parties,
  — itself exploit the franchise, or itself market the goods or services which are the subject-matter of the franchise under a similar formula,
  — itself supply the franchisor's goods to third parties;

(*b*) an obligation to the master franchisee not to conclude franchise agreements with third parties outside its contract territory;

(*c*) an obligation on the franchisee to exploit the franchise only from the contract premises;

(*d*) an obligation on the franchisee to refrain, outside the contract territory, from seeking customers for the goods or the services which are the subject-matter of the franchise;

(*e*) an obligation on the franchisee not to manufacture, sell or use in the course of the provision of services, goods competing with the franchisor's goods which are the subject-matter of the franchise; where the subject-matter of the franchise is the sale or use in the course of the provision of services both certain types of goods and spare parts or accessories therefor, that obligation may not be imposed in respect of these spare parts or accessories.

Article 3

1   Article 1 shall apply notwithstanding the presence of any of the following obligations on the franchisee, in so far as they are necessary to protect the franchisor's industrial or intellectual property rights or to maintain the common identity and reputation of the franchised network:

(*a*) to sell, or use in the course of the provision of services, exclusively goods matching minimum objective quality specifications laid down by the franchisor;

(*b*) to sell, or use in the course of the provision of services, goods which are manufactured only by the franchisor or by third parties designed by it, where it is impracticable, owing to the nature of the goods which are the subject-matter of the franchise, to apply objective quality specifications;

(*c*) not to engage, directly or indirectly, in any similar business in a territory where it would compete with a member of the franchised network, including the franchisor; the franchisee may be held to this obligation after termination of the agreement, for a reasonable period which may not exceed one year, in the territory where it has exploited the franchise;

(*d*) not to acquire financial interests in the capital of a competing undertaking, which would give the franchisee the power to influence the economic conduct of such undertaking;

(*e*) to sell the goods which are the subject-matter of the franchise only to end users, to other franchisees and to resellers within other channels of distribution supplied by the manufacturer of these goods or with its consent;

(*f*) to use its best endeavours to sell the goods or provide the services that are the subject-matter of the franchise; to offer for sale a minimum range of goods, achieve a minimum turnover, plan its orders in advance, keep minimum stocks and provide customer and warranty services;

(*g*) to pay to the franchisor a specified proportion of its revenue for advertising and itself carry out advertising for the nature of which it shall obtain the franchisor's approval.

2   Article 1 shall apply notwithstanding the presence of any of the following obligations on the franchisee:

(*a*) not to disclose to third parties the know-how provided by the franchisor; the franchisee may be held to this obligation after termination of the agreement;

(*b*) to communicate to the franchisor any experience gained in exploiting the franchise and to grant it, and other franchisees, a non-exclusive licence for the know-how resulting from that experience;

(*c*) to inform the franchisor of infringements of licensed industrial or intellectual property rights, to take legal action against infringers or to assist the franchisor in any legal actions against infringers;

(*d*) not to use know-how licensed by the franchisor for purposes other than the exploitation of the franchise; the franchisee may be held to this obligation after termination of the agreement;

(*e*) to attend or have its staff attend training courses arranged by the franchisor;

(*f*) to apply the commercial methods devised by the franchisor, including any subsequent modification thereof, and use the licensed industrial or intellectual property rights;

(*g*) to comply with the franchisor's standards for the equipment and presentation of the contract premises and/or means of transport;

(*h*) to allow the franchisor to carry out checks of the contract premises and/or means of transport, including the goods sold and the services provided, and the inventory and accounts of the franchisee;

(*i*) not without the franchisor's consent to change the location of the contract premises;

(*j*) not without the franchisor's consent to assign the rights and obligations under the franchise agreement.

3 In the event that, because of particular circumstances, obligations referred to in paragraph 2 fall within the scope of Article 85(1), they shall also be exempted even if they are not accompanied by any of the obligations exempted by Article 1.

Article 4

The exemption provided for in Article 1 shall apply on condition that:

(*a*) the franchisee is free to obtain the goods that are the subject-matter of the franchise from other franchisees; where such goods are also distributed through another network of authorised distributors, the franchisee must be free to obtain goods from the latter;

(*b*) where the franchisor obliges the franchisee to honour guarantees for the franchisor's goods, that obligation shall apply in respect of such goods supplied by any member of the franchised network or other distributors which give a similar guarantee, in the common market;

(*c*) the franchisee is obliged to indicate its status as an independent undertaking; this indication shall however not interfere with the common identity of the franchised network resulting in particular from the common name or shop sign and uniform appearance of the contract premises and/or means of transport.

Article 5

The exemption granted by Article 1 shall not apply where:

(*a*) undertakings producing goods or providing services which are identical or are considered by users as equivalent in view of their characteristics, price and intended use, enter into franchise agreements in respect of such goods or services;

(*b*) without prejudice in Article 2(*e*) and Article 3(1)(*b*), the franchisee is prevented from obtaining supplies of goods of a quality equivalent to those offered by the franchisor;

(*c*) without prejudice to Article 2(*e*), the franchisee is obliged to sell, or use in the process of providing services, goods manufactured by the franchisor or third parties designated by the franchisor and the franchisor refuses, for reasons other than protecting the franchisor's industrial or intellectual property rights, or maintaining the common identity and reputation of the franchised network, to designate as authorised manufacturers third parties proposed by the franchisee;

(*d*) the franchisee is prevented from continuing to use the licensed know-how after termination of the agreement where the know-how has become generally known or easily accessible, other than by breach of an obligation by the franchisee;

(*e*) the franchisee is restricted by the franchisor, directly or indirectly, in the determination of sale prices for the goods or services which are the subject-matter of the franchise, without prejudice to the possibility for the franchisor of recommending sale prices;

(*f*) the franchisor prohibits the franchisee from challenging the validity of the industrial or intellectual property rights which form part of the franchise, without prejudice to the possibility for the franchisor of terminating the agreement in such a case;

(*g*) franchisees are obliged not to supply within the common market the goods or services which are the subject-matter of the franchise to end users because of their place of residence.

Article 6

1 The exemption provided for in Article 1 shall also apply to franchise agreements which fulfil the conditions laid down in Article 4 and include obligations restrictive of competition which are not covered by Articles 2 and 3(3) and do not fall within the scope of Article 5, on condition that the agreements in question are notified to the Commission in accordance with the provisions of Commission Regulation No 27 and that the Commission does not oppose such exemption within a period of six months.

2   The period of six months shall run from the date on which the notification is received by the Commission. Where, however, the notification is made by registered post, the period shall run from the date shown on the postmark of the place of posting.

3   Paragraph 1 shall apply only if:

(*a*) express reference is made to this Article in the notification or in a communication accompanying it; and

(*b*) the information furnished with the notification is complete and in accordance with the facts.

4   The benefit of paragraph 1 can be claimed for agreements notified before the entry into force of this Regulation by submitting a communication to the Commission referring expressly to this Article and to the notification. Paragraphs 2 and 3(*b*) shall apply *mutatis mutandis*.

5   The Commission may oppose exemption. It shall oppose exemption if it receives a request to do so from a Member State within three months of the forwarding to the Member State of the notification referred to in paragraph 1 or the communication referred to in paragraph 4. This request must be justified on the basis of considerations relating to the competition rules of the Treaty.

6   The Commission may withdraw its opposition to the exemption at any time. However, where that opposition was raised at the request of a Member State, it may be withdrawn only after consultation of the advisory Committee on Restrictive Practices and Dominant Positions.

7   If the opposition is withdrawn because the undertakings concerned have shown that the conditions of Article 85(3) are fulfilled, the exemption shall apply from the date of the notification.

8   If the opposition is withdrawn because the undertakings concerned have amended the agreement so that the conditions of Article 85(3) are fulfilled, the exemption shall apply from the date on which the amendments take effect.

9   If the Commission opposes exemption and its opposition is not withdrawn, the effects of the notification shall be governed by the provisions of Regulation No 17.

Article 7

1   Information acquired pursuant to Article 6 shall be used only for the purposes of this Regulation.

2   The Commission and the authorities of the Member States, their officials and other servants shall not disclose information acquired by them pursuant to this Regulation of a kind that is covered by the obligation of professional secrecy.

3 Paragraphs 1 and 2 shall not prevent publication of general information or surveys which do not contain information relating to particular undertakings or associations of undertakings.

Article 8

The Commission may withdraw the benefit of this Regulation, pursuant to Article 7 of Regulation No 19/65/EEC, where it finds in a particular case that an agreement exempted by this Regulation nevertheless has certain effects which are incompatible with the conditions laid down in Article 85(3) of the EEC Treaty, and in particular where territorial protection is awarded to the franchisee and:

(*a*) access to the relevant market or competition therein is significantly restricted by the cumulative effect of parallel networks of similar agreements established by competing manufacturers or distributors;

(*b*) the goods or services which are the subject-matter of the franchise do not face, in a substantial part of the common market, effective competition from goods or services which are identical or considered by users as equivalent in view of their characteristics, price and intended use;

(*c*) the parties, or one of them, prevent end users, because of their place of residence, from obtaining, directly or through intermediaries, the goods or services which are the subject-matter of the franchise within the common market, or use differences in specifications concerning those goods or services in different Member States, to isolate markets;

(*d*) franchisees engaged in concerted practices relating to the sale prices of the goods or services which are the subject-matter of the franchise;

(*e*) the franchisor uses its right to check the contract premises and means of transport, or refuses its agreement to requests by the franchisee to move the contract premises or assign its rights and obligations under the franchise agreement, for reasons other than protecting the franchisor's industrial or intellectual property rights, maintaining the common identity and reputation of the franchised network or verifying that the franchise abides by its obligations under the agreement.

Article 9

This Regulation shall enter into force on 1 February 1989.

It shall remain in force until 31 December 1999.

This Regulation shall be binding in its entirety and directly applicable in all Member States.

Done at Brussels, 30 November 1988.

For the Commission
Peter SUTHERLAND
Member of the Commission

419

Appendix 2

British Franchise Association
Code of Ethical Conduct

ISSUE NO 4 JANUARY 1992

This *Code of Ethical Conduct* in franchising takes as its foundation the Code developed by the European Franchise Federation. In adopting the Code, the Federation recognised that national requirements may necessitate certain other clauses or provisions and delegated responsibility for the presentation and implementation of the Code in their own country to individual member National Franchise Associations.

The *Extension and Interpretation* which follows the European Code has been adopted by the British Franchise Association, and agreed by the European Franchise Federation, for the application of the *European Code of Ethics for Franchising* by the British Franchise Association within the United Kingdom of Great Britain and Northern Ireland.

EUROPEAN CODE OF ETHICS FOR FRANCHISING

PREFACE

The European Franchise Federation, EFF, was constituted on 23 September 1972.

Its members are national franchise associations or federations established in Europe.

The EFF also accepts affiliates, ie non European franchise associations or federations, and other professional persons, interested in or concerned with franchising. Affiliates have no voting rights and cannot be appointed officers of the EFF.

The objects of the EFF are, among others, the ongoing unbiased and scientific study of franchising in every respect, the co-ordination of its members' actions,

421

the promotion of the franchise industry in general and of its members' interests in particular.

The EFF also comprises a Legal Committee, composed of two lawyers from each national member association or federation and highly qualified in franchise matters.

The EFF has, furthermore, installed a Franchise Arbitration Committee which is at the disposal of parties preferring to submit their disputes to the latter's determination.

The evolution and the ever growing importance of franchising in the EC economy as well as the EC Block Exemption Regulation for franchise agreements, entered into force on 1 February 1989, prompted the EFF to revise its existing *Code of Ethics*.

This *Code of Ethics* is meant to be a practical ensemble of essential provisions of fair behaviour for franchise practitioners in Europe, but not to replace possibly related national or EC law.

This *Code of Ethics* is the end-product of work carried out by the European Franchise Federation and its member associations (Austria, Belgium, Denmark, Germany, France, Italy, the Netherlands, Portugal and the United Kingdom) in conjunction with the Commission of the European Community. It shall replace the previous *European Code of Ethics* as well as all national and regional Codes existing at that time in Europe.

By subscribing to the EFF, its members accept the *European Code of Ethics* and undertake not to delete or amend it in any way. It is, however, recognised that national requirements may necessitate certain other clauses or provisions and, providing these do not conflict with or detract from the Code and are attached to the Code in a separate document, permission to do this will not be withheld by the EFF.

By adhering to the EFF its members commit themselves to impose on their own members the obligation to respect and apply the provions of this *Code of Ethics for Franchising*.

1 DEFINITION OF FRANCHISING

Franchising is a system of marketing goods and/or services and/or technology, which is based upon a close and ongoing collaboration between legally and financially separate and independent undertakings, the Franchisor and its Individual Franchisees, whereby the Franchisor grants its Individual Franchisees the right, and imposes the obligation, to conduct a business in accordance with the Franchisor's concept. The right entitles and compels the individual Franchisee, in exchange for a direct or indirect financial consideration, to use the Franchisor's trade name, and/or trade mark and/or service mark, know-how(*), business and technical methods, procedural system, and other industrial and/or intellectual property rights, supported by continuing provision of commercial and technical assistance, within the framework and for the term of a written franchise agreement, concluded between parties for this purpose.

(*)'Know-how' means a body of non patented practical information, resulting from experience and testing by the Franchisor, which is secret, substantial and identified;

— 'secret', means that the know-how, as a body or in the precise configuration and assembly of its components, is not generally known or easily accessible; it is not limited in the narrow sense that each individual component of the know-how should be totally unknown or unobtainable outside the Franchisor's business;

— 'substantial' means that the know-how includes information which is of importance for the sale of goods or the provision of services to end users, and in particular for the presentation of goods for sale, the processing of goods in connection with the provision of services, methods of dealing with customers, and administration and financial management; the know-how must be useful for the Franchisee by being capable, at the date of conclusion of the agreement, of improving the competitive position of the Franchisee, in particular by improving the Franchisee's performance or helping it to enter a new market.

— 'identified' means that the know-how must be described in a sufficiently comprehensive manner so as to make it possible to verify that it fulfils the criteria of secrecy and substantiality; the description of the know-how can either be set out in the franchise agreement or in a separate document or recorded in any other appropriate form.

2 GUIDING PRINCIPLES

2.1 The Franchisor is the initiator of a franchise network, composed of itself and its Individual Franchisees, of which the Franchisor is the long term guardian.

2.2 **The obligations of the Franchisor:**

The Franchisor shall
— have operated a business concept with success, for a reasonable time and in at least one pilot unit before starting its franchise network;
— be the owner, or have legal rights to the use, of its network's trade name, trade mark or other distinguishing identification;
— provide the Individual Franchisee with initial training and continuing commercial and/or technical assistance during the entire life of the agreement.

2.3 **The obligations of the Individual Franchisee:**

The Individual Franchisee shall

— devote its best endeavours to the growth of the franchise business and to the maintenance of the common identity and reputation of the franchise network;

— supply the Franchisor with verifiable operating data to facilitate the determination of performance and the financial statements necessary for effective management guidance, and allow the Franchisor, and/or its agents, to have access to the individual Franchisee's premises and records at the Franchisor's request and at reasonable times;

— not disclose to third parties the know-how provided by the franchisor, neither during nor after termination of the agreement.

2.4 **The ongoing obligations of both parties:**

Parties shall exercise fairness in their dealings with each other. The Franchisor shall give written notice to its Individual Franchisees of any contractual breach and, where appropriate, grant reasonable time to remedy default.

Parties should resolve complaints, grievances and disputes with good faith and goodwill through fair and reasonable direct communication and negotiation.

3 **RECRUITMENT, ADVERTISING AND DISCLOSURE**

3.1 Advertising for the recruitment of Individual Franchisees shall be free of ambiguity and misleading statements.

3.2 Any publicly available recruitment, advertising and publicity material, containing direct or indirect references to future possible results, figures or earnings to be expected by Individual Franchisees, shall be objective and shall not be misleading.

3.3 In order to allow prospective Individual Franchisees to enter into any binding document with full knowledge, they shall be given a copy of the present *Code of Ethics* as well as full and accurate written disclosure of all information material to the franchise relationship, within a reasonable time prior to the execution of these binding documents.

3.4 If a Franchisor imposes a Pre-contract on a candidate Individual Franchisee, the following principles should be respected:

— prior to the signing of any pre-contract, the candidate Individual Franchisee should be given written information on its purpose and on any consideration he may be required to pay to the Franchisor to cover the latter's actual expenses, incurred during and with respect to the pre-contract phase; if the Franchise agreement is executed, the said consideration should be reimbursed by the Franchisor or set off against a possible entry fee to be paid by the Individual Franchisee;

— the Pre-contract shall define its term and include a termination clause;

— the Franchisor can impose non-competition and/or secrecy clauses to protect its know-how and identity.

4 SELECTION OF INDIVIDUAL FRANCHISEES

A Franchisor should select and accept as Individual Franchisees only those who, upon reasonable investigation, appear to possess the basic skills, education, personal qualities and financial resources sufficient to carry on the franchised business.

5 THE FRANCHISE AGREEMENT

5.1 The Franchise agreement should comply with the National law, European Community law and this *Code of Ethics*.

5.2 The agreement shall reflect the interests of the members of the franchised network in protecting the Franchisor's industrial and intellectual property rights and in maintaining the common identity and reputation of the franchised network. All agreements and all contractual arrangements in connection with the franchise relationship should be written in or translated by a sworn translator into the official language of the country the Individual Franchisee is established in, and signed agreements shall be given immediately to the Individual Franchisee.

5.3 The Franchise agreement shall set forth without ambiguity, the respective obligations and responsibilities of the parties and all other material terms of the relationship.

5.4 The essential minimum terms of the agreement shall be the following:

— the rights granted to the Franchisor;
— the rights granted to the Individual Franchisee;
— the goods and/or services to be provided to the Individual Franchisee;
— the obligations of the Franchisor;
— the obligations of the Individual Franchisee;

— the terms of payment by the Individual Franchisee;

— the duration of the agreement which should be long enough to allow Individual Franchisees to amortise their initial investments specific to the franchise;

— the basis for any renewal of the agreement;

— the terms upon which the Individual Franchisee may sell or transfer the franchised business and the Franchisor's possible pre-emption rights in this respect;

— provisions relevant to the use by the Individual Franchisee of the Franchisor's distinctive signs, trade name, service mark, store sign, logo or other distinguishing identification;

— the Franchisor's right to adapt the franchise sytstem to new or changed methods;

— provisions for termination of the agreement;

— provisions for surrendering promptly upon termination of the franchise agreement any tangible and intangible property belonging to the Franchisor or other owner thereof.

6 THE CODE OF ETHICS AND THE MASTER FRANCHISE SYSTEM

This *Code of Ethics* shall apply to the relationship between the Franchisor and its Individual Franchisees and equally between the Master Franchisee and its Individual Franchisees. It shall not apply to the relationship between the Franchisor and its Master Franchisees.

EXTENSION AND INTERPRETATION

This *Extension and Interpretation* forms an integral part of the *Code of Ethical Conduct* adopted by the British Franchise Association and to which its members adhere.

APPLICATION

1 This *Code of Ethical Conduct* forms part of the membership agreement between the British Franchise Association and its member companies. It does not form any part of the contractual agreement between franchisor and franchisee unless expressly stated to do so by the franchisor. Neither should anything in this Code be construed as limiting a franchisor's right to sell or assign its interest in a franchised business.

DISCLOSURE

2 The objectivity of recruitment literature (Clause 3.2) refers *specifically* to publicly available material. It is recognised that in discussing individual

business projections with franchisees, franchisors are invariably involved in making assumptions which can only be tested by the passage of time.

CONFIDENTIALITY

3 For the generality of this *Code of Ethical Conduct*, 'know-how' is taken as being as defined in the European Block exemption to Article 85 of the Treaty of Rome. However, for the purposes of Article 3.4 of the *European Code of Ethics* it is accepted that franchisors may impose non-competition and secrecy clauses to protect other information and systems where they may be reasonably regarded as material to the operation of the franchise.

CONTRACT LANGUAGE

4 Franchisors should seek to ensure that they offer to franchisees contracts in a language in which the franchisee is competent.

CONTRACT TERM

5 In suggesting in Article 5.4 of the *European Code of Ethics* that the minimum term for a franchise contract should be the period necessary to amortise those of a franchisee's initial investment which are specific to the franchise, it is recognised:

(a) that for a minority of the largest franchise opportunities amortising initial investments may not be a primary objective for the franchisee. In such cases the objective should be to adopt a contract period which reasonably balances the interests of the parties to the contract.

(b) that this section could be subject to national laws concerning the restraint of trade and may need to be met through renewal clauses.

CONTRACT RENEWAL

6 The basis for contract renewal should take into account the length of the original term, the extent to which the contract empowers the franchisor to require investments from the franchisee for refurbishment or renovation, and the extent to which the franchisor may vary the terms of a contract on renewal. The overriding objective is to ensure that the franchisee has the opportunity to recover his franchise specific initial and subsequent investments and to exploit the franchised business for as long as the contract persists.

ADOPTION

7 This *Code of Ethical Conduct* comprising this *Extension and Interpretation* and the *European Code of Ethics for Franchising* was adopted by the British Franchise Association, replacing its previous *Code of Ethics* on 30 August 1990, subject to a transitional period for full compliance ending 31 December 1991. During the transitional period members of the Association are nonetheless required to comply at least with the *Code of Ethics* previously in force. In October 1991 the Association agreed with the European Franchise Federation some amendments to the Code agreed in August 1990 and at the same time extended the transitional period to full compliance to 31 December 1992.

The Code of Ethical Conduct is reproduced with the kind permission of the British Franchise Association.

Appendix 3

Chartered Institute of Arbitrators British Franchise Association Arbitration Scheme Rules

(1987) EDITION—AMENDED

These Rules provide an inexpensive and informal method of resolving disputes between Franchisors and Franchisees which the parties cannot resolve amicably between themselves. The Rules will apply to arbitrations commenced under the Scheme after 1 May 1987.

INTRODUCTION

1   In these Rules:

    (i)   'the Institute' shall mean the Chartered Institute of Arbitrators of 75 Cannon Street, London EC4N 5BH.

    (ii) 'the BFA' shall mean the British Franchise Association of Franchise Chambers, Thames View, Newtown Road, Henley on Thames, Oxon RG9 1HG.

    (iii) 'the Arbitrator' shall mean a sole and independent arbitrator appointed by the President or a Vice President of the Institute in an arbitration under this Scheme.

    (iv) 'the Franchisor' shall mean a company, firm or person who is the franchisor in respect of any agreement under which a dispute arises and is referred to arbitration under this Scheme.

    (v) 'the Franchisee' shall mean a company, firm or person who is the franchisee in respect of any agreement under which a dispute arises and is referred to arbitration under this Scheme.

    (vi) 'the costs of the arbitration' shall mean the total of the Arbitrator's fees and expenses, the Institute's administrative costs and the cost of any independent examination under Rule 8 (iv).

    (vii) 'costs in the reference' shall mean legal or other costs incurred by a party in connection with an arbitration under this Scheme.

2   The Franchisee may apply for arbitration under this Scheme as an alternative to court action. He must decide at the outset whether to use this Scheme or to seek his remedy through the courts. If he uses this Scheme he will not be able to start again with court action, because awards made under the Scheme are final and binding on the parties.

3   (i)   Application for arbitration must be made on the prescribed application form which may be obtained from the BFA.

       (ii)   A deposit of £150 is payable by each party when an application for arbitration is submitted. These deposits may be refunded or may be applied in whole or in part towards defraying the costs of the arbitration, at the discretion of the Arbitrator.

4   (i)   The application form should be completed by the Franchisee and returned to the BFA with the Franchisee's deposit.

       (ii)   The BFA will then refer the application form to the Franchisor, to be completed and returned to the BFA with the Franchisor's deposit.

       (iii) The Franchisor's agreement to arbitration is necessary for the application to proceed. The BFA will encourage the Franchisor to agree, but he is not obliged to do so. If the Franchisor does not agree to arbitration, he is required to inform the BFA accordingly. The Franchisee's deposit will be returned and he may seek his remedy through the courts.

INSTITUTION OF ARBITRATION PROCEEDINGS

5   Provided the application form has been signed by both parties and is accompanied by the appropriate deposits, it will be forwarded to the Institute by the BFA with the deposits.

6   The arbitration commences for the purposes of these Rules when the Institute despatches to the parties written notice of acceptance of the application. The notice sent to the party making the claim will be accompanied by a claim form.

PROCEDURE

7   *General*

Subject to any directions issued by the Arbitrator the procedure will be as follows:

       (i)   The Franchisee is required, within 28 days of receipt of the claim form, to send the completed form, together with any supporting documents in duplicate, to the Institute. The Franchisee is also required to notify the Institute at this stage if he requests an attended hearing. (The Franchisee may not, without the consent of the Arbitrator, claim an amount greater than that specified on the application for arbitration.)

(ii) A copy of the claim documents will be sent by the Institute to the Franchisor, who is required, within 28 days of receipt of the documents, to send to the Institute his written defence to the claim, together with any supporting documents in duplicate. (The Franchisor may include with his defence a counterclaim in respect of any balance of payment alleged to be due on the contract between the parties, or in respect of any other matter notified to the Franchisee before the Franchisee applied for arbitration.)

(iii) A copy of the defence documents will be sent by the Institute to the Franchisee, who is entitled to send to the Institute any written comments which he wishes to make on the defence documents within 14 days of their receipt. Such comments should be in duplicate. They must be restricted to points arising from the Franchisor's defence and may not introduce any new matters or points of claim.

(iv) The President or a Vice-President of the Institute, at such stage of the proceedings as the Institute considers appropriate, will appoint the Arbitrator, taking into account the nature of the dispute and the location of the Franchisee's trading premises. The Institute will notify the parties of the Arbitrator's appointment.

(v) The Arbitrator may in his discretion call the parties to an attended hearing and shall do so if the Franchisee has so requested in accordance with Rule 7(i). Subject to that, the Arbitrator will make his award with reference to the documents submitted by the parties.

(vi) The Arbitrator will send his award to the Institute for publication. Unless the parties otherwise agree, the Arbitrator's reasons will be set out or referred to in his award.

(vii) The Institute will notify the parties when it receives the award from the Arbitrator and will also notify the Franchisor of any costs of the arbitration payable under Rule 11. On payment of such costs, the Institute will publish the award by sending copies to each of the parties. The Institute will also send a copy to the BFA.

(viii) After publication of the award the Institute will return the Franchisee's deposit in whole or in part if so directed by the Arbitrator.

(ix) Unless directed otherwise in the award, within 21 days of despatch by the Institute to the parties a copy award, payment shall be made of any monies directed by the award to be paid by one party to the other. Such payment shall be made by the party liable direct to the party entitled, and not through the Institute or the BFA.

(x)   If either party has sent original documents in support of its case to the Institute that party may, within six weeks of publication of the award, request the return of those documents. Subject to that, case papers will be retained by the Institute and may in due course be disposed of in accordance with the Institute's policies from time to time.

8   *Supplementary*

(i)   Attended hearings shall be conducted in private at a place to be notified to the parties by the Institute on behalf of the Arbitrator, who shall use his best endeavours to take into account the convenience of the parties. The parties may attend a hearing in person or be represented by an employee (but not a person employed to give legal advice) unless the Arbitrator agrees that they may be legally represented.

(ii) The Arbitrator may, through the Institute, request the provision of any further documents/information which he considers would assist him in his decision. If the documents/information are not supplied to the Institute within such time as it prescribes, the Arbitrator will proceed with the reference on the basis of documents already before him.

(iii) Where, in the opinion of the Arbitrator, it is desirable, he may make an examination of the subject matter of the dispute without holding an attended hearing. The parties shall afford the Arbitrator all necessary assistance and facilities for the conduct of this examination.

(iv) Where, in the opinion of the Arbitrator, it is desirable that independent examination of the subject matter of the dispute be made, an independent examiner will be appointed by the Institute to make such examination and a written report thereon. The parties shall afford the examiner all necessary assistance and facilities for the conduct of this examination and copies of his report shall be sent by the Institute to the parties who will then be given 14 days in which to comment thereon.

(v)   If the Franchisee does not furnish his claim within the time allowed and does not remedy his default within 14 days after despatch to him by the Institute of notice of that default, he will be treated as having abandoned his claim. The arbitration will not proceed and the Franchisee's deposit will be returned less the Institute's administrative costs to date. The Franchisor's deposit will be returned in full.

(vi) If the Franchisor does not furnish his defence within the time allowed and does not remedy his default within 14 days after despatch to him by the Institute of notice of that default, the

Arbitrator will be appointed, and subject to any directions he may give, the dispute may be decided by him by reference to the documents submitted by the Franchisee.

(vii) If a party fails to attend or be represented at an attended hearing, the Arbitrator shall either make an award *ex parte* or, if he so decides, adjourn the hearing for such time as he considers reasonable and serve notice on the party failing to attend that the matter will be dealt with *ex parte* at the adjourned hearing.

COSTS

9   The Franchisor shall be responsible for the costs of the arbitration less any amount which the Arbitrator may order the Franchisee to pay but the Franchisor shall in any event be responsible for not less than two-thirds of the costs of the arbitration. Where the arbitration is conducted on the basis of documents only, the Arbitrator will not order the Franchisee to pay a contribution to the costs of the arbitration in excess of £150 unless he considers the application by the Franchisee to have been frivolous or vexatious. In the case of an attended hearing, if the costs of the arbitration exceed £300, the Arbitrator may order the Franchisee to pay part of such excess in addition to the sum of £150 (or more if he considers the application frivolous or vexatious).

10   The Arbitrator may order the Franchisor to pay some or all of the Franchisee's costs in the reference and may order the Franchisee to pay up to one-third of the Franchisor's costs in the reference.

11   The Franchisor agrees to pay to the Institute within 14 days of notice from the Institute of receipt of the award and of the amount of the costs of the arbitration, a total sum equal to the costs of the arbitration less the amount of any deposits ordered to be utilised towards payment of the fees and expenses. This is without prejudice to any right which the Franchisor may have to recover from the Franchisee a contribution to the costs of the arbitration or the Franchisor's costs in the reference, ordered in the Arbitrator's award to be paid by the Franchisee.

MISCELLANEOUS

12   (i)   The law to apply (English, Scots etc) shall be determined by the Arbitrator if the parties fail to agree.

      (ii) Where Scots law applies, any reference in these Rules to an arbitrator shall be construed as a reference to an arbiter.

13   The Institute reserves the right to appoint a substitute Arbitrator if the Arbitrator originally appointed dies or is incapacitated or is for any

reason unable to deal expeditiously with the dispute. The parties shall be notified of any substitution.

14 Awards made under the Scheme are final and binding on the parties. Subject to the right of a party to request the Institute to draw the Arbitrator's attention to any accidental slip or omission which he has the power to correct, neither the Institute nor the Arbitrator can enter into correspondence regarding awards made under the Scheme.

15 Rights of application or appeal (if any) to the courts are as under the relevant Arbitration Acts provided that the special costs provisions of the Scheme shall not apply to any such application or appeal.

16 Neither the Institute nor the Arbitrator shall be liable to any party for any act or omission in connection with any arbitration conducted under these Rules save that the Arbitrator (but not the Institute) shall be liable for any conscious or deliberate wrongdoing on his own part.

The Chartered Institute of Arbitrators
International Arbitration Centre
75 Cannon Street
London EC4N 5BH
Tel: 0171-236 8761
Fax: 0171-236 5204
Telex: 893466 CIARB G

THE CHARTERED INSTITUTE OF ARBITRATORS
BRITISH FRANCHISE ASSOCIATION ARBITRATION SCHEME
APPLICATION FOR ARBITRATION

To: The Chartered Institute of Arbitrators
(to be submitted through the British Franchise Association)

1 .... Franchisee

of .... Phone: ....

and

.... Franchisor

of .... Phone: ....

Hereby apply to the Chartered Institute of Arbitrators for the following dispute to be referred to arbitration under the Rules of the British Franchise Association Arbitration Scheme for the time being in force for determination by an arbitrator appointed for that purpose by the Institute.

2   The dispute has arisen in connection with the following:

....
....
....
....

(NOTE: Only an outline is required here to enable the dispute to be identified by the parties. The Franchisee will be asked to submit his specific claim in detail as soon as the arbitration request has been accepted by the Institute.)

3   We, the parties to this application, are each in possession of the current (1987) Rules of the Scheme. We agree to be bound by these Rules (or any amendment thereof for the time being in force that may be notified to us) and by the Award of the arbitrator appointed to determine the dispute.

4   A cheque for the sum of £150* in respect of the Franchisee's deposit, and a cheque for the same amount in respect of the Franchisor's deposit are enclosed.

We agree to the disposal of these deposits in accordance with the Rules of the Scheme.

Signed .... Date ....
            (Franchisee)
Signed .... Date ....
            (Franchisor)

* Cheques should be in favour of 'The Chartered Institute of Arbitrators'

The Arbitration Scheme Rules are reproduced with the kind permission of the British Franchise Association.

Index

445